New Perspectives on

Microsoft®
Word 97

COMPREHENSIVE—ENHANCED

The New Perspectives Series

The New Perspectives Series consists of texts and technology that teach computer concepts and microcomputer applications (listed below). You can order these New Perspectives texts in many different lengths, software releases, custom-bound combinations, CourseKits™ and Custom Editions®. Contact your Course Technology sales representative or customer service representative for the most up-to-date details.

The New Perspectives Series

Computer Concepts

Borland® dBASE®

Borland® Paradox®

Corel® Presentations™

Corel® Quattro Pro®

Corel® WordPerfect®

DOS

HTML

Lotus® 1-2-3®

Microsoft® Access

Microsoft® Excel

Microsoft® Internet Explorer

Microsoft® Office Professional

Microsoft® PowerPoint®

Microsoft® Windows® 3.1

Microsoft® Windows® 95

Microsoft® Windows NT® Server 4.0

Microsoft® Windows NT® Workstation 4.0

Microsoft® Word

Microsoft® Works

Netscape Navigator™

Netscape Navigator™ Gold

Microsoft® Visual Basic® 4 and 5

New Perspectives on
Microsoft®
Word 97

COMPREHENSIVE—ENHANCED

Beverly B. Zimmerman
Brigham Young University

S. Scott Zimmerman
Brigham Young University

Ann Shaffer

COURSE
TECHNOLOGY

ONE MAIN STREET, CAMBRIDGE, MA 02142

an International Thomson Publishing company I(T)P®

Cambridge • Albany • Bonn • Boston • Cincinnati • London • Madrid • Melbourne • Mexico City
New York • Paris • San Francisco • Singapore • Tokyo • Toronto • Washington

New Perspectives on Microsoft Word® 97—Comprehensive—Enhanced is published by Course Technology.

Associate Publisher	Mac Mendelsohn
Series Consulting Editor	Susan Solomon
Acquisitions Editor	Mark Reimold
Developmental Editor	Robin Geller
Production Editor	Seth Andrews
Text and Cover Designer	Ella Hanna
Cover Illustrator	Douglas Goodman

© 1998 by Course Technology — I(T)P®

For more information contact:

Course Technology
One Main Street
Cambridge, MA 02142

ITP Europe
Berkshire House 168-173
High Holborn
London WCIV 7AA
England

Nelson ITP, Australia
102 Dodds Street
South Melbourne, 3205
Victoria, Australia

ITP Nelson Canada
1120 Birchmount Road
Scarborough, Ontario
Canada M1K 5G4

International Thomson Editores
Seneca, 53
Colonia Polanco
11560 Mexico D.F. Mexico

ITP GmbH
Königswinterer Strasse 418
53227 Bonn
Germany

ITP Asia
60 Albert Street, #15-01
Albert Complex
Singapore 189969

ITP Japan
Hirakawacho Kyowa Building, 3F
2-2-1 Hirakawacho
Chiyoda-ku, Tokyo 102
Japan

Trademarks
Course Technology and the Open Book logo are registered trademarks and CourseKits is a trademark of Course Technology. Custom Editions and the ITP logo are registered trademarks of International Thomson Publishing Inc.

Microsoft and the Office logo are either registered trademarks or trademarks of Microsoft Corporation in the United States and/or other countries. Course Technology is an independent entity from Microsoft Corporation, and not affiliated with Microsoft in any manner. This text may be used in assisting students to prepare for a Certified Microsoft Office User Exam. Neither Microsoft Corporation, its designated review company, nor Course Technology warrants that use of this text will ensure passing the relevant CMOU Exam.

Some of the product names and company names used in this book have been used for identification purposes only and may be trademarks or registered trademarks of their respective manufacturers and sellers.

Disclaimer
Course Technology reserves the right to revise this publication and make changes from time to time in its content without notice.

ISBN 0-7600-7380-2

Printed in the United States of America

2 3 4 5 6 7 8 9 10 BM 01 00 99 98

At Course Technology we have one foot in education and the other in technology. We believe that technology is transforming the way people teach and learn, and we are excited about providing instructors and students with materials that use technology to teach about technology.

Our development process is unparalleled in the higher education publishing industry. Every product we create goes through an exacting process of design, development, review, and testing.

Reviewers give us direction and insight that shape our manuscripts and bring them up to the latest standards. Every manuscript is quality tested. Students whose backgrounds match the intended audience work through every keystroke, carefully checking for clarity and pointing out errors in logic and sequence. Together with our own technical reviewers, these testers help us ensure that everything that carries our name is error-free and easy to use.

We show both how and why technology is critical to solving problems in college and in whatever field you choose to teach or pursue. Our time-tested, step-by-step instructions provide unparalleled clarity. Examples and applications are chosen and crafted to motivate students.

As the New Perspectives Series team at Course Technology, our goal is to produce the most timely, accurate, creative, and technologically sound product in the entire college publishing industry. We strive for consistent high quality. This takes a lot of communication, coordination, and hard work. But we love what we do. We are determined to be the best. Write to us and let us know what you think. You can also e-mail us at NewPerspectives@course.com.

The New Perspectives Series Team

Joseph J. Adamski	Jessica Evans	William Newman
Judy Adamski	Marilyn Freedman	Dan Oja
Roy Ageloff	Kathy Finnegan	David Paradice
Tim Ashe	Robin Geller	June Parsons
David Auer	Donna Gridley	Harry Phillips
Daphne Barbas	Kate Habib	Sandra Poindexter
Dirk Baldwin	Roger Hayen	Mark Reimold
Rachel Bunin	Charles Hommel	Ann Shaffer
Joan Carey	Cindy Johnson	Karen Shortill
Patrick Carey	Janice Jutras	Susan Solomon
Sharon Caswell	Chris Kelly	Susanne Walker
Barbara Clemens	Mary Kemper	John Zeanchock
Rachel Crapser	Stacy Klein	Beverly Zimmerman
Kim Crowley	Terry Ann Kremer	Scott Zimmerman
Melissa Dezotell	John Leschke	
Michael Ekedahl	Mac Mendelsohn	

Preface The New Perspectives Series

What is the New Perspectives Series?

Course Technology's **New Perspectives Series** is an integrated system of instruction that combines text and technology products to teach computer concepts and microcomputer applications. Users consistently praise this series for innovative pedagogy, creativity, supportive and engaging style, accuracy, and use of interactive technology. The first New Perspectives text was published in January of 1993. Since then, the series has grown to more than 100 titles and has become the best-selling series on computer concepts and microcomputer applications. Others have imitated the New Perspectives features, design, and technologies, but none have replicated its quality and its ability to consistently anticipate and meet the needs of instructors and students.

What is the Integrated System of Instruction?

New Perspectives textbooks are part of a truly Integrated System of Instruction: text, graphics, video, sound, animation, and simulations that are linked and that provide a flexible, unified, and interactive system to help you teach and help your students learn. Specifically, the *New Perspectives Integrated System of Instruction* includes a Course Technology textbook in addition to some or all of the following items: Course Labs, Course Test Manager, Online Companions, and Course Presenter. These components—shown in the graphic on the back cover of this book—have been developed to work together to provide a complete, integrative teaching and learning experience.

How is the New Perspectives Series different from other microcomputer concepts and applications series?

The **New Perspectives Series** distinguishes itself from other series in at least four substantial ways: sound instructional design, consistent quality, innovative technology, and proven pedagogy. The applications texts in this series consist of two or more tutorials, which are based on sound instructional design. Each tutorial is motivated by a realistic case that is meaningful to students. Rather than learn a laundry list of features, students learn the features in the context of solving a problem. This process motivates all concepts and skills by demonstrating to students *why* they would want to know them.

Instructors and students have come to rely on the high quality of the **New Perspectives Series** and to consistently praise its accuracy. This accuracy is a result of Course Technology's unique multi-step quality assurance process that incorporates student testing at at least two stages of development, using hardware and software configurations appropriate to the product. All solutions, test questions, and other supplements are tested using similar procedures. Instructors who adopt this series report that students can work through the tutorials independently with minimum intervention or "damage control" by instructors or staff. This consistent quality has meant that if instructors are pleased with one product from the series, they can rely on the same quality with any other New Perspectives product.

The **New Perspectives Series** also distinguishes itself by its innovative technology. This series innovated Course Labs, truly *interactive* learning applications. These have set the standard for interactive learning.

How do I know that the New Perspectives Series will work?

Some instructors who use this series report a significant difference between how much their students learn and retain with this series as compared to other series. With other series, instructors often find that students can work through the book and do well on homework and tests, but still not demonstrate competency when asked to perform particular tasks outside the context of the text's sample case or project. With the **New Perspectives Series**, however, instructors report that students have a complete, integrative learning experience that stays with them. They credit this high retention and competency to the fact that this series incorporates critical thinking and problem-solving with computer skills mastery.

How does this book I'm holding fit into the New Perspectives Series?

New Perspectives applications books are available in the following categories:

Brief books are typically about 150 pages long, contain two to four tutorials, and are intended to teach the basics of an application.

Introductory books are typically about 300 pages long and consist of four to seven tutorials that go beyond the basics. These books often build out of the Brief editions by providing two or three additional tutorials.

Comprehensive books are typically about 600 pages long and consist of all of the tutorials in the Introductory books, plus a few more tutorials covering higher-level topics. Comprehensive books typically also include two Windows tutorials and three or four Additional Cases. The book you are holding is a Comprehensive book.

Advanced books cover topics similar to those in the Comprehensive books, but go into more depth. Advanced books present the most high-level coverage in the series.

Custom Books The New Perspectives Series offers you two ways to customize a New Perspectives text to fit your course exactly: *CourseKits*™, two or more texts packaged together in a box, and *Custom Editions*®, your choice of books bound together. Custom Editions offer you unparalleled flexibility in designing your concepts and applications courses. You can build your own book by ordering a combination of titles bound together to cover only the topics you want. Your students save because they buy only the materials they need. There is no minimum order, and books are spiral bound. Both CourseKits and Custom Editions offer significant price discounts. Contact your Course Technology sales representative for more information.

New Perspectives Series Microcomputer Applications				
■ **Brief Titles or Modules**	■ **Introductory Titles or Modules**	■ **Intermediate Tutorials**	■ **Advanced Titles or Modules**	■ **Other Modules**
Brief	**Introductory**	**Comprehensive**	**Advanced**	**Custom Editions**
2 to 4 tutorials	6 or 7 tutorials, or Brief + 2 or 3 more tutorials	Introductory + 3 to 6 more tutorials. Includes Brief Windows tutorials and Additional Cases	Quick Review of basics + in-depth, high-level coverage	Choose from any of the above to build your own Custom Editions® or CourseKits™

In what kind of course could I use this book?

This book can be used in any course in which you want students to learn all the most important topics of Microsoft Word 97, including customizing toolbars and templates, recording macros, creating on-screen forms, managing long documents with master documents, faxing and routing documents, and drawing watermarks and 3-D objects. It is particularly recommended for a full-semester course on Microsoft Word 97. This book also includes coverage of basic Windows 95 navigation and file management skills from the Windows 95 tutorials.

Windows 98 Preview Following the Brief Windows 95 tutorials of this text, students are presented with a brief explanation of what to expect with Windows 98. This introductory tour explains some of the new features of the operating system, by comparing them to the Windows 95 system. Students are encouraged to look critically at these new features in order to decide whether to upgrade their systems.

This book has been approved by Microsoft as courseware for the Certified Microsoft Office User (CMOU) program. After completing the tutorials and exercises in this book, students will be prepared to take the Expert level CMOU exam for Microsoft Word 97. By passing the certification exam for a Microsoft software program, students demonstrate proficiency in that program to employers. For more information about certification, please visit the CMOU program World Wide Web site at http://www.microsoft.com/office/train_cert.

How do the Windows 95 editions differ from the Windows 3.1 editions?

Sessions We've divided the tutorials into sessions. Each session is designed to be completed in about 45 minutes to an hour (depending, of course, upon student needs and the speed of your lab equipment). With sessions, learning is broken up into more easily assimilated portions. You can more accurately allocate time in your syllabus, and students can better manage the available lab time. Each session begins with a "session box," which quickly describes the skills students will learn in the session. Furthermore, each session is numbered, which makes it easier for you and your students to navigate and communicate about the tutorial. Look on page W 1.5 for the session box that opens Session 1.1.

Quick Checks Each session concludes with meaningful, conceptual Quick Check questions that test students' understanding of what they learned in the session. Answers to the Quick Check questions in this book are provided on pages W 4.31 through W 4.35, W 7.45 through W 7.46, and W 10.59 through W 10.62.

New Design We have retained the best of the old design to help students differentiate between what they are to *do* and what they are to *read*. The steps are clearly identified by their shaded background and numbered steps. Furthermore, this new design presents steps and screen shots in a larger, easier to read format. Some good examples of our new design are pages W 2.4 and W 2.5.

What features are retained in the Windows 95 editions of the New Perspectives Series?

"Read This Before You Begin" Page This page is consistent with Course Technology's unequaled commitment to helping instructors introduce technology into the classroom. Technical considerations and assumptions about software are listed to help instructors save time and eliminate unnecessary aggravation. See pages W 1.2, W 5.2, and W 8.2 for the "Read This Before You Begin" pages in this book.

Tutorial Case Each tutorial begins with a problem presented in a case that is meaningful to students. The problem turns the task of learning how to use an application into a problem-solving process. The problems increase in complexity with each tutorial. These cases touch on multicultural, international, and ethical issues—so important to today's business curriculum. See page W 1.3 for the case that begins Tutorial 1.

1.
2.
3.

Step-by-Step Methodology This unique Course Technology methodology keeps students on track. They enter data, click buttons, or press keys always within the context of solving the problem posed in the tutorial case. The text constantly guides students, letting them know where they are in the course of solving the problem. In addition, the numerous screen shots include labels that direct students' attention to what they should look at on the screen. On almost every page in this book, you can find an example of how steps, screen shots, and labels work together.

TROUBLE?

TROUBLE? Paragraphs These paragraphs anticipate the mistakes or problems that students are likely to have and help them recover and continue with the tutorial. By putting these paragraphs in the book, rather than in the Instructor's Manual, we facilitate independent learning and free the instructor to focus on substantive conceptual issues rather than on common procedural errors. Some representative examples of TROUBLE? paragraphs appear on page W 1.6.

Reference Windows Reference Windows appear throughout the text. They are succinct summaries of the most important tasks covered in the tutorials. Reference Windows are specially designed and written so students can refer to them when doing the Tutorial Assignments and Case Problems, and after completing the course. Page W 5.21 contains the Reference Window for Creating and Editing Outlines.

Task Reference The Task Reference contains a summary of how to perform common tasks using the most efficient method, as well as references to pages where the task is discussed in more detail. It appears as a table at the end of the book.

Tutorial Assignments, Case Problems, and Lab Assignments Each tutorial concludes with Tutorial Assignments, which provide students with additional hands-on practice of the skills they learned in the tutorial. See pages W 4.25 through W 4.26 for examples of Tutorial Assignments. The Tutorial Assignments are followed by four Case Problems that have approximately the same scope as the tutorial case. In the Windows 95 applications texts, the last Case Problem of each tutorial typically requires students to solve the problem independently, either "from scratch" or with minimum guidance. See pages W 4.27 through W 4.30 for examples of Case Problems. Finally, if a Course Lab accompanies a tutorial, Lab Assignments are included after the Case Problems. See page W 1.31 for examples of Lab Assignments.

Exploration Exercises The Windows environment allows students to learn by exploring and discovering what they can do. Exploration Exercises can be Tutorial Assignments or Case Problems that challenge students, encourage them to explore the capabilities of the program they are using, and extend their knowledge using the Help facility and other reference materials. Page W 5.49 contains Exploration Exercises for Tutorial 5.

What supplements are available with this textbook?

Course Labs: Now, Concepts Come to Life Computer skills and concepts come to life with the New Perspectives Course Labs—highly-interactive tutorials that combine illustrations, animations, digital images, and simulations. The Labs guide students step-by-step, present them with Quick Check questions, let them explore on their own, test their comprehension, and provide printed feedback. Lab icons at the beginning of the tutorial and in the tutorial margins indicate when a topic has a corresponding Lab. Lab Assignments are included at the end of each relevant tutorial. The Labs available with this book and the tutorials in which they appear are:

TUTORIAL 1 Windows 95	TUTORIAL 1 Windows 95	TUTORIAL 2 Windows 95	TUTORIAL 1	TUTORIAL 7
			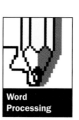	
Using a Keyboard	Using a Mouse	Using Files	Word Processing	The Internet World Wide Web

Course Test Manager Course Test Manager is a powerful testing and assessment package that enables instructors to create and print tests from test banks designed specifically for Course Technology titles. In addition, instructors with access to a networked computer lab (LAN) can administer, grade, and track tests online. Students can also take online practice tests, which generate customized study guides that indicate where in the text students can find more information on each question.

Skills Assessment Manager (SAM) This ground-breaking new assessment tool tests students' ability to perform real-world tasks live in the Microsoft Office 97 applications. Designed to be administered over a network, SAM tracks every action students perform in Microsoft Office 97 as they work through an exam. Upon completion of an exam, SAM assesses not only the *results* of students' work, but also the *way* students arrived at each answer and *how efficiently* they worked. Instructors may use SAM to create their own custom exams, or they may select from a library of pre-made exams, including exams that map to the content in this text as well as the Microsoft Office User Specialist certification program. SAM is available to test students who have purchased this text. Instructors interested in using SAM to test students out of a course, or to place them into a course, should contact their Course Technology sales representative.

Figures on CD-ROM This lecture presentation tool allows instructors to create electronic slide shows or traditional overhead transparencies using the figure files from the book. Instructors can customize, edit, save, and display figures from the text in order to illustrate key topics or concepts in class.

Online Companions: Dedicated to Keeping You and Your Students Up To Date When you use a New Perspectives product, you can access Course Technology's faculty sites and student sites on the World Wide Web. You can browse the password-protected Faculty Online Companion to obtain an online Instructor's Manual, Solution Files, Student Files, and more. Please see your Instructor's Manual or call your Course Technology customer service representative for more information. Student and Faculty Online Companions are accessible through the Course Technology home page at http://www.course.com.

Internet Assignments   The Instructor's Manual that accompanies this book includes additional assignments that integrate the World Wide Web with the word processing skills students learn in the tutorials. To complete these assignments, students will need to search the Web and follow the links from the *New Perspectives on Microsoft Word 97* home page. The Word 97 home page is accessible through the Student Online Companion link on the Course Technology home page at http:\\www.course.com. Please refer to the Instructor's Manual for more information.

Instructor's Manual   New Perspectives Series Instructor's Manuals contain instructor's notes and printed solutions for each tutorial. Instructor's notes provide tutorial overviews and outlines, technical notes, lecture notes, and extra Case Problems. Printed solutions include solutions to Tutorial Assignments, Case Problems, Additional Cases, and Lab Assignments.

Student Files   Student Files contain all of the data that students will use to complete the tutorials, Tutorial Assignments, Case Problems, and Additional Cases. A Readme file includes technical tips for lab management. See the inside covers of this book and the "Read This Before You Begin" pages for more information on Student Files.

Solution Files   Solution Files contain every file students are asked to create or modify in the tutorials, Tutorial Assignments, Case Problems, and Additional Cases.

The following supplements are included in the Instructor's Resource Kit that accompanies this textbook:

- electronic Instructor's Manual
- Solution Files
- Student Files
- Course Labs
- Course Test Manager Testbank
- Course Test Manager Engine
- Figures on CD-ROM

Some of the supplements listed above are also available over the World Wide Web through Course Technology's password-protected Faculty Online Companions. Please see your Instructor's Manual or call your Course Technology customer service representative for more information.

Acknowledgments

We would like to recognize the people whose contributions were essential in creating this book: our reviewers Jacqueline Artmayer, Oklahoma City Community College; Andrea Wachter, Point Park College; Patricia Lynn Wermers, North Shore Community College; Susan Hanns, Vincennes University; and Sylvia Charland, Fitchburg State University, for their thoughtful reviews; Mark Reimold and Donna Gridley for their excellent project management; Robin Geller, Barbara Clemens, and Joan Carey, whose fine editorial skills helped shape the book; Quality Assurance Project Leader Greg Bigelow and Quality Assurance Manuscript Reviewers John McCarthy and Brian McCooey, who ensured its accuracy with their detailed reviews; Roxanne Alexander for her careful production editing; and Gex for their usual excellent composition work. We could not have produced this book without them.

Beverly B. Zimmerman
S. Scott Zimmerman
Ann Shaffer

Brief Contents

Table of **Contents**

New Perspectives on

Microsoft® Windows® 95

BRIEF

TUTORIALS

Read This **Before You Begin**

STUDENT DISKS

To complete the tutorials and Tutorial Assignments, you need a Student Disk. Your instructor will either provide you with a Student Disk or ask you to make your own.

If you are supposed to make your own Student Disk, you will need a blank, formatted high-density disk. Follow the instructions in the section called "Creating Your Student Disk" in Tutorial 2 to use the Make Student Disk program to create your own Student Disk. See the inside front or inside back cover of this book for more information on Student Disk files, or ask your instructor or technical support person for assistance.

COURSE LABS

This book features three interactive Course Labs to help you understand Windows concepts. There are Lab Assignments at the end of each tutorial that relate to these Labs. To start a Lab, click the Start button on the Windows 95 taskbar, point to Programs, point to CTI Windows 95 Applications, point to Windows 95 New Perspectives Brief, and click the name of the Lab you want to use.

USING YOUR OWN COMPUTER

If you are going to work through this book using your own computer, you need:

■ **Computer System** Windows 95 must be installed on your computer. This book assumes a complete installation of Windows 95.

■ **Student Disk** Ask your instructor or lab manager for details on how to get the Student Disk. You will not be able to complete the tutorials or exercises in this book using your own computer until you have the Student Disk. The student files may also be obtained electronically over the Internet. See the inside front or inside back cover of this book for more details.

■ **Course Labs** See your instructor or technical support person to obtain the Course Lab software for use on your own computer.

To complete the tutorials and Tutorial Assignments in this book, your students must use a set of files on a Student Disk. The Instructor's Resource Kit for this book includes either two Student Files Setup Disks or a CD-ROM containing the student disk setup program. Follow the instructions on the disk label or in the Readme file to install the Make Student Disk program onto your server or standalone computers. Your students can then use the Windows 95 Start menu to run the program that will create their Student Disk. Tutorial 2 contains steps that instruct your students on how to generate student disks.

If you prefer to provide Student Disks rather than letting students generate them, you can run the Make Student Disk program yourself following the instructions in Tutorial 2.

COURSE LAB SOFTWARE

This book features three online, interactive Course Labs that introduce basic Windows concepts. The Instructor's Resource Kit for this book contains the Lab software either on four Course Labs Setup Disks or on a CD-ROM. Follow the instructions on the disk label or in the Readme file to install the Lab software on your server or standalone computers. Refer also to the Readme file for essential technical notes related to running the labs in a multiuser environment.
Once you have installed the Course Lab software, your students can start the Labs from the Windows 95 desktop by clicking the Start button on the Windows 95 taskbar, pointing to Programs, pointing to CTI Windows 95 Applications, pointing to Windows 95 New Perspectives Brief, and then clicking the name of the Lab they want to use.

CT LAB SOFTWARE AND STUDENT FILES

You are granted a license to copy the Student Files and Course Labs to any computer or computer network used by students who have purchased this book.

TUTORIAL 1

Exploring the Basics

Investigating the Windows 95 Operating System in the Computer Lab

LABS

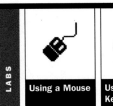

Using a Mouse

Using a Keyboard

CASE

Your First Day in the Lab

You walk into the computer lab and sit down at a desk. There's a computer in front of you, and you find yourself staring dubiously at the stack of software manuals. Where to start? As if in answer to your question, your friend Steve Laslow appears.

Gesturing to the stack of manuals, you tell Steve that you were just wondering where to start.

"You start with the operating system," says Steve. Noticing your slightly puzzled look, Steve explains that the **operating system** is software that helps the computer carry out basic operating tasks such as displaying information on the computer screen and saving data on your disks. Your computer uses the **Microsoft Windows 95** operating system—Windows 95, for short.

Steve tells you that Windows 95 has a "gooey" or **graphical user interface (GUI)**, which uses pictures of familiar objects, such as file folders and documents, to represent a desktop on your screen. Microsoft Windows 95 gets its name from the rectangular-shaped work areas, called "windows," that appear on your screen.

Steve continues to talk as he sorts through the stack of manuals on your desk. He says there are two things he really likes about Windows 95. First, lots of software is available for computers that have the Windows 95 operating system and all this software has a standard graphical user interface. That means once you have learned how to use one Windows software package, such as word-processing software, you are well on your way to understanding how to use other Windows software. Second, Windows 95 lets you use more than one software package at a time, so you can easily switch between your word-processing software and your appointment book software, for example. All in all, Windows 95 makes your computer an effective and easy-to-use productivity tool.

Steve recommends that you get started right away by using some tutorials that will teach you the skills essential for using Microsoft Windows 95. He hands you a book and assures you that everything on your computer system is set up and ready to go.

You mention that last summer you worked in an advertising agency where the employees used something called Windows 3.1. Steve explains that Windows 3.1 is an earlier version of the Windows operating system. Windows 95 and Windows 3.1 are similar, but Windows 95 is more powerful and easier to use. Steve says that as you work through the tutorials you will see notes that point out the important differences between Windows 95 and Windows 3.1.

Steve has a class, but he says he'll check back later to see how you are doing.

Using the Tutorials Effectively

These tutorials will help you learn about Windows 95. The tutorials are designed to be used at a computer. Each tutorial is divided into sessions. Watch for the session headings, such as Session 1.1 and Session 1.2. Each session is designed to be completed in about 45 minutes, but take as much time as you need. It's also a good idea to take a break between sessions.

Before you begin, read the following questions and answers. They are designed to help you use the tutorials effectively.

Where do I start?

Each tutorial begins with a case, which sets the scene for the tutorial and gives you background information to help you understand what you will be doing in the tutorial. Read the case before you go to the lab. In the lab, begin with the first session of the tutorial.

How do I know what to do on the computer?

Each session contains steps that you will perform on the computer to learn how to use Windows 95. Read the text that introduces each series of steps. The steps you need to do at a computer are numbered and are set against a color background. Read each step carefully and completely before you try it.

How do I know if I did the step correctly?

As you work, compare your computer screen with the corresponding figure in the tutorial. Don't worry if your screen display is somewhat different from the figure. The important parts of the screen display are labeled in each figure. Check to make sure these parts are on your screen.

What if I make a mistake?

Don't worry about making mistakes—they are part of the learning process. Paragraphs labeled "**TROUBLE?**" identify common problems and explain how to get back on track. Follow the steps in a **TROUBLE?** paragraph *only* if you are having the problem described. If you run into other problems:

- Carefully consider the current state of your system, the position of the pointer, and any messages on the screen.
- Complete the sentence, "Now I want to...." Be specific, because you are identifying your goal.
- Develop a plan for accomplishing your goal, and put your plan into action.

How do I use the Reference Windows?

Reference Windows summarize the procedures you learn in the tutorial steps. Do not complete the actions in the Reference Windows when you are working through the tutorial. Instead, refer to the Reference Windows while you are working on the assignments at the end of the tutorial.

How can I test my understanding of the material I learned in the tutorial?

At the end of each session, you can answer the Quick Check questions. The answers for the Quick Checks are at the end of the book.

After you have completed the entire tutorial, you should complete the Tutorial Assignments. The Tutorial Assignments are carefully structured so you will review what you have learned and then apply your knowledge to new situations.

What if I can't remember how to do something?

You should refer to the Task Reference at the end of the book; it summarizes how to accomplish commonly performed tasks.

What are the 3.1 Notes?

The 3.1 Notes are helpful if you have used Windows 3.1. The notes point out the key similarities and differences between Windows 3.1 and Windows 95.

What are the Interactive Labs, and how should I use them?

Interactive Labs help you review concepts and practice skills that you learn in the tutorial. Lab icons at the beginning of each tutorial and in the margins of the tutorials indicate topics that have corresponding Labs. The Lab Assignments section includes instructions for how to use each Lab.

Now that you understand how to use the tutorials effectively, you are ready to begin.

SESSION

1.1

In this session, in addition to learning basic Windows terminology, you will learn how to use a mouse, to start and stop a program, and to use more than one program at a time. With the skills you learn in this session, you will be able to use Windows 95 to start software programs.

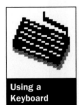

Using a Keyboard

Starting Windows 95

Windows 95 automatically starts when you turn on the computer. Depending on the way your computer is set up, you might be asked to enter your user name and password. If prompted to do so, type your assigned user name and press the Enter key. Then type your password and press the Enter key to continue.

To start Windows 95:

1. Turn on your computer.

TROUBLE? If the Welcome to Windows 95 box appears on your screen, press the Enter key to close it.

The Windows 95 Desktop

In Windows terminology, the screen represents a **desktop**—a workspace for projects and the tools needed to manipulate those projects. Look at your screen display and locate the objects labeled in Figure 1-1 on the following page.

Because it is easy to customize the Windows environment, your screen might not look exactly the same as Figure 1-1. You should, however, be able to locate objects on your screen similar to those in Figure 1-1.

Icons are small pictures that represent objects such as your computer, your computer network, a specific computer program, or a document. Your desktop probably contains several icons, such as My Computer, Network Neighborhood, and the Recycle Bin. You'll use these icons in later tutorials to work with files stored on your computer or on other computers on the network.

Figure 1-1 ◄
The Windows
95 desktop

The **desktop** is
your workspace
on the screen.

The **Start** button
is one of the
most important
controls in
Windows 95.
You use the
Start button
to access essential
Windows 95
functions, programs,
and documents.

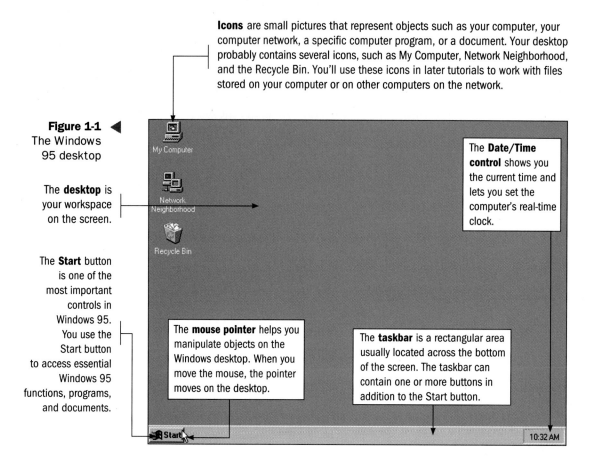

The **Date/Time control** shows you the current time and lets you set the computer's real-time clock.

The **mouse pointer** helps you manipulate objects on the Windows desktop. When you move the mouse, the pointer moves on the desktop.

The **taskbar** is a rectangular area usually located across the bottom of the screen. The taskbar can contain one or more buttons in addition to the Start button.

My Computer
Network Neighborhood
Recycle Bin
Start   10:32 AM

TROUBLE? If the screen goes blank or starts to display a moving design, press any key to restore the image.

Using the Mouse

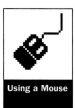

Using a Mouse

A **mouse**, like those shown in Figure 1-2, is a pointing device that helps you interact with objects on the screen. In Windows 95 you need to know how to use the mouse to point, click, and drag. In this session you will learn about pointing and clicking. In Session 1.2 you will learn how to use the mouse to drag objects.

You can also interact with objects by using the keyboard; however, the mouse is much more convenient for most tasks, so the tutorials in this book assume you are using one.

Pointing

The **pointer**, or **mouse pointer**, is a small object that moves on the screen when you move the mouse. The pointer is usually shaped like an arrow. As you move the mouse on a flat surface, the pointer on the screen moves in the direction corresponding to the movement of the mouse. The pointer sometimes changes shape depending on where it is on the screen or the action the computer is completing.

Find the arrow-shaped pointer on your screen. If you do not see the pointer, move your mouse until the pointer comes into view.

Figure 1-2 ◄
The mouse

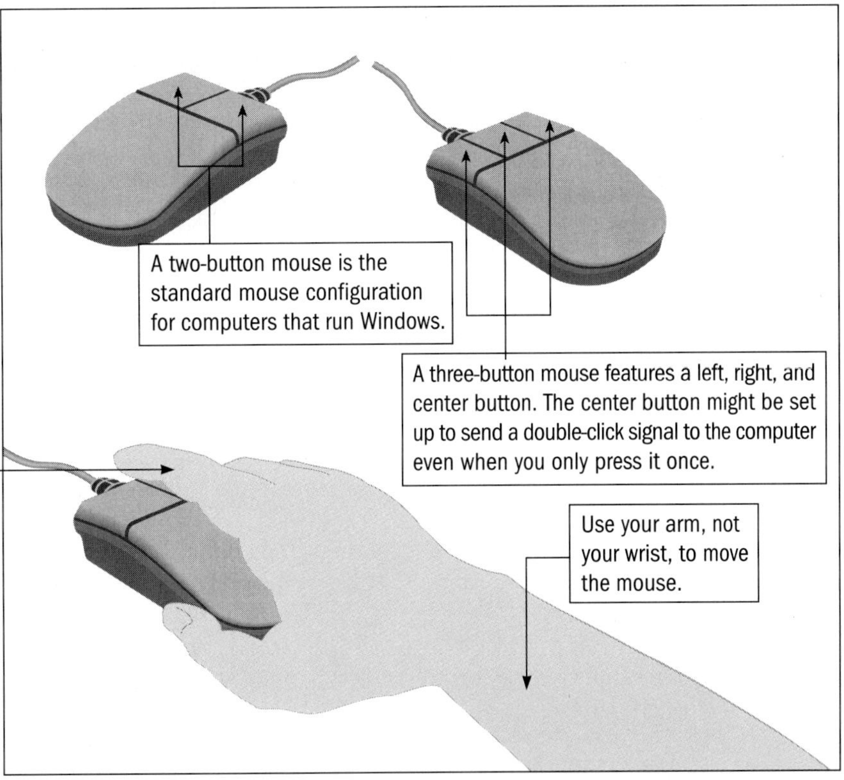

To hold the
mouse, place
your forefinger
over the left mouse
button. Place your
thumb on the left side
of the mouse. Your
ring and small
fingers should be
on the right side
of the mouse.

A two-button mouse is the standard mouse configuration for computers that run Windows.

A three-button mouse features a left, right, and center button. The center button might be set up to send a double-click signal to the computer even when you only press it once.

Use your arm, not your wrist, to move the mouse.

Basic "mousing" skills depend on your ability to position the pointer. You begin most Windows operations by positioning the pointer over a specific part of the screen. This is called **pointing**.

To move the pointer:

1. Position your right index finger over the left mouse button, as shown in Figure 1-2. Lightly grasp the sides of the mouse with your thumb and little finger.

   TROUBLE? If you want to use the mouse with your left hand, ask your instructor or technical support person to help you use the Control Panel to change the mouse settings to swap the left and right mouse buttons. Be sure you find out how to change back to the right-handed mouse setting, so you can reset the mouse each time you are finished in the lab.

2. Locate the arrow-shaped pointer on the screen.

3. Move the mouse and watch the movement of the pointer.

If you run out of room to move your mouse, lift the mouse and move it to a clear area on your desk, then place the mouse back on the desk. Notice that the pointer does not move when the mouse is not in contact with the desk.

When you position the mouse pointer over certain objects, such as the objects on the taskbar, a "tip" appears. These "tips" are called **ToolTips**, and they tell you the purpose or function of an object.

To view ToolTips:

1. Use the mouse to point to the **Start** button 🏁 Start. After a few seconds, you see the tip "Click here to begin" as shown in Figure 1-3 on the following page.

Figure 1-3 ◀
Viewing ToolTips

Start button ———

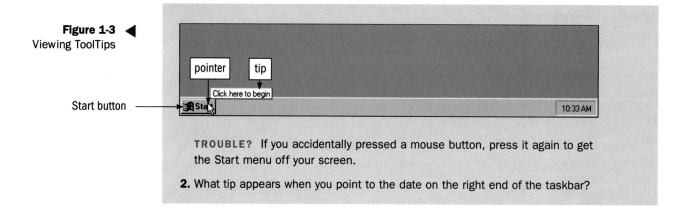

TROUBLE? If you accidentally pressed a mouse button, press it again to get the Start menu off your screen.

2. What tip appears when you point to the date on the right end of the taskbar?

Clicking

When you press a mouse button and immediately release it, it is called **clicking**. Clicking the mouse selects an object on the desktop. *You usually click the left mouse button, so* unless the instructions tell you otherwise, always click the left mouse button.

Windows 95 shows you which object is selected by highlighting it, usually by changing the object's color, putting a box around it, or making the object appear to be pushed in, as shown in Figure 1-4.

Figure 1-4 ◀
Selected objects

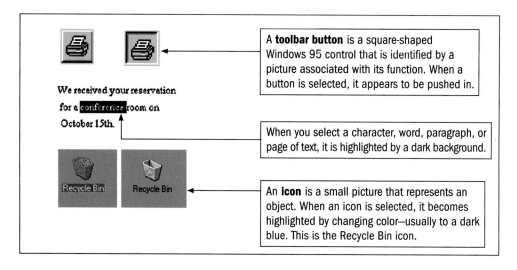

A **toolbar button** is a square-shaped Windows 95 control that is identified by a picture associated with its function. When a button is selected, it appears to be pushed in.

We received your reservation for a **conference** room on October 15th.

When you select a character, word, paragraph, or page of text, it is highlighted by a dark background.

An **icon** is a small picture that represents an object. When an icon is selected, it becomes highlighted by changing color—usually to a dark blue. This is the Recycle Bin icon.

To select the Recycle Bin icon:

1. Position the pointer over the **Recycle Bin** icon.

2. Click the mouse button and notice how the color of the icon changes to show that it is selected.

Starting and Closing a Program

The software you use is sometimes referred to as a program or an application. To use a program, such as a word-processing program, you must first start it. With Windows 95 you start a program by clicking the Start button. The Start button displays a menu.

A **menu** is a list of options. Windows 95 has a **Start menu** that provides you with access to programs, data, and configuration options. One of the Start menu's most important functions is to let you start a program.

The Reference Window below explains how to start a program. Don't do the steps in the Reference Window now; they are for your later reference.

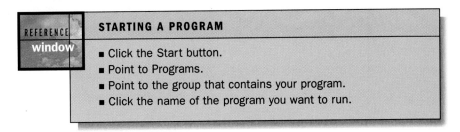

REFERENCE window	**STARTING A PROGRAM**
	■ Click the Start button.
	■ Point to Programs.
	■ Point to the group that contains your program.
	■ Click the name of the program you want to run.

3.1 NOTE

WordPad is similar to Write in Windows 3.1.

Windows 95 includes an easy-to-use word-processing program called WordPad. Suppose you want to start the WordPad program and use it to write a letter or report.

To start the WordPad program from the Start menu:

1. Click the **Start** button ![Start] as shown in Figure 1-5. A menu appears.

Figure 1-5 ◄
Starting the WordPad program

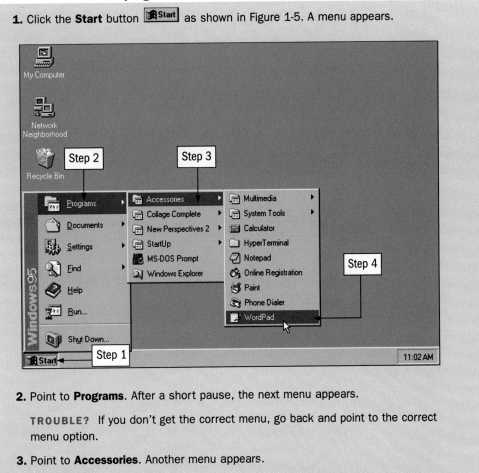

2. Point to **Programs**. After a short pause, the next menu appears.

   TROUBLE? If you don't get the correct menu, go back and point to the correct menu option.

3. Point to **Accessories**. Another menu appears.

4. Click **WordPad**. Make sure you can see the WordPad program as shown in Figure 1-6 on the following page.

Figure 1-6
The WordPad
program

WordPad program
window

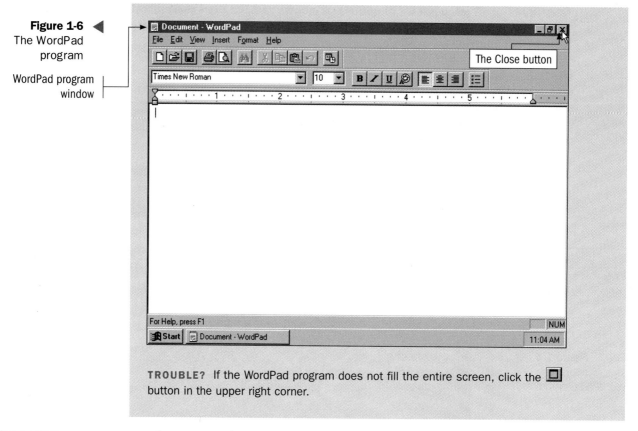

TROUBLE? If the WordPad program does not fill the entire screen, click the ☐ button in the upper right corner.

3.1 NOTE

As with Windows 3.1, in Windows 95 you can also exit a program using the Exit option from the File menu.

When you are finished using a program, the easiest way to return to the Windows 95 desktop is to click the Close button ☒.

To exit the WordPad program:

1. Click the **Close** button ☒. See Figure 1-6. You will be returned to the Windows 95 desktop.

Running More than One Program at the Same Time

3.1 NOTE

Paint in Windows 95 is similar to Paintbrush in WIndows 3.1.

One of the most useful features of Windows 95 is its ability to run multiple programs at the same time. This feature, known as **multi-tasking**, allows you to work on more than one task at a time and to quickly switch between tasks. For example, you can start WordPad and leave it running while you then start the Paint program.

To run WordPad and Paint at the same time:

1. Start WordPad.

   TROUBLE? You learned how to start WordPad earlier in the tutorial: Click the Start button, point to Programs, point to Accessories, and then click WordPad.

2. Now you can start the Paint program. Click the **Start** button 🏁 Start again.

3. Point to **Programs**.

4. Point to **Accessories**.

5. Click **Paint**. The Paint program appears as shown in Figure 1-7. Now two programs are running at the same time.

TROUBLE? If the Paint program does not fill the entire screen, click the ⬜ button in the upper right corner.

Figure 1-7 ◄
The Paint
Program

Paint program
window

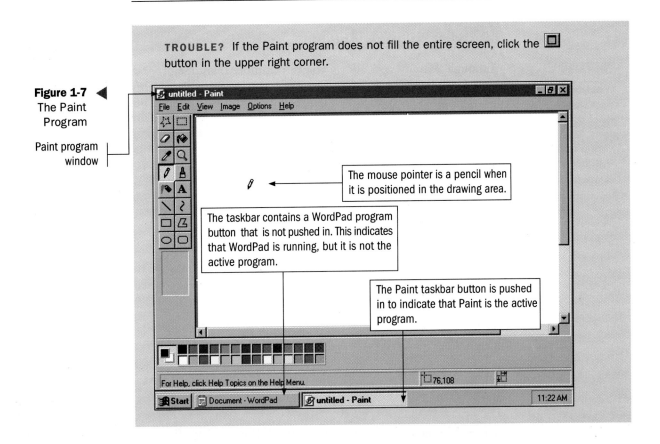

The mouse pointer is a pencil when it is positioned in the drawing area.

The taskbar contains a WordPad program button that is not pushed in. This indicates that WordPad is running, but it is not the active program.

The Paint taskbar button is pushed in to indicate that Paint is the active program.

3.1 NOTE

With Windows 3.1, some users had difficulty finding program windows on the desktop. The buttons on the Windows 95 taskbar make it much easier to keep track of which programs are running.

What happened to WordPad? The WordPad button is still on the taskbar, so even if you can't see it, WordPad is still running. You can imagine that it is stacked behind the Paint program, as shown in Figure 1-8.

Other projects might be hidden under the project you are working on. For example, you might have worked on a letter earlier, but it is now under the picture you are currently drawing.

You might keep other projects handy on your desk. Anytime you want to work with one of them, you bring it to the center of your desk.

Figure 1-8 ◄
Programs
stacked on top
of a desk

Think of your screen
as the main work
area of your desk.

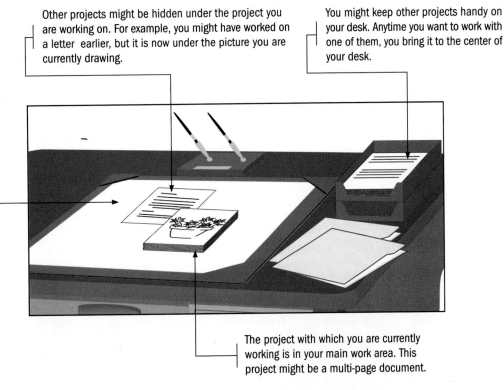

The project with which you are currently working is in your main work area. This project might be a multi-page document.

Switching Between Programs

3.1 NOTE

In Windows 95, you can still use Alt-Tab to switch between programs. You can also click any open window to switch to it.

Although Windows 95 allows you to run more than one program, only one program at a time is active. The **active** program is the program with which you are currently working. The easiest way to switch between programs is to use the buttons on the taskbar.

 REFERENCE window

SWITCHING BETWEEN PROGRAMS

■ Click the taskbar button that contains the name of the program to which you want to switch.

To switch between WordPad and Paint:

1. Click the button labeled **Document - WordPad** on the taskbar. The Document - WordPad button now looks like it has been pushed in to indicate it is the active program.

2. Next, click the button labeled **untitled - Paint** on the taskbar to switch to the Paint program.

Closing WordPad and Paint

It is good practice to close each program when you are finished using it. Each program uses computer resources such as memory, so Windows 95 works more efficiently when only the programs you need are open.

To close WordPad and Paint:

1. Click the **Close** button ☒ for the Paint program. The button labeled "untitled - Paint" disappears from the taskbar.

2. Click the **Close** button ☒ for the WordPad program. The WordPad button disappears from the taskbar, and you return to the Windows 95 desktop.

Shutting Down Windows 95

It is very important to shut down Windows 95 before you turn off the computer. If you turn off your computer without correctly shutting down, you might lose data and damage your files.

To shut down Windows 95:

1. Click the **Start** button ⊞Start on the taskbar to display the Start menu.

2. Click the **Shut Down** menu option to display the Shut Down Windows dialog box.

3. Make sure the **Shut down the computer?** option is selected.

4. Click the **Yes** button.

5. Wait until you see a message indicating it is safe to turn off your computer, then switch off your computer.

You should typically use the option "Shut down the computer?" when you want to turn off your computer. However, other shut-down options are available. For example, your school might prefer that you select the option to "Close all programs and log on as a different user." This option logs you out of Windows 95, leaves the computer turned on, and allows another user to log on without restarting the computer. Check with your instructor or technical support person for the preferred method for your school's computer lab.

Quick Check

1. Label the components of the Windows 95 desktop in the figure below:

Figure 1-9 ◀

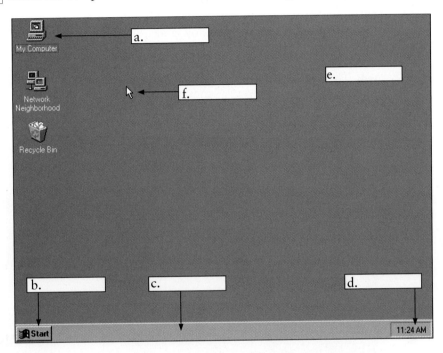

2. The _____ feature of Windows 95 allows you to run more than one program at a time.

3. The _____ is a list of options that provides you with access to programs, data, and configuration options.

4. What should you do if you are trying to move the pointer to the left edge of your screen, but your mouse runs into the keyboard?

5. Windows 95 shows you that an icon is selected by _____ it.

6. Even if you can't see a program, it might be running. How can you tell if a program is running?

7. Why is it good practice to close each program when you are finished using it?

8. Why do you need to shut down Windows 95 before you turn off your computer?

SESSION

1.2

In this session you will learn how to use many of the Windows 95 controls to manipulate windows and programs. You will learn how to change the size and shape of a window and to move a window so that you can customize your screen-based workspace. You will also learn how to use menus, dialog boxes, tabs, buttons, and lists to specify how you want a program to carry out a task.

Anatomy of a Window

When you run a program in Windows 95, it appears in a window. A **window** is a rectangular area of the screen that contains a program or data. A window also contains controls for manipulating the window and using the program. WordPad is a good example of how a window works.

Windows, spelled with an uppercase "W," is the name of the Microsoft operating system. The word "window" with a lowercase "w" refers to one of the rectangular windows on the screen.

To look at window controls:

1. Make sure Windows 95 is running and you are at the Windows 95 desktop screen.

2. Start WordPad.

   TROUBLE? To start WordPad, click the Start button, point to Programs, point to Accessories, and then click WordPad.

3. Make sure WordPad takes up the entire screen.

   TROUBLE? If WordPad does not take up the entire screen, click the ▢ button in the upper right corner.

4. On your screen, identify the controls labeled in Figure 1-10.

Figure 1-10 ◀
Window
controls

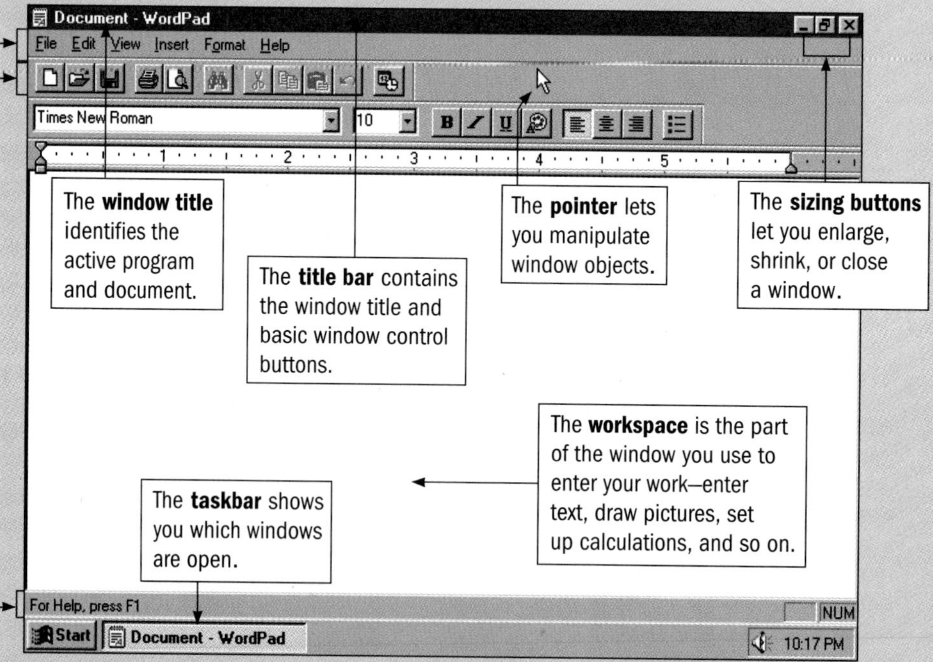

The **menu bar** contains the titles of menus, such as File, Edit, and Help.

The **toolbar** contains buttons that provide you with a shortcut to the commands listed on the menus.

The **status bar** provides you with abbreviated help relevant to the task you are doing.

The **window title** identifies the active program and document.

The **title bar** contains the window title and basic window control buttons.

The **pointer** lets you manipulate window objects.

The **sizing buttons** let you enlarge, shrink, or close a window.

The **workspace** is the part of the window you use to enter your work—enter text, draw pictures, set up calculations, and so on.

The **taskbar** shows you which windows are open.

Manipulating a Window

There are three buttons located on the right side of the title bar. You are already familiar with the Close button. The Minimize button hides the window. The other button either maximizes the window or restores it to a predefined size. Figure 1-11 shows how these buttons work.

Figure 1-11 ◀
Minimize,
Maximize and
Restore buttons

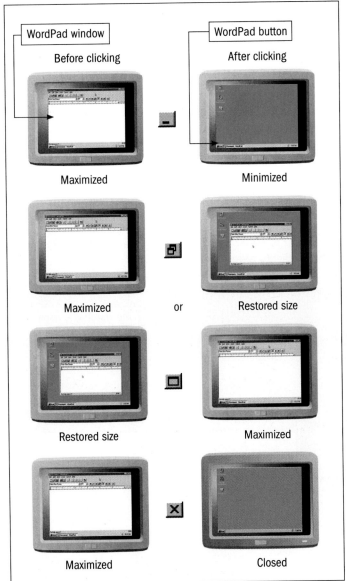

The **Minimize button** [—]
shrinks the window,
so you only see its
button on the taskbar.

The middle button appears as
a **Restore button** [◱]
or a **Maximize button.** [□]
When the window is maximized,
the Restore button appears. It
can be used to reduce the size
of the window to a predetermined
or "normal" size. When the
window does not fill the entire
screen, the Maximize button
appears. Clicking the Maximize
button enlarges the window to fill
the screen.

The **Close button** [✕]
closes the window and removes
its button from the taskbar at the
bottom of the screen.

Minimizing a Window

The **Minimize button** [—] shrinks the current window so that only the button on the taskbar remains visible. You can use the Minimize button when you want to temporarily hide a window but keep the program running.

To minimize the WordPad window:

1. Click the **Minimize** button [—]. The WordPad window shrinks so only the Document - WordPad button on the taskbar is visible.

   TROUBLE? If you accidentally clicked the Close button and closed the window, use the Start button to start WordPad again.

Redisplaying a Window

You can redisplay a minimized window by clicking the program's button on the taskbar. When you redisplay a window, it becomes the active window.

To redisplay the WordPad window:

1. Click the **Document - WordPad** button on the taskbar. The WordPad window is restored to its previous size. The Document - WordPad button looks pushed in as a visual clue that it is now the active window.

Restoring a Window

The **Restore** button 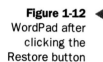 reduces the window so it is smaller than the entire screen. This is useful if you want to see more than one window at a time. Also, because of its small size, you can drag the window to another location on the screen or change its dimensions.

To restore a window:

1. Click the **Restore** button 🗗 on the WordPad title bar. The WordPad window will look similar to Figure 1-12, but the exact size of the window on your screen might be slightly different.

Figure 1-12 ◄
WordPad after
clicking the
Restore button

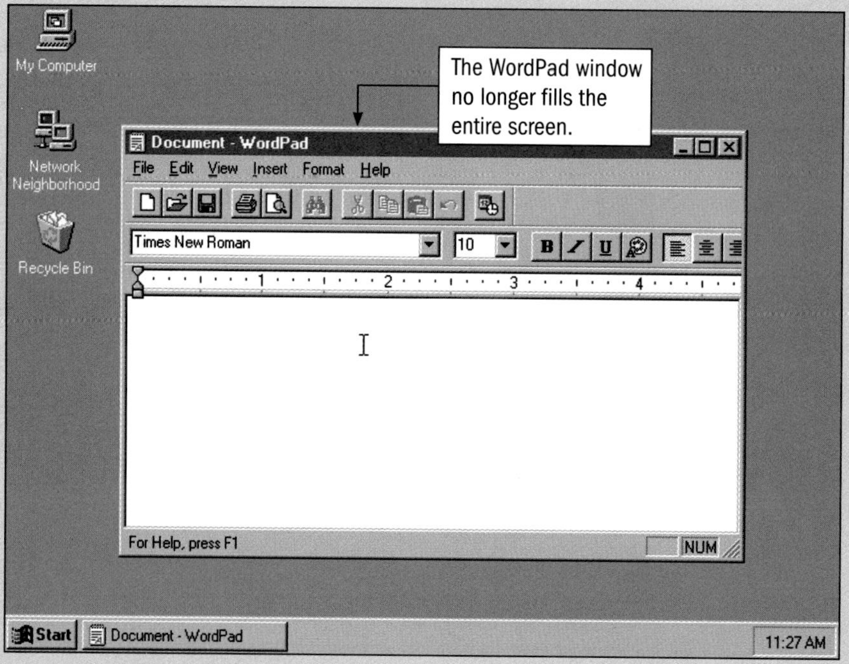

> The WordPad window no longer fills the entire screen.

Moving a Window

You can use the mouse to **move** a window to a new position on the screen. When you hold down the mouse button while moving the mouse, it is called **dragging**. You can move objects on the screen by dragging them to a new location. If you want to move a window, you drag its title bar.

To drag the WordPad window to a new location:

1. Position the mouse pointer on the WordPad window title bar.

2. While you hold down the left mouse button, move the mouse to drag the window. A rectangle representing the window moves as you move the mouse.

3. Position the rectangle anywhere on the screen, then release the left mouse button. The WordPad window appears in the new location.

4. Now drag the WordPad window to the upper-left corner of the screen.

Changing the Size of a Window

3.1 NOTE

You can also change the size of a window by dragging the top, bottom, sides, and corners of the window, as you did in Windows 3.1.

You can also use the mouse to change the size of a window. Notice the sizing handle at the lower right corner of the window. The **sizing handle** provides a visible control for changing the size of a current window.

To change the size of the WordPad window:

1. Position the pointer over the sizing handle . The pointer changes to a diagonal arrow .

2. While holding down the mouse button, drag the sizing handle down and to the right.

3. Release the mouse button. Now the window is larger.

4. Practice using the sizing handle to make the WordPad window larger or smaller.

Maximizing a Window

The **Maximize button** enlarges a window so that it fills the entire screen. You will probably do most of your work using maximized windows because you can see more of your program and data.

To maximize the WordPad window:

1. Click the **Maximize** button on the WordPad title bar.

Using Program Menus

Most Windows programs use menus to provide an easy way for you to select program commands. The **menu bar** is typically located at the top of the program window and shows the titles of menus such as File, Edit, and Help.

Windows menus are relatively standardized—most Windows programs include similar menu options. It's easy to learn new programs, because you can make a pretty good guess about which menu contains the command you want.

Selecting Commands from a Menu

When you click any menu title, choices for that menu appear below the menu bar. These choices are referred to as **menu options**. To select a menu option, you click it. For example, the File menu is a standard feature in most Windows programs and contains the options related to working with a file: creating, opening, saving, and printing a file or document.

To select Print Preview from the File menu:

1. Click **File** in the WordPad menu bar to display the File menu.

   TROUBLE? If you open a menu but decide not to select any of the menu options, you can close the menu by clicking its title again.

2. Click **Print Preview** to open the preview screen and view your document as it will appear when printed. This document is blank because you didn't enter any text.

3. After examining the screen, click the button labeled "Close" to return to your document.

Not all menu options immediately carry out an action—some show submenus or ask you for more information about what you want to do. The menu gives you hints about what to expect when you select an option. These hints are sometimes referred to as **menu conventions**. Study Figures 1-13a and 1-13b so you will recognize the Windows 95 menu conventions.

Figure 1-13a ◀
Menu
Conventions

Some menu options are toggle switches that can be either "on" or "off." When a feature is turned on, a **check mark** appears next to the menu option. When the feature is turned off, there is no check mark.

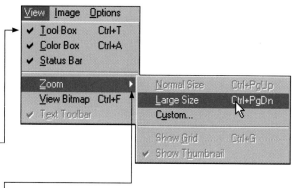

Certain menu selections lead you to an additional menu, called a **submenu**. A triangle on the right side of the menu choice indicates menu options that lead to submenus. When you move the pointer to a menu option with a triangle next to it, the submenu automatically appears.

Figure 1-13b ◀
Menu
conventions
(continued)

Some menu options are followed by a series of three dots, called an **ellipsis**. The dots indicate that you must make additional selections from a dialog box after you select that option. Options without dots do not require additional choices—they take effect as soon a you click them.

Sometimes certain menu options are unavailable. For example, a word-processing program might prevent you from trying to delete text if a document is blank. When a menu option is not available, it is usually **"grayed-out"** to provide you with a visual cue that the function is not available.

A **dialog box** lets you enter specification for how you want a task carried out.

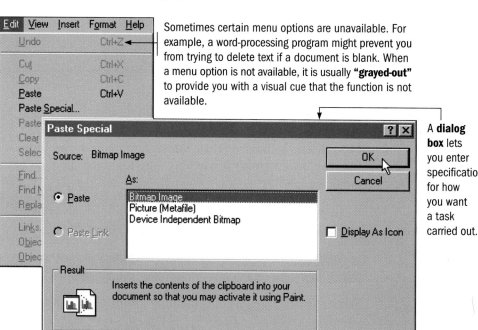

Using Toolbars

A **toolbar** contains buttons that provide quick access to important program commands. Although you can usually perform all program commands using the menus, the toolbar provides convenient one-click access to frequently-used commands. For most Windows 95 functions, there is usually more than one way to accomplish a task. To simplify your introduction to Windows 95 in this tutorial, you will learn only one method for performing a task. As you become more accomplished using Windows 95, you can explore alternative methods.

In Session 1.1 you learned that Windows 95 programs include ToolTips that indicate the purpose and function of a tool. Now is a good time to explore the WordPad toolbar buttons by looking at their ToolTips.

To find out a toolbar button's function:

1. Position the pointer over any button on the toolbar, such as the Print Preview icon 🔍. After a short pause, the name of the button appears in a box and a description of the button appears in the status bar just above the Start button.

2. Move the pointer to each button on the toolbar to see its name and purpose.

You select a toolbar button by clicking it.

To select the Print Preview toolbar button:

1. Click the **Print Preview** button 🔍. The Print Preview dialog box appears. This is the same dialog box that appeared when you selected File, Print Preview from the menu bar.

2. Click ⌊ Close ⌋ to close the Print Preview dialog box.

Using List Boxes and Scroll Bars

As you might guess from the name, a **list box** displays a list of choices. In WordPad, date and time formats are shown in the Date/Time list box. List box controls include arrow buttons, a scroll bar, and a scroll box, as shown in Figure 1-14.

Figure 1-14 ◀
List box

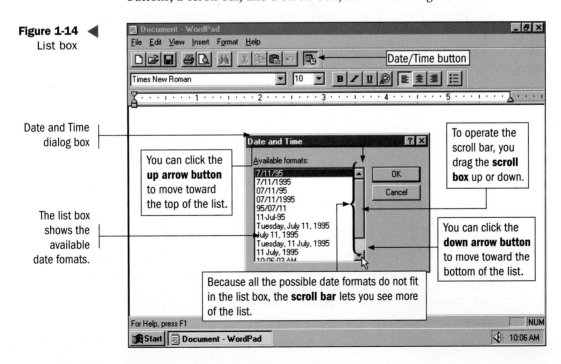

Date and Time dialog box

The list box shows the available date fomats.

You can click the **up arrow button** to move toward the top of the list.

To operate the scroll bar, you drag the **scroll box** up or down.

You can click the **down arrow button** to move toward the bottom of the list.

Because all the possible date formats do not fit in the list box, the **scroll bar** lets you see more of the list.

To use the Date/Time list box:

1. Click the **Date/Time** button to display the Date and Time dialog box. See Figure 1-14.

2. To scroll down the list, click the **down arrow** button . See Figure 1-14.

3. Find the scroll box on your screen. See Figure 1-14.

4. Drag the **scroll box** to the top of the scroll bar. Notice how the list scrolls back to the beginning.

5. Find a date format similar to "October 2, 1997." Click that date format to select it.

6. Click the **OK** button to close the Date and Time list box. This inserts the current date in your document.

A variation of the list box, called a **drop-down list box**, usually shows only one choice, but can expand down to display additional choices on the list.

To use the Font Size drop-down list:

1. Click the **down arrow** button shown in Figure 1-15.

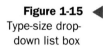

Figure 1-15
Type-size drop-down list box

2. Click **18**. The drop-down list disappears and the font size you selected appears at the top of the pull-down list.

3. Type a few characters to test the new font size.

4. Click the **down arrow** button in the Font Size drop-down list box again.

5. Click **12**.

6. Type a few characters to test this type size.

7. Click the **Close** button to close WordPad.

8. When you see the message "Save changes to Document?" click the **No** button.

Using Tab Controls, Radio Buttons, and Check Boxes

Dialog boxes often use tabs, radio buttons, or check boxes to collect information about how you want a program to perform a task. A **tab control** is patterned after the tabs on file folders. You click the appropriate tab to view different pages of information or choices. Tab controls are often used as containers for other Windows 95 controls such as list boxes, radio buttons, and check boxes.

Radio buttons, also called **option buttons**, allow you to select a single option from among one or more options. **Check boxes** allow you to select many options at the same time. Figure 1-16 explains how to use these controls.

Figure 1-16 ◀
Tabs, radio buttons, and check boxes

A **tab** indicates an "index card" that contains information or a group of controls, usually with related functions. To look at the functions on an index card, click the tab.

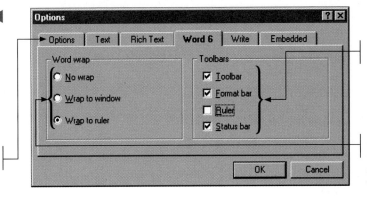

Check boxes allow you to select one or more options from a group. When you click a check box, a check mark appears in it. To remove a check mark from a box, click it again.

Radio buttons are round and usually come in groups of two or more. You can select only one radio button from a group. Your selection is indicated by a black dot.

Using Help

Windows 95 **Help** provides on-screen information about the program you are using. Help for the Windows 95 operating system is available by clicking the Start button on the taskbar, then selecting Help from the Start menu. If you want Help for a program, such as WordPad, you must first start the program, then use the Help menu at the top of the screen.

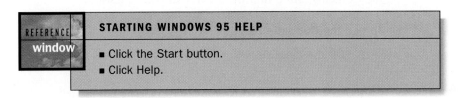

REFERENCE window

STARTING WINDOWS 95 HELP

- Click the Start button.
- Click Help.

To start Windows 95 Help:

1. Click the **Start** button.

2. Click **Help.**

Help uses tabs for each section of Help. Windows 95 Help tabs include Contents, Index, and Find as shown in Figure 1-17 on the following page.

Figure 1-17 ◀
Windows 95
Help

Each section of
Help is divided
into "books."
To open a book,
you click the
book, then click
the Open button.

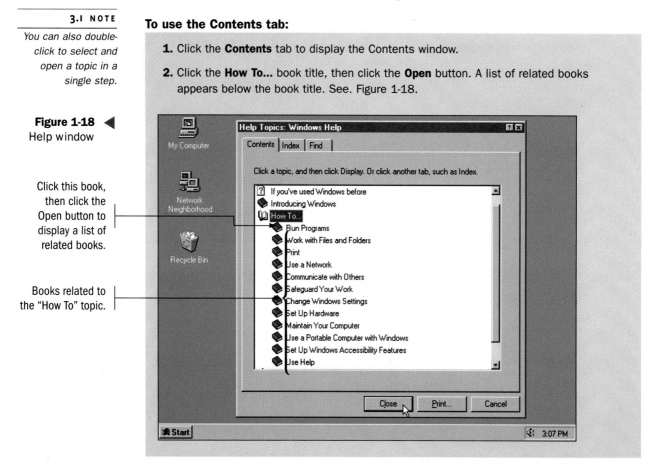

The Contents tab groups Help topics into a series of books. You select a book, which then provides you with a list of related topics from which you can choose. The **Index tab** displays an alphabetical list of all the Help topics from which you can choose. The **Find tab** lets you search for any word or phrase in Help.

Suppose you're wondering if there is an alternative way to start programs. You can use the Contents tab to find the answer to your question.

3.1 NOTE

You can also double-click to select and open a topic in a single step.

To use the Contents tab:

1. Click the **Contents** tab to display the Contents window.

2. Click the **How To...** book title, then click the **Open** button. A list of related books appears below the book title. See. Figure 1-18.

Figure 1-18 ◀
Help window

Click this book,
then click the
Open button to
display a list of
related books.

Books related to
the "How To" topic.

3. Click the **Run Programs** book, then click the **Open** button. The table of contents for this Help book is displayed.

4. Click the topic **Starting a Program**, then click the **Display** button. A Help window appears and explains how to start a program.

Help also provides you with definitions of technical terms. You can click any underlined term to see its definition.

To see a definition of the term "taskbar":

1. Point to the underlined term, <u>**taskbar**</u> until the pointer changes to a hand. Then click.

2. After you have read the definition, click the definition to deselect it.

3. Click the **Close** button ☒ on the Help window.

The **Index tab** allows you to jump to a Help topic by selecting a topic from an indexed list. For example, you can use the Index tab to learn how to arrange the open windows on your desktop.

To find a Help topic using the Index tab:

1. Click the **Start** button.

2. Click **Help**.

3. Click the **Index** tab.

4. A long list of indexed Help topics appears. Drag the scroll box down to view additional topics.

5. You can quickly jump to any part of the list by typing the first few characters of a word or phrase in the line above the Index list. Type **desktop** to display topics related to the Windows 95 desktop.

6. Click the topic **arranging open windows on** in the bottom window.

7. Click the **Display** button as shown in Figure 1-19.

Figure 1-19 ◀
Displaying a
Help Topic

Click here to type
words or phrases.

Index topics are
displayed here.
Click the topic to
select it.

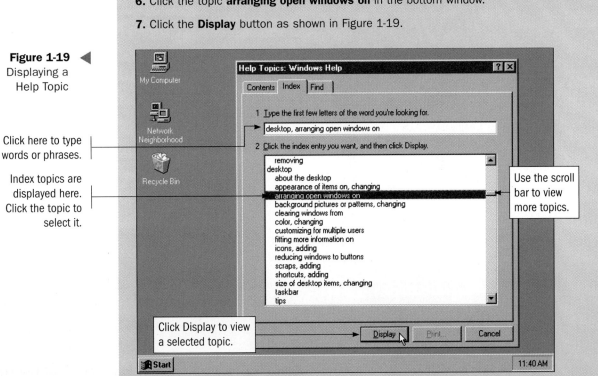

8. Click the **Close** button ⊠ to close the Windows Help window.

The **Find tab** contains an index of all words in Windows 95 Help. You can use it to search for Help pages that contain a particular word or phrase. For example, suppose you heard that a screen saver blanks out your screen when you are not using it. You could use the Find tab to find out more about screen savers.

To find a Help topic using the Find tab:

1. Click the **Start** button 📶 Start.

2. Click **Help**.

3. Click the **Find** tab.

 TROUBLE? If the Find index has not yet been created on your computer, the computer will prompt you through several steps to create the index. Continue with Step 4 below after the Find index is created.

4. Type **screen** to display a list of all topics that start with the letters "screen."

5. Click **screen-saver** in the middle window to display the topics that contain the word "screen-saver."

6. Click **Having your monitor automatically turn off**, then click the **Display** button.

7. Click the **Help window** button shown in Figure 1-20. The screen saver is shown on a simulated monitor.

 TROUBLE? If you see an error message, your lab does not allow students to modify screen savers. Click the OK button and go to Step 9.

Figure 1-20 ◄
Clicking a
Button in Help

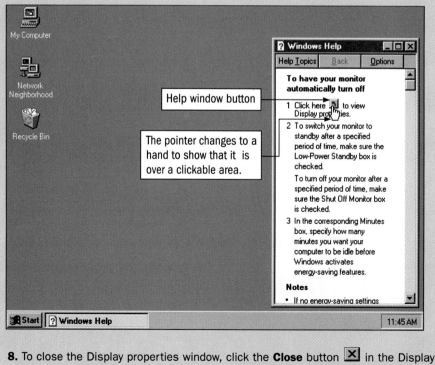

8. To close the Display properties window, click the **Close** button ⊠ in the Display Properties window.

9. Click the **Close** button ⊠ to close the Help window.

Now that you know how Windows 95 Help works, don't forget to use it! Use Help when you need to perform a new task or when you forget how to complete a procedure.

Quick Check

1 Label the parts of the window shown in Figure 1-21.

Figure 1-21 ◀

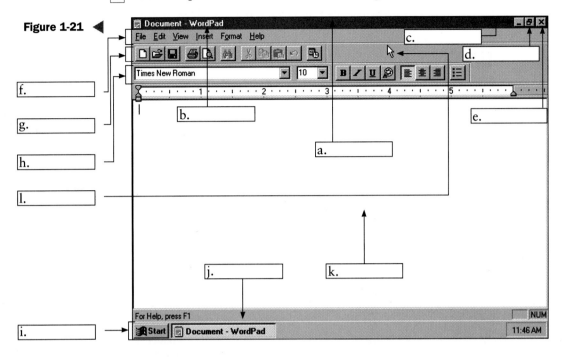

f.
g.
h.
l.
i.

2 Provide the name and purpose of each button:
a.
b.
c.
d.

3 Explain each of the following menu conventions:
a. Ellipsis...
b. Grayed out
c. ▶
d. ✔

4 A(n) _____ consists of a group of buttons, each of which provides one-click access to important program functions.

5 Label each part of the dialog box below:

Figure 1-22 ◀

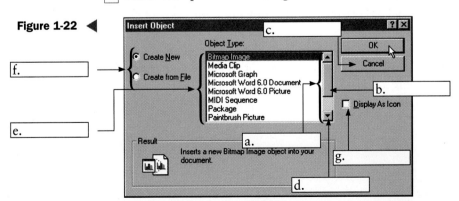

f.
e.

6   Radio buttons allow you to select _____ option(s) at a time, but _____ allow you to select one or more options.

7   It is a good idea to use _____ when you need to learn how to perform new tasks, simplify tedious procedures, and correct actions that did not turn out as you expected.

End Note

You've finished the tutorial, but Steve Laslow still hasn't returned. Take a moment to review what you have learned. You now know how to start a program using the Start button. You can run more than one program at a time and switch between programs using the buttons on the taskbar. You have learned the names and functions of window controls and Windows 95 menu conventions. You can now use toolbar buttons, list boxes, drop-down lists, radio buttons, check boxes, and scroll bars. Finally, you can use the Contents, Index, and Find tabs in Help to extend your knowledge of how to use Windows 95.

Tutorial Assignments

1. Running Two Programs and Switching Between Them In this tutorial you learned how to run more than one program at a time using WordPad and Paint. You can run other programs at the same time, too. Complete the following steps and write out your answers to questions b through f:

    a. Start the computer. Enter your user name and password if prompted to do so.
    b. Click the Start button. How many menu options are on the Start menu?
    c. Run the program Calculator program located on the Programs, Accessories menu. How many buttons are now on the taskbar?
    d. Run the Paint program and maximize the Paint window. How many application programs are running now?
    e. Switch to Calculator. What are the two visual clues that tell you that Calculator is the active program?
    f. Multiply 576 by 1457. What is the result?
    g. Close Calculator, then close Paint.

2. WordPad Help In Tutorial 1 you learned how to use Windows 95 Help. Just about every Windows 95 program has a help feature. Many computer users can learn to use a program just by using Help. To use Help, you would start the program, then click the Help menu at the top of the screen. Try using WordPad Help:

    a. Start WordPad.
    b. Click Help on the WordPad menu bar, then click Help Topics.
    c. Using WordPad help, write out your answers to questions 1 through 3.
        1. How do you create a bulleted list?
        2. How do you set the margins in a document?
        3. What happens if you hold down the Alt key and press the Print Screen key?
    d. Close WordPad.

3. Using Help to Explore Paint In this assignment, you will use the Paint Help to learn how to use the Paint program. Your goal is to create and print a picture that looks like the one in Figure 1-23.

Figure 1-23 ◄

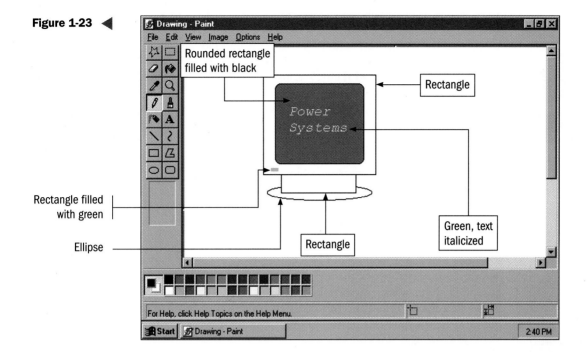

a. Start Paint.
b. Click Help, then click Help Topics.
c. Use Paint Help to learn how to put text in a picture and how to draw rectangles and circles.
d. Draw a picture of a monitor using rectangles, circles, and text as shown in Figure 1-23.
e. Print your picture.
f. Close Paint.

4. The Windows 95 Tutorial Windows 95 includes a five part on-line tutorial. In Tutorial 1 you learned about starting programs, switching windows, and using Help. You can use the on-line Windows 95 Tutorial to review what you learned and pick up some new tips for using Windows 95. Complete the following steps and write out your answers to questions f, g, and h:

a. Click the Start button to display the Start menu.
b. Click Help to display Windows help.
c. Click the Contents tab.
d. From the Contents screen, click Tour: Ten minutes to using Windows.
e. Click the Display button. If an error message appears, the Tour is probably not loaded on your computer. You will not be able to complete this assignment. Click Cancel, then click OK to cancel and check with your instructor or technical support person.
f. Click Starting a Program and complete the tutorial. What are the names of the seven programs on the Accessories menu in the tutorial?
g. Click Switching Windows and complete the on-line tutorial. What does the Minimize button do?
h. Click Using Help and complete the tutorial. What is the purpose of the 🔲 button?
i. Click the Exit button to close the Tour window.
j. Click the Exit Tour button to exit the Tour and return to the Windows 95 desktop.

Lab Assignments

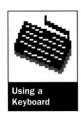

Using a Keyboard

1. Learning to Use the Keyboard If you are not familiar with computer keyboards, you will find the Keyboard Lab helpful. This Lab will give you a structured introduction to special computer keys and their function in Windows 95. As you work through the Lab, you will be asked to answer Quick Check questions about what you have learned. At the end of the lab, you will see a summary report of your answers. If your instructor wants you to print out your answers to these questions, click the Print button on the summary report screen.

    a. Click the Start button.
    b. Point to Programs, then point to CTI Windows 95 Applications.
    c. Click Windows 95 New Perspectives Brief.
    d. Click Using a Keyboard. If you cannot find Windows 95 New Perspectives Brief or Using a Keyboard, ask for help from your instructor or technical support person.

Using a Mouse

2. Mouse Practice If you would like more practice using a mouse, you can complete the Mouse Lab. As you work through the Lab, you will be asked to answer Quick Check questions about what you have learned. At the end of the lab, the Quick Check Report shows you how you did. If your instructor wants you to print out your answers to these questions, click the Print button on the summary report screen.

    a. Click the Start button.
    b. Point to Programs, then point to CTI Windows 95.
    c. Point to Windows 95 New Perspectives Brief.
    d. Click Using a Mouse. If you cannot find Windows 95 New Perspectives Brief or Using a Mouse, ask for help from your instructor or technical support person.

Working with Files

In this tutorial you will learn to:

- Format a disk

- Enter, select, insert, and delete text

- Create and save a file

- Open and edit a file

- Print a file

- Create a Student Disk

- View the list of files on your disk

- Move, copy, delete, and rename a file

- Make a backup of your floppy disk

LABS

Using Files

CASE

Your First Day in the Lab—Continued

Steve Laslow is back from class, grinning. "I see you're making progress!"

"That's right," you reply. "I know how to run programs, control windows, and use Help. I guess I'm ready to work with my word-processing and spreadsheet software now."

Steve hesitates before he continues, "You could, but there are a few more things about Windows 95 that you should learn first."

Steve explains that most of the software you have on your computer—your word-processing, spreadsheet, scheduling, and graphing software—was created especially for the Windows 95 operating system. This software is referred to as **Windows 95 applications** or **Windows 95 programs**. You can also use software designed for Windows 3.1, but Windows 95 applications give you more flexibility. For example, when you name a document in a Windows 95 application, you can use descriptive filenames with up to 255 characters, whereas in Windows 3.1 you are limited to eight-character names.

You typically use Windows 95 applications to create files. A **file** is a collection of data that has a name and is stored in a computer. You typically create files that contain documents, pictures, and graphs when you use software packages. For example, you might use word-processing software to create a file containing a document. Once you create a file, you can open it, edit its contents, print it, and save it again—usually using the same application program you used to create it.

Another advantage of Windows 95 is that once you know how to save, open, and print files with one Windows 95 application, you can perform those same functions in *any* Windows 95 application. This is because Windows 95 applications have similar controls. For example, your word-processing and spreadsheet software will have identical menu commands to save, open, and print documents. Steve suggests that it would be worth a few minutes of your time to become familiar with these menus in Windows 95 applications.

You agree, but before you can get to work, Steve gives you one final suggestion: you should also learn how to keep track of the files on your disk. For instance, you might need to find a file you have not used for a while or you might want to delete a file if your disk is getting full. You will definitely want to make a backup copy of your disk in case something happens to the original. Steve's advice seems practical, and you're eager to explore these functions so you can get to work!

Tutorial 2 will help you learn how to work with Windows 95 applications and keep track of the files on your disk. When you've completed this tutorial, you'll be ready to tackle all kinds of Windows 95 software!

In Session 2.1 you will learn how to format a disk so it can store files. You will create, save, open, and print a file. You will find out how the insertion point is different from the mouse pointer, and you will learn the basic skills for Windows 95 text entry, such as inserting, deleting, and selecting.
For this tutorial you will need two blank 3 ½-inch disks.

Formatting a Disk

Before you can save files on a disk, the disk must be formatted. When the computer **formats** a disk, the magnetic particles on the disk surface are arranged so data can be stored on the disk. Today, many disks are sold preformatted and can be used right out of the box. However, if you purchase an unformatted disk, or if you have an old disk that you want to completely erase and reuse, you can format the disk using the Windows 95 Format command.

The following steps tell you how to format a 3 ½-inch high-density disk using drive A. Your instructor will tell you how to revise the instructions given in these steps if the procedure is different for your lab equipment.

All data on the disk you format will be erased, so don't perform these steps using a disk that contains important files.

To format a disk:

1. Start Windows 95, if necessary.

2. Write your name on the label of a 3 ½-inch disk.

3. Insert your disk in drive A. See Figure 2-1.

Figure 2-1 ◀
Inserting a
disk into the
disk drive

floppy disk drive

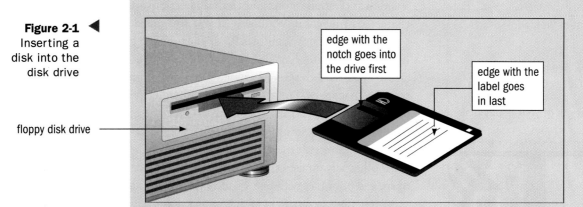

edge with the
notch goes into
the drive first

edge with the
label goes
in last

TROUBLE? If your disk does not fit in drive A, put it in drive B and substitute drive B for drive A in all of the steps for the rest of the tutorial.

4. Click the **My Computer** icon to select it, then press the **Enter** key. Make sure you can see the My Computer window. See Figure 2-2.

TROUBLE? If you see a list instead of icons like those in Figure 2-2, click View. Then click Large Icon.

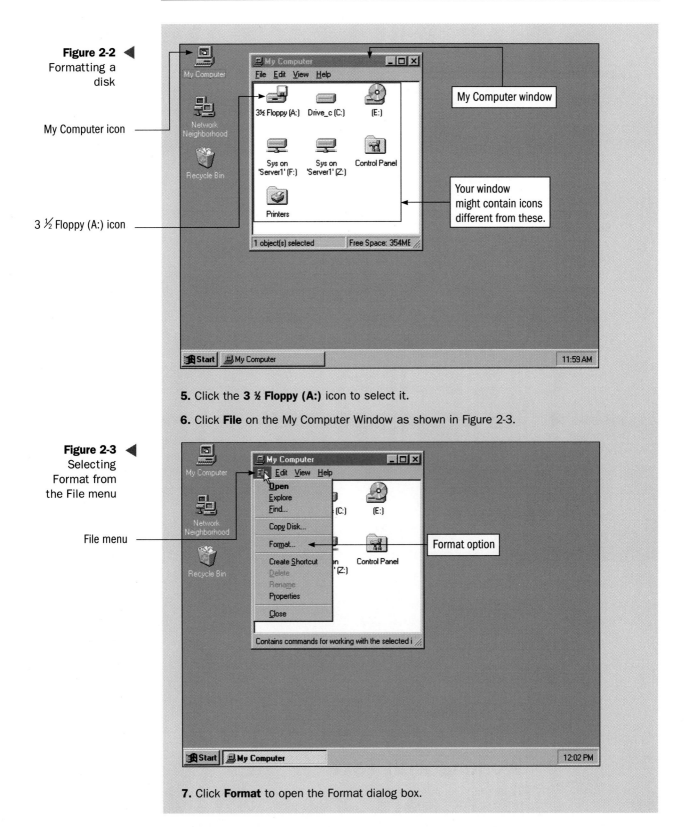

Figure 2-2
Formatting a
disk

My Computer icon

3 ½ Floppy (A:) icon

My Computer window

Your window
might contain icons
different from these.

5. Click the **3 ½ Floppy (A:)** icon to select it.

6. Click **File** on the My Computer Window as shown in Figure 2-3.

Figure 2-3
Selecting
Format from
the File menu

File menu

Format option

7. Click **Format** to open the Format dialog box.

8. Make sure the dialog box settings on your screen match those in Figure 2-4.

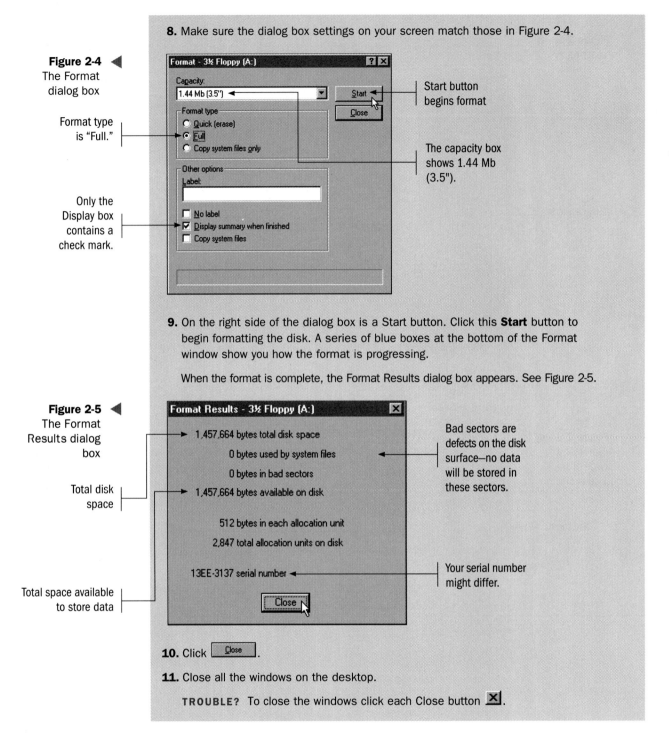

Figure 2-4
The Format
dialog box

Format type
is "Full."

Only the
Display box
contains a
check mark.

Start button
begins format

The capacity box
shows 1.44 Mb
(3.5").

9. On the right side of the dialog box is a Start button. Click this **Start** button to begin formatting the disk. A series of blue boxes at the bottom of the Format window show you how the format is progressing.

When the format is complete, the Format Results dialog box appears. See Figure 2-5.

Figure 2-5
The Format
Results dialog
box

Total disk
space

Total space available
to store data

Bad sectors are
defects on the disk
surface—no data
will be stored in
these sectors.

Your serial number
might differ.

10. Click ⬛ Close .

11. Close all the windows on the desktop.

TROUBLE? To close the windows click each Close button ❌.

Working with Text

To accomplish many computing tasks, you need to type text in documents and text boxes. Windows 95 facilitates basic text entry by providing a text-entry area, by showing you where your text will appear on the screen, by helping you move around on the screen, and by providing insert and delete functions.

When you type sentences and paragraphs of text, do *not* press the Enter key when you reach the right margin. The software contains a feature called **word wrap** that automatically continues your text on the next line. Therefore, you should press Enter only when you have completed a paragraph.

If you type the wrong character, press the Backspace key to backup and delete the character. You can also use the Delete key. What's the difference between the Backspace and the Delete keys? The Backspace key deletes the character to left. The Delete key deletes the character to the right.

Now you will type some text using WordPad to learn about text entry.

To type text in WordPad:

> **1.** Start WordPad.
>
>   **TROUBLE?** If the WordPad window does not fill the screen, click the Maximize button 🔲.
>
> **2.** Notice the flashing vertical bar, called the **insertion point**, in the upper-left corner of the document window. The insertion point indicates where the characters you type will appear.
>
> **3.** Type your name, using the Shift key to type uppercase letters and using the spacebar to type spaces, just like on a typewriter.
>
> **4.** Press the **Enter** key to end the current paragraph and move the insertion point down to the next line.
>
> **5.** As you type the following sentences, watch what happens when the insertion point reaches the right edge of the screen:
>
>   **This is a sample typed in WordPad. See what happens when the insertion point reaches the right edge of the screen.**
>
>   **TROUBLE?** If you make a mistake, delete the incorrect character(s) by pressing the Backspace key on your keyboard. Then type the correct character(s).

The Insertion Point versus the Pointer

The insertion point is not the same as the mouse pointer. When the mouse pointer is in the text-entry area, it is called the **I-beam pointer** and looks like I. Figure 2-6 explains the difference between the insertion point and the I-beam pointer.

Figure 2-6 ◀
The insertion point vs. the pointer

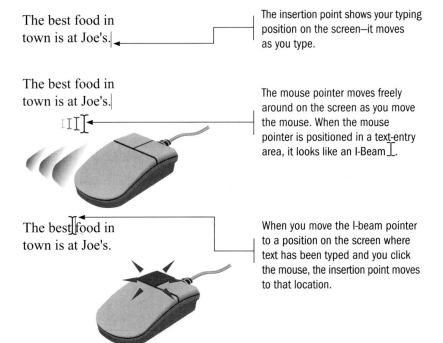

The best food in town is at Joe's.|

The insertion point shows your typing position on the screen—it moves as you type.

The best food in town is at Joe's.|

The mouse pointer moves freely around on the screen as you move the mouse. When the mouse pointer is positioned in a text-entry area, it looks like an I-Beam I.

The best food in town is at Joe's.

When you move the I-beam pointer to a position on the screen where text has been typed and you click the mouse, the insertion point moves to that location.

To move the insertion point:

1. Check the location of the insertion point and the I-beam pointer. The insertion point should be at the end of the sentence you typed in the last set of steps.

   TROUBLE? If you don't see the I-beam pointer, move your mouse until you see it.

2. Use the mouse to move the I-beam pointer to the word "sample," then click the left mouse button. The insertion point jumps to the location of the I-beam pointer.

3. Move the I-beam pointer to a blank area near the bottom of the work space and click the left mouse button. *Notice that the insertion point does not jump to the location of the I-beam pointer.* Instead the insertion point jumps to the end of the last sentence. The insertion point can move only within existing text. It cannot be moved out of the existing text area.

Selecting Text

Many text operations are performed on a **block** of text, which is one or more consecutive words, sentences, or paragraphs. Once you select a block of text, you can delete it, move it, replace it, underline it, and so on. As you select a block of text, the computer highlights it. If you want to remove the highlighting, just click in the margin of your document.

   Suppose you want to replace the phrase "See what happens" with "You can watch word wrap in action." You do not have to delete the text one character at a time. Instead you can highlight the entire phrase and begin to type the replacement text.

To select and replace a block of text:

1. Move the I-beam pointer just to the left of the word "See."

2. While holding down the left mouse button, drag the I-beam pointer over the text to the end of the word "happens." The phrase "See what happens" should now be highlighted. See Figure 2-7.

Figure 2-7 ◀
Highlighting
text

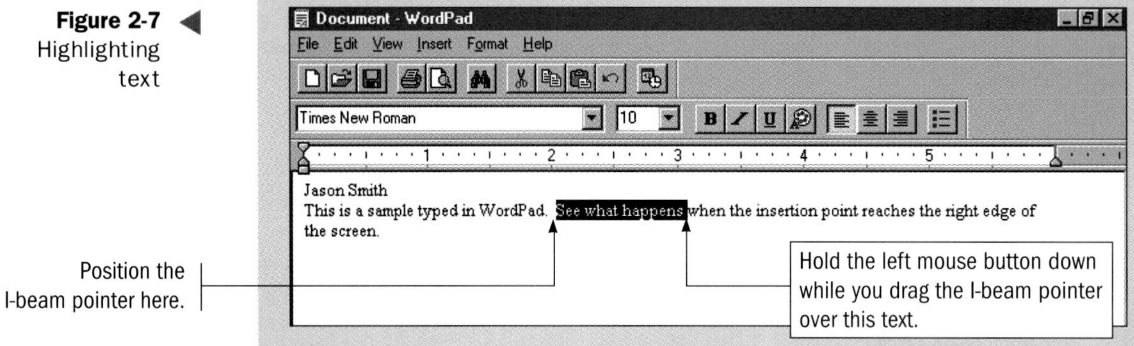

Position the
I-beam pointer here.

Hold the left mouse button down while you drag the I-beam pointer over this text.

3. Release the left mouse button.

   TROUBLE? If the phrase is not highlighted correctly, repeat Steps 1 through 3.

4. Type: **You can watch word wrap in action**

   The text you typed replaces the highlighted text. Notice that you did not need to delete the highlighted text before you typed the replacement text.

Inserting a Character

Windows 95 programs usually operate in **insert mode**—when you type a new character, all characters to the right of the cursor are pushed over to make room.

Suppose you want to insert the word "sentence" before the word "typed."

To insert characters:

> **1.** Position the I-beam pointer just before the word "typed," then click.
>
> **2.** Type: **sentence**.
>
> **3.** Press the **spacebar**.

3.1 NOTE

When you save a file with a long filename, Windows 95 also creates an eight-character filename that can be used by Windows 3.1 applications. The eight-character filename is created by using the first six non-space characters from the long filename, then adding a tilde (~) and a number. For example, the filename Car Sales for 1997 would be converted to Carsal~1.

Notice how the letters in the first line are pushed to the right to make room for the new characters. When a word gets pushed past the right margin, the word-wrap feature pushes it down to the beginning of the next line.

Saving a File

As you type text, it is held temporarily in the computer's memory. For permanent storage, you need to save your work on a disk. In the computer lab, you will probably save your work on a floppy disk in drive A.

When you save a file, you must give it a name. Windows 95 allows you to use filenames containing up to 255 characters, and you may use spaces and punctuation symbols. You cannot use the symbols \ ? : * " < > | in a filename, but other symbols such as &, -, and $ are allowed.

Most filenames have an extension. An **extension** is a suffix of up to three characters that is separated from the filename by a period, as shown in Figure 2-8.

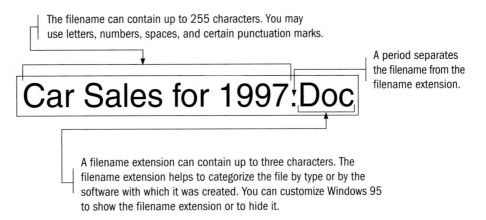

The filename can contain up to 255 characters. You may use letters, numbers, spaces, and certain punctuation marks.

A period separates the filename from the filename extension.

Figure 2-8 ◀
Filename and extension

A filename extension can contain up to three characters. The filename extension helps to categorize the file by type or by the software with which it was created. You can customize Windows 95 to show the filename extension or to hide it.

The file extension indicates which application you used to create the file. For example, files created with Microsoft Word software have a .Doc extension. In general, you will not add an extension to your filenames, because the application software automatically does this for you.

Windows 95 keeps track of file extensions, but does not always display them. The steps in these tutorials refer to files using the filename, but not its extension. So if you see the filename Sample Text in the steps, but "Sample Text.Doc" on your screen, don't worry—these are the same files.

Now you can save the document you typed.

To save a document:

1. Click the **Save** button 💾 on the toolbar. Figure 2-9 shows the location of this button and the Save As dialog box that appears after you click it.

Figure 2-9 ◀
The Save button

Save button

Save As
dialog box
appears after
you click the
Save button

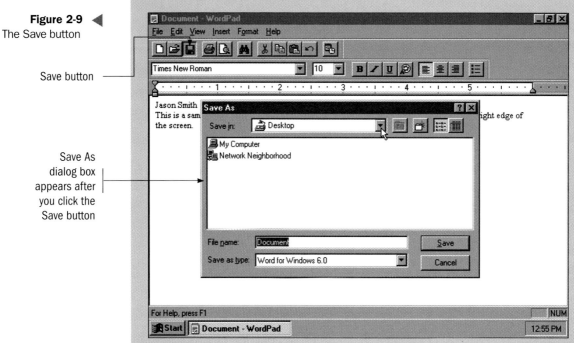

2. Click ▼ on the side of the Save in: box to display a list of drives. See Figure 2-10.

Figure 2-10 ◀
Selecting the
drive

3 ½ Floppy (A:)
drive menu
option

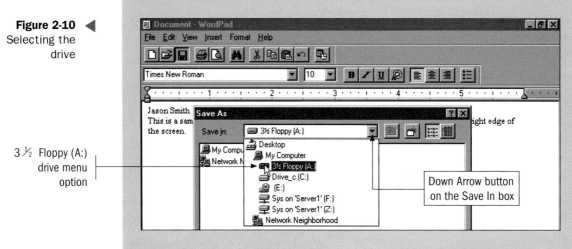

3. Click **3½ Floppy (A:)**.

4. Select the text in the File Name box.

> **TROUBLE?** To select the text, position the I-beam pointer at the beginning of the word "Document." While you hold down the mouse button, drag the I-beam pointer to the end of the word.

5. Type **Sample Text** in the File Name box.

6. Click the **Save** button. Your file is saved on your Student Disk and the document title, "Sample Text," appears on the WordPad title bar.

What if you tried to close WordPad *before* you saved your file? Windows 95 would display a message—"Save changes to Document?" If you answer "Yes," Windows displays the Save As dialog box so you can give the document a name. If you answer "No," Windows 95 closes WordPad without saving the document.

After you save a file, you can work on another document or close WordPad. Since you have already saved your Sample Text document, you should continue this tutorial by closing WordPad.

To close WordPad:

1. Click the **Close** button ☒ to close the WordPad window.

Opening a File

Suppose you save and close the Sample Text file, then later you want to revise it. To revise a file you must first open it. When you **open** a file, its contents are copied into the computer's memory. If you revise the file, you need to save the changes before you close the application or work on a different file. If you close a revised file without saving your changes, you will lose the revisions.

Typically, you would use one of two methods to open a file. You could select the file from the Documents list or the My Computer window, or you could start an application program and then use the Open button to open the file. Each method has advantages and disadvantages. You will have an opportunity to try both methods.

The first method for opening the Sample Text file simply requires you to select the file from the Documents list or the My Computer window. With this method the document, not the application program, is central to the task; hence this method is sometimes referred to as *document-centric*. You only need to remember the name of your document or file—you do not need to remember which application you used to create the document.

The Documents list contains the names of the last 15 documents used. You access this list from the Start menu. When you have your own computer, the Documents list is very handy. In a computer lab, however, the files other students use quickly replace yours on the list.

If your file is not in the Documents list, you can open the file by selecting it from the My Computer window. Windows 95 starts an application program that you can use to revise the file, then automatically opens the file. The advantage of this method is its simplicity. The disadvantage is that Windows 95 might not start the application you expect. For example, when you select Sample Text, you might expect Windows 95 to start WordPad because you used WordPad to type the text of the document. Depending on the software installed on your computer system, however, Windows 95 might start the Microsoft Word application instead. Usually this is not a problem. Although the application might not be the one you expect, you can still use it to revise your file.

To open the Sample Text file by selecting it from My Computer:

1. Click the **My Computer** icon. Press the **Enter** key. The My Computer window opens.

2. Click the **3½ Floppy (A:)** icon, then press the **Enter** key. The 3½ Floppy (A:) window opens.

TROUBLE? If the My Computer window disappears when you open the 3½ floppy (A:) window, click View, click Options, then click the Folder tab, if necessary. Click the radio button labelled "Browse Folders using a separate window for each folder." Then click the OK button.

3. Click the **Sample Text** file icon, then press the **Enter** key. Windows 95 starts an application program, then automatically opens the Sample Text file.

TROUBLE? If Windows 95 starts Microsoft Word instead of WordPad, don't worry. You can use Microsoft Word to revise the Sample Text document.

Now that Windows 95 has started an application and opened the Sample Text file, you could make revisions to the document. Instead, you should close all the windows on your desktop so you can try the other method for opening files.

To close all the windows on the desktop:

1. Click ☒ on each of the windows.

   TROUBLE? If you see a message, "Save changes to Document?" click the No button.

The second method for opening the Sample Text file requires you to open WordPad, then use the Open button to select the Sample Text file. The advantage of this method is that you can specify the application program you want to use—WordPad in this case. This method, however, involves more steps than the method you tried previously.

To start WordPad and open the Sample Text file using the Open button:

1. Start WordPad.

2. Click the **Open** button 📂 on the toolbar. Figure 2-11 shows the location of this button and the dialog box that appears after you click it.

Figure 2-11 ◄
The Open button
and dialog box

Open button

Open dialog box

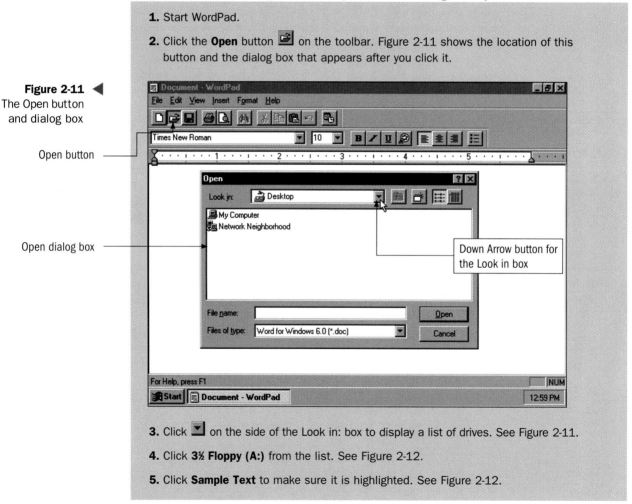

3. Click ▼ on the side of the Look in: box to display a list of drives. See Figure 2-11.

4. Click **3½ Floppy (A:)** from the list. See Figure 2-12.

5. Click **Sample Text** to make sure it is highlighted. See Figure 2-12.

Figure 2-12
Opening the
Sample Text file

Sample Text
icon

Open button

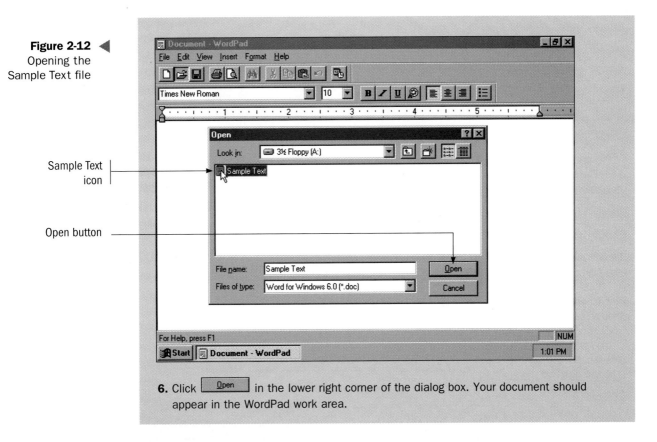

6. Click [Open] in the lower right corner of the dialog box. Your document should appear in the WordPad work area.

Printing a File

Now that the Sample Text file is open, you can print it. It is a good idea to use Print Preview before you send your document to the printer. **Print Preview** shows on screen exactly how your document will appear on paper. You can check your page layout so you don't waste paper printing a document that is not quite the way you want it. Your instructor or technical support person might supply you with additional instructions for printing in your school's computer lab.

To preview, then print the Sample Text file:

1. Click the **Print Preview** button 🔳 on the toolbar.

2. Look at your print preview. Before you print the document and use paper, you should make sure that the font, margins, and other document features look the way you want them to.

   TROUBLE? If you can't read the document text on screen, click the Zoom In button.

3. Click the **Print** button. A Print dialog box appears.

4. Study Figure 2-13 to familiarize yourself with the controls in the Print dialog box.

This is the name of the printer that Windows 95 will use for this printout. If you are using a network, you might have a choice of printers. If you need to select a different printer, ask your instructor or your technical support person for help.

The Properties button lets you modify the way your printer is set up. Do not change any of the settings on your school printer without the consent of your instructor or technical support person.

Figure 2-13 ◀
The Print dialog box

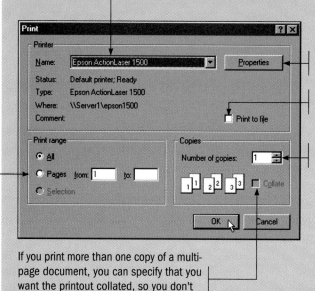

When you click this check box, your printout will go on your disk instead of to the printer.

In the Print range box, you specify how much of the document you want to print. If you want to print only part of a document, click the Pages radio button and then enter the starting and ending pages for the printout.

You can specify how many copies you want by typing the number in this box. Alternatively, you can use the arrow buttons to increase or decrease the number in the box.

If you print more than one copy of a multi-page document, you can specify that you want the printout collated, so you don't have to collate the pages manually.

5. Make sure your screen shows the Print range set to "All" and the number of copies set to "1."

6. Click the **OK** button to print your document. If a message appears telling you printing is complete, click the **OK** button.

TROUBLE? If your document does not print, make sure the printer has paper and the printer on-line light is on. If your document still doesn't print, ask your instructor or technical support person for help.

7. Close WordPad.

TROUBLE? If you see the message "Save changes to Document?" click the "No" button.

Quick Check

1. A(n) _____ is a collection of data that has a name and is stored on a disk or other storage medium.

2. _____ erases all the data on a disk and arranges the magnetic particles on the disk surface so the disk can store data.

3. When you are working in a text box, the pointer shape changes to a(n) _____.

4. The _____ shows you where each character you type will appear.

5. _____ automatically moves text down to the beginning of the next line when you reach the right margin.

6. Explain how you select a block of text: _____.

7. Which of these characters are not allowed in Windows 95 file names: \ ? : * " < > | ! @ # $ % ^ & ; + - ( ) /

8 In the filename New Equipment.Doc, .Doc is a(n) ——————.

9 Suppose you created a graph using the Harvard Graphics software and then you stored the graph on your floppy disk under the name Projected 1997 Sales - Graph. The next day, you use Harvard Graphics to open the file and change the graph. If you want the new version of the file on your disk, you need to ——————.

10 You can save —————— by using the Print Preview feature.

SESSION

2.2

In this session, you will learn how to manage the files on your disk—a skill that can prevent you from losing important documents. You will learn how to list information about the files on your disk; organize the files into folders; and move, delete, copy, and rename files.

Creating Your Student Disk

For this session of the tutorial, you must create a Student Disk that contains some sample files. *You can use the disk you formatted in the previous session.*

If you are using your own computer, the CTI Windows 95 Applications menu selection will not be available. Before you proceed, you must go to your school's computer lab and find a computer that has the CTI Windows 95 Applications installed. Once you have made your own Student Disk, you can use it to complete this tutorial on any computer you choose.

To add the sample files to your Student Disk:

1. Write "Windows 95 Student Disk" on the label of your formatted disk.

2. Place the disk in Drive A.

   TROUBLE? If your 3½-inch disk drive is B, place your formatted disk in that drive instead, and for the rest of this session substitute Drive B where ever you see Drive A.

3. Click the **Start** button [Start]. See Figure 2-14.

Figure 2-14 ◀
Making your
Student Disk

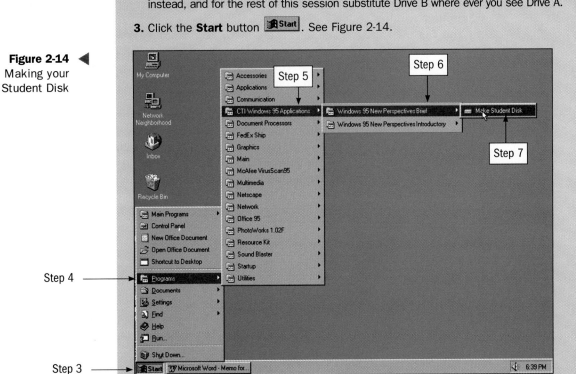

4. Point to **Programs.**

5. Point to **CTI Windows 95 Applications.**

TROUBLE? If CTI Windows 95 Applications is not listed, contact your instructor or technical support person.

6. Point to **Windows 95 New Perspectives Brief.**

7. Select **Make Student Disk.**

A dialog box opens, asking you to indicate the drive that contains your formatted disk.

8. If it is not already selected, click the Drive radio button that corresponds to the drive containing your student disk.

9. Click the **OK** button.

The sample files are copied to your formatted disk. A message tells you when all the files have been copied.

10. Click **OK.**

11. If necessary, close all the open windows on your screen.

Your Student Disk now contains sample files that you will use throughout the rest of this tutorial.

My Computer

The **My Computer** icon represents your computer, its storage devices, and its printers. The My Computer icon opens into the My Computer window, which contains an icon for each of the storage devices on your computer. On most computer systems the My Computer window also contains Control Panel and Printers folders, which help you add printers, control peripheral devices, and customize your Windows 95 work environment. Figure 2-15 on the following page explains more about the My Computer window.

You can use the My Computer window to keep track of where your files are stored and to organize your files. In this section of the tutorial you will move and delete files on your Student Disk in drive A. If you use your own computer at home or computer at work, you would probably store your files on drive C, instead of drive A. However, in a school lab environment you usually don't know which computer you will use, so you need to carry your files with you on a floppy disk that you use in drive A. In this session, therefore, you will learn how to work with the files on drive A. Most of what you learn will also work on your home or work computer when you use drive C.

In this session you will work with several icons, including My Computer. As a general procedure, when you want to open an icon, you click it and then press the Enter key.

Figure 2-15 ◄
Information
about My
Computer

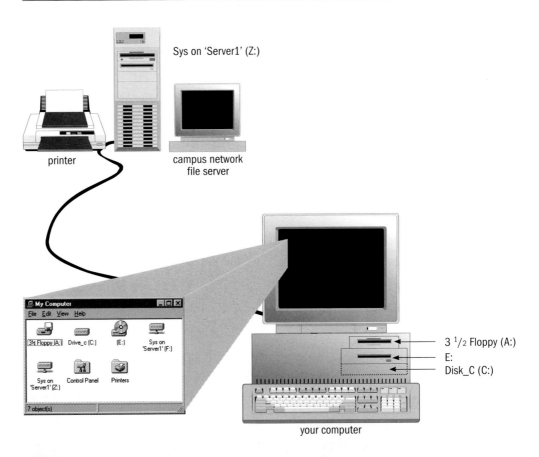

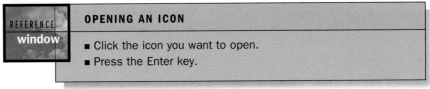

Now you should open the My Computer icon.

To open the My Computer icon:

1. Click the **My Computer** icon to select it.

2. Press the **Enter** key. The My Computer window opens.

Now that you have opened the My Computer window, you can find out what is on
your Student Disk in drive A.

To find out what is on your Student Disk:

1. Open the **3½ Floppy (A:)** icon by clicking it, then pressing the **Enter** key. A window appears showing the contents of drive A:. See Figure 2-16.

Figure 2-16 ◀
Contents of
Student Disk

Icons show contents
of drive A

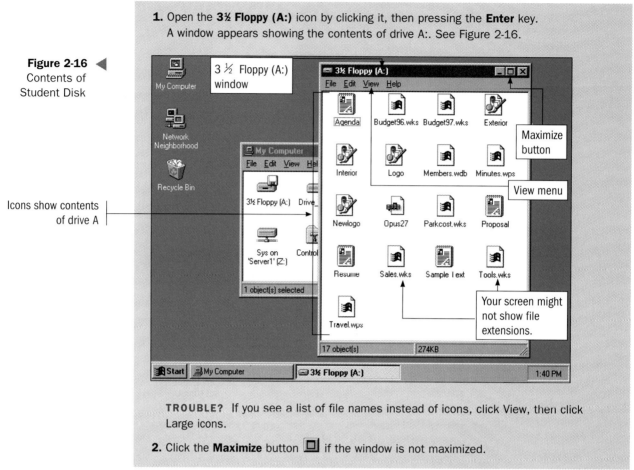

TROUBLE? If you see a list of file names instead of icons, click View, then click Large icons.

2. Click the **Maximize** button ▣ if the window is not maximized.

Windows 95 provides four ways to view the contents of a disk—large icons, small icons, list, or details. The standard view, shown on your screen, displays a large icon and title for each file. The icon provides a visual cue to the type and contents of the file, as Figure 2-17 illustrates.

Figure 2-17 ◀
Program and
file icons

Text files that you can open and read using the WordPad or NotePad software are represented by notepad icons.

The icons for Windows programs usually depict an object related to the function of the program. For example, an icon that looks like a calculator signifies the Windows Calc program; an icon that looks like a computer signifies the Windows Explorer program.

Many of the files you create are represented by page icons. Here the page icon for the Circles file shows some graphics tools to indicate the file contains a graphic. The Page icon for the Access file contains the Windows logo, indicating that Windows does not know if the file contains a document, graphics, or data base.

Folders provide a way to group and organize files. A folder icon contains other icons for folders and files. Here, the System folder contains files used by the Windows operating system.

Non-Windows programs are represented by this icon of a blank window.

The **Details** view shows more information than the large icon, small icon, and list views. Details view shows the file icon, the filename, the file size, the application you used to create the file, and the date/time the file was created or last modified.

To view a detailed list of files:

1. Click **View** then click **Details** to display details for the files on your disk as shown in Figure 2-18.

Figure 2-18 ◀
Detailed file list

File icon ——

Filename ——

Your screen might not
show file extensions

Total number of
files and folders
in the window

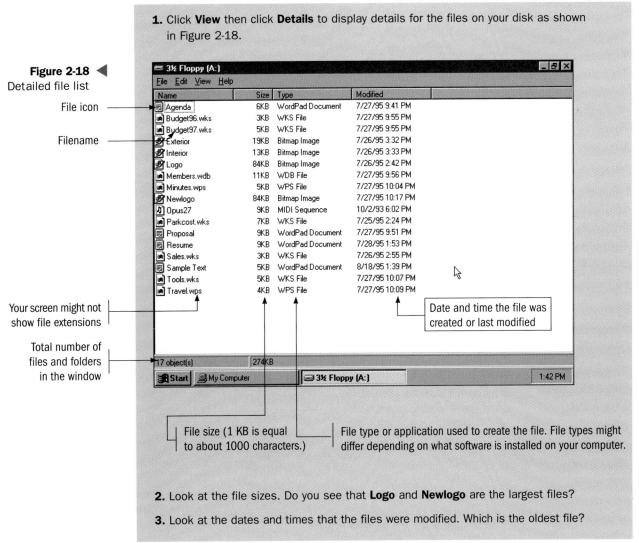

File size (1 KB is equal
to about 1000 characters.)

File type or application used to create the file. File types might
differ depending on what software is installed on your computer.

Date and time the file was
created or last modified

2. Look at the file sizes. Do you see that **Logo** and **Newlogo** are the largest files?

3. Look at the dates and times that the files were modified. Which is the oldest file?

Now that you have looked at the file details, switch back to the large icon view.

To switch to the large icon view:

1. Click **View** then click **Large Icons** to return to the large icon display.

Folders and Directories

A list of files is referred to as a **directory**. The main directory of a disk is sometimes called the **root directory**. The root directory is created when you format a disk and is shown in parentheses at the top of the window. For example, at the top of your screen you should see "3 ½ Floppy (A:)." The root directory is A:. In some situations, the root directory is indicated by a backslash after the drive letter and colon, such as A:\. All of the files on your Student Disk are currently in the root directory.

If too many files are stored in a directory, the directory list becomes very long and difficult to manage. A directory can be divided into **folders** (also called **subdirectories**), into which you group similar files. The directory of files for each folder then becomes much shorter and easier to manage. For example, you might create a folder for all the papers you write for an English 111 class as shown in Figure 2-19.

A folder appears on the screen as a folder icon. When you open the folder icon, the folder is represented by a window. The ENG111 folder appears as the ENG111 window on the screen. The contents of the folder are represented by icons in the window.

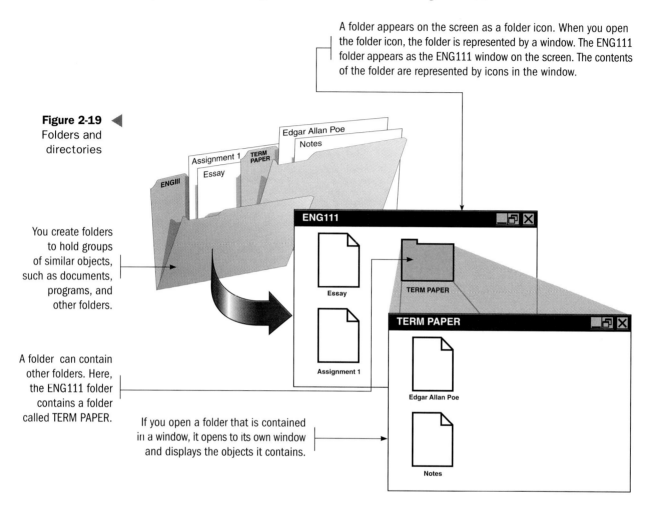

Figure 2-19 ◀
Folders and
directories

You create folders to hold groups of similar objects, such as documents, programs, and other folders.

A folder can contain other folders. Here, the ENG111 folder contains a folder called TERM PAPER.

If you open a folder that is contained in a window, it opens to its own window and displays the objects it contains.

Now, you'll create a folder called My Documents to hold your document files.

To create a My Documents folder:

1. Click **File** then point to **New** to display the submenu.

2. Click **Folder**. A folder icon with the label "New Folder" appears.

3. Type **My Documents** as the name of the folder.

4. Press the **Enter** key.

When you first create a folder, it doesn't contain any files. In the next set of steps you will move a file from the root directory to the My Documents folder.

REFERENCE window	**CREATING A NEW FOLDER**
	■ Open the My Computer icon to display the My Computer window.
	■ Open the icon for the drive on which you want to create the folder.
	■ Click File then point to New.
	■ From the submenu click Folder.
	■ Type the name for the new folder.
	■ Press the Enter key.

Moving and Copying a File

You can move a file from one directory to another or from one disk to another. When you move a file it is copied to the new location you specify, then the version in the old location is erased. The move feature is handy for organizing or reorganizing the files on your disk by moving them into appropriate folders. The easiest way to move a file is to hold down the *right* mouse button and drag the file from the old location to the new location. A menu appears and you select Move Here.

You can also copy a file from one directory to another, or from one disk to another. When you copy a file, you create an exact duplicate of an existing file in whatever disk or folder you specify. To copy a file from one folder to another on your floppy disk, you use the same procedure as for moving a file, except that you select Copy Here from the menu.

Suppose you want to move the Minutes file from the root directory to the My Documents folder. Depending on the software applications installed on your computer, this file is either called Minutes or Minutes.wps. In the steps it is referred to simply as Minutes.

To move the Minutes file to the My Documents folder:

1. Click the **Minutes** icon to select it.

2. Press and hold the right mouse button while you drag the **Minutes** icon to the My Documents folder. See Figure 2-20.

Figure 2-20 ◀
Moving a file

Minutes file ──────

My Documents folder ──────

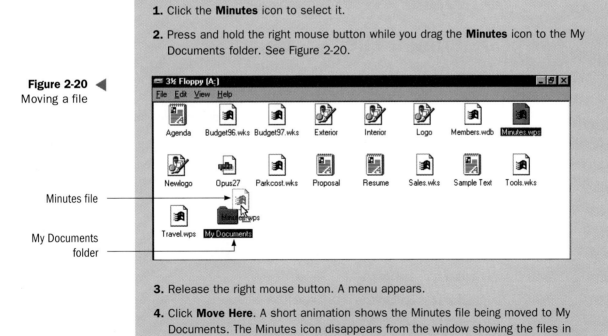

3. Release the right mouse button. A menu appears.

4. Click **Move Here**. A short animation shows the Minutes file being moved to My Documents. The Minutes icon disappears from the window showing the files in the root directory.

REFERENCE window

MOVING A FILE

- Open the My Computer icon to display the My Computer window.
- If the document you want to move is in a folder, open the folder.
- Hold down the *right* mouse button while you drag the file icon to its new folder or disk location.
- Click Move Here.
- If you want to move more than one file at a time, hold down the Ctrl key while you click the icons for all the files you want to move.

3.1 NOTE

Windows 3.1 users be careful! When you delete or move an icon in the Windows 95 My Computer window you are actually deleting or moving the file. This is quite different from the way the Windows 3.1 Program Manager worked.

Anything you do to an icon in the My Computer window is actually done to the file represented by that icon. If you move an icon, the file is moved; if you delete an icon, the file is deleted.

After you move a file, it is a good idea to make sure it was moved to the correct location. You can easily verify that a file is in its new folder by displaying the folder contents.

To verify that the Minutes file was moved to My Documents:

1. Click the **My Documents** folder, then press **Enter**. The My Documents window appears and it contains one file—Minutes.

2. Click the My Documents window **Close** button ☒.

   TROUBLE? If the My Computer window is no longer visible, click the My Computer icon, then press Enter. You might also need to open the 3 ½ Floppy (A:) icon.

Deleting a File

You delete a file or folder by deleting its icon. However, be careful when you delete a *folder*, because you also delete all the files it contains! When you delete a file from the hard drive, the filename is deleted from the directory but the file contents are held in the Recycle Bin. If you change your mind and want to retrieve the deleted file, you can recover it by clicking the Recycle Bin.

When you delete a file from a floppy disk, it does not go into the Recycle Bin. Instead it is deleted as soon as its icon disappears. Try deleting the file named Agenda from your Student Disk. Because this file is on the floppy disk and not on the hard disk, it will not go into the Recycle Bin.

To delete the file Agenda:

1. Click the icon for the file **Agenda**.

2. Press the **Delete** key.

3. If a message appears asking, "Are sure you want to delete Agenda?", click **Yes**. An animation, which might play too quickly to be seen, shows the file being deleted.

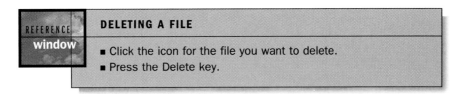

REFERENCE window

DELETING A FILE

- Click the icon for the file you want to delete.
- Press the Delete key.

Renaming a File

You can easily change the name of a file using the Rename option on the File menu or by using the file's label. Remember that when you choose a filename it can contain up to 255 characters, including spaces, but it cannot contain \ ? : " < > | characters.

Practice using this feature by renaming the Sales file to give it a more descriptive filename.

To rename Sales:

1. Click the **Sales** file to select it.

2. Click the label "Sales". After a short pause a solid box outlines the label and an insertion point appears.

3. Type **Preliminary Sales Summary** as the new filename.

4. Press the **Enter key**.

5. Click the **Close** button ☒ to close the 3 ½-inch Floppy (A:) window.

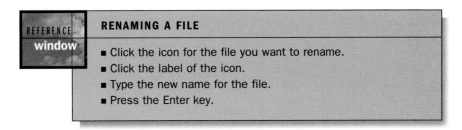

REFERENCE window

RENAMING A FILE

- Click the icon for the file you want to rename.
- Click the label of the icon.
- Type the new name for the file.
- Press the Enter key.

Copying an Entire Floppy Disk

You can have trouble accessing the data on your floppy disk if the disk gets damaged, exposed to magnetic fields, or picks up a computer virus. If the damaged disk contains important files, you will have to spend many hours to try to reconstruct those files. To avoid losing all your data, it is a good idea to make a copy of your floppy disk. This copy is called a **backup** copy.

If you wanted to make a copy of an audio cassette, your cassette player would need two cassette drives. You might wonder, therefore, how your computer can make a copy of your disk if you have only one disk drive. Figure 2-21 illustrates how the computer uses only one disk drive to make a copy of a disk.

Figure 2-21 ◀
Using one disk
drive to make a
copy of a disk

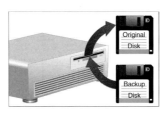

1. First, the computer
copies the data from your
original disk into memory.

2. Once the data is in
memory, you remove your
original disk from the drive
and replace it with your
backup disk.

3. The computer moves the
data from memory onto
your backup disk.

REFERENCE window

MAKING A BACKUP OF YOUR FLOPPY DISK

- Click My Computer then press the Enter key.
- Insert the disk you want to copy in drive A.
- Click the 3 ½ Floppy (A:) icon 3½ Floppy (A:) to select it.
- Click File then click Copy Disk to display the Copy Disk dialog box.
- Click Start to begin the copy process.
- When prompted, remove the disk you want to copy. Place your backup disk in drive A.
- Click OK.
- When the copy is complete, close the Copy Disk dialog box.
- Close the My Computer dialog box.

If you have two floppy disks, you can make a backup of your Student Disk now. Make sure you periodically follow the backup procedure, so your backup is up-to-date.

To back up your Student Disk:

1. Write your name and "Backup" on the label of your second disk. This will be your backup disk.

2. Make sure your Student Disk is in drive A.

3. Make sure the My Computer window is open. See Figure 2-22.

Figure 2-22 ◀
The My
Computer
window

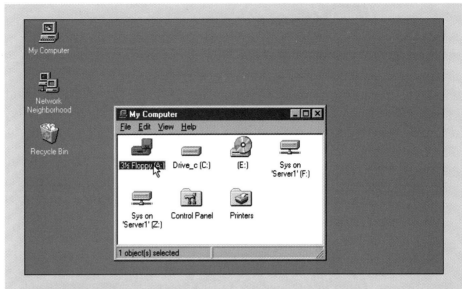

4. Click the **3 ½ Floppy (A:)** icon  to select it.

   TROUBLE? If you mistakenly open the 3½ Floppy (A:) *window*, click ☒ .

5. Click **File**.

6. Click **Copy Disk** to display the Copy Disk dialog box as shown in Figure 2-23.

Figure 2-23 ◀
The Copy Disk
dialog box

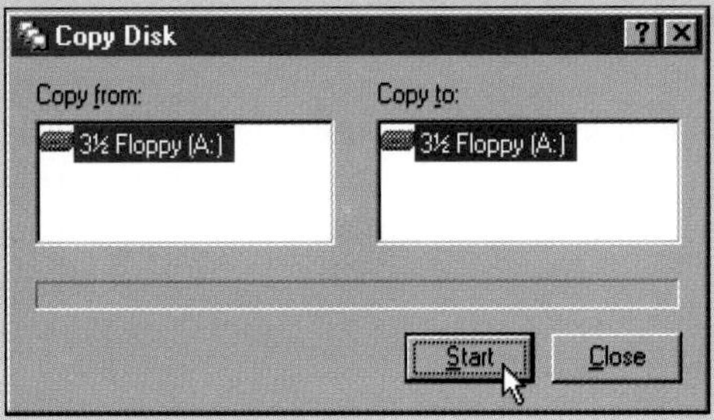

7. On the lower right side of the dialog box, you'll see a Start button. Click this **Start** button to begin the copy process.

8. When the message, "Insert the disk you want to copy from (source disk)..." appears, click the **OK** button.

9. When the message, "Insert the disk you want to copy to (destination disk)..." appears, insert your backup disk in drive A.

10. Click the **OK** button. When the copy is complete, you will see the message "Copy completed successfully."

11. After the data is copied to your backup disk, click ☒ on the blue title bar of the Copy Disk dialog box.

12. Click ☒ on the My Computer window to close the My Computer window.

13. Remove your disk from the drive.

Each time you make a backup, the data on your backup disk is erased, and replaced with the data from your updated Student Disk. Now that you know how to copy an entire disk, make a backup whenever you have completed a tutorial or you have spent a long time working on a file.

Quick Check

1. If you want to find out about the storage devices and printers connected to your computer, click the _____ icon.

2. If you have only one floppy disk drive on your computer, it is identified by the letter _____.

3. The letter C: is typically used for the _____ drive of a computer.

4. What are the five pieces of information that the Details view supplies about each of your files?

5. The main directory of a disk is referred to as the _____ directory.

6. You can divide a directory into _____.

7. If you delete the icon for a file, what happens to the file?

8. If you have one floppy disk drive, but you have two disks, can you copy a file from one floppy disk to another?

End Note

Just as you complete the Quick Check for Session 2.2, Steve appears. He asks how you are doing. You summarize what you remember from the tutorial, telling him that you learned how to insert, delete, and select text. You also learned how to work with files using Windows 95 software—you now know how to save, open, revise, and print a document. You tell him that you like the idea that these file operations are the same for almost all Windows 95 software. Steve agrees that this makes work a lot easier.

When Steve asks you if you have a supply of disks, you tell him you do, and that you just learned how to format a disk and view a list of files on your disk. Steve wants you to remember that you can use the Details view to see the filename, size, date, and time. You assure him that you remember that feature—and also how to move, delete, and rename a file.

Steve seems pleased with your progress and agrees that you're now ready to use software applications. But he can't resist giving you one last warning—don't forget to back up your files frequently!

Tutorial Assignments

1. Opening, Editing, and Printing a Document In this tutorial you learned how to create a document using WordPad. You also learned how to save, open, and print a document. Practice these skills by opening the document on your Student Disk called Resume, which is a résumé for Jamie Woods. Make the changes shown in Figure 2-24, and then print the document. After you print, save your revisions.

Figure 2-24 ◀

Change this to your name, address, and phone number. If you don't have an office number delete this.

Change this to the name of your university or college.

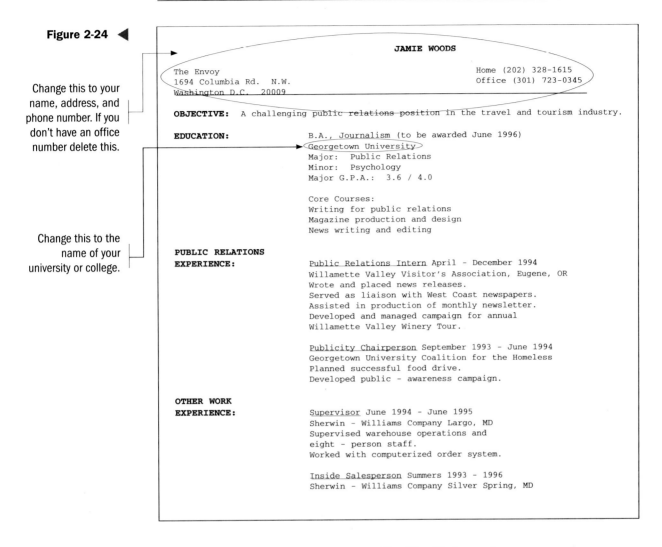

```
                                    JAMIE WOODS

          The Envoy                           Home (202) 328-1615
          1694 Columbia Rd.  N.W.             Office (301) 723-0345
          Washington D.C.  20009

          OBJECTIVE:    A challenging public relations position in the travel and tourism industry.

          EDUCATION:              B.A., Journalism (to be awarded June 1996)
                                  Georgetown University
                                  Major:  Public Relations
                                  Minor:  Psychology
                                  Major G.P.A.:  3.6 / 4.0

                                  Core Courses:
                                  Writing for public relations
                                  Magazine production and design
                                  News writing and editing

          PUBLIC RELATIONS
          EXPERIENCE:             Public Relations Intern April - December 1994
                                  Willamette Valley Visitor's Association, Eugene, OR
                                  Wrote and placed news releases.
                                  Served as liaison with West Coast newspapers.
                                  Assisted in production of monthly newsletter.
                                  Developed and managed campaign for annual
                                  Willamette Valley Winery Tour.

                                  Publicity Chairperson September 1993 - June 1994
                                  Georgetown University Coalition for the Homeless
                                  Planned successful food drive.
                                  Developed public - awareness campaign.

          OTHER WORK
          EXPERIENCE:             Supervisor June 1994 - June 1995
                                  Sherwin - Williams Company Largo, MD
                                  Supervised warehouse operations and
                                  eight - person staff.
                                  Worked with computerized order system.

                                  Inside Salesperson Summers 1993 - 1996
                                  Sherwin - Williams Company Silver Spring, MD
```

2. Creating, Saving, and Printing a Letter Use WordPad to write a one-page letter to a relative or a friend. Save the document in the My Documents folder with the name "Letter." Use the Print Preview feature to look at the format of your finished letter, then print it, and be sure you sign it.

3. Managing Files and Folders Earlier in this tutorial you created a folder and moved the file called Minutes into it. Now complete a through g below to practice your file management skills.

    a. Create a folder called Spreadsheets on your Student Disk.

    b. Move the files ParkCost, Budget96, Budget97, and Sales into the Spreadsheets folder.

    c. Create a folder called Park Project.

    d. Move the files Proposal, Members, Tools, Logo, and Newlogo into the Park Project folder.

    e. Move the ParkCost file from the Spreadsheets folder to the Park Project folder.

    f. Delete the file called Travel.

    g. Switch to the Details view and answer the following questions:

Write out your answers to questions a through e.

    a. What is the largest file in the Park Project folder?

    b. What is the newest file in the Spreadsheets folder?

    c. How many files are in the root directory?

    d. How are the Members and Resume icons different?

    e. What is the file with the most recent date on the entire disk?

4. More Practice with Files and Folders For this assignment, you will format your disk again and put a fresh version of the Student Disk files on it. Complete a through h below to practice your file management skills.

    a. Format a disk.

    b. Create a Student Disk. Refer to the section "Creating Your Student Disk" in Session 2.2.

    c. Create three folders on your new Student Disk: Documents, Budgets, and Graphics.

    d. Move the files Interior, Exterior, Logo, and Newlogo to the Graphics folder.

    e. Move the files Travel, Members and Minutes to the Documents folder.

    f. Move Budget96 and Budget97 to the Budgets folder.

    g. Switch to the Details view.

Answer questions a through f.

    a. What is the largest file in the Graphics folder?

    b. How many WordPad documents are in the root directory?

    c. What is the newest file in the root directory?

    d. How many files in all folders are 5KB in size?

    e. How many files in the Documents folder are WKS files?

    f. Do all the files in the Graphics folder have the same icon?

5. Finding a File Microsoft Windows 95 contains an on-line Tour that explains how to find files on a disk without looking through all the folders. Start the Windows 95 Tour (if you don't remember how, look at the instructions for Tutorial Assignment 1 in Tutorial 1), then click Finding a File, and answer the following questions:

    a. To display the Find dialog box, you must click the _____ button, then select _____ from the menu, and finally click _____ from the submenu.

    b. Do you need to type in the entire filename to find the file?

    c. When the computer has found your file, what are the steps you have to follow if you want to display the contents of the file?

6. Help with Files and Folders In Tutorial 2 you learned how to work with Windows 95 files and folders. What additional information on this topic does Windows 95 Help provide? Use the Start button to access Help. Use the Index tab to locate topics related to files and folders. Find at least two tips or procedures for working with files and folders that were not covered in the tutorial. Write out the tip in your own words and indicate the title of the Help screen that contains the information.

Lab Assignments

Using Files

1. Using Files Lab In Tutorial 2 you learned how to create, save, open, and print files. The Using Files Lab will help you review what happens in the computer when you perform these file tasks. To start the Lab, follow these steps:

    a. Click the Start button.

    b. Point to Programs, then point to CTI Windows 95 Applications.

    c. Point to Windows 95 New Perspectives Brief.

    d. Click Using Files. If you can't find Windows 95 New Perspectives Brief or Using Files, ask for help from your instructor or technical support person.

Answer the Quick Check questions that appear as you work through the Lab. You can print your answers at the end of the Lab.

Answers to Quick Check Questions

SESSION 1.1

1 a. icon b. Start button c. taskbar d. Date/Time control e. desktop f. pointer

2 Multitasking

3 Start menu

4 Lift up the mouse, move it to the right, then put it down, and slide it left until the pointer reaches the left edge of the screen.

5 Highlighting

6 If a program is running, its button is displayed on the taskbar.

7 Each program that is running uses system resources, so Windows 95 runs more efficiently when only the programs you are using are open.

8 Answer: If you do not perform the shut down procedure, you might lose data.

SESSION 1.2

1 a. title bar b. program title c. Minimize button d. Restore button e. Close button
f. menu bar g. toolbar h. formatting bar i. taskbar j. status bar k. workspace l. pointer

2 a. Minimize button—hides the program so only its button is showing on the taskbar.
b. Maximize button—enlarges the program to fill the entire screen.
c. Restore button—sets the program to a pre-defined size.
d. Close button—stops the program and removes its button from the taskbar.

3 a. Ellipses—indicate a dialog box will appear.
b. Grayed out—the menu option is not currently available.
c. Submenu—indicates a submenu will appear.
d. Check mark—indicates a menu option is currently in effect.

4 Toolbar

5 a. scroll bar b. scroll box c. Cancel button d. down arrow button e. list box f. radio button g. check box

6 one, check boxes

7 On-line Help

SESSION 2.1

1 file

2 formatting

3 I-beam

4 insertion point

5 word wrap

6 You drag the I-beam pointer over
the text to highlight it.

7 \ ? : * < > | "

8 extension

9 save the file again

10 paper

SESSION 2.2

1 My Computer

2 A (or A:)

3 Hard (or hard disk)

4 Filename, file type, file size, date, time

5 Root

6 Folders (or subdirectories)

7 It is deleted from the disk.

8 Yes

NEW
PERSPECTIVES
SERIES

Microsoft
Windows® 98
Preview

TUTORIAL

Microsoft Windows 98 Preview

A Brief Comparison of the Windows 95 and Windows 98 Operating Systems

OBJECTIVES

In this tutorial, you will:

- Explore the differences between the Windows 95 and Windows 98 desktop

- Compare the Windows 95 and Windows 98 Start menus

- Compare mouse operations under Windows 95 and Windows 98

- Examine Active Desktop capabilities

- Explore Web view

- Preview additional Windows 98 features

Upgrading to a New Operating System

If you have worked with computers for very long, you already know that computer owners regularly face the decision to upgrade. **Upgrading** is the process of placing a more recent version of a product onto your computer. Upgrades to **hardware**, the physical components of a computer, occur when a computer user decides to purchase a newer computer or computer component that will add features, space, or speed to his or her computer system.

Upgrades to **software**, the set of instructions that make a computer perform a specific task, occur when a user decides to take advantage of improvements in a more recent version of a software product. Software developers produce new versions of software for a variety of reasons. Because hardware is constantly changing as new technology emerges, software developers need to ensure that their software takes full advantage of the latest hardware technology. For example, when it became cheaper and easier to expand the amount of memory on personal computers, many software companies developed their software to take advantage of extra memory. Another important reason for software revisions is usability. Developers are constantly trying to make their software easier to learn and use. For example, when it became clear that people found a graphical interface easy to work with, most software companies provided such an interface to their software. Software revisions also occur when a new software technology emerges. Developers update their products so they can compete against newer products that use newer technology. For example, with the recent explosion in popularity of the World Wide Web, many software companies hastened to include Web features in their products.

Microsoft Corporation's operating system revision from Windows 95 to Windows 98 is a response to these and other trends. For example, hardware now exists that makes it possible for you to run your computer through your television set, so Windows 98 includes a software accessory, TV Viewer, that lets you use this technology if you have the appropriate hardware. Windows 98 features such as automated disk maintenance are a response to the demand for ease of use. To take advantage of emerging software technology, Microsoft designed Windows 98 around features of the World Wide Web.

The decision to upgrade your operating system can be difficult to make. Upgrades can be expensive. To take full advantage of the Windows 98 upgrade, you might need to purchase new hardware, such as an Internet connection via a modem, a TV tuner card, or additional memory. Some revisions don't greatly affect how a software product is used, but other revisions change the interface so significantly that computer owners need to evaluate whether the advantages of upgrading are greater than the disadvantages of having to learn a practically new product. Users also consider the newness of the technology before they upgrade; some like to wait until the dust settles and the technology is tested and proven before they risk using it on their own computers.

In this tutorial, you'll examine how the upgrade to Windows 98 from Windows 95 affects what you see as you use the interface. This tutorial was developed using a prerelease version of Windows 98, so there might be slight differences between what you see in the figures and what you see in the final product. If you want more information about a feature that seems to be operating differently from what you see here, click the Start button and then click Help. Use the online Help system to learn more about the feature.

The Windows 98 Desktop

When you first turn on your computer, you might not notice much difference between the Windows 95 and Windows 98 desktops. Recall that the **desktop** is the workspace on your screen. Because it's easy to customize the desktop, someone might have changed your desktop so that it looks different from the one shown in the figures in this tutorial. You should, however, be able to locate objects similar to those in the figures. Figure 1 shows the Windows 95 desktop. Remember that you might see additional icons, and your screen might show a different background.

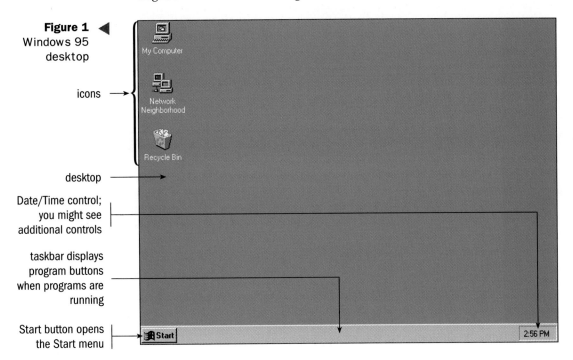

Figure 1 ◀
Windows 95 desktop

icons →

desktop →

Date/Time control; you might see additional controls

taskbar displays program buttons when programs are running

Start button opens the Start menu

Figure 2 shows the Windows 98 desktop. Notice that the Start button, taskbar, Date/Time control, and icons all look the same as their Windows 95 counterparts. Your Windows 98 desktop might show additional objects; you'll learn more about these shortly.

Figure 2
Windows 98
desktop

icon labels are
underlined

desktop looks
the same

Date/Time control
looks the same

Quick Launch toolbar
is new

Start button looks
the same

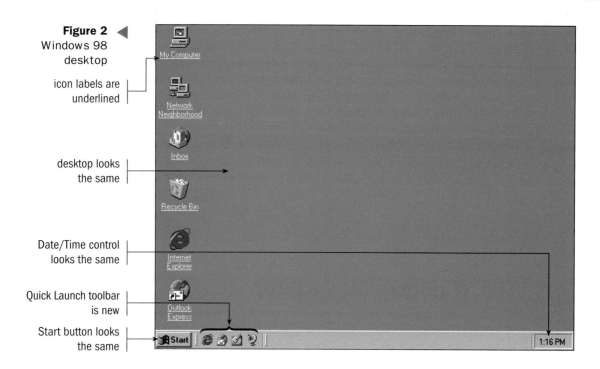

There are really only two visible differences between the basic Windows 95 and Windows 98 desktops:

■ Windows 98 includes the Quick Launch toolbar.

■ In Windows 98, icon names can appear underlined.

If you have access to the Internet and the Web, and if your desktop has been customized, it's possible you'll see additional desktop objects. Windows 98 makes it possible to integrate your Web experience into your desktop, as you'll see shortly.

Underlined Icon Names

The underlined icon names you see are evidence of Microsoft's attempt to make your experience with the Windows 98 desktop more like your experience with the Web. The **World Wide Web**, or just the **Web**, is a service on the Internet that allows you to view documents on computers around the world. Documents on the Web are called **Web pages**. Web pages contain elements known as **links** that you can select, usually by clicking a mouse, to move to another part of the document or another document altogether. A link can be a word, a phrase, or a graphic image. When a link consists of text, the text link usually appears underlined and in a different color.

To view Web pages, you use a program called a **browser**. When you click a link on a Web page in your browser, you jump to a different location—perhaps to a page stored on another computer, as shown in Figure 3.

Windows 98

Web page on
rock climbing

Figure 3 ◄
Clicking Web
page links

click this link
to jump to a
different document

this Web page
appears when you
click the <u>Tour</u> link

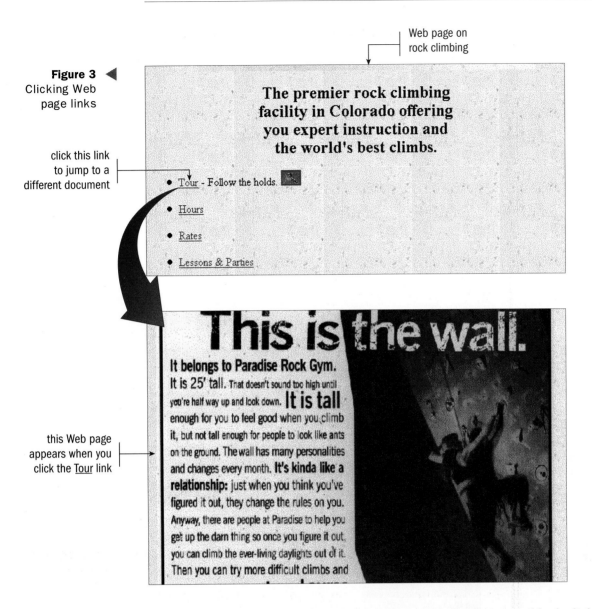

On the Windows 98 desktop, icon labels are underlined to resemble the links you see on Web pages. By attempting to mimic the Web experience, Microsoft is trying to simplify how you interact with your computer. If the actions you take on the desktop are similar to those you take in your browser, you have to learn only one set of techniques.

Thus, when you click one of the icon labels on the Windows 98 desktop, you "jump" to that icon's destination. For example, in Windows 95, to open My Computer, you had to double-click its icon (or click its icon to select it and then press Enter). In Windows 98, however, the My Computer icon label is underlined just like a link. When you point at the icon label, the pointer changes from ⌖ to 🖑, just as it would if you pointed at a link in your browser. When you click the underlined icon label, you "jump" to the My Computer window. The result is the same: The My Computer window opens, but the Windows 98 technique is more like the technique you use on the Web. Figure 4 illustrates this difference.

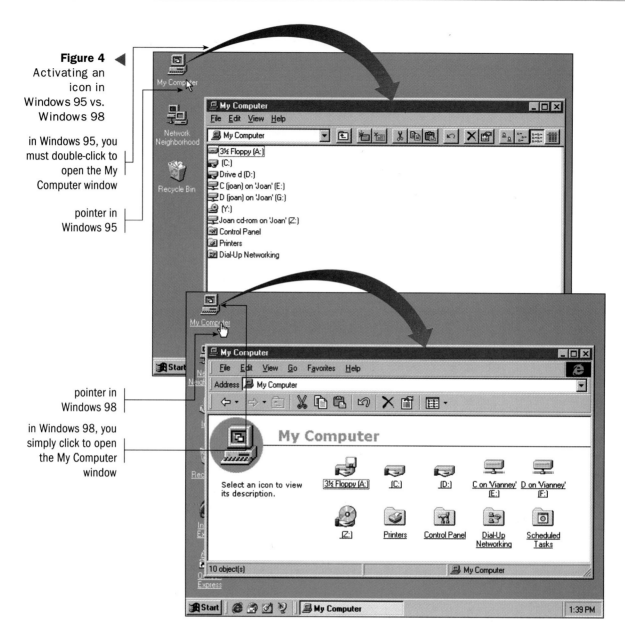

Figure 4
Activating an
icon in
Windows 95 vs.
Windows 98

in Windows 95, you
must double-click to
open the My
Computer window

pointer in
Windows 95

pointer in
Windows 98

in Windows 98, you
simply click to open
the My Computer
window

As you work with the Windows 98 operating system, you'll see that underlined text appears not just on the desktop but in numerous places—the My Computer window, the folder windows, and the Windows Explorer window, just to name a few. You can also display Windows 98 icons in the traditional Windows 95 manner: From My Computer, click View, click Folder Options, and then on the General tab, click the Classic style option button.

The Quick Launch Toolbar

The Windows 95 taskbar displays the Start button, buttons that correspond to active programs or open documents, and the tray area that includes the Date/Time control and any other active controls. The Windows 98 taskbar looks the same except for one difference: You can now display toolbars on the taskbar. Figure 5 shows the Windows 95 taskbar, and below it, the Windows 98 taskbar.

Windows 98

Figure 5 ◄
Taskbars in
Windows 95
and
Windows 98

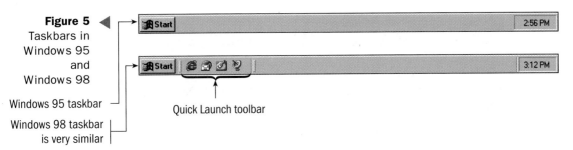

Windows 95 taskbar ─┐

Quick Launch toolbar

Windows 98 taskbar ─┐
is very similar

Unless a user has customized his or her taskbar, only the Quick Launch toolbar appears on the Windows 98 taskbar, but you can also display three other taskbar toolbars. Like a toolbar in an application, the taskbar toolbars give you single-click access to common operations.

Figure 6 summarizes the Windows 98 taskbar toolbars.

Figure 6 ◄
Windows 98
taskbar
toolbars

Toolbar	Description
Address	As in a browser, allows you to select or enter an address, such as a URL, to open the browser to that location.
Links	As in a browser, displays buttons for popular Web pages, such as the Microsoft home page. When you click a button on the Links toolbar, your browser opens and displays the location you clicked.
Desktop	Displays a button for each desktop icon on the taskbar.
Quick Launch	Displays buttons for Internet services and for a direct route to the desktop.

The Quick Launch toolbar is the only toolbar to appear by default; the others you can enable by right-clicking the taskbar, pointing at the Toolbars menu option, and clicking the toolbar you want. Figure 7 shows a Windows 98 taskbar with the Address and Links toolbars visible in addition to the Quick Launch toolbar.

scroll arrow appears
when there are
additional objects
on a toolbar

Figure 7 ◄
Windows 98
taskbar with
multiple
toolbars

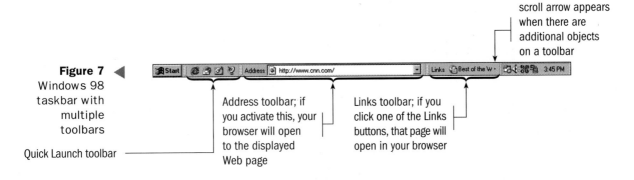

Quick Launch toolbar ─────

Address toolbar; if
you activate this, your
browser will open
to the displayed
Web page

Links toolbar; if you
click one of the Links
buttons, that page will
open in your browser

Figure 8 describes the default buttons on the Quick Launch toolbar.

Figure 8 ◀
Quick Launch
toolbar buttons

Icon	Name	Description
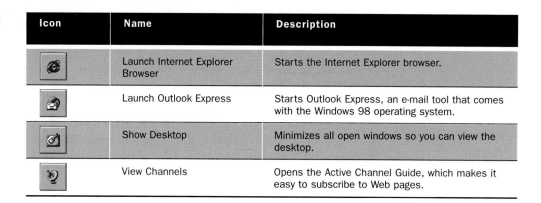	Launch Internet Explorer Browser	Starts the Internet Explorer browser.
	Launch Outlook Express	Starts Outlook Express, an e-mail tool that comes with the Windows 98 operating system.
	Show Desktop	Minimizes all open windows so you can view the desktop.
	View Channels	Opens the Active Channel Guide, which makes it easy to subscribe to Web pages.

You can easily customize the taskbar toolbars by adding and removing buttons. Figure 9, for example, shows a taskbar whose Quick Launch toolbar includes buttons for popular applications.

Figure 9 ◀
Quick Launch
toolbar with
application
buttons

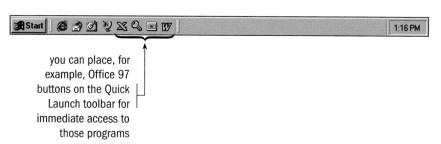

you can place, for example, Office 97 buttons on the Quick Launch toolbar for immediate access to those programs

To add a button to the Windows 98 Quick Launch toolbar, you simply drag the object you want to the toolbar.

The Start Menu

The Windows 98 Start menu looks similar to the Windows 95 Start menu. The only difference is that the Windows 98 Start menu includes a Favorites folder and a Windows Update link to Microsoft's Web site. Figure 10 shows the two Start menus. Again, since you can customize Start menus, yours might look different.

Figure 10 ◀
Windows 95
and
Windows 98
Start menus

Windows Update opens the browser to display the Microsoft resource site

Favorites folder has been added to the Windows 98 Start menu

your Start menu might include a Log Off command if you are on a network

Windows 95 Start menu

Windows 98 Start menu

The Favorites folder that Microsoft has added to the Windows 98 Start menu duplicates the Favorites folder in your browser. In your browser, you create a Favorites folder by collecting and saving a list of favorite Web pages. Once a Web page is in your Favorites folder, you can return to it in your browser by simply selecting the page from the folder. By duplicating the browser's list of favorite Web pages on the Windows 98 Start menu, Microsoft allows you to reach your favorite Web pages without having to go through the interim steps of starting your browser and opening the Favorites folder. To view a favorite Web page in Windows 98, you simply click Start, point at the Favorites option, and then click the Web page you want. Your browser launches automatically and connects you directly to that page.

The Windows Update link that appears on the Windows 98 Start menu is a Microsoft resource site on the Web that you connect to by clicking Windows Update on the Start menu. Your browser displays the Windows Update page, which helps you ensure that your system is running the most recent and efficient system software possible.

You might notice one final difference between the Windows 95 and Windows 98 Start menus. If you have more items on your Start menu than can be displayed on the screen, Windows 95 doubles the width of the menu to display the entire list of Start menu objects. Windows 98, however, adds to the bottom of the Start menu an arrow to which you can point to see additional objects.

Mouse Operation

You won't notice a difference between how your mouse operates in Office 97 or your other Windows 95 applications when you run them under the Windows 98 operating system. But if you work with certain Windows 98 windows, such as My Computer or Windows Explorer, be aware that Microsoft has simplified the actions you need to take with the mouse.

You've already seen that the icons on your desktop now behave like links and are, therefore, activated with a single-click rather than a double-click. In fact, in Windows 98, single-clicking completely replaces double-clicking on the desktop. In Windows 95, you generally selected an object by clicking it, but in Windows 98, you select an object by simply pointing to it for a moment. Windows 98 uses the term **hover** to describe pointing to an object, such as an icon, long enough to select it. Passing the pointer over an icon does not select it; you need to hover the pointer over the object long enough for Windows 98 to realize that you mean to select it. Once you've practiced hovering, you'll find it easy. Figure 11 summarizes how mouse functions have changed from Windows 95 to Windows 98.

Figure 11 ◄
Comparing
mouse
functions

Task	Windows 95	Windows 98
Select	Click	Hover
Open or run	Double-click (or click and press Enter)	Click
Select multiple contiguous objects	Shift+click	Shift+hover
Select multiple noncontiguous objects	Ctrl+click	Ctrl+hover

Changes in mouse operation do not affect Windows 98 dialog boxes: They affect only the desktop, My Computer, Windows Explorer, and similar windows.

Active Desktop

In Windows 95, to experience the Web you generally must first start your browser (although new generations of Internet communications software products are now bypassing the browser and placing Web information directly on the desktop even without the Windows 98 operating system). Users with Web access will find Windows 98 **Active Desktop** technology brings Web content directly to the desktop, without requiring extra communications software, allowing your desktop to act like your personal Web page.

You can enable Active Desktop by right-clicking the desktop, pointing to Active Desktop, and then clicking View As Web Page. Active Desktop integrates your Web experience with the Windows 98 desktop in two primary ways: with background wallpaper and with Web components. You can use a Web page as the desktop's background, and you can place Web components (updateable information from the Web) on the desktop.

Using a Web Page as Background Wallpaper

If you've ever worked with the Desktop Properties dialog box in Windows 95 (which you access by right-clicking the desktop and then clicking Properties), you might have experimented with the look of your desktop by changing the color or pattern of the default background wallpaper.

Windows 95 limits you to using image files as your background wallpaper. Trying to create a desktop background that integrated text and images and other objects is impossible. Windows 98, however, extends your control over your desktop's background by allowing you to use Web pages as wallpaper. To write Web pages, you use a language called **HTML**, which stands for Hypertext Markup Language. HTML uses special codes to describe how the page should appear on the screen. A document created using the HTML language is called an **HTML file** and is saved with the htm or html extension.

Because Windows 98 enables you to use an HTML file as your background wallpaper, your Windows 98 desktop background can feature text, images, links, and multimedia objects. You can use Microsoft Word to save a document as an HTML file; also, you can use the HTML editor included with Windows 98, FrontPage Express, to create more complex and sophisticated HTML files. Alternatively, you can use the Internet Explorer browser to save an existing Web page as an HTML file that you can then use as your wallpaper. To use a Web page as your wallpaper, right-click the desktop, click Properties, click the Background tab, click the Browse button, locate and select the HTML file you want to use, then click the OK button.

The added control Windows 98 gives you over background wallpaper makes it possible to make the desktop a launch pad for your most important projects. A corporation, for example, might create an HTML file that contains important company information, an updateable company calendar, links to company documents, a sound clip welcoming new employees to the company, and so on.

Figure 12 shows a sample Windows 98 desktop that might appear on the computers of a gift shop chain's main headquarters.

Figure 12 ◄
Windows 98 desktop with a background HTML file

embedded updateable program

embedded image file

embedded video clip

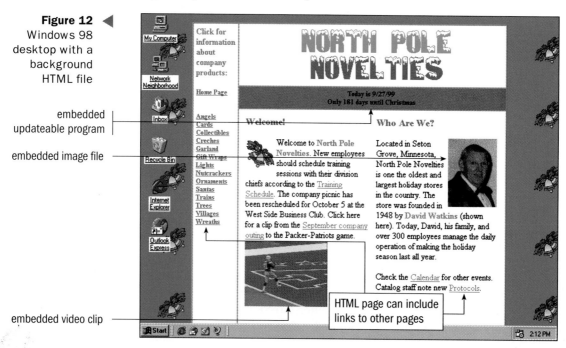

This company created a wallpaper that includes links to product groups, information about the company, a video clip of a recent company outing, and links to current events, company protocols, and training procedures.

Web Components on the Desktop

In addition to using a Web page as a background, you can also add Web components to the Windows 98 desktop in resizable, movable windows. A **Web component** is an object on the desktop that you can set to update automatically via your Web connection. For example, you might place a weather map, an investor ticker, or a news component on your desktop. You can schedule when each component will update itself and the information will be delivered to your desktop without your having to look for it.

Windows 95 users can purchase separate software that performs a similar function, such as the Internet Explorer 4.0 browser, Netscape Communicator's Netcaster component, or a product such as PointCast. But with Windows 98, the ability to place update-able Web information on the desktop is actually *integrated* into the operating system.

Figure 13 shows a Windows 98 desktop with several such Web components.

Figure 13 ◄
Windows 98
desktop with
Web
components

CNN news ⟶

Wall Street Journal news

weather ⟶

investment ticker ⟶

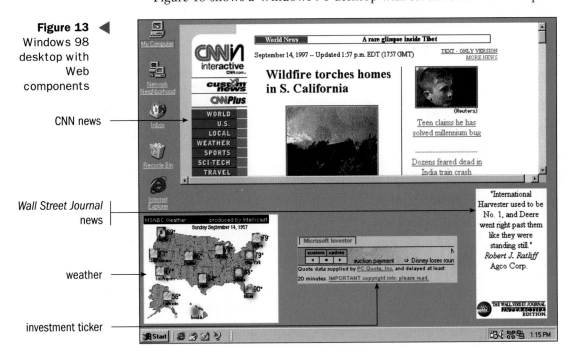

Every morning when this user checks her desktop, each component will have been automatically updated (if, that is, she has set the update schedules that way). The weather map will show the morning's weather instead of weather from the night before, her news service will display the most recent news, and the other Web components will update in a similar fashion. If she wants a more detailed look at, for example, the news, she can select and enlarge one of the Web component windows.

There are three ways to add Web components to the Windows 98 desktop:

- The Active Desktop Gallery offers a small set of useful Web components, including the weather map, investment ticker, clock, and so on. To access the Active Desktop Gallery, right-click the desktop, point to Active Desktop, and then click Customize my Desktop. A list of current Web components appears on the Web tab of the Display Properties dialog box. To add new ones, click the New button and follow the prompts to locate the Active Desktop Gallery.

- The Channel Bar lists companies that have agreements with Microsoft to deliver information directly to the desktops of those who subscribe to the Active Channel service. (A site that offers regularly updated information that can be delivered to the desktop on a predetermined schedule is called a **channel**.) When you subscribe to a channel delivery service, you request that information be "broadcast" to you from that channel at whatever schedule you specify. To add a channel from the Channel Bar, you must first enable the Channel Bar from the Web tab of the Display Properties dialog box. Once you can see the Channel Bar, click the channel you want to add. Follow the prompts to add the channel to your list of channels.

- You can add your own components by connecting to channel sites not necessarily associated with Microsoft and then subscribing to those channels. In most cases, you do this by connecting to the site with your browser. Sites that support channel delivery include a link that asks if you want to subscribe to the site. Click the link and follow the prompts; they vary from site to site.

If any of these components are on your desktop, a rectangular block appears that seems to be a part of the background. When you select that component, however, a window border appears that you can resize and move.

Web View in Explorer Windows

In addition to the Web components that appear on the desktop, the Windows 98 Explorer windows also have changed to extend the Web experience to folder navigation. The term **Explorer windows** is a general term that applies to windows such as Windows Explorer, My Computer, the folder and drive windows, and the Printer window. In other words, any window that displays and allows you to navigate the object hierarchy of your computer is an Explorer window.

With Windows 98 Explorer windows, you can enable **Web view**, which does the following:

- Displays objects on your computer as links

- Allows single-click navigation

- Adds to the window an HTML document with customizable links and information

- Enables you to use the Explorer window as a browser

Figure 14 shows the My Computer window as it looks in Windows 95 and in Windows 98.

Figure 14 ◀
My Computer in
Windows 95
and
Windows 98

Windows 95 My
Computer window

Windows 98
My Computer window

toolbars are different

list of objects is the
same as in Windows
95, except labels are
underlined and
perform like links

Web view HTML
document contains
text and images that
you can customize

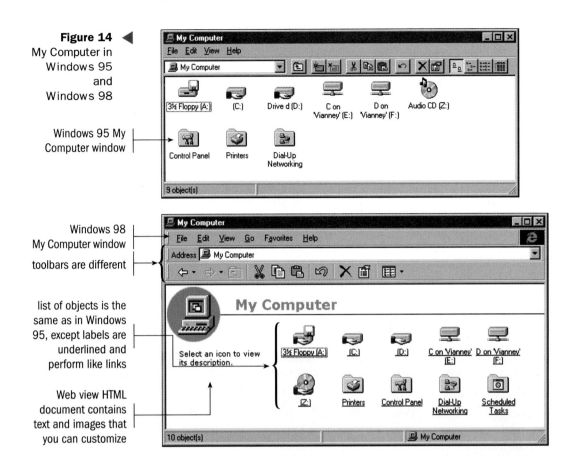

The Windows 95 window shows the familiar object list, but Windows 98 Explorer windows now have HTML documents in the background that you can customize. The ability to customize the Explorer windows by editing their background HTML page makes it easier than ever for you to work efficiently. For example, you could customize a network folder's HTML page so that anyone who accesses that Explorer window sees a description of the folder's contents, links to the most important objects in that window, and links to related objects. You might customize a network folder containing 1999 corporate reports so that it contains links to corporate reports for 1998 and 1997.

The objects that your computer displays look like the links you see on a Web page. As on the desktop, a single click suffices to open the object. For example, if you click the Floppy (A:) icon, the A: window opens. If you are used to thinking of a link as something that targets an object on the Web, you'll have to expand your vision. In Windows 98, links target any object accessible to your computer—not just Web pages, but also local drives, network folders, and files.

Web View Toolbars

In the Explorer windows, the Windows 95 Standard toolbar has been updated to include buttons that enable you to use the Explorer windows as browsers. The Address toolbar looks like the Address bar in a browser, and the Standard toolbar includes buttons that allow you to navigate through the hierarchy of drives and folders just as you would move through pages on the Web in your browser. Figure 15 first shows the Windows 95 Standard toolbar and then the Windows 98 Address and Standard toolbars on separate lines so you can see all the buttons.

Figure 15
My Computer
toolbars in
Windows 95
and
Windows 98

Windows 98 adds the
Address toolbar

As you move from one location on your computer to another, Windows 98 "remembers" where you've been, just as in your browser you can move back to previously viewed Web pages. You can use the navigation buttons to move easily through the hierarchy of your computer's objects.

Suppose you want to view the contents of a folder on drive A:. You could open My Computer and click the A: icon. The A: Explorer window would open. Then you could click the folder whose contents you want to view. The folder's Explorer window would open. To return to My Computer, you'd simply click the Back button twice.

Additionally, you can display the Links toolbar in Web view. When you click one of the buttons on the Links toolbar, the Explorer window functions just like your browser to display the page you selected.

Using Windows Explorer to Browse the Web

In both Windows 95 and Windows 98, Windows Explorer displays a hierarchy of objects on your computer. Windows 98 includes the Internet icon 🅴 as one of those objects. You might recognize this icon as the one that appears on the desktop in Windows 95; if you have an Internet service set up on your computer, double-clicking that icon on the Windows 95 desktop starts your browser. In Windows 98, however, when you click 🅴 in the Windows Explorer window, your browser's home page appears in the Exploring window. Figure 16 shows Windows Explorer with the object hierarchy on the left and a Web page off the Internet on the right.

Figure 16
Using Windows
Explorer as a
browser

current location is
a Web page

click to connect to
your home page

Notice that when you select a Web page in Windows Explorer, the standard Explorer toolbars and menus are replaced with toolbars and menus that are more browser-oriented. Indeed, you could use Windows Explorer as a Web-browsing tool.

Windows 98

Additional Windows 98 Features

This tutorial has focused primarily on how upgrading to Windows 98 affects the way you interact with the operating system. But Windows 98 offers many other features that replace or expand Windows 95 functions, as well as some completely new features. Figure 17 describes some of the most intriguing updated, expanded, or new features. You might not understand the technology behind all these features, but they should give you an idea of what you can do if you are running Windows 98 with the latest hardware.

Figure 17 ◄
Additional
Windows 98
features

Feature	Description
Digital Versatile Disc (DVD) support	The successor to CD-ROM disks, DVD stores many times the capacity of a CD-ROM, enough to store full-length digitized movies that you can then view on your monitor or TV screen if you have the appropriate hardware.
Disk space	The space available on your hard disk is limited by the type of file system you use. Windows 95 employs the FAT 16 file system. With Windows 98 FAT 32, you can store up to 30 percent more data on your disk, and you can work with drives that are much larger than those available to FAT 16. The FAT 32 converter utility also makes it easy to upgrade your file system.
Internet communications	Windows 98 ships with Internet Explorer, an Internet communications software suite that offers state-of-the-art integrated browsing, e-mail, newsgroup, Web page editing, and conferencing software—and much more!
Internet Connection Wizard	Establishing a connection to the Internet is much easier with this wizard, which works with your Internet service provider to configure your Internet connection properly.
On-line Help	Information about the Windows 98 operating system now appears as a Web page, and is continually updated by Microsoft. You can access the Windows 98 Help Desk to receive online technical support.
Peripheral device support	Windows 98 supports Universal serial bus (USB) technology, a hardware device that plugs into a single port from which you can run multiple peripheral devices.
Power management	If you own a new PC that supports OnNow hardware technology, your PC will start much more quickly, and you will consume less power if you take advantage of power-down features.
Speed	Windows 98 runs your applications faster, saving you time.
Tune-Up Wizard	In an effort to simplify and streamline your computer maintenance program, the Tune-Up Wizard analyzes your system and helps you schedule maintenance tasks such as defragmentation, disk scan, and backup. Most of the maintenance tools have also been improved.
TV Viewer	This accessory brings television to the PC—not just regular TV signals, but also content-rich broadcasts that provide interactivity on your TV. For example, a cooking show might include links to recipes that you could download over your TV satellite or cable connection.
Video playback	ActiveMovie expands the multimedia capabilities of your computer, featuring improved video playback.
Windows Update	Accessed directly from the Windows 98 Start menu, this Microsoft site features a service that scans your system and allows you to update it with the most recent software. This site also helps you troubleshoot problems.

When computer owners consider whether or not to upgrade, they review feature lists and comparisons such as the ones you've seen in this tutorial. They then assess their needs and budget to determine whether to make the upgrade.

Now that you've had a chance to explore how Windows 98 changes the operating system landscape, you can see why users must balance the advantages against the sometimes uncertain world of switching to a new operating system and a new way of working with computers. Many users believe, however, that Windows 98 raises personal computing to new heights, and the benefits far outweigh the challenges.

Tutorial Assignments

1. Based on what you've read in this tutorial, if you were a Windows 95 user, would you make the upgrade to Windows 98? Write a one-page essay that answers this question. In your essay, you'll need to define your computing needs, address how Windows 95 fulfills those needs, and evaluate the degree to which Windows 98 could better meet those needs. Be sure to itemize the features that influence you the most —both pro and con.

2. Using the resources available to you, either online or through your library, locate information about the release of Windows 98. Computing trade magazines, both hard copy and online, are an excellent source of information about software. Read several articles about Windows 98 and then write a one-page essay that discusses the features that seem most important to the people who evaluated the software. If you find reviews of the software, mention the features that reviewers had the strongest reaction to, pro or con.

3. Write a single-page essay defending or refuting the following proposition: "Software developers upgrade their software only to make money."

4. Interview two people you know who are well-informed computer users. Ask them how they decide when to upgrade a software product. If they are using a PC with the Windows 3.X, 95, or 98 operating system, ask them why they did or did not upgrade to Windows 98. Write a single-page essay summarizing what you learned from these interviews about making the decision to upgrade.

5. Based on what you learned about Windows 98 in this tutorial, what Windows 98 features interest you the most? The least? Write two paragraphs describing those features and explaining why you do or do not find them interesting.

6. How has Windows 98 changed the concept of the "home computer"? Research the Windows 98 features that might benefit home users, such as its TV and appliance capabilities, and write two paragraphs summarizing those features and assessing how they could impact home life.

Microsoft®
Word 97

LEVEL I

TUTORIALS

Read This **Before You Begin**

STUDENT DISK

To complete Word 97 Tutorials 1-4, you need a Student Disk. Your instructor will either provide you with a Student Disk or ask you to make your own.

If you are supposed to make your own Student Disk, you will need one blank, formatted, high-density disk. You will need to copy a set of folders from a file server or standalone computer onto your disk. Your instructor will tell you which computer, drive letter, and folders contain the files you need. The following table shows you which folders go on your disk:

Student Disk	Write this on the disk label	Put these folders on the disk
1	Student Disk 1: Word 97 Tutorials 1-4	Tutorial.01, Tutorial.02, Tutorial.03, Tutorial.04

See the inside front or inside back cover of this book for more information on Student Disk files, or ask your instructor or technical support person for assistance.

COURSE LAB

Tutorial 1 features an interactive Course Lab to help you understand word processing concepts. There are Lab Assignments at the end of the tutorial that relate to this Lab. To start the Lab, click the Start button on the Windows 95 Taskbar, point to Programs, point to Course Labs, point to New Perspectives Applications, and click Word Processing.

USING YOUR OWN COMPUTER

If you are going to work through this book using your own computer, you need:
- **Computer System** Microsoft Windows 95 or Microsoft Windows NT Workstation 4.0 (or a later version) and Microsoft Word 97 must be installed on your computer. This book assumes a typical installation of Microsoft Word 97.
- **Student Disk** Ask your instructor or lab manager for details on how to get the Student Disk. You will not be able to complete the tutorials or end-of-tutorial assignments in this book using your own computer until you have a Student Disk. The Student Files may also be obtained electronically over the Internet. See the inside front or inside back cover of this book for more details.
- **Course Lab** See your instructor or technical support person to obtain the Course Lab software for use on your own computer.

To complete Word 97 Tutorials 1-4, your students must use a set of files on a Student Disk. These files are included in the Instructor's Resource Kit, and they may also be obtained electronically over the Internet. See the inside front or inside back cover of this book for more details. Follow the instructions in the Readme file to copy the files to your server or standalone computer. You can view the Readme file using WordPad. Once the files are copied, you can make Student Disks for the students yourself, or you can tell students where to find the files so they can make their own Student Disks.

COURSE LAB SOFTWARE

The Course Lab software is distributed on a CD-ROM included in the Instructor's Resource Kit. To install the Course Lab software, follow the setup instructions in the Readme file on the CD-ROM. Refer also to the Readme file for essential technical notes related to running the Lab in a multi-user environment. Once you have installed the Course Lab software, your students can start the Lab from the Windows 95 desktop by following the instructions in the Course Labs section above.

COURSE TECHNOLOGY STUDENT FILES AND LAB SOFTWARE

You are granted a license to copy the Student Files and Lab software to any computer or computer network used by students who have purchased this book.

TUTORIAL 1

Creating a Document

Writing a Business Letter for Crossroads

Word

OBJECTIVES

In this tutorial you will:

- Start and exit Word

- Identify the components of the Word window

- Choose commands using the toolbars and menus

- Correct spelling errors with AutoCorrect

- Scroll through a document

- Create, save, and print a document

- Use the Word Help system to get Help

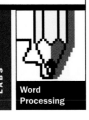

LABS

Word Processing

CASE

Crossroads

Karen Liu is executive director of Crossroads, a small, non-profit organization in Tacoma, Washington. Crossroads distributes business clothing to low-income clients who are returning to the job market or starting new careers. To make potential clients in the community more aware of their services, Crossroads reserves an exhibit booth each year at a local job fair sponsored by the Tacoma Chamber of Commerce. Crossroads needs to find out the date and location of this year's fair, as well as some other logistical information, before they can reserve a booth. Karen asks you to write a letter requesting this information from the Tacoma Chamber of Commerce.

In this tutorial you will create Karen's letter using Microsoft Word 97, a popular word-processing program. Before you begin typing the letter, you will learn to start the Word program, identify and use the elements of the Word screen, and adjust some Word settings. You will then go on to create a new Word document, type in the text of the Crossroads letter, save the letter, and then print the letter for Karen. In the process of entering the text, you'll learn several ways of correcting typing errors. You'll also learn how to use the Word Help system, which allows you to quickly find answers to your questions about the program.

Using the Tutorials Effectively

These tutorials are designed to be used at a computer. Each tutorial is divided into sessions. Watch for the session headings, such as "Session 1.1" and "Session 1.2." Each session is designed to be completed in about 45 minutes, but take as much time as you need. When you've completed a session, it's a good idea to exit the program and take a break. You can exit Microsoft Word by clicking the Close button in the top-right corner of the program window.

Before you begin, read the following questions and answers. They are designed to help you use the tutorials effectively.

Where do I start?

Each tutorial begins with a case, which sets the scene for the tutorial and gives you background information to help you understand what you will be doing in the tutorial. Read the case before you go to the lab. In the lab, begin with the first session of the tutorial.

How do I know what to do on the computer?

Each session contains steps that you will perform on the computer to learn how to use Microsoft Word. The steps are numbered and are set against a colored background. Read the text that introduces each series of steps, and read each step carefully and completely before you try it.

How do I know if I did the step correctly?

As you work, compare your computer screen with the corresponding figure in the tutorial. Don't worry if your screen display is somewhat different from the figure. The important parts of the screen display are labeled in each figure. Check to make sure these parts are on your screen.

What if I make a mistake?

Don't worry about making mistakes—they are part of the learning process. Paragraphs labeled "TROUBLE?" identify common problems and explain how to get back on track. Follow the steps in a TROUBLE? paragraph *only* if you are having the problem described. If you run into other problems, carefully consider the current state of your system, the position of the pointer, and any messages on the screen.

How do I use the Reference Windows?

Reference Windows summarize the procedures you learn in the tutorial steps. Do not complete the actions in the Reference Windows when you are working through the tutorial. Instead, refer to the Reference Windows while you are working on the assignments at the end of the tutorial.

How can I test my understanding of the material I learned in the tutorial?

At the end of each session, you can answer the Quick Check questions. If necessary, refer to the Answers to Quick Check Questions to check your work.

After you have completed the entire tutorial, you should complete the Tutorial Assignments and Case Problems. These exercises are carefully structured so you will review what you have learned and then apply your knowledge to new situations.

What if I can't remember how to do something?

You should refer to the Task Reference at the end of the book; it summarizes how to accomplish commonly performed tasks.

What is the Word Processing Course Lab, and how should I use it?

This interactive Lab helps you review word processing concepts and practice skills that you learn in Tutorial 1. The Lab Assignments section at the end of Tutorial 1 includes instructions for using the Lab.

Now that you've seen how to use the tutorials effectively, you are ready to begin.

SESSION

1.1

In this session you will learn how to start Word, how to identify and use the parts of the Word screen, and how to adjust some Word settings. With the skills you learn in this session, you'll be prepared to use Word to create a variety of documents, such as letters, reports, and memos.

Four Steps to a Professional Document

Word helps you produce quality work in minimal time. Not only can you type a document, you can quickly make editing changes and corrections, adjust margins and spacing, create columns and tables, and add graphics to your documents. The most efficient way to produce a document is to follow these four steps: 1) planning and creating, 2) editing, 3) formatting, and 4) printing.

In the long run, *planning* saves you time and effort. First, you should determine what you want to say. State your purpose clearly and include enough information to achieve that purpose without overwhelming or boring your reader. Be sure to *organize* your ideas logically. Also, decide how you want your document to look—its *presentation*. In this case, your letter to the Tacoma Chamber of Commerce will take the form of a standard business letter. Karen has given you a handwritten note with all her questions for the Tacoma Chamber of Commerce, as shown in Figure 1-1.

Figure 1-1 ◀
Karen's
questions about
the job fair

> Please write the Tacoma Chamber of Commerce and find out the following:
>
> What are the location and dates for this year's job fair?
>
> Is a map of the exhibit area available? What size booths are available and how can we reserve a booth?
>
> Who do we contact about what physical facilities are available at each booth?
>
> Send the letter to the Chamber's president. The address is 210 Shoreline Vista, Suite 1103, Tacoma WA 98402.

After you've planned your document, you can go ahead and *create* it using Word. The next step, *editing*, consists of reading through the document you've created, then correcting your errors, and finally adding or deleting text to make the document easy to read.

Once your document is error-free, you can *format* it to make it visually appealing. As you'll learn in Tutorial 2, formatting features, such as white space (blank areas of a page), line spacing, boldface, and italics can help make your document easier to read. *Printing* is the final phase in creating an effective document. In this tutorial, you will preview your document before you spend time and resources to print it.

Starting Word

Before you can apply these four steps to produce the letter using Word, you need to start Word and learn about the general organization of the Word screen. You'll do that now.

To start Microsoft Word:

1. Make sure Windows 95 is running on your computer and the Windows 95 desktop appears on your screen.

TROUBLE? If you're running Windows NT Workstation 4.0 (or a later version) on your computer or network, don't worry. Although the figures in this book were created while running Windows 95, Windows NT 4.0 and Windows 95 share the same interface, and Word 97 runs equally well under either operating system.

2. Click the **Start** button on the taskbar to display the Start menu, and then point to **Programs** to display the Programs menu.

3. Point to **Microsoft Word** on the Programs menu. See Figure 1-2.

Figure 1-2 ◀
Starting
Microsoft Word

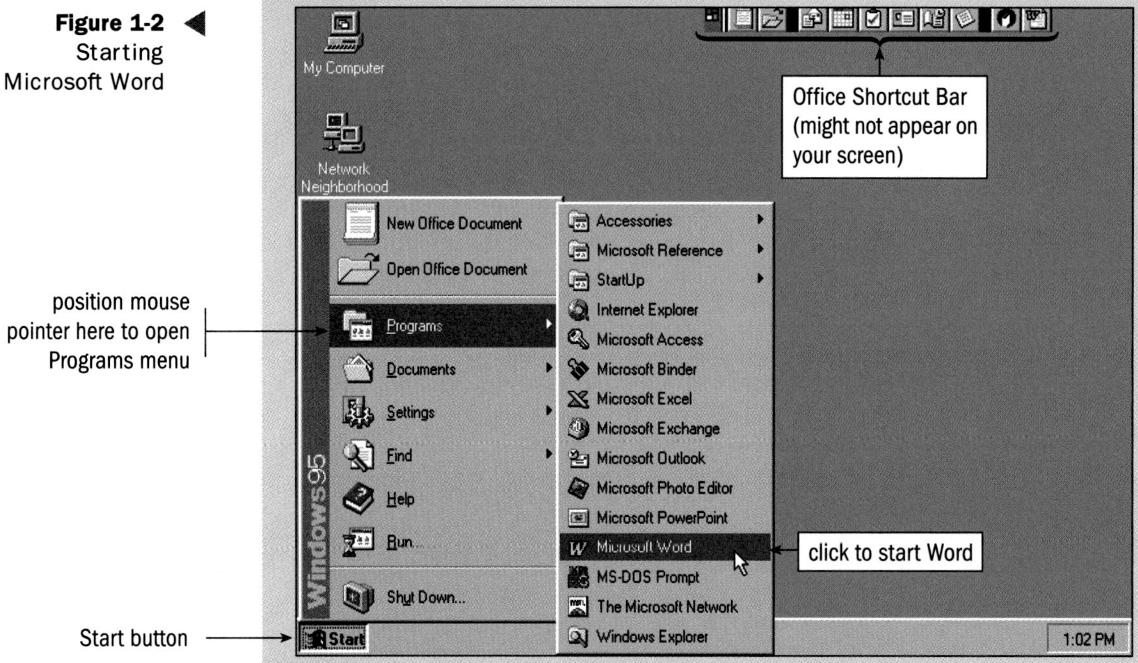

position mouse
pointer here to open
Programs menu

Start button

TROUBLE? If you don't see the Microsoft Word option on the Programs menu, ask your instructor or technical support person for help.

TROUBLE? The Office Shortcut Bar, which appears along the top border of the desktop in Figure 1-2, might look different on your screen, or it might not appear at all, depending on how your system is set up. Since the Office Shortcut Bar is not required to complete these tutorials, it has been omitted from the remaining figures in this text.

4. Click **Microsoft Word**. After a short pause, the Microsoft Word copyright information appears in a message box and remains on the screen until the Word program window, containing a blank Word document, is displayed. See Figure 1-3.

Word

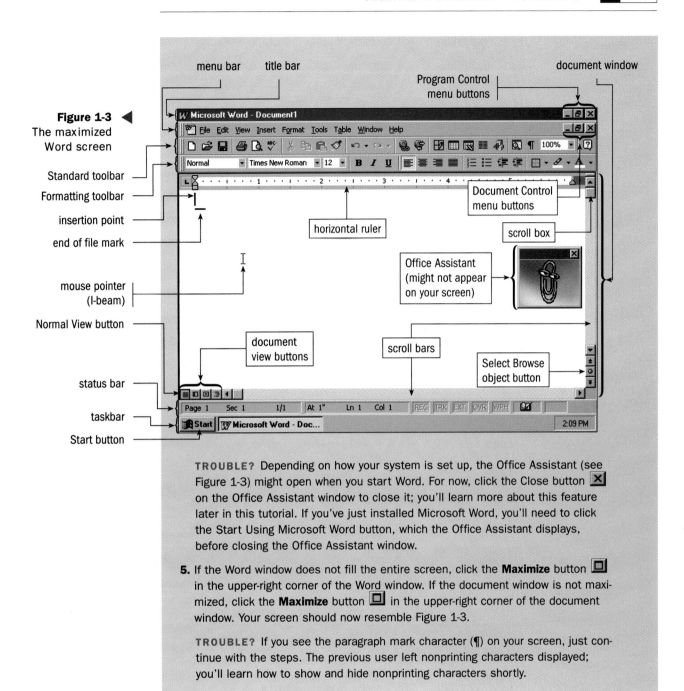

Figure 1-3 ◀
The maximized
Word screen

Standard toolbar

Formatting toolbar

insertion point

end of file mark

mouse pointer
(I-beam)

Normal View button

status bar

taskbar

Start button

menu bar   title bar   Program Control menu buttons   document window

Document Control menu buttons

horizontal ruler

scroll box

Office Assistant (might not appear on your screen)

document view buttons

scroll bars

Select Browse object button

TROUBLE? Depending on how your system is set up, the Office Assistant (see Figure 1-3) might open when you start Word. For now, click the Close button ☒ on the Office Assistant window to close it; you'll learn more about this feature later in this tutorial. If you've just installed Microsoft Word, you'll need to click the Start Using Microsoft Word button, which the Office Assistant displays, before closing the Office Assistant window.

5. If the Word window does not fill the entire screen, click the **Maximize** button 🔲 in the upper-right corner of the Word window. If the document window is not maximized, click the **Maximize** button 🔲 in the upper-right corner of the document window. Your screen should now resemble Figure 1-3.

TROUBLE? If you see the paragraph mark character (¶) on your screen, just continue with the steps. The previous user left nonprinting characters displayed; you'll learn how to show and hide nonprinting characters shortly.

Word is now running and ready to use.

The Word Screen

The Word screen is made up of both a program window and a document window. The **program window**, also called the Word window, opens automatically when you start Word and contains all the toolbars and menus. The **document window**, which opens within the Word window, is where you type and edit documents.

Figure 1-3 shows the Word screen with both windows maximized. If your screen doesn't look exactly like Figure 1-3, just continue for now. Figure 1-4 lists each element of the Word screen and summarizes its function. You are already familiar with some of these elements, such as the menu bar, title bar, and status bar, because they are common to all Windows screens.

Figure 1-4 ◀
Summary
of functions of
Word screen

Screen Element	Function
Title bar	Identifies the current application (i.e., Microsoft Word); shows the filename of the current document
Control menu buttons	Program Control menu buttons size and close the Word window; Document Control menu buttons size and close the current document window
Menu bar	Contains lists or menus of all the Word commands
Standard toolbar	Contains buttons to activate frequently used commands
Formatting toolbar	Contains buttons to activate common font and paragraph formatting commands
Select Browse object button	Displays buttons that allow you to move quickly through the document
Horizontal ruler	Adjusts margins, tabs, and column widths; vertical ruler appears in page layout view
Document window	Area where you enter text and graphics
Document view buttons	Show document in four different views: normal view, online layout view, page layout view, and outline view
Status bar	Provides information regarding the location of the insertion point
Taskbar	Shows programs that are running and allows you to switch quickly from one program to another
Mouse pointer	Changes shape depending on its location on the screen (i.e., I-beam pointer in text area; arrow in nontext areas)
Insertion point	Indicates location where characters will be inserted or deleted
Scroll bars	Shift text vertically and horizontally on the screen so you can see different parts of the document
Scroll box	Helps you move quickly to other pages of your document
Start button	Starts a program, opens a document, provides quick access to Windows 95 Help

If at any time you would like to check the name of a Word toolbar button, just position the mouse pointer over the button without clicking. A **ScreenTip**, a small yellow box with the name of the button, will appear.

Checking the Screen Before You Begin Each Tutorial

Word provides a set of standard settings, called **default settings**, that are appropriate for most documents. The setup of your Word document might have different default settings from those shown in the figures. This often happens when you share a computer and another user changes the appearance of the Word screen. The rest of this section explains what your screen should look like and how to make it match those in the tutorials.

Setting the Document View to Normal

You can view your document in one of four ways—normal, online layout, page layout, or outline. **Online layout** and **outline view** are designed for special situations that you don't need to worry about now. You will, however, learn more about **page layout view**—which allows you to see a page's design and format—in later tutorials. In most cases you'll want to use **normal view** when completing these tutorials. Depending on the document view selected by the last person who used Word, you might need to change the document back to normal view.

To make sure the document window is in normal view:

1. Click the **Normal View** button 📄 to the left of the horizontal scroll bar. See Figure 1-5. If your document window was not in normal view, it changes to normal view now.

Figure 1-5 ◀
Changing to
normal view

Normal View button

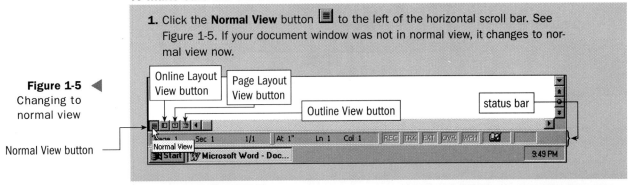

Online Layout View button · Page Layout View button · Outline View button · status bar · Normal View

Displaying the Toolbars and Ruler

These tutorials frequently use the Standard toolbar and the Formatting toolbar to help you work more efficiently. Each time you start Word, check to make sure both toolbars appear on your screen. If either toolbar is missing, or if other toolbars are displayed, perform the steps below.

To display or hide a toolbar:

1. Position the pointer over any visible toolbar and click the right mouse button. A shortcut menu appears. The menu lists all available toolbars, and displays a check mark next to those currently displayed.

2. If the Standard or Formatting toolbar is not visible, click its name on the shortcut menu to place a check mark next to it. If any toolbars besides the Formatting and Standard toolbars have checkmarks, click each one to remove the check mark and hide the toolbar.

As you complete these tutorials, the ruler should also be visible to help you place items precisely. If your ruler is not visible, perform the next step.

To display the ruler:

1. Click **View** on the menu bar, and then click **Ruler** to place a check mark next to it.

Setting the Font and Font Size

A **font** is a set of characters that has a certain design, shape, and appearance. Each font has a name, such as Courier, Times New Roman, or Arial. The **font size** is the actual height of a character, measured in points, where one point equals $\frac{1}{72}$ of an inch in height. You'll learn more about fonts and font sizes in Tutorial 2, but for now simply keep in mind that most of the documents you'll create will use the Times New Roman font in a font size of 12 points. Word usually uses a default setting of 10-point font size in new documents. This font size, however, is not as easy to read as the larger 12-point font. If your font setting is not Times New Roman 12 point, you should change the default setting now. You'll use the menu bar to choose the desired commands.

To change the default font and font size:

1. Click **Format** on the menu bar, and then click **Font** to open the Font dialog box. If necessary, click the Font tab. See Figure 1-6.

Figure 1-6 ◀
Font dialog box

use this font ──────▶

click to make
selected font ────
settings the defaults

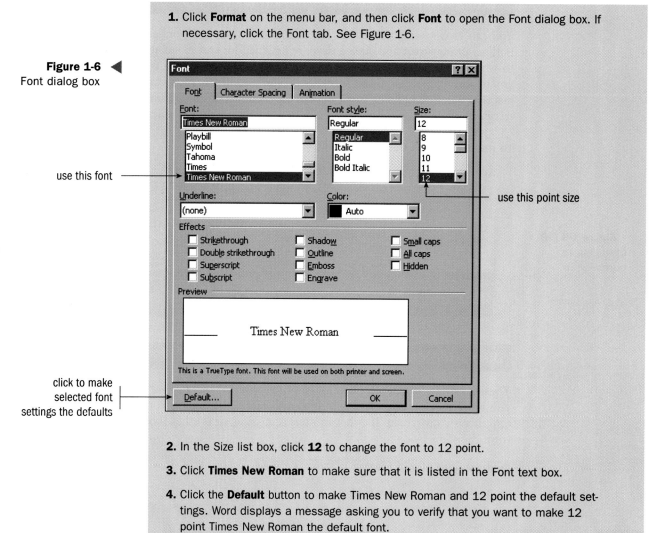

use this point size

2. In the Size list box, click **12** to change the font to 12 point.

3. Click **Times New Roman** to make sure that it is listed in the Font text box.

4. Click the **Default** button to make Times New Roman and 12 point the default settings. Word displays a message asking you to verify that you want to make 12 point Times New Roman the default font.

5. Click the **Yes** button.

Displaying Nonprinting Characters

Nonprinting characters are symbols that can be displayed on the screen but that do not show up when you print your document. You can display them when you are working on the appearance, or **format**, of your document. For example, one nonprinting character marks the end of a paragraph (¶), while another marks the space between words (•). It's sometimes helpful to display nonprinting characters so you can actually see whether you've typed an extra space, ended a paragraph, typed spaces instead of tabs, and so on. In general, in these tutorials, you will display nonprinting characters only when you are formatting a document. You'll display them now, though, so you can use them as guides when typing your first letter.

To display nonprinting characters:

1. Click the **Show/Hide ¶** button 🔳 on the Standard toolbar to display the nonprinting characters. A paragraph mark (¶) appears at the top of the document window. See Figure 1-7.

Word

Figure 1-7 ◀
Nonprinting
characters
activated

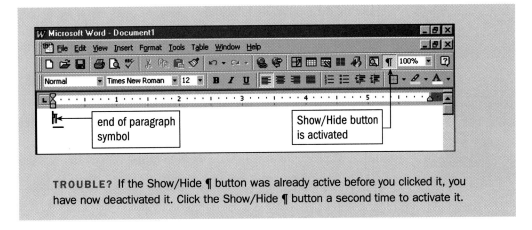

TROUBLE? If the Show/Hide ¶ button was already active before you clicked it, you have now deactivated it. Click the Show/Hide ¶ button a second time to activate it.

To make sure your screen always matches the figures in this book, remember to complete the checklist in Figure 1-8 each time you sit down at the computer.

Figure 1-8 ◀
Word screen
session
checklist

Screen Element	Setting	Check
Document view	Normal	
Program and document windows	Maximized	
Standard toolbar	Displayed	
Formatting toolbar	Displayed	
Other toolbars	Hidden	
Nonprinting characters	Hidden	
Font	Times New Roman	
Point size	12 point	
Ruler	Displayed	

Quick Check

1 In your own words, list and describe the steps in creating a document.

2 How do you start Word from the Windows 95 desktop?

3 Define each of the following in your own words:
   a. Standard toolbar
   b. ruler
   c. insertion point
   d. font
   e. default settings

4 How do you change the default font size?

5 How do you display or hide the Standard toolbar?

6 How do you display or hide nonprinting characters?

Now that you have planned a document, opened the Word program, identified screen elements, and adjusted settings, you are ready to create a new document. In the next session, you will create Karen's letter to the Tacoma Chamber of Commerce.

SESSION

1.2

In this session you will create a one-page document using Word. You'll learn how to correct errors and scroll through your document. You'll also learn how to name, save, preview, and print the document, and how to use the Word Help system.

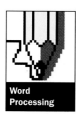

Word Processing

Typing a Letter

You're ready to type Karen's letter to the Tacoma Chamber of Commerce. Figure 1-9 shows the completed letter printed on the company letterhead. You'll begin by opening a new blank page (in case you accidentally typed something in the current page). Then you'll move the insertion point to about 2½ inches from the top margin of the paper to allow space for the Crossroads letterhead.

Figure 1-9 ◀
Job fair letter

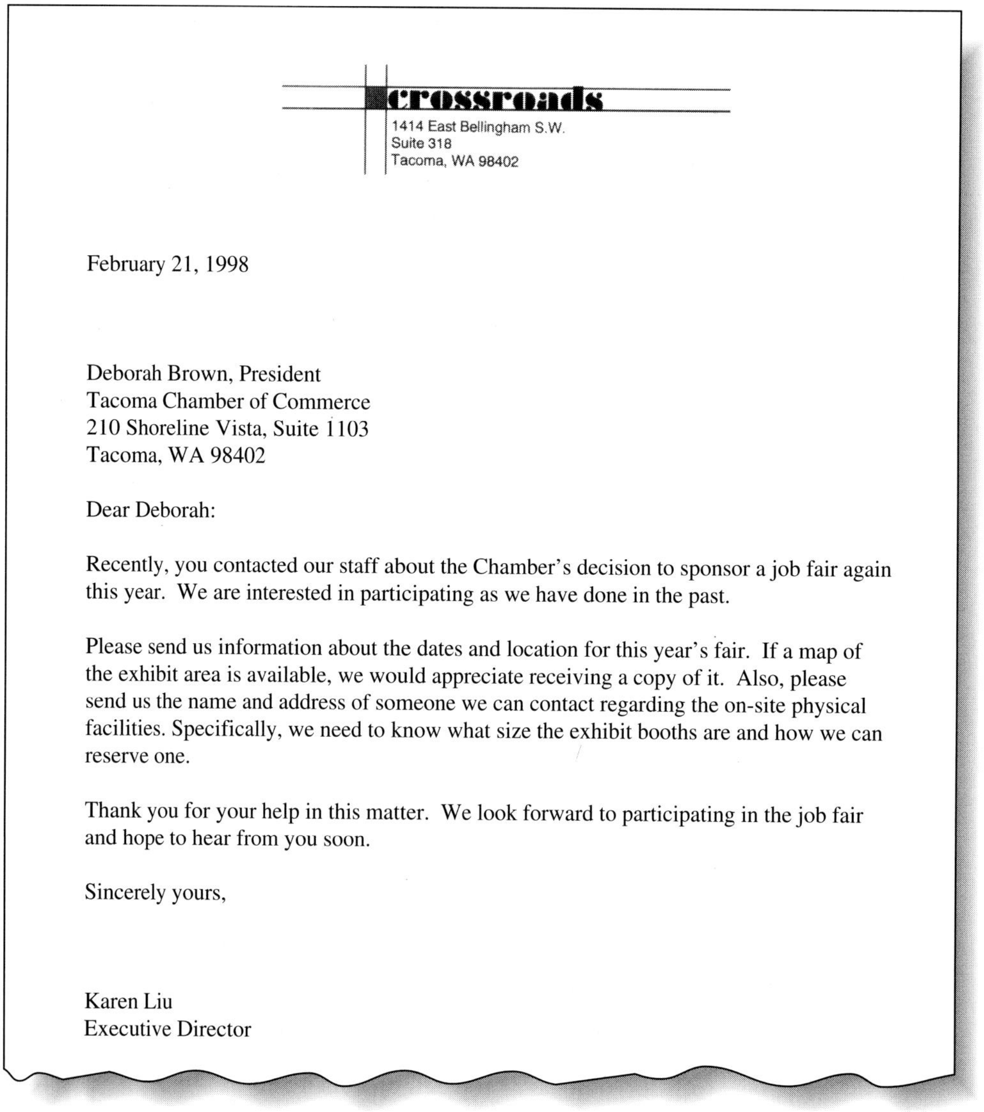

crossroads
1414 East Bellingham S.W.
Suite 318
Tacoma, WA 98402

February 21, 1998

Deborah Brown, President
Tacoma Chamber of Commerce
210 Shoreline Vista, Suite 1103
Tacoma, WA 98402

Dear Deborah:

Recently, you contacted our staff about the Chamber's decision to sponsor a job fair again this year. We are interested in participating as we have done in the past.

Please send us information about the dates and location for this year's fair. If a map of the exhibit area is available, we would appreciate receiving a copy of it. Also, please send us the name and address of someone we can contact regarding the on-site physical facilities. Specifically, we need to know what size the exhibit booths are and how we can reserve one.

Thank you for your help in this matter. We look forward to participating in the job fair and hope to hear from you soon.

Sincerely yours,

Karen Liu
Executive Director

To open a new document:

1. If you took a break after the last session, make sure the Word program is running, that nonprinting characters are displayed, and that the font settings in the Formatting toolbar are set to 12 point Times New Roman.

2. Click the **New** button 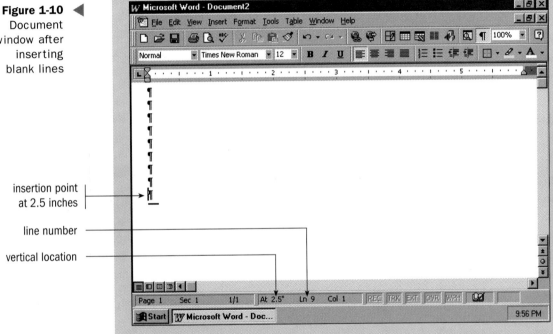 on the Standard toolbar to open a new, blank document.

3. Press the **Enter** key eight times. Each time you press the Enter key, a nonprinting paragraph mark appears. In the status bar (at the bottom of the document window) you should see the setting "At 2.5"", indicating that the insertion point is 2½ inches from the top of the page. Another setting in the status bar should read "Ln 9", indicating the insertion point is in line 9 of the document. See Figure 1-10.

Figure 1-10
Document window after inserting blank lines

insertion point at 2.5 inches

line number

vertical location

TROUBLE? If the paragraph mark doesn't appear each time you press the Enter key, the nonprinting characters might be hidden. To show the nonprinting characters, click the Show/Hide ¶ button ¶.

TROUBLE? If you pressed the Enter key too many times, just press the Backspace key to delete each extra line and paragraph mark. If you're on line 9 but the At number is not 2.5", don't worry. Different fonts and monitors produce slightly different measurements when you press the Enter key.

Using AutoText Tips

Now you're ready to type the date. As you do it, you'll take advantage of Word's **AutoText** feature, which automatically types dates and other regularly used words and text for you.

To insert the date using an AutoText tip:

1. Type **Febr** (the first four letters of February). An AutoText tip appears above the line, as shown in Figure 1-11.

Figure 1-11 ◀
AutoText tip

tip shows the
rest of the word

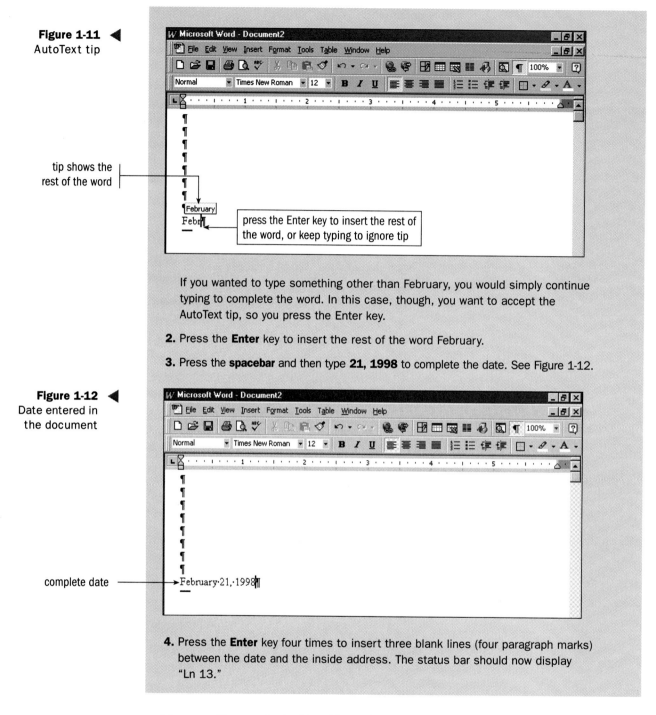

press the Enter key to insert the rest of
the word, or keep typing to ignore tip

If you wanted to type something other than February, you would simply continue
typing to complete the word. In this case, though, you want to accept the
AutoText tip, so you press the Enter key.

2. Press the **Enter** key to insert the rest of the word February.

3. Press the **spacebar** and then type **21, 1998** to complete the date. See Figure 1-12.

Figure 1-12 ◀
Date entered in
the document

complete date

4. Press the **Enter** key four times to insert three blank lines (four paragraph marks)
between the date and the inside address. The status bar should now display
"Ln 13."

Next, you'll enter the inside address shown on Karen's note.

Entering Text

You'll enter the inside address by typing it. If you type a wrong character, simply press the
Backspace key to delete the mistake and then retype it.

To type the inside address:

1. Type **Deborah Brown, President** and press the **Enter** key. As you type, the nonprinting character (•) appears between words to indicate a space.

TROUBLE? If a wavy red or green line appears beneath a word, check to make sure you typed the text correctly. If you did not, use the Backspace key to remove the error, and then retype the text correctly.

2. Type the following text, pressing the **Enter** key after each line to enter the inside address.

Tacoma Chamber of Commerce
210 Shoreline Vista, Suite 1103
Tacoma, WA 98402

3. Press the **Enter** key again to add a blank line between the inside address and the salutation. See Figure 1-13.

Figure 1-13 ◀
Document window showing inside address

inside address ——

extra blank line ——

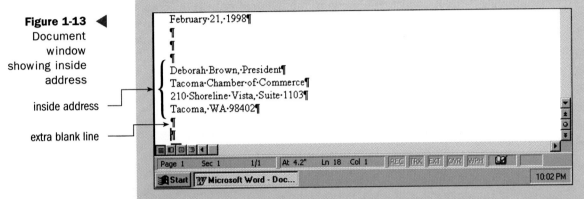

4. Type **Dear Deborah:** and press the **Enter** key twice to double space between the salutation and the body of the letter.

When you press the Enter key the first time, the Office Assistant appears and asks if you would like help writing your letter. See Figure 1-14.

Figure 1-14 ◀
Office Assistant

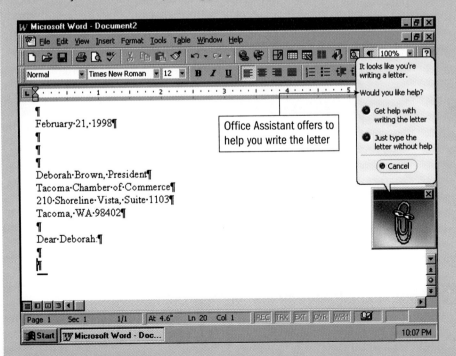

Office Assistant offers to help you write the letter

The Office Assistant is a special feature that sometimes appears to offer help on routine tasks. In this case, you could click the "Get help with writing the letter button" and have the Office Assistant lead you through a series of dialog boxes designed to set up the basic elements of your letter automatically. You'll learn more about the

Office Assistant later in this tutorial. Then, in the Tutorial Assignments, you'll have a chance to create a letter with the help of the Office Assistant. For now, though, you'll close the Office Assistant and continue writing your letter.

5. Click the **Just type the letter without help** button to close the Office Assistant.

You have completed the date, the inside address, and the salutation of Karen's letter, using a standard business letter format. You're ready to complete the letter. Before you do, however, you should save what you have typed so far.

Saving a Document

The letter on which you are working is stored only in the computer's memory, not on a disk. If you were to exit Word, turn off your computer, or experience an accidental power failure, the part of Karen's letter that you just typed would be lost. You should get in the habit of frequently saving your document to a disk.

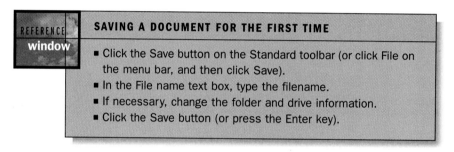

REFERENCE window	**SAVING A DOCUMENT FOR THE FIRST TIME**
	■ Click the Save button on the Standard toolbar (or click File on the menu bar, and then click Save).
	■ In the File name text box, type the filename.
	■ If necessary, change the folder and drive information.
	■ Click the Save button (or press the Enter key).

After you name your document, Word automatically appends the .doc filename extension to identify the file as a Microsoft Word document. However, depending on how Windows 95 is set up (or configured) on your computer, you might not actually see .doc extension. These tutorials assume that filename extensions are hidden.

To save the document:

1. Place your Student Disk in the appropriate disk drive.

TROUBLE? If you don't have a Student Disk, you need to get one before you can proceed. Your instructor or technical support person will either give you one or ask you to make your own by following the instructions on the "Read This Before You Begin" page at the beginning of this tutorial. See your instructor or technical support person for more information.

2. Click the **Save** button 🔲 on the Standard toolbar. The Save As dialog box opens. See Figure 1-15.

Figure 1-15 ◀
Save As
dialog box

change folder to
Tutorial.01

type filename here

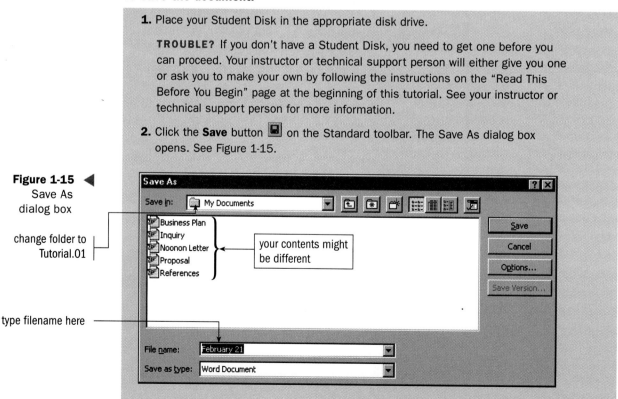

3. Type **Tacoma Job Fair Letter** in the File name text box.

4. Click the **Save in** list arrow, click the drive containing your Student Disk, and then double-click the **Tutorial.01** folder. The Tutorial.01 folder is now open for saving the file. See Figure 1-16.

Figure 1-16 ◀
Save As dialog
box with
Tutorial.01
folder open

folder on
Student Disk

filename

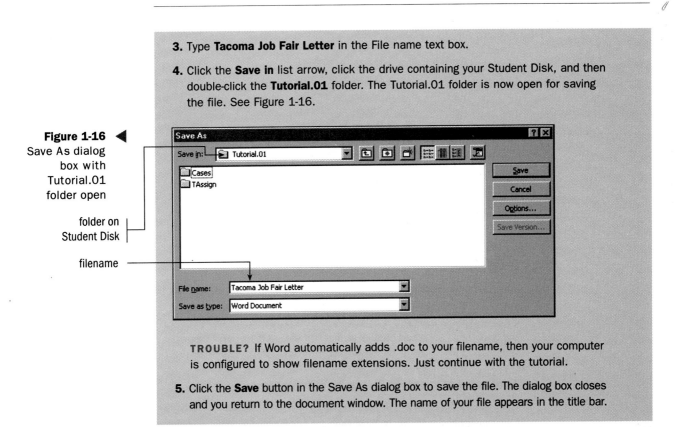

TROUBLE? If Word automatically adds .doc to your filename, then your computer is configured to show filename extensions. Just continue with the tutorial.

5. Click the **Save** button in the Save As dialog box to save the file. The dialog box closes and you return to the document window. The name of your file appears in the title bar.

Word Wrap

With your document saved, you're ready to complete Karen's letter. As you type the body of the letter, do not press the Enter key at the end of each line. When you type a word that extends into the right margin, both the insertion point and the word move automatically to the next line. This automatic text line breaking is called **word wrap**. You'll see how word wrap works as you type the body of Karen's letter.

To observe word wrap while typing a paragraph:

1. Make sure the insertion point is at Ln 20 Col 1 (according to the settings in the status bar). If it's not, move it to that location by pressing the arrow keys.

2. Type the following sentence slowly and watch when the insertion point automatically jumps to the next line: **Recently, you contacted our staff about the Chamber's decision to sponsor a job fair again this year.** Notice how Word automatically moves the last few words to a new line. See Figure 1-17.

Figure 1-17 ◀
Word wrapping
text

beginning of first
paragraph

word wrapped
to new line

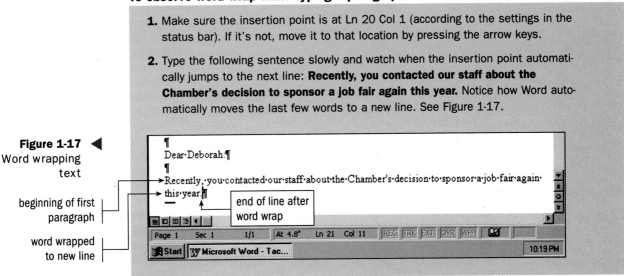

TROUBLE? If your screen does not match Figure 1-17 exactly, don't be concerned. The word or letter at which word wrap occurred in your document and the status bar values might be different from Figure 1-17 because fonts have varying letter widths and produce slightly different measurements on monitors. Continue with Step 3. If you see any other AutoText tips as you type, ignore them.

3. Press the **spacebar** twice, and type **We are interested in participating as we have done in the past.** (including the period) to enter the rest of the first paragraph of the letter.

4. Press the **Enter** key to end the first paragraph, and then press the **Enter** key again to double space between the first and second paragraphs.

Scrolling

After you finish the last set of steps, the insertion point will probably be at the bottom of your document window. It might seem that no room is left in the document window to type the rest of Karen's letter. However, as you continue to add text at the end of your document, the text that you typed earlier will scroll (or shift up) and disappear from the top of the document window. You'll see how scrolling works as you enter the final text of Karen's letter.

To observe scrolling while you're entering text:

1. Make sure the insertion point is at the bottom of the screen, to the left of the second paragraph mark in the body of the letter.

2. Type the second paragraph, as shown in Figure 1-18, and then press the **Enter** key twice to insert a blank line. Notice that as you type the paragraph, the top of the letter scrolls off the top of the document window. Don't worry if you make a mistake in your typing. You'll learn a number of ways to correct errors in the next section.

Figure 1-18 ◀
Text scrolled
off the screen

date and inside
address scrolled
off the screen

second paragraph

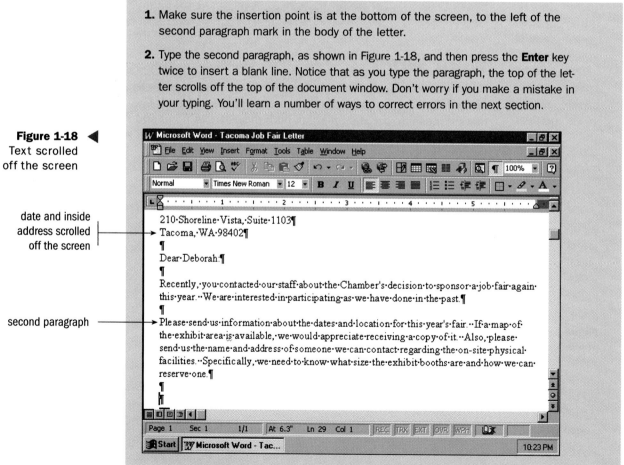

Correcting Errors

Have you made any typing mistakes yet? If so, don't worry. The advantage of using a word processor is that you can correct mistakes quickly and efficiently. Word provides several ways to correct errors when you're entering text.

Word

If you discover a typing error as soon as you make it, you can press the Backspace key to erase the characters and spaces to the left of the insertion point one at a time. Backspacing will erase both printing and nonprinting characters. After you erase the error, you can type the correct characters.

Word also provides a feature, called **AutoCorrect**, that checks for errors in your document as you type and automatically corrects common typing errors, such as "adn" for "and." If the spelling of a particular word doesn't appear as it would in the Word electronic dictionary or isn't in the dictionary (for example, a person's name), a wavy *red* line appears beneath the word. If you accidentally type an extra space between words or make a grammatical error (such as typing "he walk" instead of "he walks"), a wavy *green* line appears beneath the error. You'll see how AutoCorrect works when you intentionally make some typing errors.

To find common typing errors:

1. Carefully and slowly type the following sentence exactly as it is shown, including the spelling errors and the extra space between the last two words: **Word corects teh common typing misTakes you make.** Press the **Enter** key when you are finished typing. Notice that as you press the spacebar after the words "corects" and "misTakes," a wavy red line appears on the screen beneath each word, indicating that the word might be misspelled. Notice also that when you pressed the spacebar after the word "teh," Word automatically corrected the spelling to "the." After you pressed the Enter key, a wavy green line appeared under the last two words, alerting you to the extra space. See Figure 1-19.

Figure 1-19 ◀
Document window showing typing errors

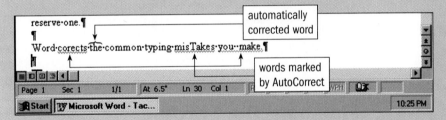

TROUBLE? If red and green wavy lines do not appear beneath mistakes, Word is probably not set to automatically check spelling and grammar as you type. Click Tools on the menu bar, and then click Options to open the Options dialog box. Click the Spelling and Grammar tab. Make sure there are check marks in the Check spelling as you type and the Check grammar as you type check boxes, and click OK. If Word does not automatically correct the incorrect spelling of "the," click Tools on the menu bar, click AutoCorrect, and make sure that all five boxes at the top of the AutoCorrect tab have check marks. Then scroll down the AutoCorrect list to make sure that there is an entry that changes "teh" to "the," and click OK.

TROUBLE? If the Office Assistant appears with a tip on correcting errors, you can close the Office Assistant window by clicking its Close button ✖.

2. Position the pointer I over the word "corects" and click the right mouse button. A list box appears with suggested spellings. See Figure 1-20.

Figure 1-20 ◀
List box showing AutoCorrect suggested spellings

click to replace misspelled word

insertion point after right-clicking misspelled word

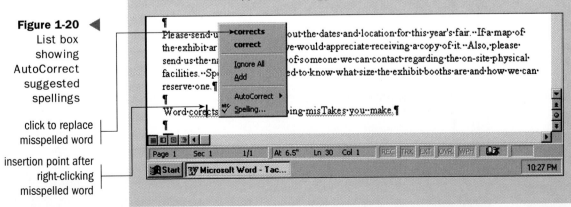

> **TROUBLE?** If the list box doesn't appear, repeat Step 2 making sure you click the right mouse button, not the left one.
>
> **3.** Click **corrects** in the list box. The list box disappears and the correct spelling appears in your document. Notice that the wavy red line disappears after you correct the error.
>
> **4.** Position the pointer I directly over the word "misTakes" and click the right mouse button. A list box appears with suggested spellings.
>
> **5.** Click **mistakes** in the list box. The list box disappears and the correct spelling appears in your document.
>
> **6.** Press the → key until the insertion point is to the right of the letter "u" in the word "you." Press the **Delete** key to delete the extra space.

You can see how quick and easy it is to correct common typing errors with AutoCorrect. Use it or the Backspace or Delete keys now to correct mistakes you might have made when typing the first part of the letter. Before you continue typing Karen's letter, you'll need to delete your practice sentence.

To delete the practice sentence:

> **1.** Click between the period and the paragraph mark at the end of the sentence.
>
> **2.** Press and hold the **Backspace** key until the entire sentence is deleted. Then press the **Delete** key to delete the extra paragraph mark.
>
> **3.** Make sure the insertion point is in line 29. There should be one nonprinting paragraph mark between the second paragraph and the paragraph you will type next.

Finishing the Letter

You're ready to complete the rest of the letter. As you type, you can use any of the techniques you learned in the previous section to correct mistakes.

To complete the letter:

> **1.** Type the final paragraph of the body of the letter, as shown in Figure 1-21, and then press the **Enter** key twice. Accept or ignore AutoText tips as necessary. Your screen should look like Figure 1-21. Notice that the date and the inside address now scroll off the top of the document window.

Figure 1-21 ◀
Final paragraph

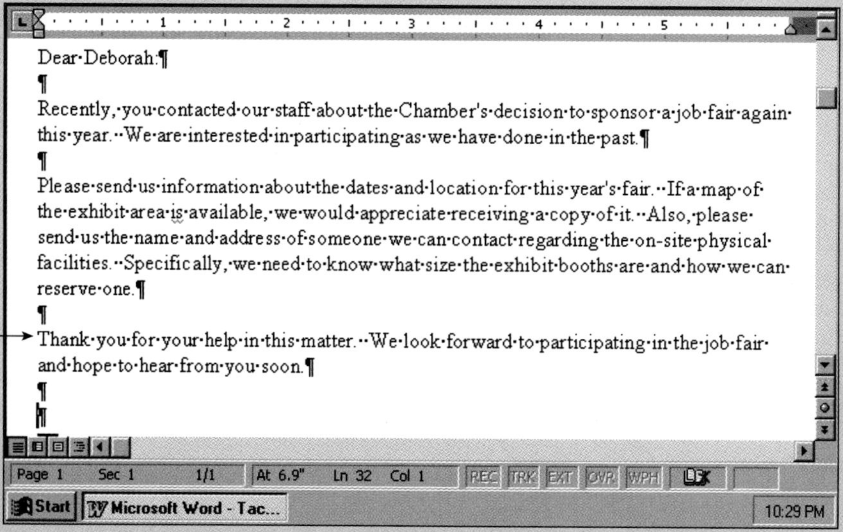

third paragraph

TROUBLE? If your screen does not match Figure 1-21 exactly, don't be concerned. Because of variations in font sizes and monitors, more or less text might have scrolled off your screen. Just continue with Step 2.

2. Type **Sincerely yours,** (including the comma) to enter the complimentary close.

3. Press the **Enter** key four times to allow space for Karen's signature.

4. Type **Karen Liu**, press the **Enter** key, and then type **Executive Director** to complete your letter. See Figure 1-22.

Figure 1-22 ◀
Complimentary
closing of letter

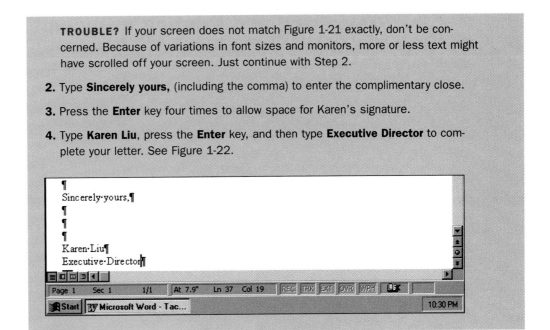

In the last set of steps, you watched the text at the top of your document move off your screen. You can scroll this hidden text back into view so you can read the beginning of the letter. When you do, the text at the bottom of the screen will scroll out of view.

To scroll the text using the scroll bar:

1. Position the mouse pointer ⬚ on the up arrow on the vertical scroll bar. Press and hold the mouse button to scroll the text. When the text stops scrolling, you have reached the top of the document and can see the beginning of the letter.

Now that you have completed the letter, you'll save the completed document.

Saving the Completed Letter

Although you saved the letter earlier, the text that you typed since then exists only in the computer's memory. That means you need to save your document again. It's especially important to save your document before printing. Then, if you experience problems that cause your computer to stop working while you are printing, you will still have a copy of the document containing your most recent additions and changes on your disk.

To save the completed letter:

1. Make sure your Student Disk is still in the appropriate disk drive.

2. Click the **Save** button 🖫 on the Standard toolbar. Because you named and saved this file earlier, you can save the document without being prompted for information. Word saves your letter with the same name you gave it earlier.

Previewing and Printing a Document

The current document window displays the text, but you cannot see an entire page without scrolling. To see how the page will look when printed, you need to use the Print Preview window.

To preview the document:

1. Click the **Print Preview** button 🔍 on the Standard toolbar. The Print Preview window opens and displays a full-page version of your letter, as shown in Figure 1-23. This shows how the letter will fit on the printed page.

Figure 1-23 ◀
Print preview
version of
the letter

one page button —

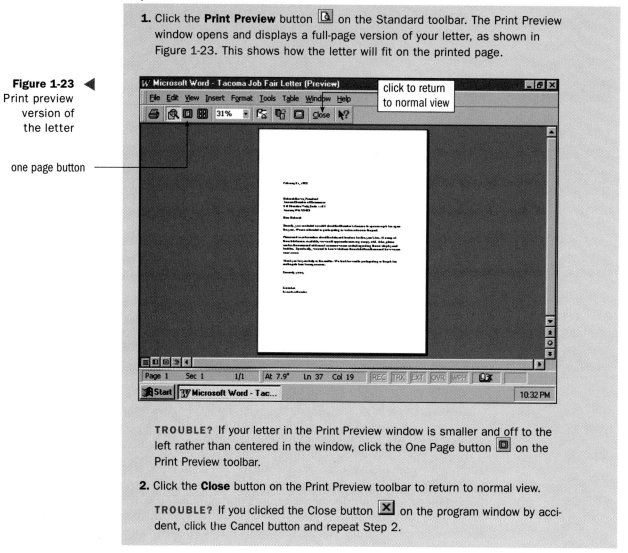

TROUBLE? If your letter in the Print Preview window is smaller and off to the left rather than centered in the window, click the One Page button 🔲 on the Print Preview toolbar.

2. Click the **Close** button on the Print Preview toolbar to return to normal view.

TROUBLE? If you clicked the Close button ✖ on the program window by accident, click the Cancel button and repeat Step 2.

You've seen how the letter will appear on the printed page. The text looks well-spaced and the letterhead will fit at the top of the page. You're ready to print the letter.

In each session, the first time you print from a shared computer, you should check the settings in the Print dialog box and make sure the number of copies is set to one. After that, you can *use* the Print button on the Standard toolbar to send your document directly to the printer without displaying the Print dialog box.

To print a document:

1. Make sure your printer is turned on and paper is in the printer.

2. Click **File** on the menu bar, and then click **Print**. The Print dialog box opens. See Figure 1-24.

Word

Figure 1-24 ◀
Print dialog box

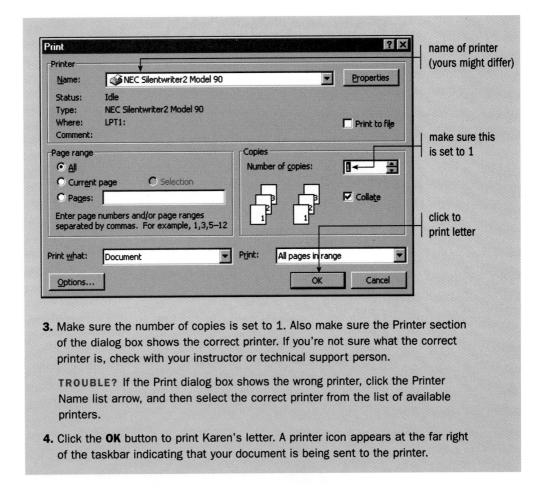

name of printer
(yours might differ)

make sure this
is set to 1

click to
print letter

3. Make sure the number of copies is set to 1. Also make sure the Printer section of the dialog box shows the correct printer. If you're not sure what the correct printer is, check with your instructor or technical support person.

   TROUBLE? If the Print dialog box shows the wrong printer, click the Printer Name list arrow, and then select the correct printer from the list of available printers.

4. Click the **OK** button to print Karen's letter. A printer icon appears at the far right of the taskbar indicating that your document is being sent to the printer.

Your printed letter should look similar to Figure 1-9 only without the Crossroads letterhead. The word wraps, or line breaks, might not appear in the same places on your letter because the size and spacing of characters vary slightly from one printer to the next.

Karen also needs an envelope to mail her letter in. Printing an envelope is an easy task in Word. You'll have a chance to try it in the Tutorial Assignments at the end of this tutorial. If you wanted to learn how to print an envelope yourself, you could use the Word Help system, which you'll learn about in the next section.

Getting Help

The Word Help system provides quick access to information about commands, features, and screen elements. The Contents and Index command on the Help menu displays the Help Topics window, which offers several options. You can look up a specific entry on the Index tab, search by general topics on the Contents tab, or search for information on a specific topic using the Find tab.

The What's This? command on the Help menu provides context-sensitive Help information. When you choose this command, the pointer changes to the Help pointer �W?, which you can then use to click any object or option on the screen to see a description of the object.

You've already encountered another form of help, the Office Assistant, an animated figure that automatically offers advice on current tasks. You'll learn how to use the Office Assistant in the next section.

Getting Help with the Office Assistant

The **Office Assistant** is an interactive guide to finding information on the Help system. You can ask the Office Assistant a question, and it will look through the Help system to find an answer.

REFERENCE window	**USING THE OFFICE ASSISTANT** ■ Click the Office Assistant button on the Standard toolbar (or choose Microsoft Word Help from the Help menu). ■ Type your question and then click the Search button. ■ Click a topic from the list of topics displayed. ■ To hide the Office Assistant, click its Close button.

You'll use the Office Assistant now to learn how to print an envelope.

To use the Office Assistant to learn how to print an envelope:

1. Click the **Office Assistant** button ⏹ on the Standard toolbar. The Office Assistant opens, offering help on topics related to the task you most recently performed (if any), and asking what you'd like to do. See Figure 1-25.

Figure 1-25 ◄
Office
Assistant

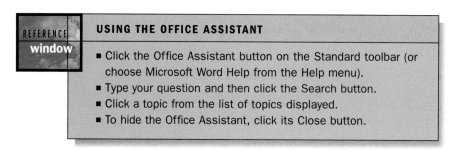

your options might be in a different order

Office Assistant suggests topics related to printing because you just printed a document

type your question here

don't worry if you see a different animated figure

your Office Assistant might display a lightbulb, indicating a tip is available

2. Type **How do I print an envelope?** and then click the **Search** button.

3. Another dialog box opens, with more specific print topics. Click the **Print an address on an envelope** button to display information on that topic. See Figure 1-26.

Figure 1-26 ◀
Help window on
printing an
envelope

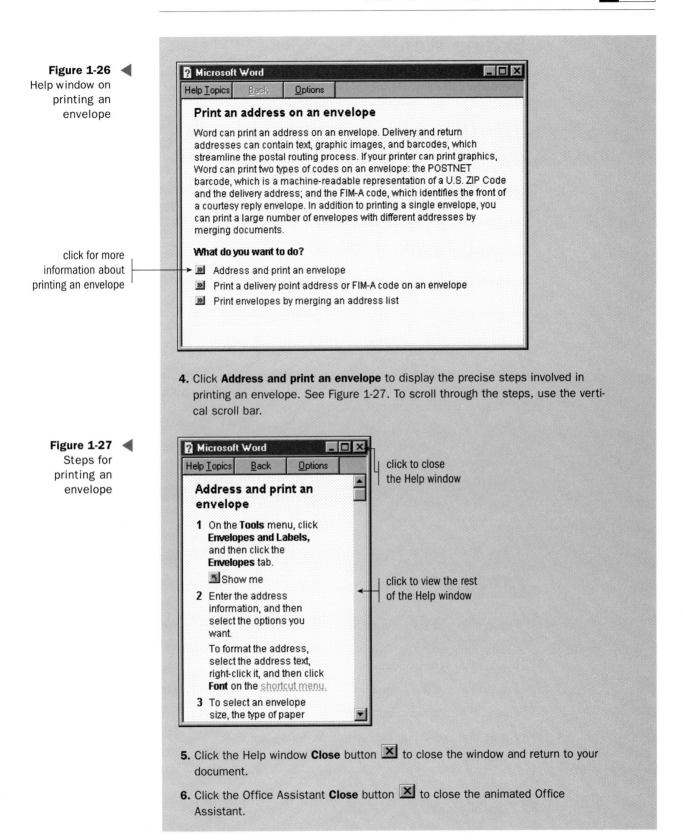

click for more
information about
printing an envelope

4. Click **Address and print an envelope** to display the precise steps involved in printing an envelope. See Figure 1-27. To scroll through the steps, use the vertical scroll bar.

Figure 1-27 ◀
Steps for
printing an
envelope

click to close
the Help window

click to view the rest
of the Help window

5. Click the Help window **Close** button [X] to close the window and return to your document.

6. Click the Office Assistant **Close** button [X] to close the animated Office Assistant.

Some Help windows have different formats than those you've just seen. However, they all provide the information you need to complete any task in Word.

Exiting Word

You have now finished typing and printing the letter to the Tacoma Chamber of Commerce, and you are ready to **exit**, or quit, Word to close the program.

REFERENCE window	**EXITING WORD**
	■ Click the Close button in the upper-right corner of the Word window (or click File on the menu bar, and then click Exit). ■ If you're prompted to save changes to the document, click the Yes button; then, if necessary, type a name of the document and click the OK button.

Because you've completed the first draft of Karen's letter, you can close the document window and exit Word now.

To exit Word:

1. Click the **Close** button ☒ on the document window to close the letter.

   TROUBLE? If you see a dialog box with the message "Do you want to save changes to Tacoma Job Fair Letter?", you have made changes to the document since the last time you saved it. Click the Yes button to save the current version and close it.

2. Click the **Close** button ☒ in the upper-right corner of the Word window. Word closes and you return to the Windows 95 desktop.

   TROUBLE? If you see a dialog box with the message "Do you want to save changes to Document1?", click the No button.

You give the letter for the Tacoma Chamber of Commerce to Karen for her to review.

Quick Check

1 Why should you save a document to your disk several times, even if you haven't finished typing it?

2 How do you save a document for the first time?

3 How do you see the portion of the document that has scrolled from sight?

4 What is Print Preview and when should you use it?

5 In your own words, define each of the following:

   a. scrolling

   b. word wrap

   c. AutoCorrect

   d. Office Assistant

6 How do you exit Word?

Now that you have created and saved Karen's letter, you are ready to learn about editing and formatting a document in the next tutorial.

Tutorial Assignments

Karen received a response from the Chamber of Commerce containing the information she requested about the job fair, and Crossroads has firmed up its plans to participate as exhibitors. Karen now needs to staff the booth with Crossroads employees for each day of the five-day fair. She sends a memo to employees asking them to commit to a date. Create the memo shown in Figure 1-28 by completing the following:

1. If necessary, start Word and make sure your Student Disk is in the appropriate disk drive, and check your screen to make sure your settings match those in the tutorials.

2. Click the New button on the Standard toolbar to display a new, blank document.

3. Press the Caps Lock key and type "MEMORANDUM" (without the quotation marks) in capital letters and then press the Caps Lock key again.

4. Press the Enter key twice, type "Date:" (without the quotation marks), press the Tab key, and then insert today's date from your computer clock by clicking Insert on the menu bar, clicking Date and Time, and then clicking the date format that corresponds to February 21, 1998.

5. Continue typing the rest of the memo exactly as shown in Figure 1-28, including any misspellings and extra words. (This will give you a chance to practice correcting errors in Step 7.) Instead of Karen Liu's name after "From", however, type your own. Press the Tab key after "To:" "From:", and RE:" to align the memo heading evenly. If the Office Assistant appears, close it by clicking its Close button.

Figure 1-28 ◀
Sample memo

MEMORANDUM

Date: February 21, 1998

To: Staff Members

From: Karen Liu

RE: Dates for 1998 Job Fair

The the 1998 Job Fair sponsored by the Tacoma Chamber of Commerce will be held September 15-20 from 10:00 a.m. to 5:30 p.m.. This fiar provvides us with an oportunity to inform Tacoma residents about our services. In the past, we have each spent one day helping at the exhibit. Please let me know by tomorrow which day you would prefer this year.

Thanks.

6. Save your work as Fair Date Memo in the TAssign folder for Tutorial 1.

7. Correct the misspelled words, indicated by the wavy red lines. To ignore an AutoCorrect suggestion, click Ignore All. Then correct any grammatical or other errors indicated by wavy green lines. Use the Backspace key to delete any extra words.

8. Scroll to the beginning of the letter. Click at the beginning of the first line and insert room for the letterhead by pressing the Enter key until the first line is at about line 14.

9. Save your most recent changes.

10. Preview and print the memo.

11. Use the Office Assistant to find the steps necessary for printing an address on an envelope. On a piece of paper, write down the necessary steps.

12. Print an envelope by following the steps you discovered in step 11. (Check with your instructor or technical support person to make sure you can print envelopes. If not, print on an $8\frac{1}{2} \times 11$-inch sheet of paper.)

13. Close the document without saving your most recent changes.

14. Click the New button on the Standard toolbar to open a new, blank document.

15. Write a letter to Deborah Brown at the Tacoma Chamber of Commerce, asking for information about food service at the job fair. Enter the date, the inside address, and the salutation as you did in the tutorial. Press the Enter key, and, when the Office Assistant opens, click the Get Help with writing the letter button. Following the Office Assistant's instructions, choose the desired options in the Letter Wizard dialog boxes. Click the Next button to move from one dialog box to the next. Type the text of your letter in the document window. Save the letter as Food Service in the TAssign folder for Tutorial 1, and print it.

16. Use the What's This? feature to learn about the program's ability to count the words in your document. Click Help on the menu bar, and then click What's This? The mouse pointer changes to an arrow with a question mark. Click Tools on the menu bar, click Word Count, and then read the text box contents. When you are finished reading, click the text box to close it.

Case Problems

1. Letter to Confirm a Conference Date As convention director for the Tallahassee Convention and Visitors Bureau, you are responsible for promoting and scheduling the convention center. The Southern Georgia chapter of the National Purchasing Management Association has reserved the convention center for their annual conference on October 24–25, 1998 and has requested a written confirmation of their reservation.

Create the letter using the skills you learned in the tutorial. Remember to include today's date, the inside address, the salutation, the date of the reservation, the complimentary close, and your name and title. If the instructions show quotation marks around text you type, do not include the quotation marks in your letter. To complete the letter, do the following:

1. If necessary, start Word, make sure your Student Disk in the appropriate disk drive, and check your screen to make sure your settings match those in the tutorials.

2. Open a new blank page, and press the Enter key six times to insert enough space for a letterhead.

3. Use AutoText to type today's date at the insertion point.

4. Insert three blank lines after the date, and, using the proper business letter format, type the inside address: "Danetta Blackwelder, 618 Live Oak Plantation Road, Valdosta, GA 31355."

5. Insert a blank line after the inside address, type the salutation "Dear Ms. Blackwelder:", and then insert another blank line. If the Office Assistant appears click the Cancel button.

6. Write one paragraph confirming the reservation for October 24–25, 1998.

7. Insert a blank line and type the complimentary close "Sincerely," (include the comma).

8. Add four blank lines to leave room for the signature, and then type your name and title.

9. Use Word's Contents and Index command on the Help menu to find out how to center a line of text. Then center your name and title.

10. Save the letter as Confirmation Letter in the Cases folder for Tutorial 1.

11. Reread your letter carefully and correct any errors.

12. Save any new changes.

13. Preview the letter using the Print Preview button on the Standard toolbar.

14. Print the letter.

15. Close the document.

2. Letter to Request Information About a "Learning to Fly" Franchise You are the manager of the UpTown Sports Mall and are interested in obtaining a franchise for "Learning to Fly," a free-fall bungee jumping venture marketed by Ultimate Sports, Inc. After reading an advertisement for the franchise, you decide to write for more information.
  Create the letter by doing the following:

1. If necessary, start Word, make sure your Student Disk in the appropriate disk drive, and check your screen to make sure your settings match those in the tutorials.

2. Open a new, blank document, and press the Enter key six times to insert sufficient space for a letterhead.

3. Use AutoText to type today's date at the insertion point.

4. Insert three blank lines after the date, and, using the proper business letter format, type the inside address: "Ultimate Sports, Inc., 4161 Comanche Drive, Colorado Springs, CO 80906."

5. Insert a blank line after the inside address, type the salutation "Dear Franchise Representative:", and then insert another blank line. Close the Office Assistant if necessary.

6. Type the first paragraph as follows: "I'm interested in learning more about the Learning to Fly bungee jumping franchise. As manager of UpTown Sports Mall, I've had success with similar programs, including both rock climbing and snowboarding franchises."(Do not include the quotation marks.)

7. Save your work as Bungee Request Letter in the Cases folder for Tutorial 1.

8. Insert one blank line, and type the following: "Please answer the following questions:". Then press the Enter key and type these questions on separate lines: "How much does your franchise cost?" "Does the price include the cost for installing the 70-foot tower illustrated in your advertisement?" "Does the price include the cost for purchasing the ropes and harnesses?" Then use the Office Assistant to find out how to add bullets, and, following its instructions, insert a bullet in front of each question.

9. Correct any typing errors indicated by wavy lines. (*Hint:* Because "bungee" is spelled correctly, click Ignore All on the AutoCorrect menu to remove the red line under "bungee.")

10. Insert another blank line, and type the complimentary close "Sincerely," (include the comma).

11. Insert three blank lines to leave room for the signature, and type your full name and title. Then press the Enter key and type "UpTown Sports Mall."

12. Save the letter with changes.

13. Preview the letter using the Print Preview button.

14. Print the letter.

15. Close the document.

3. Memo of Congratulations Glenna Zumbrennen is owner, founder, and president of Cuisine Unlimited. She was recently recognized as the 1998 New Hampshire Woman Business Owner of the Year by the National Association of Women Business Owners. She was also named to the 1998 Small Business Administration Advisory Council. Do the following:

1. If necessary, start Word, make sure your Student Disk in the appropriate disk drive, and check your screen to make sure your settings match those in the tutorials.

2. Write a brief memo congratulating Glenna on receiving these awards. Remember to use the four-part planning process. You should plan the content, organization, and style of the memo, and use a standard memo format similar to the one shown in Figure 1-28.

3. Save the document as Awards Memo in the Cases folder for Tutorial 1.

4. Preview the memo using the Print Preview button.

5. Print the memo.

6. Close the document.

4. Writing a Personal Letter with the Letter Template Word provides templates, which are models with predefined formatting, to help you create documents quickly and effectively. For example, the Letter template helps you create letters with professional-looking letterheads and with various letter formats. Do the following:

1. If necessary, start Word, make sure your Student Disk in the appropriate disk drive, and check your screen to make sure your settings match those in the tutorials.

2. Click File on the menu bar, and then click New. The New dialog box opens.

3. Click the Letters & Faxes tab, click Contemporary Letter, and then click the OK button.

4. Follow the instructions given in the document window. You might be asked to type personal information such as your name and address.

5. For the inside (recipient's) name and address, type a real or fictitious name and address.

6. In the body of the letter, include a sentence or two explaining that you're using the Word Letter template to create this letter.

7. After typing the letter, make sure that you're listed as the person sending the letter. (Someone else's name might be listed if you're not using your own computer or the personal information is already entered into Word.)

8. Save the letter as My Template Letter (in the Cases folder for Tutorial 1) and then print it.

9. If you completed Step 11 in the Tutorial Assignments, create an envelope for this letter and print it (if necessary, on an 8½ x 11 inch sheet of paper).

10. Close the document.

Lab Assignments

These Lab Assignments are designed to accompany the interactive Course Lab called Word Processing. To start the Word Processing Lab, click the Start button on the Windows 95 taskbar, point to Programs, point to Course Labs, point to New Perspectives Applications, and click Word Processing. If you do not see Course Labs on your Programs menu, see your instructor or technical support person.

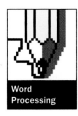

Word Processing Word processing software is the most popular computerized productivity tool. In this Lab you will learn how word processing software works.

1. Click the Steps button to learn how word processing software works. As you proceed through the Steps, answer all of the Quick Check questions that appear. After you complete the Steps, you will see a Quick Check summary report. Follow the instructions on the screen to print this report.

2. Click the Explore button to begin. Click File on the menu bar, and then click Open to display the Open dialog box. Click the file TIMBER.TEX, and then press the Enter key to open the letter to Northern Timber Company. Make the following modifications to the letter, and then print it. You do not need to save the letter.
   a. In the first and last lines of the letter, change "Jason Kidder" to your name.
   b. Change the date to today's date.
   c. Select the second paragraph, which begins "Your proposal did not include. . ." Move this paragraph so it is the last paragraph in the text of the letter.
   d. Change the cost of a permanent bridge to $20,000.
   e. Spell check the letter.

3. Using Explore, open the file STARS.TEX. Make the following modifications to the document, and then print it. You do not need to save the document.
   a. Center and bold the title.
   b. Change the title font to 16 point Arial.
   c. Bold DATE, SHOWER, and LOCATION.
   d. Move the January 2–3 line to the top of the list.
   e. Number the items in the list 1., 2., 3., and so on.
   f. Add or delete tabs to realign the columns.
   g. Double space the entire document.

4. Using Explore, compose a one-page, double-spaced letter to your parents or to a friend. Make sure you date and spell check the letter. Print the letter and sign it. You do not need to save your letter.

Editing and Formatting a Document

Preparing an Annuity Plan Description for Right-Hand Solutions

Word

OBJECTIVES

In this tutorial you will:

▪ Open, rename, and save a previously saved document

▪ Move the insertion point around the document

▪ Delete text

▪ Reverse edits using the Undo and Redo commands

▪ Move text within the document

▪ Find and replace text

▪ Change margins, alignment, and paragraph indents

▪ Copy formatting with the Format Painter

▪ Emphasize points with bullets, numbering, boldface, underlining, and italics

▪ Change fonts and adjust font sizes

CASE

Right-Hand Solutions

Reginald Thomson is a contract specialist for Right-Hand Solutions, a company that provides small businesses with financial and administrative services. Right-Hand Solutions contracts with independent insurance companies to prepare insurance plans and investment opportunities for these small businesses. Brandi Paxman, vice president of administrative services, asked Reginald to plan and write a document that describes the tax-deferred annuity plan for their clients' employee handbooks. Now that Brandi has commented on and corrected the draft, Reginald asks you to make the necessary changes and print the document.

In this tutorial, you will edit the annuity plan description according to Brandi's comments. You will open a draft of the annuity plan, resave it, and delete a phrase. You'll move text using two different methods, and find and replace one version of the company name with another.

You will also change the overall look of the document by changing margins, indenting and justifying paragraphs, and copying formatting from one paragraph to another. You'll create a bulleted list to emphasize the types of financial needs the annuity plan will cover and a numbered list for the conditions under which employees can receive funds. Then you'll make the title more prominent by centering it, changing its font, and enlarging it. You'll italicize the questions within the plan to set them off from the rest of the text, and underline an added note about how to get further information to give it emphasis. Finally, you will print a copy of the plan so you can proofread it.

SESSION

2.1

In this session you will edit Reginald's document by deleting words and by moving text within the document. Then you'll find and replace text throughout the document.

Opening the Document

Brandi's editing marks and notes on the first draft are shown in Figure 2-1. You'll begin by opening the first draft of the description, which has the filename Annuity.

Figure 2-1 ◀
Draft of annuity plan showing Brandi's edits (page 1)

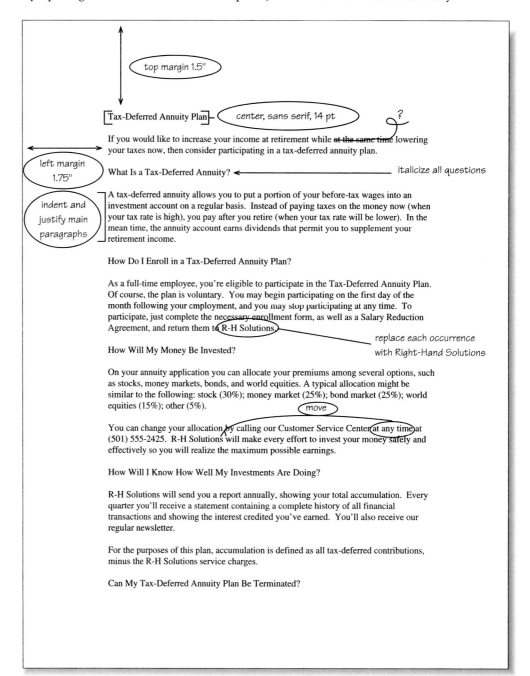

top margin 1.5"

Tax-Deferred Annuity Plan — center, sans serif, 14 pt   ?

If you would like to increase your income at retirement while ~~at the same time~~ lowering your taxes now, then consider participating in a tax-deferred annuity plan.

left margin 1.75"

What Is a Tax-Deferred Annuity? ◀———————— italicize all questions

indent and justify main paragraphs

A tax-deferred annuity allows you to put a portion of your before-tax wages into an investment account on a regular basis. Instead of paying taxes on the money now (when your tax rate is high), you pay after you retire (when your tax rate will be lower). In the mean time, the annuity account earns dividends that permit you to supplement your retirement income.

How Do I Enroll in a Tax-Deferred Annuity Plan?

As a full-time employee, you're eligible to participate in the Tax-Deferred Annuity Plan. Of course, the plan is voluntary. You may begin participating on the first day of the month following your employment, and you may stop participating at any time. To participate, just complete the necessary enrollment form, as well as a Salary Reduction Agreement, and return them to R-H Solutions.

replace each occurrence with Right-Hand Solutions

How Will My Money Be Invested?

On your annuity application you can allocate your premiums among several options, such as stocks, money markets, bonds, and world equities. A typical allocation might be similar to the following: stock (30%); money market (25%); bond market (25%); world equities (15%); other (5%).

move

You can change your allocation by calling our Customer Service Center at any time at (501) 555-2425. R-H Solutions will make every effort to invest your money safely and effectively so you will realize the maximum possible earnings.

How Will I Know How Well My Investments Are Doing?

R-H Solutions will send you a report annually, showing your total accumulation. Every quarter you'll receive a statement containing a complete history of all financial transactions and showing the interest credited you've earned. You'll also receive our regular newsletter.

For the purposes of this plan, accumulation is defined as all tax-deferred contributions, minus the R-H Solutions service charges.

Can My Tax-Deferred Annuity Plan Be Terminated?

Word

Figure 2-1 ◀
Draft of annuity
plan showing
Brandi's edits
(page 2)

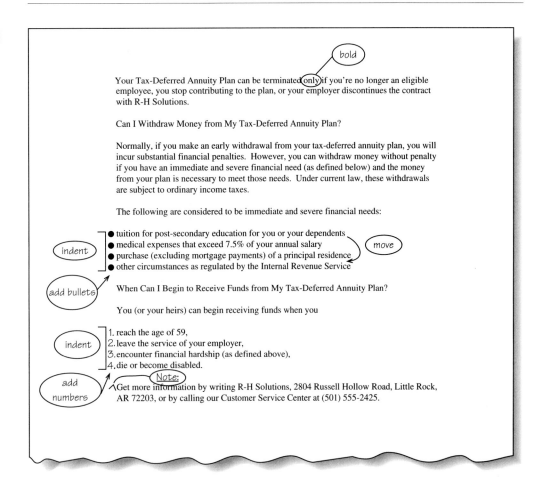

To open the document:

1. Place your Student Disk into the appropriate disk drive.

2. Start Word as usual.

3. Click the **Open** button 🖆 on the Standard toolbar to display the Open dialog box, shown in Figure 2-2.

Figure 2-2 ◀
The open
document

names and files
specified here

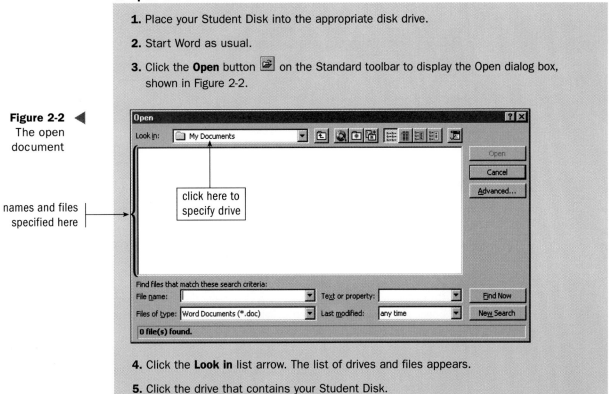

4. Click the **Look in** list arrow. The list of drives and files appears.

5. Click the drive that contains your Student Disk.

6. Double-click the **Tutorial.02** folder.

7. Click **Annuity** to select the file.

TROUBLE? If you see "Annuity.doc" in the folder, Windows 95 might be configured so that the filename extension is displayed. Click Annuity.doc and continue with Step 8. If you can't find the file with or without the filename extension, make sure you're looking in the Tutorial.02 folder and on the drive that contains your Student Disk, and check to make sure the Files of type text box displays Word Documents or All Files. If you still can't locate the file, ask your instructor or technical support person for help.

8. Click the **Open** button. The document opens, with the insertion point at the beginning of the document. See Figure 2-3.

Figure 2-3 ◀
The open
document

title

heading (question)

main paragraph
(answer)

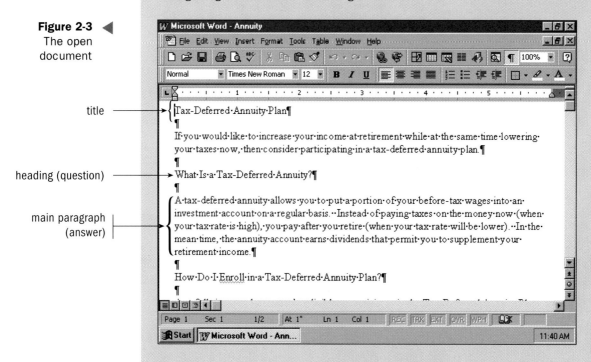

9. Check that your screen matches Figure 2-3. For this tutorial, display the nonprinting characters so that the formatting elements (tabs, paragraph marks, and so forth) are visible and easier to change.

Renaming the Document

To avoid altering the original file Annuity, you will save the document using the filename RHS Annuity Plan. Saving the document with another filename creates a copy of the file and leaves the original file unchanged in case you want to work through the tutorial again.

To save the document with a new name:

1. Click **File** on the menu bar, and then click **Save As**. The Save As dialog box opens with the current filename highlighted in the File name text box.

2. Click to the left of "Annuity" in the File name text box, type **RHS**, and then press the **spacebar**. Press the → key to move the insertion point to the right of the letter "y" in "Annuity," press the **spacebar**, and then type **Plan**. The filename changes to RHS Annuity Plan.

Word

> **3.** Click the **Save** button to save the document with the new filename.

Now you can edit the document. To make all of Brandi's edits, you'll need to learn how to quickly move the insertion point to any location in the document.

Moving the Insertion Point Around the Document

The arrow keys on your keyboard, ←, →, ↑, and ↓, allow you to move the insertion point one character at a time to the left or right, or one line at a time up or down. If you want to move more than one character or one line at a time, you can point and click in other parts of a line or the document. You can also press a combination of keys to move the insertion point. As you become more experienced with Word, you'll decide for yourself which method you prefer.

To see how quickly you can move through the document, you'll use keystrokes to move the insertion point to the beginning of the second page and to the end of the document.

To move the insertion point with keystrokes:

> **1.** Press and hold down the **Ctrl** key while you press the **Page Down** key to move the insertion point to the beginning of the next page. Notice that the status bar indicates that the insertion point is now on page 2.
>
> **2.** Press the ↑ key twice to move to the previous paragraph. Notice the automatic page break, a dotted line that Word inserts automatically to mark the beginning of the new page. See Figure 2-4. As you insert and delete text or change formatting in a document, the location of the automatic page breaks in your document continually adjust to account for the edits.

Figure 2-4 ◀
Automatic
page break

insertion point at
the end of page 1

automatic
page break

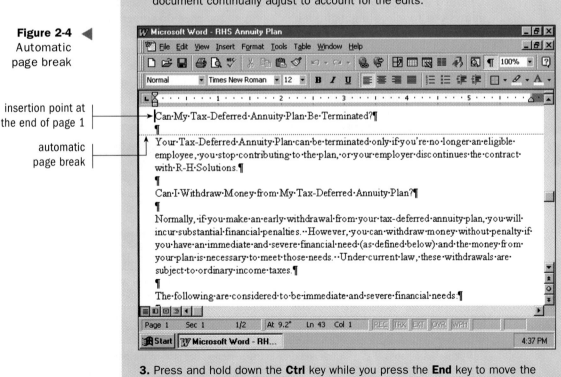

> **3.** Press and hold down the **Ctrl** key while you press the **End** key to move the insertion point to the end of the document.
>
> **4.** Press and hold down the **Ctrl** key while you press the **Home** key to move the insertion point back to the beginning of the document.

Figure 2-5 summarizes the keystrokes you can use to move the insertion point around the document.

Figure 2-5 ◀
Key strokes for
moving the
insertion point

Press	To Move Insertion Point
← or →	Left or right one character at a time
↑ or ↓	Up or down one line at a time
Ctrl + ← or Ctrl + →	Left or right one word at a time
Ctrl + ↑ or Ctrl + ↓	Up or down one paragraph at a time
Home or End	To the beginning or to the end of the current line
Ctrl + Home or Ctrl + End	To the beginning or to the end of the document
PageUp or PageDown	To the previous screen or to the next screen
Alt + Ctrl + PageUp or Alt + Ctrl + PageDown	To the top or to the bottom of the document window
Ctrl + PageUp or Ctrl + PageDown	To the beginning of the previous page or the next page

Using Select, Then Do

One of the most powerful editing features in Word is the "select, then do" feature. It allows you to select (highlight) a block of text and then do something to that text such as deleting, moving, or formatting it. You can select text using either the mouse or the keyboard; however, the mouse is usually the easier and more efficient way. You can quickly select a line or paragraph by clicking on the **selection bar**, which is the blank space in the left margin area of the document window. Figure 2-6 summarizes methods for selecting text with the mouse.

Figure 2-6 ◀
Methods for
selecting text
with the mouse

To Select	Do This
A word	Double-click the word
A line	Click in the selection bar next to the line
A sentence	Press and hold down the Ctrl key and click within the sentence
Multiple lines	Click and drag in the selection bar next to the lines
A paragraph	Double-click in the selection bar next to the paragraph, or triple-click within the paragraph
Multiple paragraphs	Click and drag in the selection bar next to the paragraphs, or triple-click and drag
The entire document	Press and hold down the Ctrl key and click in the selection bar, or triple-click in the selection bar
A block of text	Click at the beginning of a block, press and hold down the Shift key and click at the end of the block; highlights all the words in the block

Word

Deleting Text

Brandi wants you to delete the phrase "at the same time" in the first paragraph of the document. You'll use the "select, then do" feature to delete the phrase now.

To select and delete a phrase from the text:

1. Click and drag I over the phrase "at the same time" located in the first line of the first paragraph. The phrase and the space following it are highlighted, as shown in Figure 2-7. Notice that dragging the pointer over the second and successive words automatically selects the entire words and the spaces following them. This makes it much easier to select words and phrases than selecting them one character at a time.

Figure 2-7 ◀
Phrase
selected
for deletion

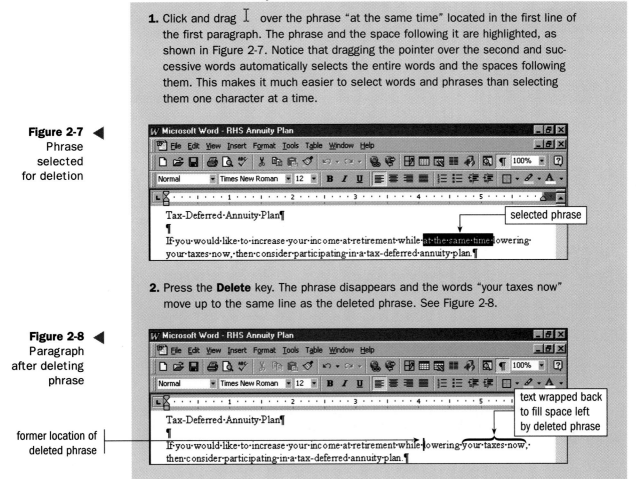

2. Press the **Delete** key. The phrase disappears and the words "your taxes now" move up to the same line as the deleted phrase. See Figure 2-8.

Figure 2-8 ◀
Paragraph
after deleting
phrase

former location of
deleted phrase

After rereading the paragraph, Reginald decides the phrase shouldn't have been deleted after all. He checks with Brandi and she agrees. You could retype the text, but there's an easier way to restore the phrase.

Using the Undo and Redo Commands

To undo (or reverse) the very last thing you did, simply click the Undo button on the Standard toolbar. If you want to reinstate your original change, the Redo button reverses the action of the Undo button (or redoes the undo). To undo anything more than your last action, you can click the Undo list arrow on the Standard toolbar. This list shows your most recent actions. Undo reverses the action only at its original location. You can't delete a word or phrase and then undo it at a different location.

USING UNDO AND REDO

- Click the Undo button on the Standard toolbar (or click Edit on the menu bar, and then click Undo) to reverse the very last thing you did.
- To reverse several previous actions, click the Undo list arrow on the Standard toolbar. Click an action on the list to reverse all actions up to and including the one you click.
- To undo your previous actions one-by-one, in the reverse order in which you performed them, click the Undo button one time for every action you want to reverse.
- If you undo an action by mistake, click the Redo button on the Standard toolbar (or click Edit on the menu bar, and then click Repeat) to reverse the undo.

Reginald suggested that you reverse your previous deletion, but left the final decision up to you. You decide to make the change to see how the sentence reads. Rather than retyping the phrase, you will reverse the edit using the Undo button.

To undo the deletion:

1. Click the **Undo** button on the Standard toolbar to undo your deletion. The phrase "at the same time" reappears in your document and is highlighted.

   TROUBLE? If the phrase doesn't reappear in your document and something else changes in your document, you probably made another edit or change to the document (such as pressing the Backspace key) between the deletion and the undo. Click the Undo button on the Standard toolbar until the phrase reappears in your document.

2. Click within the paragraph to deselect the phrase.

   As you read the sentence, you decide that it reads better without the phrase. Instead of selecting and deleting it again, you'll redo the undo.

3. Click the **Redo** button on the Standard toolbar.

   The phrase "at the same time" disappears from your document again.

4. Click the **Save** button on the Standard toolbar to save your changes to the document.

You have edited the document by deleting the text that Brandi marked for deletion. Now you are ready to make the rest of the edits she suggested.

Moving Text Within a Document

One of the most important uses of "select, then do" is moving text. For example, Brandi wants to reorder the four points Reginald made in the section "Can I Withdraw Money from My Tax-Deferred Annuity Plan?" on page 2 of his draft. You could reorder the list by deleting the sentence and then retyping it at the new location, but a much more efficient approach is to select and then move the sentence. Word has several ways to move text: drag and drop, cut and paste, and copy and paste.

Dragging and Dropping Text

The easiest way to move text within a document is called drag and drop. With **drag and drop,** you select the text you want to move, press and hold down the mouse button while you drag the pointer to a new location, and then release the mouse button.

<table>
<tr><td>REFERENCE
window</td><td>**DRAGGING AND DROPPING TEXT**</td></tr>
</table>

- Select the text to be moved.
- Press and hold down the mouse button until the drag-and-drop pointer appears, and then drag the selected text to its new location.
- Use the dashed insertion point as a guide to determine the precise spot where the text will be inserted.
- Release the mouse button to drop the text at the new location.

Brandi requested a change in the order of the items in the bulleted list on page 2 of Reginald's draft, so you'll use the drag-and-drop method to reorder the items. At the same time, you'll get some practice using the selection bar to highlight a line of text.

To move text using drag and drop:

1. Scroll through the document until you see "tuition for post-secondary education...", the first in the list of "immediate and severe financial needs:", which begins in the middle of page 2.

2. Click ⟋ in the selection bar to the left of the line beginning "tuition..." to select that line of text, including the return character. See Figure 2-9.

Figure 2-9
Selected text to drag and drop

pointer in selection bar

The·following·are·considered·to·be·immediate·and·severe·financial·needs:¶
¶
tuition·for·post-secondary·education·for·you·or·your·dependents¶   ← selected line of text
medical·expenses·that·exceed·7.5%·of·your·annual·salary¶
purchase·(excluding·mortgage·payments)·of·a·principal·residence¶
other·circumstances·as·regulated·by·the·Internal·Revenue·Service¶
¶
When·Can·I·Begin·to·Receive·Funds·from·My·Tax-Deferred·Annuity·Plan?¶
¶
You·(or·your·heirs)·can·begin·receiving·funds·when·you¶
¶
reach·the·age·of·59,¶
leave·the·service·of·your·employer,¶
encounter·financial·hardship·(as·defined·above),¶
die·or·become·disabled.¶

Page 2   Sec 1   2/2   At 3.7"   Ln 15   Col 1   REC TRK EXT OVR WPH

Start   Microsoft Word - RH...   12:10 PM

3. Position the pointer over the selected text. The shape of the pointer changes to ↖.

4. Press and hold down the mouse button until the drag-and-drop pointer ↖, which has a dashed insertion point, an arrow, and a small square called a move box, appears.

5. Drag the selected text down three lines until the dashed insertion point appears to the left of the word "other." Make sure you use the dashed insertion point to guide the text to its new location rather than the mouse pointer or the move box; the dashed insertion point marks the precise location of the drop. See Figure 2-10.

Figure 2-10 ◀
Moving text
with drag-and-
drop pointer

selected text
to be moved

dashed
insertion point

drag-and-drop pointer

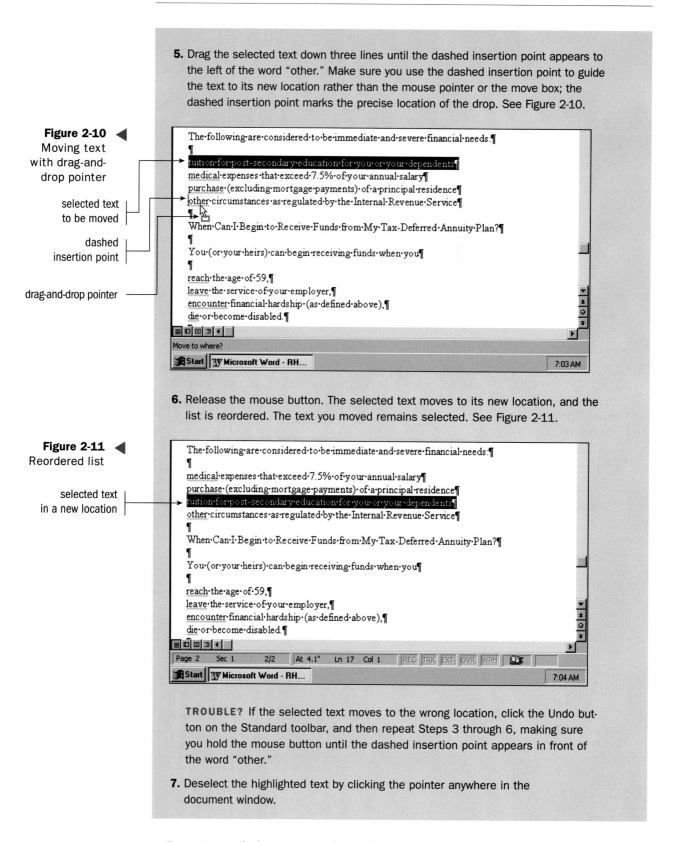

6. Release the mouse button. The selected text moves to its new location, and the list is reordered. The text you moved remains selected. See Figure 2-11.

Figure 2-11 ◀
Reordered list

selected text
in a new location

TROUBLE? If the selected text moves to the wrong location, click the Undo button on the Standard toolbar, and then repeat Steps 3 through 6, making sure you hold the mouse button until the dashed insertion point appears in front of the word "other."

7. Deselect the highlighted text by clicking the pointer anywhere in the document window.

Dragging and dropping works well if you're moving text a short distance in a document; however, Word provides another method, called cut and paste, that works well for moving text either a short distance or beyond the current screen.

Word

Cutting or Copying and Pasting Text

To **cut** means to remove text from the document and place it on the Windows Clipboard. The Clipboard stores only one item at a time; when you cut a new piece of text or a graphic, it replaces what was on the Clipboard. To **paste** means to transfer a copy of the text from the clipboard into the document at the insertion point. To perform a cut-and-paste operation, you select the text you want to move, cut (remove) it from the document, and then paste (restore) it into the document in a new location. If you don't want to remove the text from its original location, you can copy it (rather than cutting it) and then paste the copy in a new location. This procedure is known as "copy and paste."

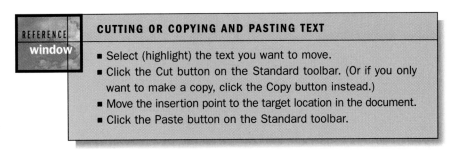

REFERENCE window

CUTTING OR COPYING AND PASTING TEXT

- Select (highlight) the text you want to move.
- Click the Cut button on the Standard toolbar. (Or if you only want to make a copy, click the Copy button instead.)
- Move the insertion point to the target location in the document.
- Click the Paste button on the Standard toolbar.

Brandi suggested moving the phrase "at any time" (in the paragraph beginning "You can change your allocation...") to a new location. You'll use cut and paste to move this phrase.

To move text using cut and paste:

1. Scroll the document up until you can see the paragraph just above the heading "How Will I Know...." on page 1.

2. Click and drag the mouse to highlight the complete phrase "at any time." See Figure 2-12.

Figure 2-12 ◀
Text to move using cut and paste

new location for text ──────

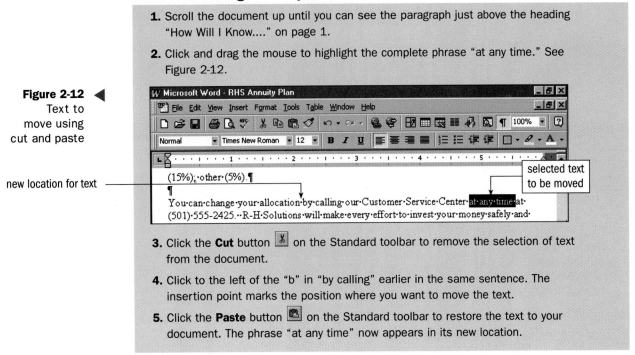

3. Click the **Cut** button 🔏 on the Standard toolbar to remove the selection of text from the document.

4. Click to the left of the "b" in "by calling" earlier in the same sentence. The insertion point marks the position where you want to move the text.

5. Click the **Paste** button 🔏 on the Standard toolbar to restore the text to your document. The phrase "at any time" now appears in its new location.

Keep in mind that you can also use the copy-and-paste method to move a copy of a block of text to another part of your document. Copy and paste works much the same way as cut and paste.

Finding and Replacing Text

When you're working with a longer document, the quickest and easiest way to locate a particular word or phrase is to use the Find command. If you want to replace characters or a phrase with something else, you can use the Replace command, which combines the Find command with a substitution feature. The Replace command searches through a document and substitutes the text you're searching for with the replacement text you specify. As Word performs the search, it will stop and highlight each occurrence of the search text and let you determine whether to substitute the replacement text by clicking the Replace button. If you want to substitute every occurrence of the search text with the replacement text, you can click the Replace All button.

REFERENCE window

FINDING AND REPLACING TEXT

- Click the Select Browse Object button on the vertical scroll bar, and then click the Find button on the Select Browse Object menu (or click Edit on the menu bar, and then click Find or Replace).
- To find text, click the Find tab, or to find and replace text, click the Replace tab.
- Type the characters you want to find in the Find what text box.
- If you are replacing text, type the replacement text in the Replace with text box.
- Click the Find Next button.
- Click the Replace button to substitute the found text with the replacement text and find the next occurrence.
- Click the Replace All button to substitute all occurrences of the found text with the replacement text.

Brandi wants the shortened version of the company name, "R-H Solutions," to be spelled out as "Right-Hand Solutions" every time it appears in the text.

To replace "R-H Solutions" with "Right-Hand Solutions:

1. Click the **Select Browse Object** button on the vertical scroll bar.

2. Click the **Find** button on the Select Browse Object menu. The Find and Replace dialog box appears.

3. Click the **Replace** tab.

4. Type **R-H Solutions** in the Find what text box, press the **Tab** key, and type **Right-Hand Solutions** in the Replace with text box. See Figure 2-13.

Figure 2-13 ◄
Find and
Replace
dialog box

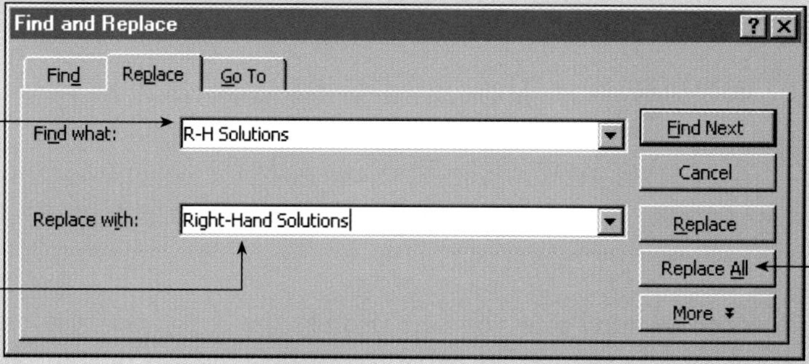

type search text here ———

type replacement
text here

click to instantly
replace all
occurrences of
search text with
replacement text

Find and Replace dialog box:
- Tabs: Find, Replace, Go To
- Find what: R-H Solutions
- Replace with: Right-Hand Solutions
- Buttons: Find Next, Cancel, Replace, Replace All, More ▾

5. Click the **Replace All** button to replace all occurrences of the search text with the replacement text. When Word finishes making the replacements, you see a dialog box telling you that 6 replacements were made.

6. Click **OK** to close the dialog box, and then click the **Close** button in the Find and Replace dialog box. The full company name has been inserted into the document, as shown in Figure 2-14.

Figure 2-14 ◀
The name
"Right-Hand
Solutions"
inserted into
the document

replacement text

replacement text

replacement text

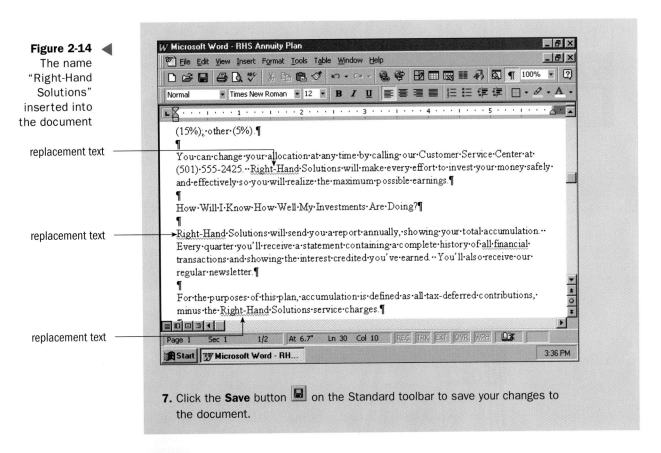

7. Click the **Save** button 🖫 on the Standard toolbar to save your changes to the document.

Quick Check

1. How do you open a document and save a copy of it with a new name?

2. Which key(s) do you press to move the insertion point to the following places:
   a. end of the document
   b. beginning of the document
   c. beginning of the next page

3. Explain how to delete text from a document.

4. Define the following terms in your own words:
   a. select, then do
   b. selection bar
   c. drag and drop

5. Explain how to select a phrase in the middle of a paragraph. Explain how to select a complete line of text.

6. What is the purpose of the Undo command? What is the purpose of the Redo command?

7. True or False: You can use the Undo command to restore deleted text at a new location in your document.

8. What is the difference between cut and paste, and copy and paste?

9. When you use the drag-and-drop method to move text, how do you know where the text will be positioned when it is dropped?

10. Explain how to find and replace text using the Select Browse Object button.

You have completed the content changes Brandi suggested, but she has some more changes for you that will improve the plan's appearance. In the next session, you'll enhance the Annuity Plan by changing the width, spacing, and alignment of text.

SESSION

2.2

In this session you will make the formatting changes Brandi suggested. You'll use a variety of formatting commands to change the margins, spacing, and tabs, and to justify and align the text. You'll also learn how to use the Format Painter, how to create bulleted and numbered lists, and how to change fonts, font sizes, and sizes.

Changing the Margins

In general, it's best to begin formatting by making the changes that affect the overall appearance of the document. In this case, you need to adjust the margin settings of the annuity plan summary.

Word uses default margins of 1.25 inches for the left and right margins, and 1 inch for the top and bottom margins. The numbers on the ruler (displayed below the Formatting toolbar) indicate the distance in inches from the left margin, not from the left edge of the paper. Unless you specify otherwise, changes you make to the margins will affect the entire document, not just the current paragraph or page.

REFERENCE window

CHANGING MARGINS FOR THE ENTIRE DOCUMENT

- With the insertion point anywhere in your document and no text selected, click File on the menu bar, then click Page Setup.
- If necessary, click the Margins tab to display the margin settings.
- Click the margins arrows to change each setting, or type a new margin value in each text box.
- Make sure the Apply to list box displays Whole document.
- Click the OK button.

You need to change the top margin to 1.5 inches and the left margin to 1.75 inches, as suggested by Brandi. The left margin needs to be wider than usual to allow space for making holes so that the document can be added to a three-ring binder. In the next set of steps, you'll change the margins with the Page Setup command. You can also change margins in page layout view; you'll practice that method in the Tutorial Assignments.

To change the margins in the annuity plan summary:

1. If you took a break after the last lesson, make sure Word is running, that the RHS Annuity Plan document is open, and that nonprinting characters are displayed.

2. Click once anywhere in the document to make sure no text is selected.

3. Click **File** on the menu bar, and then click **Page Setup** to open the Page Setup dialog box.

4. If necessary, click the **Margins** tab to display the margin settings. See Figure 2-15.

Figure 2-15 ◄
Page Setup
dialog box

margins tab selected

text box

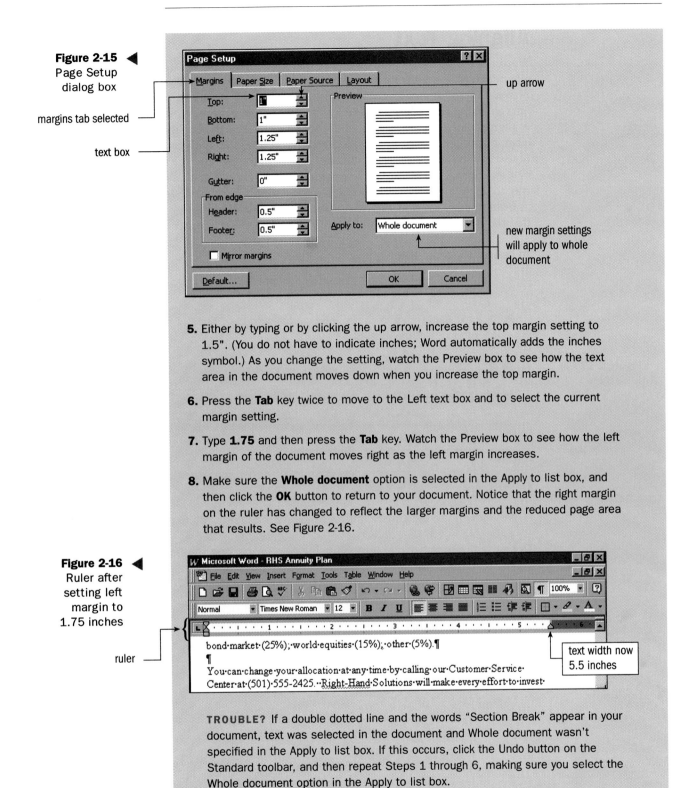

up arrow

new margin settings
will apply to whole
document

5. Either by typing or by clicking the up arrow, increase the top margin setting to 1.5". (You do not have to indicate inches; Word automatically adds the inches symbol.) As you change the setting, watch the Preview box to see how the text area in the document moves down when you increase the top margin.

6. Press the **Tab** key twice to move to the Left text box and to select the current margin setting.

7. Type **1.75** and then press the **Tab** key. Watch the Preview box to see how the left margin of the document moves right as the left margin increases.

8. Make sure the **Whole document** option is selected in the Apply to list box, and then click the **OK** button to return to your document. Notice that the right margin on the ruler has changed to reflect the larger margins and the reduced page area that results. See Figure 2-16.

Figure 2-16 ◄
Ruler after
setting left
margin to
1.75 inches

ruler

text width now
5.5 inches

TROUBLE? If a double dotted line and the words "Section Break" appear in your document, text was selected in the document and Whole document wasn't specified in the Apply to list box. If this occurs, click the Undo button on the Standard toolbar, and then repeat Steps 1 through 6, making sure you select the Whole document option in the Apply to list box.

9. Click the **Save** button on the Standard toolbar to save the document with the new margin settings.

Now you are ready to make formatting changes that affect individual paragraphs.

Aligning Text

Word defines a paragraph as any text that ends with a paragraph mark symbol (¶). The alignment of a paragraph or document refers to how the text lines up horizontally between the margins. By default, text is aligned along the left margin but is ragged, or uneven, along the right margin. This is called **left alignment**. With **right alignment**, the text is aligned along the right margin and is ragged along the left margin. With **center alignment**, text is centered between the left and right margins. With **justified alignment**, full lines of text are spaced between or aligned along both the left and the right margins (similar to that in a newspaper column). The paragraph you are reading now is justified. The easiest way to apply alignment settings is by clicking buttons on the Formatting toolbar.

Brandi indicated that the title of the annuity plan description should be centered and that the main paragraphs should be justified. First, you'll center the title.

To center align the title:

1. Click anywhere in the title "Tax-Deferred Annuity Plan" at the beginning of the document.

2. Click the **Center** button 📰 on the Formatting toolbar. The text centers between the left and right margins. See Figure 2-17.

Figure 2-17 ◄
Title centered

centered title ──────────

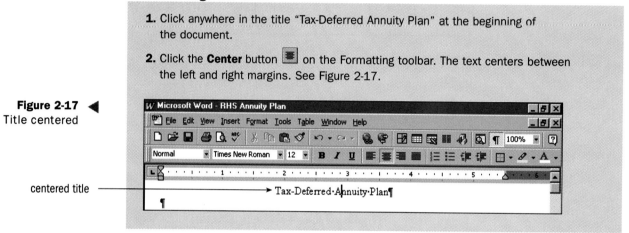

Now you'll use the Justify button to justify the text in the first two main paragraphs.

To justify the first two paragraphs using the Formatting toolbar:

1. Click anywhere in the first paragraph, which begins "If you would like to increase...", and click the Justify button 📰 on the Formatting toolbar. The justification would be easier to see if the paragraph had more lines of text. You'll see the effects more clearly after you justify the second paragraph in the document.

2. Move the insertion point to the second main paragraph, which begins "A tax-deferred annuity allows...".

3. Click 📰 again. The text is evenly spaced between the left and right margins. See Figure 2-18.

Figure 2-18 ◀
Text justified
using the
Formatting
toolbar

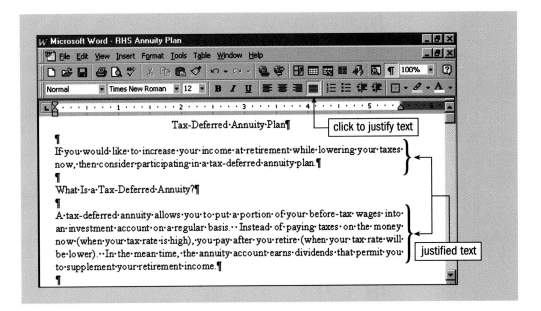

You'll justify the other paragraphs later. Now that you've learned how to change the paragraph alignment, you can turn your attention to indenting paragraphs.

Indenting a Paragraph

When you become a more experienced Word user, you might want to use some special forms of paragraph formatting, such as a hanging indent (where the first line of the paragraph extends into the left margin) or a right indent (where all lines of the paragraph are indented from the right margin). In this document, though, you'll only need to indent the main paragraphs 0.5 inches from the left margin. This is a simple kind of paragraph indent, requiring only a quick click on the Formatting toolbar's Increase Indent button. According to Brandi's notes, you need to indent all of the main paragraphs, starting with the second paragraph.

To indent a paragraph using the Increase Indent button:

1. Make sure the insertion point is still located anywhere within the second paragraph, which begins "A tax-deferred annuity allows...".

2. Click the **Increase Indent** button ⊞ on the Formatting toolbar twice. (Don't click the Decrease Indent button by mistake.) The entire paragraph moves right .5" each time you click the Increase Indent button. The paragraph is indented 1", .5" more than Brandi wants.

3. Click the **Decrease Indent** button ⊞ on the Formatting toolbar to move the paragraph left .5". The paragraph is now indented 0.5 inches from the left margin, as shown in Figure 2-19.

Figure 2-19 ◀
Indented
paragraph

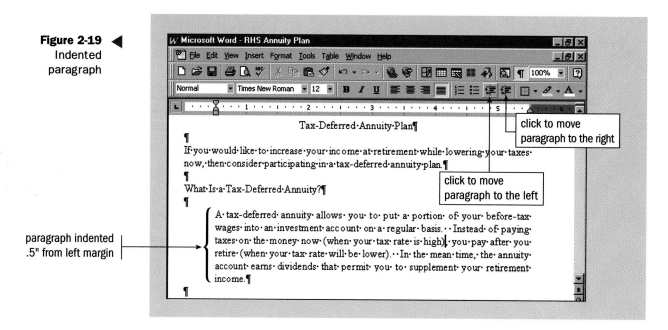

paragraph indented
.5" from left margin

You could continue to indent, and then justify, each paragraph individually, but there's an easier way—the Format Painter command. The Format Painter allows you to copy both the indentation and alignment changes to all the other main paragraphs in the document.

In addition to changing the horizontal alignment of text on the page, you can also change the vertical spacing, called **line spacing**. You can easily make the text double-spaced or, if you want the lines a little closer together, one-and-a-half spaced. You'll practice this in an Exploration Exercise in the Tutorial Assignment at the end of the tutorial.

Using Format Painter

The Format Painter makes it easy to copy all the formatting features of one paragraph to one or more other paragraphs. You'll use the Format Painter now to copy the formatting of the second paragraph to other main paragraphs. You'll begin by highlighting the paragraph whose format you want to copy. (Notice that you can't simply move the insertion point to that paragraph.)

To copy paragraph formatting with the Format Painter:

1. Double-click in the selection bar to select the second paragraph, which is indented and justified and begins "A tax-deferred annuity...".

2. Double-click the **Format Painter** button 🖌 on the Standard toolbar. Notice that the Format Painter button stays pressed. When you move the pointer over text it changes to 🖌I to indicate that the format of the selected paragraph can be painted (or copied) onto another paragraph.

3. Scroll down, and then click anywhere in the third paragraph, which begins "As a full-time employee...". The format of the third paragraph shifts to match the format of the selected paragraph. See Figure 2-20. As you can see, both paragraphs are now indented and justified. The pointer remains as the Format Painter pointer.

Figure 2-20
Formats copied
with Format
Painter

Format Painter
pointer

paragraph with
new formatting

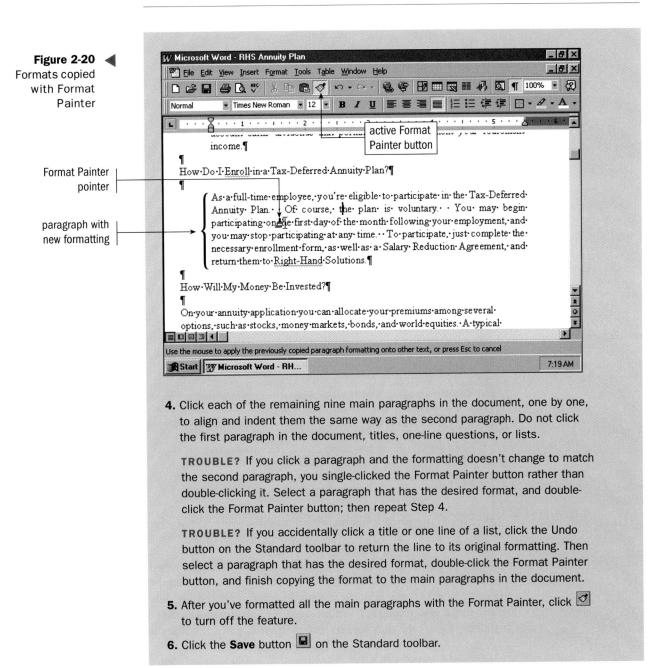

4. Click each of the remaining nine main paragraphs in the document, one by one, to align and indent them the same way as the second paragraph. Do not click the first paragraph in the document, titles, one-line questions, or lists.

   TROUBLE? If you click a paragraph and the formatting doesn't change to match the second paragraph, you single-clicked the Format Painter button rather than double-clicking it. Select a paragraph that has the desired format, and double-click the Format Painter button; then repeat Step 4.

   TROUBLE? If you accidentally click a title or one line of a list, click the Undo button on the Standard toolbar to return the line to its original formatting. Then select a paragraph that has the desired format, double-click the Format Painter button, and finish copying the format to the main paragraphs in the document.

5. After you've formatted all the main paragraphs with the Format Painter, click ⬦ to turn off the feature.

6. Click the **Save** button 🖫 on the Standard toolbar.

All the main paragraphs in the document are formatted with the correct indentation and alignment. Your next job is to make the lists easier to read by adding bullets and numbers.

Adding Bullets and Numbers

Bullets (•) or numbers are useful whenever you need to emphasize a particular list of items. Brandi requested that you add bullets to the list of financial needs on page 2 to make them stand out.

To apply bullets to a list of items:

1. Scroll the document until you see the list of financial needs below the sentence "The following are considered to be immediate and severe financial needs:".

2. Select the four items that appear in the middle of page 2 (from "Medical expenses" to "Internal Revenue Service"). The text doesn't need to be fully highlighted; as long as you select a single character in a line, you can apply bullets to the paragraph.

3. Click the **Bullets** button 📄 on the Formatting toolbar to activate the Bullets feature. A rounded bullet, a special character, appears in front of each item, and each line indents to make room for the bullet.

4. Click the **Increase Indent** button 📄 to align the bullet text at the one-half inch mark, just below the left edge of the paragraphs above them.

TROUBLE? If the bullets in your document are already indented, you probably indented the list when you indented the main paragraphs earlier; don't click the Increase Indent button. If the bulleted list is now indented too much, click the Decrease Indent button until the bullet text is at the .5" mark on the ruler.

5. Click anywhere within the document window to deselect the text. Figure 2-21 shows the indented bulleted list. Note that the text itself, not the bullets, is indented.

Figure 2-21 ◀
Indented
bulleted list

bulleted list ⟶

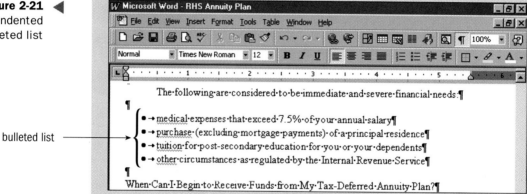

Next, you need to add numbers to the list that identifies when benefits can be received in the section below the bulleted list. For this you'll use the Numbering button, which automatically numbers the selected paragraphs with consecutive numbers and aligns them. If you insert a new paragraph, delete a paragraph, or reorder the paragraphs, Word automatically adjusts the numbers to make sure they remain consecutive.

To apply numbers to the list of items:

1. Scroll down to the next section, and then select the list that begins "Reach the age..." and ends with "...become disabled."

2. Click the **Increase Indent** button 📄 on the Formatting toolbar to indent the paragraph one-half inch. Notice that you can indent paragraphs before or after adding bullets or numbers. The order doesn't matter.

3. Click the **Numbering** button 📄 on the Formatting toolbar. Consecutive numbers appear in front of each item in the indented list.

4. Click anywhere in the document to deselect the text. Figure 2-22 shows the indented and numbered list.

Figure 2-22
Indented
numbered list

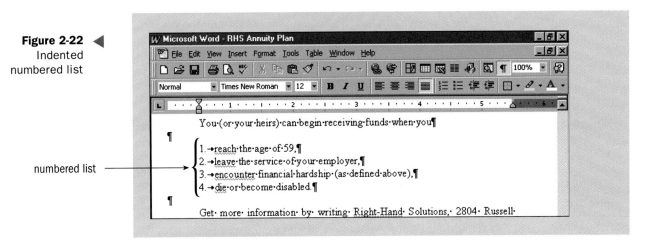

numbered list

The text of the document is now properly aligned and indented. The bullets and numbers make the lists easy to read and give readers visual clues as to what type of information they contain. Next, you need to adjust the formatting of individual words.

Changing the Font and Font Size

All of Brandi's remaining changes have to do with changing fonts, adjusting font sizes, and emphasizing text with font styles. The first step is to change the font of the title from 12-point Times New Roman to a 14-point bold Arial. This will make the title stand out from the rest of the text.

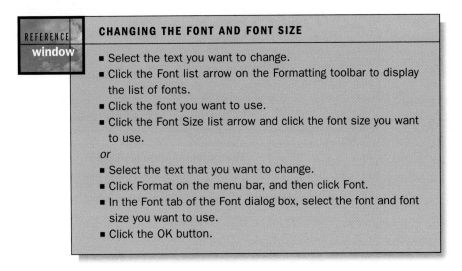

REFERENCE
window

CHANGING THE FONT AND FONT SIZE

- Select the text you want to change.
- Click the Font list arrow on the Formatting toolbar to display the list of fonts.
- Click the font you want to use.
- Click the Font Size list arrow and click the font size you want to use.

or

- Select the text that you want to change.
- Click Format on the menu bar, and then click Font.
- In the Font tab of the Font dialog box, select the font and font size you want to use.
- Click the OK button.

Brandi wants you to change not only the font of the title, but also its size and style. To do this, you'll use the Formatting toolbar. She wants you to use a **sans serif** font, which is a font that does not have the small horizontal lines at the tops and bottoms of the letters. Sans serif fonts are often used in titles so they contrast with the body text. Times New Roman is a serif font, and Arial is a sans serif font. The text you are reading now is a serif font, and the text in the steps below is a sans serif font.

To change the attributes of the title using the Font command:

1. Press **Ctrl** + **Home** to move to the beginning of the document, and then select the title.

2. Click the **Font** list arrow on the Formatting toolbar. A list of available fonts appears in alphabetical order, with the name of the current font highlighted in the font list and in the Font text box. See Figure 2-23. Your list of fonts might be different from those shown in the figure. Fonts that have been used recently appear above the double line.

Figure 2-23 ◀
Font list

current font ——

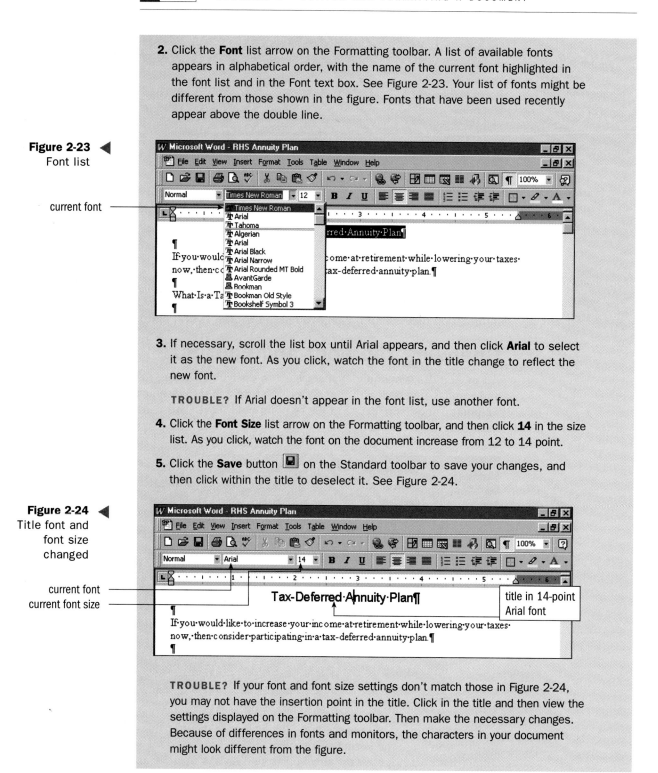

3. If necessary, scroll the list box until Arial appears, and then click **Arial** to select it as the new font. As you click, watch the font in the title change to reflect the new font.

TROUBLE? If Arial doesn't appear in the font list, use another font.

4. Click the **Font Size** list arrow on the Formatting toolbar, and then click **14** in the size list. As you click, watch the font on the document increase from 12 to 14 point.

5. Click the **Save** button 🖫 on the Standard toolbar to save your changes, and then click within the title to deselect it. See Figure 2-24.

Figure 2-24 ◀
Title font and
font size
changed

current font
current font size

TROUBLE? If your font and font size settings don't match those in Figure 2-24, you may not have the insertion point in the title. Click in the title and then view the settings displayed on the Formatting toolbar. Then make the necessary changes. Because of differences in fonts and monitors, the characters in your document might look different from the figure.

Emphasizing Text with Boldface, Underlining, and Italics

You can emphasize words in your document with boldface, underlining, or italics. These styles help you make specific thoughts, ideas, words, or phrases stand out. Brandi marked a few words on Reginald's draft that need this kind of special emphasis.

Word

Bolding Text

Brandi wants to make sure that clients' employees see that the tax-deferred annuity plan can be terminated only under certain conditions. You will do this by bolding the word "only."

To change the font style to boldface:

1. Scroll down so you can view the first line of the paragraph beneath the question "Can My Tax-Deferred Annuity Plan Be Terminated?" on page 2.

2. Select the word "only" (immediately after the word "terminated").

3. Click the **Bold** button B on the Formatting toolbar, and then click anywhere in the document to deselect the text. The word appears in bold, as shown in Figure 2-25.

Figure 2-25 ◀
Word in boldface

Bold button

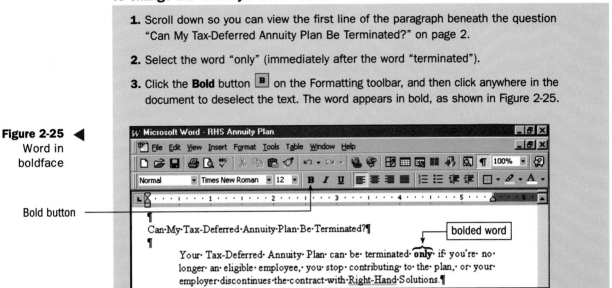

Underlining Text

The Underline command works in the same way as the Bold command. Brandi's edits indicate that the word "Note" should be inserted and underlined at the beginning of the final paragraph. You'll make both of these changes at once using the Underline command.

To underline text:

1. Press **Ctrl + End** to move the insertion point to the end of the document. Then move the insertion point to the left of the word "Get" in the first line of the final paragraph.

2. Click the **Underline** button U on the Formatting toolbar to turn on underlining. Notice that the Underline button remains pressed. Now, whatever text you type will be underlined on your screen and in your printed document.

3. Type **Note** and then click U to turn off underlining. Notice that the Underline button is no longer pressed, and the word "Note" is underlined.

4. Type **:** (a colon) and then press the **spacebar** twice. See Figure 2-26.

Figure 2-26 ◀
Word typed with underline

underlined word

Underline button

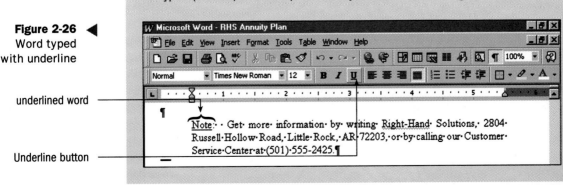

Italicizing Text

Next, you'll make annuity plan document conform with the other documents that Right-Hand Solutions produces by changing each question (heading) in the document to italics. This makes the document easier to read by clearly separating the sections. You'll begin with the first heading.

To italicize the question headings:

1. Press **Ctrl** + **Home** to return to the beginning of the document, and then select the text of the first heading, "What Is a Tax-Deferred Annuity?", by triple-clicking the text.

2. Click the **Italic** button *I* on the Formatting toolbar. The heading changes from regular to italic text.

3. Repeat Steps 1 and 2 to italicize the next heading. Now try a shorter way to italicize the text by repeating the formatting you just applied.

4. Select the next heading and then press the **F4** key. Repeat for each of the remaining five questions (headings) in the document. The italicized headings stand out from the rest of the text and help give the document a visual structure.

5. Click the **Save** button 🖫 on the Standard toolbar to save your work.

You have made all the editing and formatting changes that Brandi requested for the annuity plan description. You are ready to print a copy of the document. You don't need to change any print settings, so you can use the Print button on the Standard toolbar.

To preview and print the document:

1. Click the **Print Preview** button on the Standard toolbar, and examine the document's appearance.

2. Click the **Print** button on the Print Preview toolbar. After a pause, the document prints.

3. Click the **Close** button on the Print Preview toolbar, then click the **Close** button ☒ on the program window to close your document and exit Word.

You now have a hard copy of the final annuity plan description, as shown in Figure 2-27.

Figure 2-27 ◀
Final version of
RHS annuity
plan (page 1)

Tax-Deferred Annuity Plan

If you would like to increase your income at retirement while lowering your taxes now, then consider participating in a tax-deferred annuity plan.

What Is a Tax-Deferred Annuity?

A tax-deferred annuity allows you to put a portion of your before-tax wages into an investment account on a regular basis. Instead of paying taxes on the money now (when your tax rate is high), you pay after you retire (when your tax rate will be lower). In the mean time, the annuity account earns dividends that permit you to supplement your retirement income.

How Do I Enroll in a Tax-Deferred Annuity Plan?

As a full-time employee, you're eligible to participate in the Tax-Deferred Annuity Plan. Of course, the plan is voluntary. You may begin participating on the first day of the month following your employment, and you may stop participating at any time. To participate, just complete the necessary enrollment form, as well as a Salary Reduction Agreement, and return them to Right-Hand Solutions.

How Will My Money Be Invested?

On your annuity application you can allocate your premiums among several options, such as stocks, money markets, bonds, and world equities. A typical allocation might be similar to the following: stock (30%); money market (25%); bond market (25%); world equities (15%); other (5%).

You can change your allocation at any time by calling our Customer Service Center at (501) 555-2425. Right-Hand Solutions will make every effort to invest your money safely and effectively so you will realize the maximum possible earnings.

How Will I Know How Well My Investments Are Doing?

Right-Hand Solutions will send you a report annually, showing your total accumulation. Every quarter you'll receive a statement containing a complete history of all financial transactions and showing the interest credited you've earned. You'll also receive our regular newsletter.

Figure 2-27 ◀
Final version of
RHS annuity
plan (page 2)

For the purposes of this plan, accumulation is defined as all tax-deferred contributions, minus the Right-Hand Solutions service charges.

Can My Tax-Deferred Annuity Plan Be Terminated?

Your Tax-Deferred Annuity Plan can be terminated **only** if you're no longer an eligible employee, you stop contributing to the plan, or your employer discontinues the contract with Right-Hand Solutions.

Can I Withdraw Money from My Tax-Deferred Annuity Plan?

Normally, if you make an early withdrawal from your tax-deferred annuity plan, you will incur substantial financial penalties. However, you can withdraw money without penalty if you have an immediate and severe financial need (as defined below) and the money from your plan is necessary to meet those needs. Under current law, these withdrawals are subject to ordinary income taxes.

The following are considered to be immediate and severe financial needs:

- medical expenses that exceed 7.5% of your annual salary
- purchase (excluding mortgage payments) of a principal residence
- tuition for post-secondary education for you or your dependents
- other circumstances as regulated by the Internal Revenue Service

When Can I Begin to Receive Funds from My Tax-Deferred Annuity Plan?

You (or your heirs) can begin receiving funds when you

1. reach the age of 59,
2. leave the service of your employer,
3. encounter financial hardship (as defined above),
4. die or become disabled.

<u>Note</u>: Get more information by writing Right-Hand Solutions, 2804 Russell Hollow Road, Little Rock, AR 72203, or by calling our Customer Service Center at (501) 555-2425.

Quick Check

1. Name and describe the four types of text alignment or justification, and how to align and justify text using Word.

2. What is the purpose of the Format Painter and how does it work?

3. Explain how to indent a paragraph 0.5 inches or more from the left margin.

4. True or False: The larger the point size, the smaller the font that will be displayed and printed.

5 How do you apply bullets to a list of items?

6 Describe the steps necessary to bold a word or phrase.

7 Describe the steps necessary to change the font of a word or phrase.

8 Explain how to find the word "strategy" in a long document and replace every occurrence with the word "plan."

9 Explain how to change a document's margins.

In this tutorial, you have helped Reginald plan, edit, and format the annuity plan that will appear in the employee handbooks of Right-Hand Solutions' clients. Now that you have fine-tuned the content, adjusted the text appearance and alignment, and added a bulleted list and a numbered list, the plan is visually appealing and easy to read.

You give the hard copy to Reginald, who makes two photocopies—one for Brandi and one for the copy center, which copies and distributes the document to all clients of Right-Hand Solutions.

Tutorial Assignments

Now that Reginald has completed the description of the annuity plan, Brandi tells him that she also wants to include a sample quarterly statement and a sample contract change notice in the client's employee handbooks to show employees how easy the statements are to read. You'll open and format this document now.

1. If necessary, start Word, make sure your Student Disk is in the appropriate disk drive, and check your screen to make sure your settings match those in the tutorial.

2. Open the file RHSQuart from the TAssign folder for Tutorial 2 on your Student Disk, and save the document as RHS Quarterly Report.

3. Make all edits and formatting changes marked on Figure 2-28. However, when you substitute Right-Hand Solutions in place of We in the first paragraph, use copy and paste, copying the company name from the top of the letter (without the paragraph mark) before you bold it.

Figure 2-28 ◀

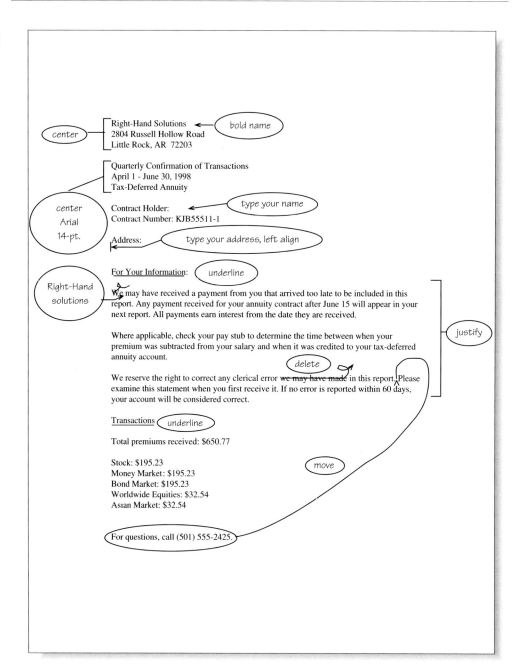

4. Save the document and print it.

5. Close the document.

6. Open the file RHSPort from the TAssign folder on your Student Disk, and save the file as RHS Portfolio Changes.

7. Make all the edits and formatting changes marked on Figure 2-29. However, instead of using the Formatting toolbar to change Current Allocation Accounts to bold 14 point, click Format on the menu bar, and then click Font to open the Font dialog box. Click the appropriate selections in the Font style and Size list boxes.

Figure 2-29 ◀

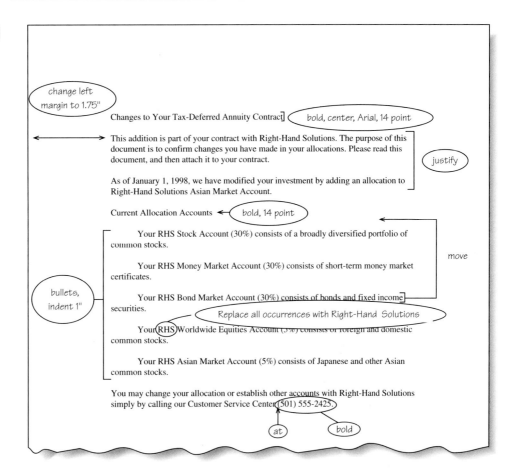

 8. Change the margins using the ruler in page layout view:
   a. Click the Page Layout View button.
   b. Select all the text in the document by pressing Ctrl + A.
   c. Position the pointer on the ruler at the right margin, which is indicated by a change from white to gray background, and then press and hold down the mouse button. The pointer changes to a two-headed arrow, which allows you to adjust the right margin. Drag the margin left to the 5" mark on the ruler, and then release the mouse button. Save the document.

 9. Change the line spacing of the text.
   a. Make sure all the text in the document is selected.
   b. Click Format on the menu bar, and then click Paragraph to open the Paragraph dialog box.
   c. Click the Indents and Spacing tab.
   d. Click the Line spacing list arrow, and then click 1.5 lines.
   e. Click the OK button.

10. Click the Print Preview button on the Standard toolbar to check your work.

 11. Use the Print command on the File menu to open the Print dialog box. Print two copies of the document by changing the Number of copies setting in the Print dialog box.

 12. You can find out the number of words in your documents by using the Word Count command on the Tools menu. Use this command to determine the number of words in the document, and then write that number in the upper-right corner of one of the printouts.

13. Save and close the document.

Case Problems

1. **Raleigh Rentals** Michele Stafford manages Raleigh Rentals, a storage facility in Huntsville, Alabama. She has written the draft of a tenant information sheet outlining Raleigh Rental's policies for new customers. She asks you to edit and format the document for her.

   1. If neccessary, start Word, make sure your Student Disk is in the appropriate disk drive, and check your screen to make sure your settings match those in the tutorials.

   2. Open the file Raleigh from the Tutorial 2 Cases folder on your Student Disk, and save it as Raleigh Rental Policies.

   3. Delete the word "general" from the first sentence of the first full paragraph. (Remember to use the Undo and Redo buttons to correct any editing mistakes as you work.)

   4. Delete the sentence at the end of the second paragraph that begins "If you renew your contract...".

   5. Insert the bolded sentence "A bill will not be sent to you." after the first sentence under the heading "Rental Payments".

   6. Delete the second paragraph under the heading "Rental Payments".

   7. Move the heading "Fees" and the sentence below it so that they appear after the "Rental Charges" section, not before it.

   8. Delete the phrase "not negotiable, and are" from the first sentence under the heading "Rental Charges".

   9. Change all of the margins (top, bottom, left, and right) to 1.5 inches.

   10. For each paragraph following a heading, indent the paragraph 0.5 inch and set the alignment to justify. (*Hint:* Format the first paragraph and then use the Format Painter to format each successive paragraph.)

   11. Use the Find tab in the Find and Replace dialog box to find the phrase "in writing" in the last sentence under the heading "Termination" and italicize it.

   12. Create bullets for the list under the heading "Delinquent Accounts," and indent the list 0.5 inch.

   13. Change both lines of the title to 16-point Arial (or another font of your choice).

   14. Center and bold both lines of the title.

   15. Bold all of the headings.

   16. Replace the misspelling "sub-let" with "sublet" wherever it appears in the document.

   17. Save, preview, and print the rental information sheet, and close the document.

2. **Synergy** Synergy provides productivity training for large companies across the country. Matt Patterson is Synergy's marketing director for the Northeast region. Matt wants to provide interested clients with a one-page summary of Synergy's productivity training.

   1. If neccessary, start Word, make sure your Student Disk is in the appropriate disk drive, and check your screen to make sure your settings match those in the tutorials.

   2. Open the file Synergy from the Tutorial 2 Cases folder on your Student Disk, and save it as Synergy Training Summary.

3. Change the title at the beginning of the document to a 14-point sans serif font. Be sure to pick a font that looks professional and is easy to read. (Remember to use the Undo and Redo buttons to correct any editing mistakes as you work.)

4. Center and bold the title.

5. Delete the word "main" from the second sentence of the first paragraph after the document title.

6. Create bullets for the list of training components following the first paragraph.

7. Under the heading "Personal Productivity Training Seminar" delete the second sentence from the first paragraph.

8. Under the heading "Personal Productivity Training Seminar" delete the phrase "in attendance at the seminar" from the first sentence in the second paragraph.

9. In the first paragraph under the heading "Management Productivity Training, move the second sentence beginning with "As a result" to the end of the paragraph.

10. Switch the order of the paragraphs under the "Field Services Technology and Training" heading.

11. Change the top margin to 1.5 inches.

12. Change the left margin to 1.75 inches.

13. Bold each of the headings.

14. Bold both occurrences of the word "free" in the second paragraph under the "Field Services Technology and Training" heading.

15. Save, preview, and print Synergy Training Summary, and then close the file.

3. **Rec-Tech** Ralph Dysktra is vice president of sales and marketing at Rec-Tech, an outdoor and sporting gear store in Conshohocken, Pennsylvania. Each quarter, Ralph and his staff mail a description of new products to Rec-Tech's regular customers. Ralph has asked you to edit and format the first few pages of this quarter's new products description.

1. If neccessary, start Word, make sure your Student Disk is in the appropriate disk drive, and check your screen to make sure your settings match those in the tutorials.

2. Open the file Backpack from the Tutorial 2 Cases folder on your Student Disk, and save it as Backpacker's Guide.

3. Delete the word "much" from the first sentence of the paragraph below the heading "Snuggle Up to These Prices". (Remember to use the Undo and Redo buttons to correct any editing mistakes as you work.)

4. Reverse the order of the last two paragraphs under the heading "You'll Eat Up the Prices of This Camp Cooking Gear!"

5. Move the last sentence at the end of the document to the end of the first full paragraph.

6. Reorder the items under the "RecTech Gear Up Ideas" heading by moving the first two product ideas to the end of the list.

7. Add bullets to the gear up product ideas.

8. Change the top margin to 2 inches.

9. Change the left margin to 1.75 inches.

10. Justify all the paragraphs in the document. (*Hint:* To select all paragraphs in the document at one time, click Edit on the menu bar, and then click Select All.)

11. Replace all occurrences of "RecTech" with "Rec-Tech."

12. Apply a 14-point sans serif font to each of the headings. Be sure to pick a font that looks professional and is easy to read.

13. Change the title's font to the same font you used for the headings, except set the size to 16 point.

14. Center and bold both lines of the title.

15. Bold the names and prices for all of the brand-name products in the Backpackers Guide.

16. Save, preview, and print the document, and then close the file.

4. Movie Review Your student newspaper has asked you to review four films currently showing in your area.

1. If neccessary, start Word, make sure your Student Disk is in the appropriate disk drive, and check your screen to make sure your settings match those in the tutorials.

2. Write a brief summary (1–2 paragraphs) for each movie and provide a rating for each movie. Correct any spelling errors. Save the document as Movie Review in the Tutorial 2 Cases folder on your Student Disk and print it.

Edit and format the document by doing the following:

3. Rearrange the order in which you discuss the movies to alphabetical order. (Remember to use the Undo and Redo buttons to correct any editing mistakes as you work.)

4. Change the top margin to 2 inches.

5. Set the left margin to 1.75 inches.

6. Add a title to your review, and then center and bold it.

7. Set the paragraph alignment to justify.

8. Italicize the title of each movie.

9. Save the edited document as Edited Movie Review.

10. Print the document.

11. Save and close your document.

Creating a Multiple-Page Report

Writing a Recommendation Report for AgriTechnology

CASE

AgriTechnology

Brittany Jones works for AgriTechnology, a biotechnology company that develops genetically engineered food products. Recently, AgriTechnology began shipping the EverRipe tomato to supermarkets. The EverRipe tomato is genetically engineered to stay ripe and fresh nearly twice as long as other varieties. Because of its longer shelf life and vine-ripened taste, supermarkets are eager to stock the new tomato, and the demand has been high. Unfortunately, the EverRipe tomato is also more susceptible to bruising than the usual varieties. Nearly 20 percent of the first year's crop was unmarketable because of damage sustained during shipping and handling. AgriTechnology's vice president, Ramon Espinoza, appointed Brittany to head a task force to determine how to increase the profitability of the EverRipe. The task force is ready to present the results of their study in the form of a report with an accompanying table. Brittany asks you to help prepare the report.

In this tutorial, you will format the report's title page so that it has a different layout from the rest of the report. The title page will contain only the title and subtitle, and will not have page numbers like the rest of the report. You will give the report a professional appearance quickly by applying a set of predefined formats that come with the Word program. You will also add a table to the AgriTechnology report that summarizes the task force's recommendations.

In this session you will review the task force's recommendation report. You will then learn how to divide a document into sections; center a page between the top and bottom margins; create a header; and number the pages in a document. Finally, you will learn how to attach a template and apply styles.

Planning the Document

As head of the task force, Brittany divided the responsibility for the report among the members of the group. Each person gathered information about one aspect of the problem and wrote the appropriate section of the report. Now Brittany must compile all the findings into a coherent and unified report. In addition, she must also follow the company's style guidelines for the content, organization, style, and format.

The report content includes the results of the study—obtained from interviews with other employees and visits to the packaging and distribution plant, trucking company, etc.—and recommendations for action.

Because Brittany knows some executives will not have time to read the entire report, she organized the report so it begins with an executive summary. The body of the report provides an in-depth statement of the problem and recommendations for solving that problem. At the end of the report, she summarizes the cost of the improvements.

The report's style follows established standards of business writing, emphasizing clarity, simplicity, and directness.

In accordance with AgriTechnology's style guide, Brittany's report will begin with a title page, with the text centered between the top and bottom margins. Every page except the title page will include a line of text at the top, giving a descriptive name for the report, as well as the page number. The text and headings will be formatted to look like all AgriTechnology's reports, following company guidelines for layout and text style.

At the end of the report, there will be a table that summarizes the costs of the proposed changes.

Opening the Draft of the Report

Brittany has already combined the individual sections into a draft of the report. You'll open the document and perform the formatting tasks indicated in Figure 3-1.

Figure 3-1 ◄
Initial draft of
task force's
report with
edits
(page 1)

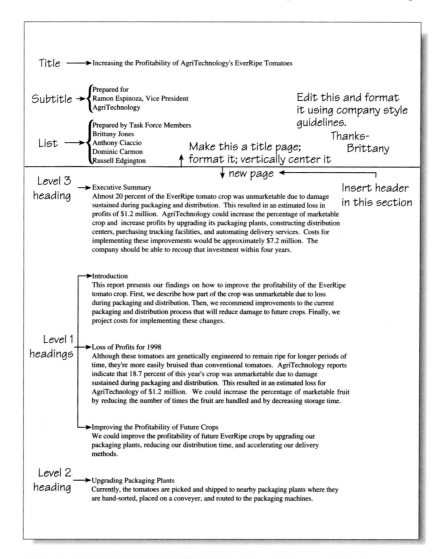

Figure 3-1 ◄
Initial draft of
task force's
report with
edits
(page 2)

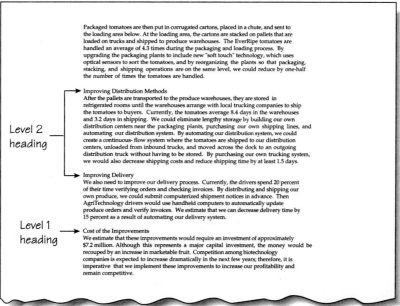

To open the document:

1. Start Word and place your Student Disk in the appropriate drive. Make sure your screen matches the figures in this tutorial. Because you'll be making large-scale formatting changes in this session, there is no need to display the nonprinting characters.

2. Open the file **EverRipe** from the **Tutorial.03** folder on your Student Disk.

3. To avoid altering the original file, save the document as **EverRipe Report** in the same folder.

Your first step is to change the layout of the title page.

Formatting the Document in Sections

According to the company guidelines, the title page of the report should be centered between the top and bottom margins of the page. In order to format the title page differently from the rest of the report, you need to divide the document into sections. A **section** is a unit or part of a document that can have its own page orientation, margins, headers, footers, and vertical alignment. Each section, in other words, is like a mini-document within a document.

To divide a document into sections, you insert a **section break**, a dotted line with the words "End of Section" that marks the point at which one section ends and another begins. Sections can start on a new page or continue on the same page. The easiest way to insert a section break is to use the Break command on the Insert menu.

To insert a section break after the title:

1. Position the insertion point immediately to the left of the "E" in the heading "Executive Summary." You want the text above this heading to be on a separate title page and the executive summary to begin the second page of the report.

2. Click **Insert** on the menu bar, and then click **Break** to open the Break dialog box. See Figure 3-2.

Figure 3-2 ◀
Break
dialog box

click here ——————

You can use this dialog box to insert several types of breaks into your document, including a page break, which places the text after it onto a new page. Instead of inserting a page break, however, you will insert a section break that indicates both a new section and a new page.

3. Click the **Next page** option button in the Section breaks area, and then click the **OK** button. A double-dotted line and the words "Section Break (Next Page)" appear before the heading "Executive Summary," indicating that you have inserted a section break. The status bar indicates that the insertion point is on page 2, section 2. See Figure 3-3.

Figure 3-3
End of
section break

insertion point
in section 2

section number

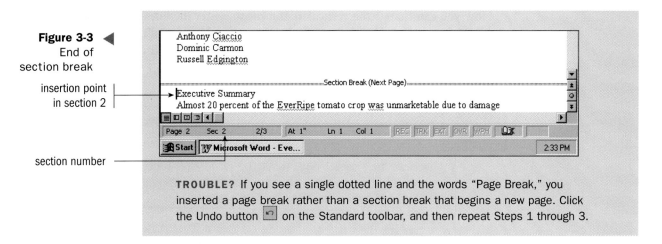

TROUBLE? If you see a single dotted line and the words "Page Break," you inserted a page break rather than a section break that begins a new page. Click the Undo button 🔄 on the Standard toolbar, and then repeat Steps 1 through 3.

Now that the title page is a separate section and page from the rest of the report, you can make changes affecting only that section, leaving the rest of the document intact.

Changing the Vertical Alignment of a Section

You're ready to center the title text vertically on the title page. But first you want to look at the layout of the report pages. To do this, you'll switch to the Print Preview window which shows the general layout of the report.

To see the document in Print Preview:

1. Click the **Print Preview** button 🔍 on the Standard toolbar to open the Print Preview window.

2. If you only see one or two pages, click the **Multiple Pages** button ⊞ on the Print Preview toolbar, and then click and drag across the top three pages in the drop-down box to select "1 × 3 Pages." The three pages of the report are reduced in size and appear side-by-side. See Figure 3-4. Although you cannot read the text on the pages, you can see their general layout.

Figure 3-4
Print Preview
of report

Print Preview toolbar

unformatted
title page

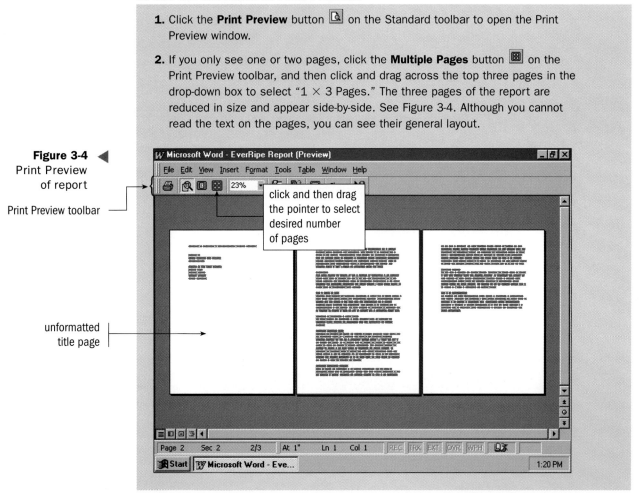

Now you can change the vertical alignment to center the lines of text between the top and bottom margins. The **vertical alignment** specifies how a page of text is positioned on the page between the top and bottom margins—flush at the top, flush at the bottom, or centered between the top and bottom margins.

REFERENCE
window

VERTICALLY ALIGNING A SECTION

- Insert a section break to create a separate section for the page you want to align.
- Move the insertion point within the section you want to align.
- Click File on the menu bar, click Page Setup, click the Layout tab, and then select the alignment option you want.
- Make sure the Apply to list box displays the This section option.
- Click the OK button.

You'll center the title page text from within the Print Preview window.

To change the vertical alignment of the title page:

1. If the Magnifier button is selected, click it once to deselect it.

2. Click the leftmost page in the Print Preview window to make sure the current page is page 1 (the title page). The status bar in the Print Preview window indicates the current page.

3. Click **File** on the menu bar, and then click **Page Setup** to open the Page Setup dialog box.

4. Click the **Layout** tab if it is not already selected. In the Apply to list box, click **This section** if it is not already selected so that the layout change affects only the first section, not both sections, of your document.

5. Click the **Vertical alignment** list arrow, and then click **Center** to center the pages of the current section—in this case just page 1—vertically between the top and bottom margins.

6. Click the **OK** button to return to the Print Preview window. The text of the title page is centered vertically, as shown in Figure 3-5.

Figure 3-5
Title page
vertically
centered

text centered
between top and
bottom margins

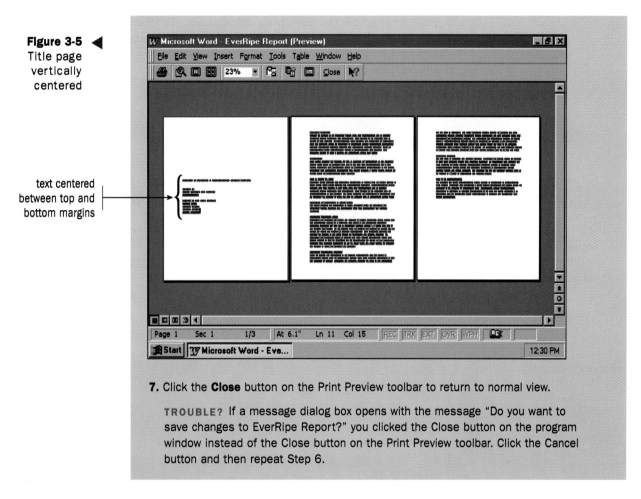

7. Click the **Close** button on the Print Preview toolbar to return to normal view.

TROUBLE? If a message dialog box opens with the message "Do you want to save changes to EverRipe Report?" you clicked the Close button on the program window instead of the Close button on the Print Preview toolbar. Click the Cancel button and then repeat Step 6.

You have successfully centered the title page text. Next, you turn your attention to placing a descriptive name for the report and the page number at the top of every page.

Adding Headers

The AgriTechnology report guidelines require a short report title and the page number to be printed at the top of every page except the title page. Text that is printed at the top of every page is called a **header**. For example, the section name, tutorial number, and page number printed at the top of the page you are reading is a header. Similarly, a **footer** is text that is printed at the bottom of every page. (You'll have a chance to work with footers in the Tutorial Assignments at the end of this tutorial.)

When you insert a header or footer into a document, you switch to Header and Footer view. The Header and Footer toolbar is displayed and the insertion point moves to the top of the document, where the header will appear. The main text is dimmed, indicating that it cannot be edited until you return to normal or page layout view.

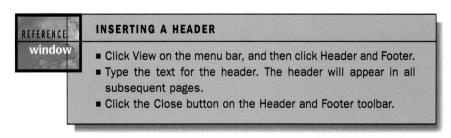

REFERENCE
window

INSERTING A HEADER

■ Click View on the menu bar, and then click Header and Footer.
■ Type the text for the header. The header will appear in all subsequent pages.
■ Click the Close button on the Header and Footer toolbar.

You'll create a header for the main body of the report (section 2) that prints "EverRipe Recommendation Report" at the left margin and the page number at the right margin.

To insert a header for section 2:

1. Make sure the insertion point is anywhere after the heading "Executive Summary" on page 2 so that the insertion point is in section 2 and not in section 1.

2. Click **View** on the menu bar, and then click **Header and Footer**. The screen changes to Header and Footer view, and the Header and Footer toolbar appears in the document window. The header area appears in the top margin of your document surrounded by a dashed line and displays the words "Header -Section 2-." See Figure 3-6.

Figure 3-6 ◄
Creating
a header

header area ——→

Header and
Footer toolbar

Same as Previous
button pressed

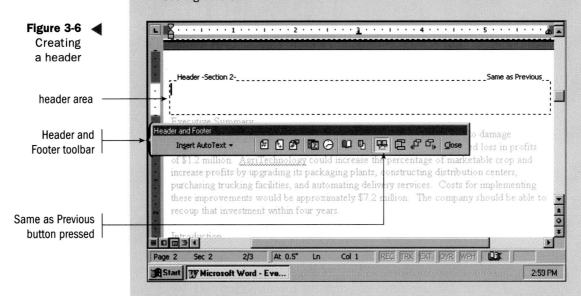

TROUBLE? If the header area displays "Header -Section 1-," click the Show Next button on the Header and Footer toolbar until the header area displays "Header -Section 2-."

TROUBLE? If the main text of the document doesn't appear on the screen, click the Show/Hide Document Text button on the Header and Footer toolbar, and continue with Step 3.

TROUBLE? If the Header and Footer toolbar covers the header area, drag the toolbar below the header area, similar to the position shown in Figure 3-6.

3. Click the **Same as Previous** button on the Header and Footer toolbar so that the button is not pressed. This ensures that the text of the current header will apply only to the current section (section 2), not to the previous section (section 1) also.

4. Type **EverRipe Recommendation Report**. The title is automatically aligned on the left. See Figure 3-7.

Figure 3-7
Text of header

report title

deselect so header
text prints only in
section 2

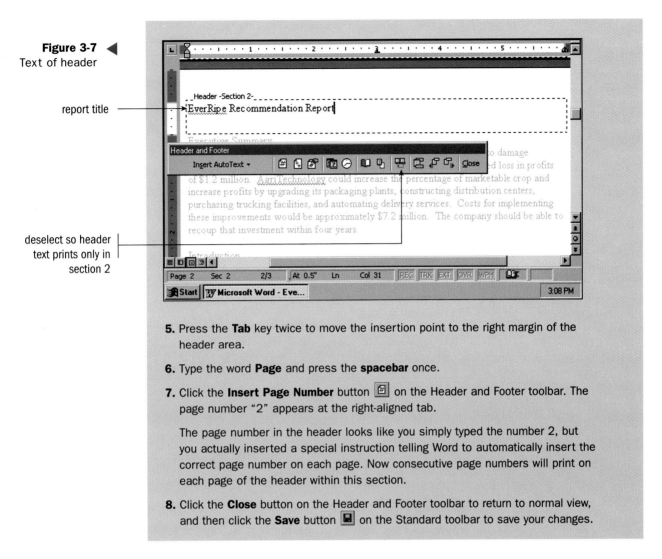

5. Press the **Tab** key twice to move the insertion point to the right margin of the header area.

6. Type the word **Page** and press the **spacebar** once.

7. Click the **Insert Page Number** button 🔲 on the Header and Footer toolbar. The page number "2" appears at the right-aligned tab.

The page number in the header looks like you simply typed the number 2, but you actually inserted a special instruction telling Word to automatically insert the correct page number on each page. Now consecutive page numbers will print on each page of the header within this section.

8. Click the **Close** button on the Header and Footer toolbar to return to normal view, and then click the **Save** button 🔲 on the Standard toolbar to save your changes.

Notice that you can't see the header in normal view. To see exactly how the header will appear on the printed page, you can switch to page layout view, which lets you read the headers and footers as well as see the margins.

To view the header and margins in page layout view:

1. Click the **Page Layout View** button 🔲.

2. Click the **Zoom Control** list arrow on the Standard toolbar, and then click **75%**. You can now see the header and the page margins. Next, you'll use the browse buttons to examine each page.

3. Click the **Select Browse Object** button 🔲 below the vertical scroll bar and click the Browse by Page button 🔲. The cursor moves to the top of the third page.

4. Click the **Previous Page** button 🔲 (just below the vertical scroll bar) twice to move to page 1.

5. Click the **Next Page** button 🔲 to move to the top of the second page.

6. Click the **Next Page** button 🔲 again to move to the top of the third page. Notice that the header appears on pages 2 and 3 but not the title page. See Figure 3-8.

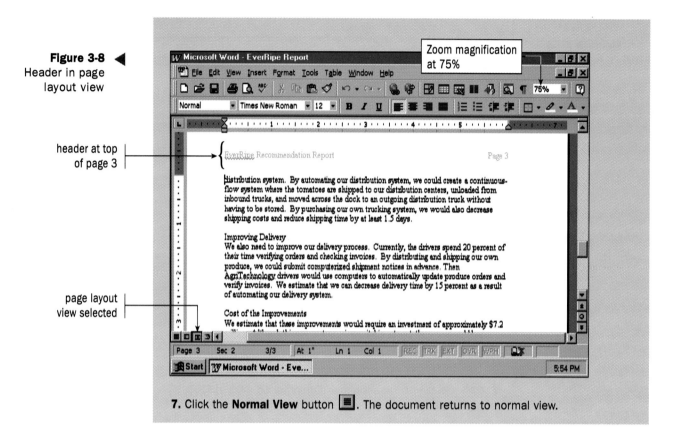

Figure 3-8
Header in page
layout view

header at top
of page 3

page layout
view selected

Zoom magnification
at 75%

7. Click the **Normal View** button. The document returns to normal view.

The recommendation report now has the required header. Your next job is to make style changes throughout the document.

Using Styles

As you know, it's often helpful to use the Format Painter to copy formatting from one paragraph to another. However, when you are working on a longer document, you'll find it easier to use a set of formats known as a **style**. Every Word document opens with a set of predefined styles which include: Normal (the default style for paragraphs in a Word document), Heading 1, Heading 2, and Heading 3. Word's default Normal style is defined as 10 point Times New Roman, left alignment, with single-line spacing. You can modify any of the predefined styles to suit the needs of your document, as you did when you changed the font size to 12 point at the beginning of the first tutorial.

The style of the current paragraph (the paragraph where the cursor is located) appears in the Style list box on the Formatting toolbar. All available styles are listed in the Style list, as shown in Figure 3-9. Styles affecting individual characters appear with a letter "a" in the gray box to the right of the style name (for example, the Page Number style in Figure 3-9); paragraph styles appear with the paragraph icon in the gray box (for example, the Heading 1 style in Figure 3-9). The font size of each style is also displayed. For example, the Page Number style is 10 point. All styles in the list appear with the formatting characteristics applied so you can see what they look like before choosing one.

Figure 3-9
List of available
default styles

click to display
list of styles

current style

font size

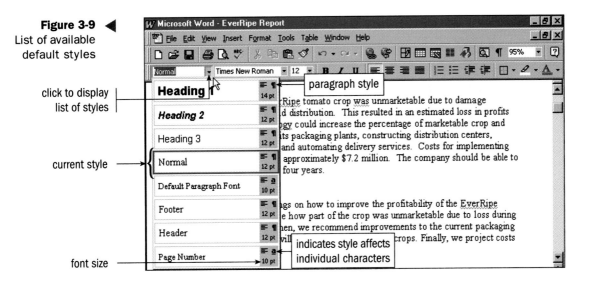

Attaching a Template to a Document

You can change the available styles by using a different template. A **template** is a set of predefined styles designed for a specific type of document. For example, Word provides templates for formatting reports, brochures, memos, letters, or resumes, among others. Word's default template, the Normal template, contains the Normal paragraph style described earlier.

There are two steps to using a template. First you need to attach the template to the document. Then you need to apply the template's styles to the various parts of the document. You'll begin by attaching a new template to the EverRipe Report document.

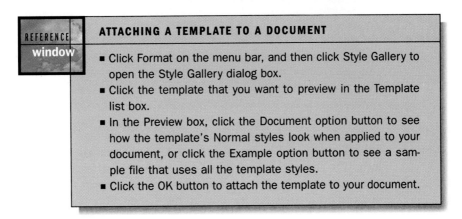

REFERENCE
window

ATTACHING A TEMPLATE TO A DOCUMENT

- Click Format on the menu bar, and then click Style Gallery to open the Style Gallery dialog box.
- Click the template that you want to preview in the Template list box.
- In the Preview box, click the Document option button to see how the template's Normal styles look when applied to your document, or click the Example option button to see a sample file that uses all the template styles.
- Click the OK button to attach the template to your document.

Brittany tells you that all reports produced at the company use Word's predefined Professional Report template. She suggests you preview the template to see what it looks like, and then attach it to the recommendation report. You'll use the Style Gallery to do this.

To preview and attach the Professional Report template to your document:

1. Click **Format** on the menu bar, and then click **Style Gallery** to open the Style Gallery dialog box. The recommendation report appears in the Preview of window and "(current)" appears in the Template list box. The report appears formatted the same way as it is in the document window.

2. Scroll to and then click **Professional Report** in the Template list box to select the template. In the Preview of Report window, the text of your document changes to reflect the new Normal style for the Professional Report template. See Figure 3-10.

Figure 3-10
Style Gallery
with preview of
Professional
Report
template

selected template

click to see
sample document

preview of document

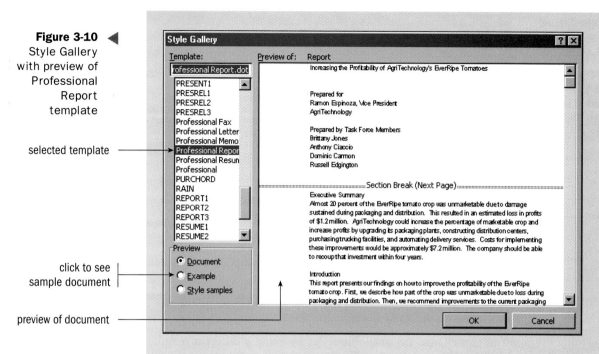

3. In the Preview box, click the **Example** option button to see a sample document that uses all the Professional Report template styles. Scroll through the sample document to preview all the styles that are available to you in this template.

4. Click the **OK** button to attach the template to the report and return to the document window. The template's default font (10-point Arial) and paragraph indentation are applied to the entire document, because the text in the document has been formatted with the Normal style, and because no other styles, such as a Heading style, have been applied to the text at this point. You'll see the Professional Report template styles when you apply them in the next section.

5. Click the **Style** list arrow on the Formatting toolbar. Scroll through the style list to verify that the styles of the Professional Report template are now available in this document, and then click the **Style** list arrow again to close the style list.

At this point, the only apparent change in the text is that the font changed from 12 point Times New Roman to 10 point Arial and that the paragraphs are left-indented 0.75 inch. (On some computers, the 10 point Arial is also condensed so that the font is actually Arial Narrow.) Now that the Professional Report template is attached to the report, you can begin applying its styles to the document.

Applying Styles

The best way to apply a template's styles to a document is to highlight individual parts of the document, and then select the appropriate style from the Style list on the Formatting toolbar. For example, to format the report title, you would highlight "Increasing the Profitability of AgriTechnology's EverRipe Tomatoes" on the title page, and then select the Title Cover style from the Style list.

You'll apply the Professional Report template styles now, beginning with the report title.

To apply styles to the report document:

1. Scroll to the title page, and then drag the pointer to select the title **Increasing the Profitability of AgriTechnology's EverRipe Tomatoes**.

2. Click the **Style** list arrow on the Formatting toolbar to open the Style list. Scroll down the list, and then click **Title Cover**. Word applies the style to the selected text. Notice that the font of the Title Cover style is 32 point Arial Black.

3. Deselect the text. See Figure 3-11. Notice that the Title Cover style dramatically emphasizes the title. You'll get a better idea of its positioning on the page when you preview and print the document.

Figure 3-11
Title formatted
with Title
Cover style

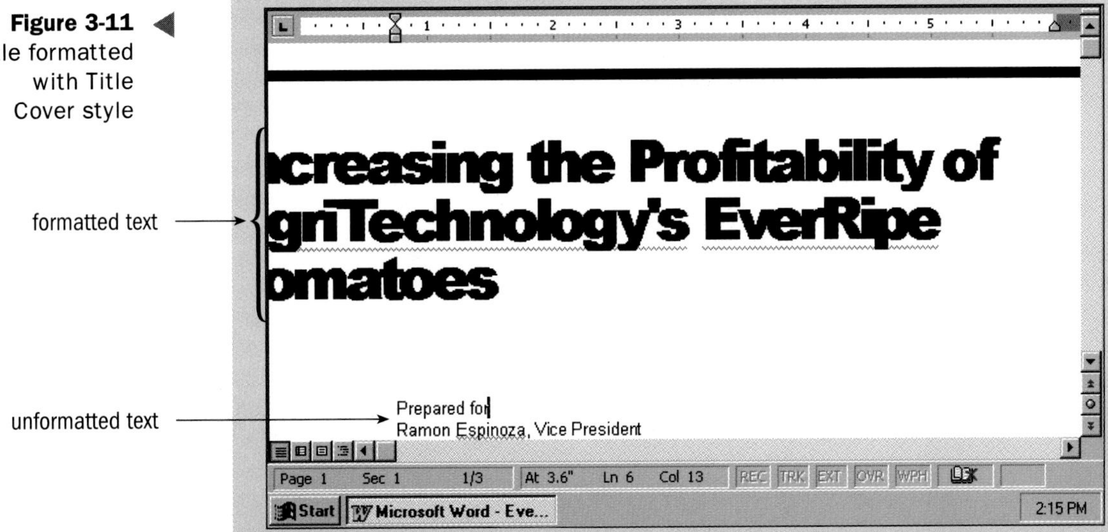

formatted text

unformatted text

icreasing the Profitability of
griTechnology's EverRipe
omatoes

Prepared for
Ramon Espinoza, Vice President

Page 1   Sec 1   1/3   At 3.6"   Ln 6   Col 13   REC TRK EXT OVR WPH

Start   Microsoft Word - Eve...   2:15 PM

4. Continue formatting the rest of the document by selecting text and applying the styles indicated in Figure 3-12. Keep in mind that you do not have to apply a new style to any text not labeled in Figure 3-12, because Word already applied the Normal style for the Professional template when you attached it to the document. Be careful to choose List 2 when formatting the name list; there are several list and list continuation styles in this template, each with a different indent. Use the Undo button to undo any mistakes. To repeat applying a style you just applied, press the F4 key. When you are finished, your document should look similar to Figure 3-12. You might not be able to see the gray background of the Block Quotation style until you print the document.

Figure 3-12 ◀
Formatted
version of
recommenda-
tion report
(title page)

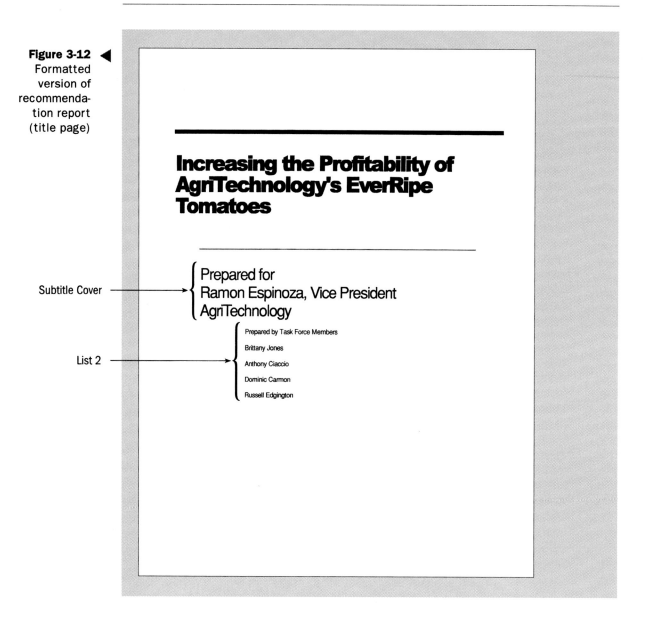

Subtitle Cover ——————→

List 2 ——————→

Figure 3-12 ◀
Formatted
version of
recommenda-
tion report
(page 2)

Heading 3

Block Quotation

Heading 1

Heading 1

Heading 1

Heading 2

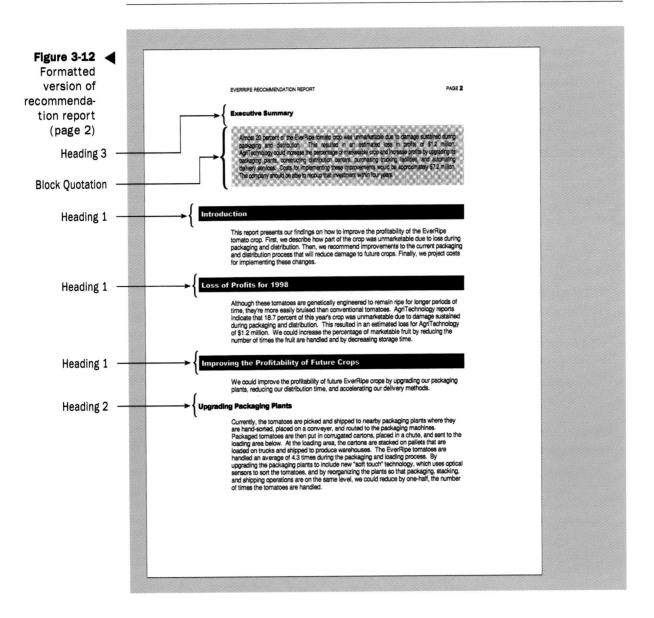

EVERRIPE RECOMMENDATION REPORT   PAGE **2**

Executive Summary

> Almost 20 percent of the EverRipe tomato crop was unmarketable due to damage sustained during packaging and distribution. This resulted in an estimated loss in profits of $1.2 million. AgriTechnology could increase the percentage of marketable crop and increase profits by upgrading its packaging plants, constructing distribution centers, purchasing trucking facilities, and automating delivery services. Costs for implementing these improvements would be approximately $7.2 million. The company should be able to recoup that investment within four years.

Introduction

This report presents our findings on how to improve the profitability of the EverRipe tomato crop. First, we describe how part of the crop was unmarketable due to loss during packaging and distribution. Then, we recommend improvements to the current packaging and distribution process that will reduce damage to future crops. Finally, we project costs for implementing these changes.

Loss of Profits for 1998

Although these tomatoes are genetically engineered to remain ripe for longer periods of time, they're more easily bruised than conventional tomatoes. AgriTechnology reports indicate that 18.7 percent of this year's crop was unmarketable due to damage sustained during packaging and distribution. This resulted in an estimated loss for AgriTechnology of $1.2 million. We could increase the percentage of marketable fruit by reducing the number of times the fruit are handled and by decreasing storage time.

Improving the Profitability of Future Crops

We could improve the profitability of future EverRipe crops by upgrading our packaging plants, reducing our distribution time, and accelerating our delivery methods.

Upgrading Packaging Plants

Currently, the tomatoes are picked and shipped to nearby packaging plants where they are hand-sorted, placed on a conveyer, and routed to the packaging machines. Packaged tomatoes are then put in corrugated cartons, placed in a chute, and sent to the loading area below. At the loading area, the cartons are stacked on pallets that are loaded on trucks and shipped to produce warehouses. The EverRipe tomatoes are handled an average of 4.3 times during the packaging and loading process. By upgrading the packaging plants to include new "soft touch" technology, which uses optical sensors to sort the tomatoes, and by reorganizing the plants so that packaging, stacking, and shipping operations are on the same level, we could reduce by one-half, the number of times the tomatoes are handled.

Word

Figure 3-12 ◄
Formatted
version of
recommenda-
tion report
(page 3)

Heading 2 ⟶

Heading 2 ⟶

Heading 1 ⟶

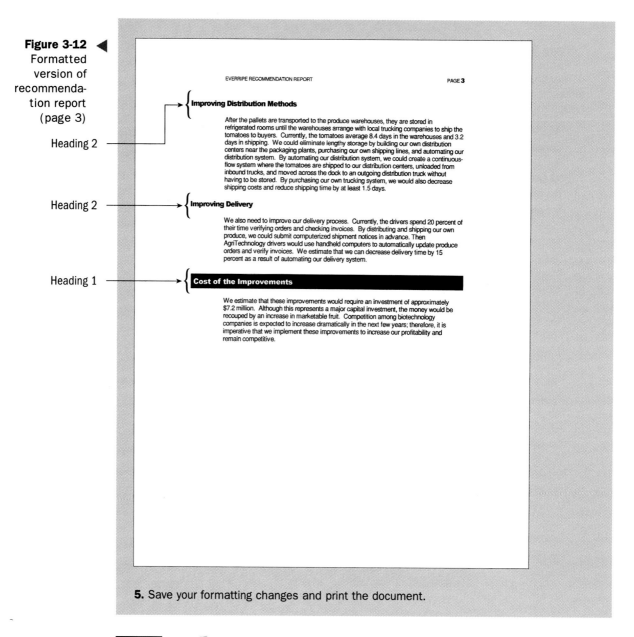

EVERRIPE RECOMMENDATION REPORT   PAGE **3**

Improving Distribution Methods

After the pallets are transported to the produce warehouses, they are stored in refrigerated rooms until the warehouses arrange with local trucking companies to ship the tomatoes to buyers. Currently, the tomatoes average 8.4 days in the warehouses and 3.2 days in shipping. We could eliminate lengthy storage by building our own distribution centers near the packaging plants, purchasing our own shipping lines, and automating our distribution system. By automating our distribution system, we could create a continuous-flow system where the tomatoes are shipped to our distribution centers, unloaded from inbound trucks, and moved across the dock to an outgoing distribution truck without having to be stored. By purchasing our own trucking system, we would also decrease shipping costs and reduce shipping time by at least 1.5 days.

Improving Delivery

We also need to improve our delivery process. Currently, the drivers spend 20 percent of their time verifying orders and checking invoices. By distributing and shipping our own produce, we could submit computerized shipment notices in advance. Then AgriTechnology drivers would use handheld computers to automatically update produce orders and verify invoices. We estimate that we can decrease delivery time by 15 percent as a result of automating our delivery system.

Cost of the Improvements

We estimate that these improvements would require an investment of approximately $7.2 million. Although this represents a major capital investment, the money would be recouped by an increase in marketable fruit. Competition among biotechnology companies is expected to increase dramatically in the next few years; therefore, it is imperative that we implement these improvements to increase our profitability and remain competitive.

5. Save your formatting changes and print the document.

Quick Check

1 Define the following in your own words:
a. style
b. template
c. Style list
d. section (of a document)
e. vertical alignment
f. header

2 Why would you need to insert a section break into a document?

3 Explain how to center the title page vertically between the top and bottom margins.

4 What is the difference between a header and a footer?

5 How do you insert the page number in a header?

6 What are the two steps involved in using a new template?

7 How do you attach a template to a document?

8 Explain how you applied styles to the EverRipe Report document.

You have planned, formatted, and printed Brittany's recommendation report so that the results are professional-looking, clearly presented, and easy to read. You have done this using the Word features that quickly add formatting to an entire section of a document: headers, templates, and styles. Next you will add and format a table that summarizes the costs and benefits of the task force's recommendations.

SESSION

3.2

In this session you will learn how to add a table to the report. Then you'll add rows to the table, widen the columns in the table, and align the text in the table. Finally you'll add shading to make the table look more professional.

Inserting Tables

The Word Table feature allows you to quickly organize data and to arrange text in an easy-to-read format of columns and rows. Figure 3-13 summarizes the elements of a Word table.

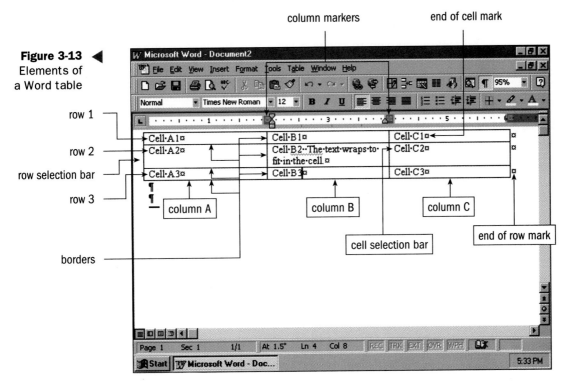

Figure 3-13
Elements of
a Word table

A **table** is information arranged in horizontal rows and vertical columns. As you can see by looking through this book, a table is an efficient way of communicating a lot of information in an easy-to-read format. It's convenient to refer to table rows as if they were labeled with numbers (row 1 at the top, row 2 below row 1, and so forth), and each column as a letter (column A on the far left, column B to the right of column A, and so forth). However, you do not see row and column numbers on the screen.

The area where a row and column intersect is called a **cell**. Each cell is identified by a column and row label. For example, the cell in the upper-left corner of a table is cell A1 (column A, row 1), the cell to the right of that is cell B1, the cell below cell A1 is A2, and so forth. The table's structure is indicated by **borders**, which are lines that outline the rows and columns. With Word's Table feature, you can create a blank table and then insert information into it, or you can convert existing text into a table. You'll begin with a blank table in the next section. In the Tutorial Assignments at the end of this tutorial, you'll have a chance to convert text into a table.

Creating a Table Using the Insert Table Button

The easiest way to create a table is by moving the insertion point to the location in your document where you want a table, clicking the Insert Table button on the Standard toolbar, and then specifying the number of rows and columns you need in your table. Word inserts a blank table structure with the number of rows and columns you specified.

REFERENCE window	CREATING A BLANK TABLE USING THE INSERT TABLE BUTTON
	■ Place the insertion point where you want the table to appear in the document.
	■ Click the Insert Table button on the Standard toolbar to display a drop-down grid.
	■ Drag the pointer to select the desired number of rows and columns, and then release the mouse button.

Brittany wants you to create a table that summarizes information in the EverRipe report, which you formatted in the previous session. Figure 3-14 shows a sketch of what Brittany wants the table to look like. The table will allow AgriTechnology's executives to see at a glance the cost and benefits of each improvement.

Figure 3-14 ◄
Sketch of
EverRipe table

Projected Improvement	Initial Cost	Percent of Total Cost	Benefit
Upgrade packaging plants	$2,500,000	35%	Reduce by one-half the number of times tomatoes are handled
Improve distribution methods	$3,700,000	51%	Decrease shipping costs and reduce shipping time by 1.5 days
Automate delivery paperwork	$1,000,000	14%	Decrease delivery time by 15%
Total	$7,200,000		

You'll use the Insert Table button to create the table.

To create a blank table using the Insert Table button:

1. If you took a break after the last session, make sure Word is running and that the EverRipe Report document is open. Because you will be working with table formatting elements in this session, make sure the nonprinting characters are displayed.

2. Position the insertion point at the end of the last paragraph in the report, and press the **Enter** key twice to insert a space between the text and the table. Word inserts the table at the location of the insertion point.

3. Click the **Insert Table** button on the Standard toolbar. A drop-down grid resembling a miniature table appears below the Insert Table button. The grid initially has four rows and five columns. You can drag the pointer to extend the grid to as many rows and columns as you need. In this case, you need only four rows and four columns.

4. Position the pointer in the upper-left cell of the grid, and then click and drag the pointer down and across the grid until you highlight four rows and four columns. As you drag the pointer across the grid, Word indicates the size of the table (rows by columns) at the bottom of the grid. See Figure 3-15.

click to insert table

Figure 3-15 ◀
Insert
Table grid

drag to select
table size

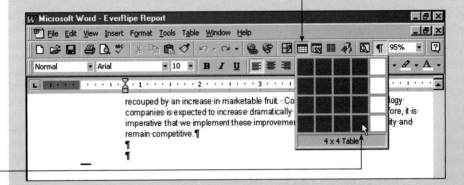

5. Release the mouse button. An empty table, four rows by four columns, appears in your document with the insertion point blinking in the upper-left corner (cell A1).

The table is outlined with borders, and the four columns are of equal width. The column widths are indicated by **column markers** on the ruler. Each cell contains an end-of-cell mark, and each row contains an end-of-row mark.

TROUBLE? If you don't see the end-of-cell and end-of-row marks, you need to show nonprinting characters. Click the Show/Hide ¶ button ¶ on the Standard toolbar to show nonprinting characters.

Now that you've created the table, you are ready to enter text and numbers summarizing the EverRipe report.

Entering Text in a Table

You can enter text in a table by moving the insertion point to a cell and typing. If the text takes up more than one line in the cell, Word automatically wraps the text to the next line and increases the height of that cell and all the cells in that row. To move the insertion point to the next cell to the right, you can either click in that cell or press the Tab key. If you want to return to the previous cell, you can press and hold down the Shift key while you press the Tab key. Figure 3-16 summarizes the keystrokes for moving within a table.

Figure 3-16 ◀
Keystrokes for
moving around
a table

Press	To move the insertion point
Tab or →	One cell to the right, or to the first cell in the next row
Shift + Tab or ←	One cell to the left, or to the last cell in the previous row
Alt + Home	To first cell of current row
Alt + End	To last cell of current row
Alt + PageUp	To top cell or current column
Alt + PageDown	To bottom cell of current column
↑	One cell up in current column
↓	One cell down in current column

Now you are ready to insert information into the table.

To insert data into the table:

   1. Make sure the insertion point is in cell A1 of the table.

   2. Type **Projected Improvement**. Watch the end-of-cell mark move to the right as you type.

   3. Press the **Tab** key to move to cell B1. See Figure 3-17.

Figure 3-17 ◀
Adding text
to the table

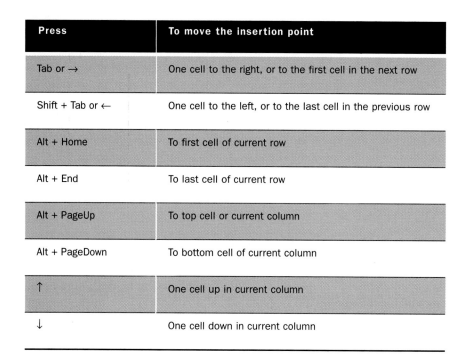

end-of-cell mark

new text

insertion point
in cell B1

   TROUBLE? If you accidentally pressed the Enter key instead of the Tab key, Word created a new paragraph within cell A1 rather than moving the insertion point to cell B1. Press the Backspace key to remove the paragraph mark, and then press the Tab key to move to cell B1.

   4. Type **Initial Cost** and then press the **Tab** key to move to cell C1.

   5. Type **Percent of Total Cost** and then press the **Tab** key to move to cell D1.

   6. Type **Benefit** and then press the **Tab** key to move the insertion point from cell D1 to cell A2. Notice that when you press the Tab key in the last column of the table, the insertion point moves to the first column in the next row.

You have entered the **heading row**, the row that identifies the information in each column.

7. Type the remaining information for the table, as shown in Figure 3-18, pressing the Tab key to move from cell to cell.

Figure 3-18 ◀
Table with
completed
information

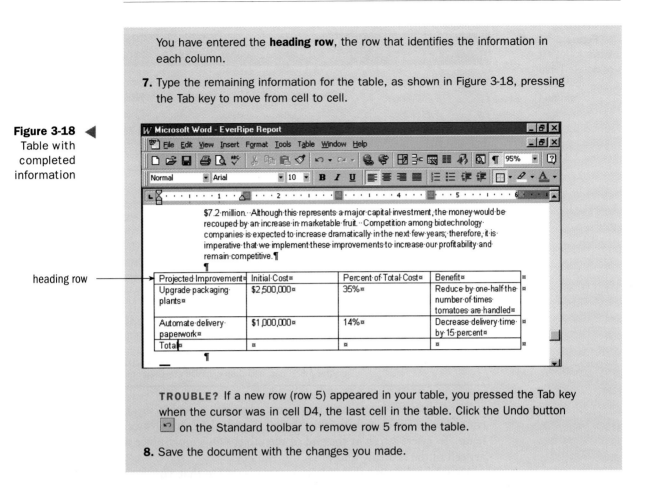

heading row

TROUBLE? If a new row (row 5) appeared in your table, you pressed the Tab key when the cursor was in cell D4, the last cell in the table. Click the Undo button 🔙 on the Standard toolbar to remove row 5 from the table.

8. Save the document with the changes you made.

Keep in mind that many of the methods you've used to edit a document, such as the Backspace key, the copy-and-paste feature, the Undo button, and the AutoCorrect feature, work the same way in a table. Just like in a paragraph, you must select text within a table in order to edit it.

Inserting Additional Rows

When creating a table, you might be unsure about how many rows or columns you will actually need. You might need to delete extra rows and columns, or, as in this case, you might need to add them. Either way, you can easily modify an existing table's structure. Figure 3-19 summarizes ways to insert or delete rows and columns in a table.

Figure 3-19 ◀
Ways to insert
or delete table
rows and
columns

To	Do this
Insert a row within a table	Select the row or position the insertion point in the row below where you want the row added, click Table on the menu bar, and then click Insert Rows. Position the insertion point in the row below where you want the row added, and then click the Insert Rows button on the Standard toolbar.
Insert a row at the end of a table	Position the insertion point in the rightmost cell of the bottom row, and then press the Tab key.
Insert a column within a table	Select the column to the right of where you want the column added, click Table on the menu bar, and then click Insert Columns. Select the column to the right of where you want the column added, and then click the Insert Columns button on the Standard toolbar.
Insert a column at the end of a table	Select the end-of-row markers to the right of the table, click Table on the menu bar, and then click Insert Columns.
Delete a row	Select the row or rows to be deleted, click Table on the menu bar, then click Delete Rows.
Delete a column	Select the column or columns to be deleted, click Table on the menu bar, and then click Delete Columns.

Word allows you to insert additional rows either within or at the end of a table. You can insert a row or rows within the table with the Insert Rows command on the Table menu. To insert a row at the end of the table, you simply place the insertion point in the last cell of the last row and press the Tab key.

After looking over the EverRipe table, you see that you forgot to include a row on improving distribution methods. You'll insert that row and the relevant data now using the Insert Rows command, which inserts a row above the current row. To insert a row above the "Automate delivery paperwork" row (row 3), you begin by selecting that row. You will insert the new row using the Table shortcut menu, which contains frequently used table commands.

To insert a row within the table:

1. Position the pointer in the margin next to cell A3 (which contains the text "Automate delivery paperwork"). This area is called the row **selection bar**. The pointer changes to ⌐⟋ .

2. Click to select row 3.

3. With the pointer ⌐⟍ positioned anywhere over the selected row, click the right mouse button. The Table shortcut menu opens. Notice that the shortcut menu includes a Delete Rows command, which you could use if you needed to delete the selected row. In this case, however, you want to insert a row. See Figure 3-20.

Figure 3-20 ◀
Table shortcut
menu

click to insert
a new row

click to delete the
selected row

click here to
select row

right-click over
highlighted
row to display
shortcut menu

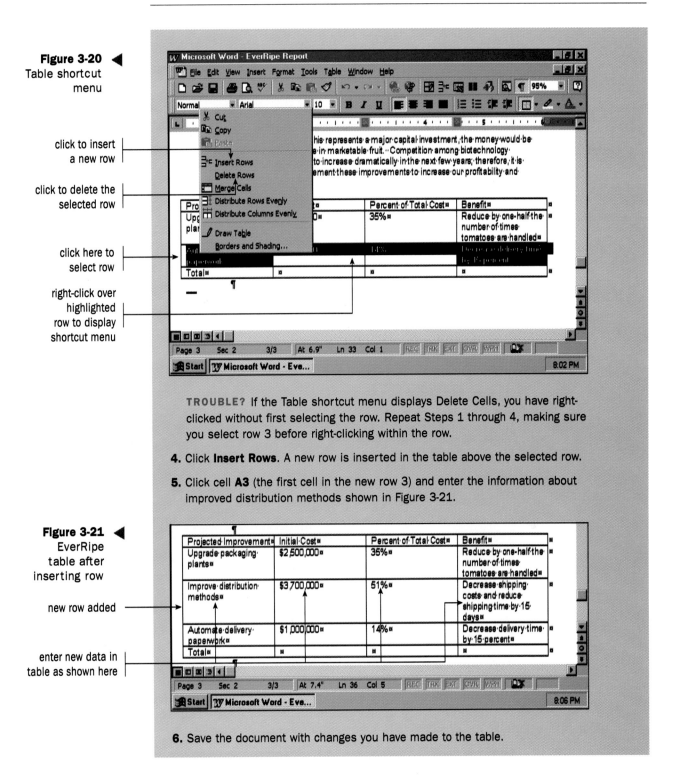

TROUBLE? If the Table shortcut menu displays Delete Cells, you have right-clicked without first selecting the row. Repeat Steps 1 through 4, making sure you select row 3 before right-clicking within the row.

4. Click **Insert Rows**. A new row is inserted in the table above the selected row.

5. Click cell **A3** (the first cell in the new row 3) and enter the information about improved distribution methods shown in Figure 3-21.

Figure 3-21 ◀
EverRipe
table after
inserting row

new row added

enter new data in
table as shown here

6. Save the document with changes you have made to the table.

Using AutoSum to Total a Table Column

Rather than calculating column totals by hand and entering them, you can easily have Word compute the totals of numeric columns in a table.

To total the values in the Cost column:

1. Click cell **B5**, the last call in the Initial Cost column.

2. Click the **Tables and Borders** button 🔲 on the Standard toolbar. The Tables and Borders toolbar appears and the document automatically changes to page layout view.

   TROUBLE? If the Office Assistant opens, displaying a hint on working with this window, just click the Cancel button to close the Office Assistant.

3. Click the **AutoSum** button Σ on the Tables and Borders toolbar. The total of the column appears in cell B5 formatted with a dollar sign and two decimal places. You want it to match the numbers above it, so you'll delete the decimal point and the two zeroes.

4. Click **Table** on the menu bar, and then click **Formula**.

5. Click the **Number Format** list arrow, and select the only format with a dollar sign.

6. In the Number Format text box, click to the right of the format and press the **Backspace** key until only $#, ##0 remains, as shown in Figure 3-22.

Figure 3-22 ◀
Formula dialog
box after
adjusting
number format

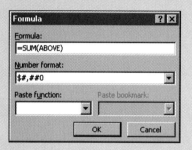

7. Click **OK**. The Initial Cost total is now formatted like the numbers above it.

8. Click the **Close** button ✕ on the Tables and Borders toolbar. If it is docked below the Formatting toolbar, and does not have a Close button, right click the toolbar and click Tables and Borders to remove the checkmark next to it.

9. Click the **Normal View** button ▤.

You have finished creating the tables and entering data. Now you can concentrate on improving the table's appearance.

Formatting Tables

Word provides a variety of ways to enhance the appearance of the tables you create: you can alter the width of the columns and the height of the rows, or change the alignment of text within the cells or the alignment of the table between the left and right margins.

After reviewing your work, Brittany decides the EverRipe table needs formatting to make it more attractive and easier to read.

Changing Column Width and Height

Sometimes you'll want to adjust the column widths in a table in order to make the text easier to read. If you want to specify an exact width for a column, you should use the Cell Height and Width command on the Table menu. However, it's usually easiest simply to drag the column's right-hand border to a new position.

The Initial Cost column (column B) and the Percent of Total Cost column (column C) are too wide for the information they contain and should be decreased. Also, the Benefit column (column D) would be easier to read if it was a little wider. You'll change these widths by dragging the column borders, using the ruler as a guide. Keep in mind that to change the width of a column, you need to drag the column's rightmost border.

To change the width of columns by dragging the borders:

1. Position the insertion point anywhere in the EverRipe table. Make sure you do not select any cells.

2. Move the pointer over the border between columns B and C (in other words, over the rightmost border of column B). The pointer changes to +⊩+ .

3. Click and drag the pointer to the left until the border reaches 2.5 inches on the ruler, and then release the mouse button. Notice that as the second column decreases in width, the width of column C increases, but the overall width of the table does not change. See Figure 3-23.

Figure 3-23 ◀
Table after decreasing the width of column B

drag this pointer to change the column width

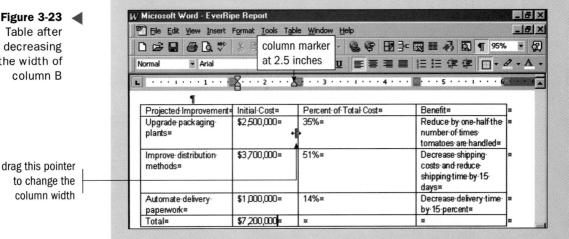

4. Click and drag the right border of column C to the left until it reaches about 3.5 inches on the ruler. Notice that Word automatically adjusted column D to compensate for the changes in columns B and C. Instead of being crowded onto several short lines, the text in column D is stretched out into one or two longer, easier-to-read lines. This means you don't have to worry about widening the last column.

You can change the height of rows by dragging a row border, just as you changed column widths by dragging a column border. You'll make row 1 taller to make it more prominent. To do this you have to change to page layout view.

To change the height of row 1:

1. Click the **Page Layout View** button 📰.

2. Position the pointer over the bottom border of the heading row. The pointer changes to ⨪ .

3. Drag the row border downward about ¼".

4. Click the **Normal View** button 📰.

The EverRipe table now looks much better with its new column widths and row height. Next you'll align the text to make the table even more attractive.

Aligning Text Within Cells

Aligning the text within the cells of a table makes the information easier to read. For example, aligning numbers and percentages along the right margin helps the reader to quickly compare the values. Centering the headings makes the columns more visually appealing. You can align text within the cells the same way you do other text—with the alignment buttons on the Formatting toolbar.

The dollar and percentage amounts in columns B and C would be much easier to read if you were to align the numbers on the right side of the cells. The table would also look better with the headings centered.

To right-align the numerical data and center the headings:

1. Drag the pointer to select cells **B2** through **C5**. See Figure 3-24.

Figure 3-24 ◄
Selected data

selected cells are
currently left-aligned

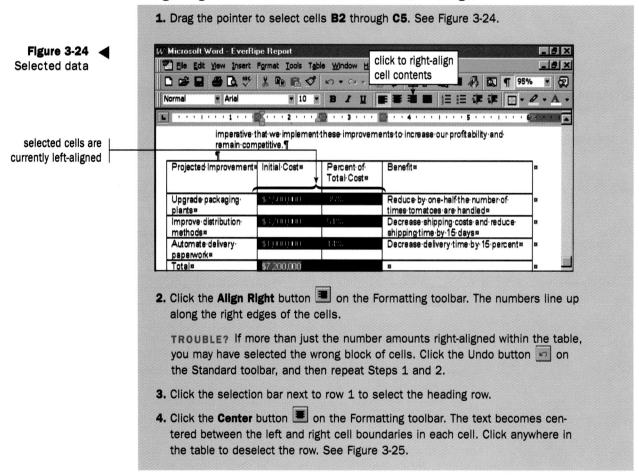

2. Click the **Align Right** button 🔲 on the Formatting toolbar. The numbers line up along the right edges of the cells.

TROUBLE? If more than just the number amounts right-aligned within the table, you may have selected the wrong block of cells. Click the Undo button 🔲 on the Standard toolbar, and then repeat Steps 1 and 2.

3. Click the selection bar next to row 1 to select the heading row.

4. Click the **Center** button 🔲 on the Formatting toolbar. The text becomes centered between the left and right cell boundaries in each cell. Click anywhere in the table to deselect the row. See Figure 3-25.

Figure 3-25 ◀
Table
with newly
aligned text

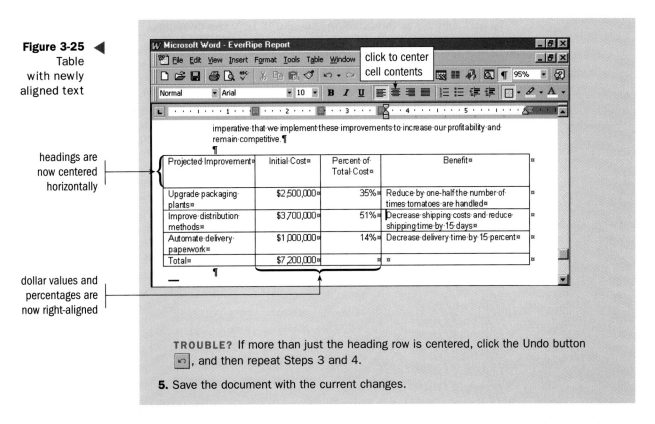

headings are
now centered
horizontally

dollar values and
percentages are
now right-aligned

TROUBLE? If more than just the heading row is centered, click the Undo button
🔄 , and then repeat Steps 3 and 4.

5. Save the document with the current changes.

The tables look better with the headings centered and the numbers right-aligned. Now you'll vertically align the text in the heading row so that it is centered between the top and bottom lines.

To align the text in the heading row vertically:

1. Click to the left of row 1 to select the heading row of the table.

2. Click the **Tables and Borders** button 🖼 on the Standard toolbar.

3. Click the **Center Vertically** button 🔲 on the Tables and Borders toolbar. The text becomes vertically centered in the row.

4. Close the Tables and Borders toolbar, and then click anywhere in the document to deselect the row.

5. Click the **Normal View** button 📄 .

You'll finish formatting the table by adding shading to the cells containing the headings.

Adding Shading

With the Borders and Shading dialog box, adding **shading** (a gray or colored background) to any text in a document is a simple task. Shading is especially useful in tables when you want to emphasize headings, totals, or other important items. In most cases, when you add shading to a table, you'll also need to bold the shaded text to make it easier to read.

You'll add a light gray shading to the heading row. You'll also bold the headings. As with most formatting tasks, you'll begin by selecting the row you want to format, and then you'll open the Borders and Shading dialog box, which is a good way to make several formatting changes at once.

To add shading to the heading row and to bold the headings:

1. Click to the left of row 1 to select the heading row of the table.

2. Click **Format** on the menu bar, and then click **Borders and Shading**. The Borders and Shading dialog box opens.

3. Click the **Shading** tab to display a list of shading options. The Fill section displays the available colors and shades of gray that you can use to shade the heading row.

4. Click the **top right square**. The label Gray-12.5% appears to the right of the color selections, and the Preview section on the right shows a sample. See Figure 3-26.

Figure 3-26 ◀
Shading tab

click this 12.5% gray

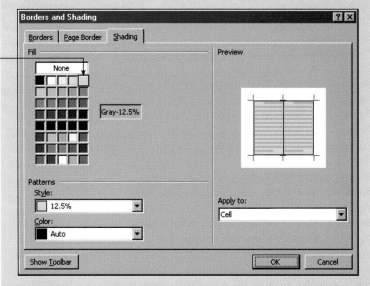

5. Click the **OK** button. A light gray background appears in the heading row. Now you need to bold the text to make the headings stand out from the shading.

6. Click the **Bold** button **B** on the Formatting toolbar to bold the headings.

   TROUBLE? If any of the headings break incorrectly (for example, if the "t" in "Cost" moves to its own line), you might need to widen columns to accommodate the bolded letters. Drag the column borders as necessary to adjust the column widths so that all the column headings are displayed correctly.

7. Click in the selection bar next to the last row to select the Total row.

8. Click the **Bold** button on the formatting toolbar to bold the total.

9. Click anywhere outside the total row to deselect it and then save your changes. Your completed table should look like Figure 3-27.

Figure 3-27
Bolded
headings
with shading

newly formatted
heading row

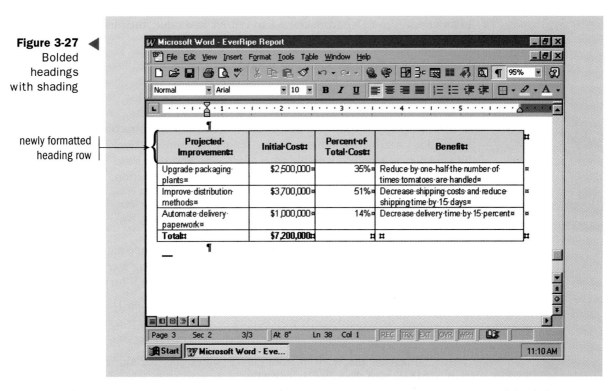

Now that you're finished with the EverRipe table, you print a copy of the full report to give to Brittany. You'll preview the report first to make sure the table fits on the third page.

To preview the table:

1. Click the **Print Preview** button on the Standard toolbar to open the Print Preview window.

2. Make sure the Magnifier button is selected and then click the table. The table looks fine, so you decide to print the report.

3. Click the **Print** button on the Print Preview toolbar to print the report; then close the document and exit Word.

You now have a hard copy of the EverRipe report including the table, which summarizes the report text. Brittany is pleased with your work.

Quick Check

1. Explain how to insert a blank table structure into a document.

2. How do you adjust the width of the columns in a table?

3. Why would you usually right-align numbers in a table?
   a. to quickly see the place value of the numbers
   b. to make the table look more attractive
   c. to make the table easier to understand
   d. all of the above

4. Define the following terms in your own words:
   a. table
   b. cell
   c. shading

5. List two ways to move from cell A1 to cell A2 in a table, then list two ways to move from cell B7 to cell B6.

6. Explain how to total a column of numbers in a table.

7. Explain how to insert a new row into a table.

In this tutorial, you have planned and formatted Brittany's recommendation report, and have added a table to summarize the report recommendations. As a result, the report information is readily available to readers who want to skim for the most important points, as well as to those who want more detailed information.

Tutorial Assignments

AgriTechnology adopted the recommendations the task force made in the EverRipe report. It is now two years later and the task force is issuing a report on the progress of the new packaging, distribution, and delivery policies. You'll format this report now.

1. If necessary, start Word and make sure your Student Disk is in the appropriate disk drive, and check your screen to make sure your settings match those in the tutorial. Display nonprinting characters as necessary

2. Open the file StatRep from the TAssign folder for Tutorial 3 on your Student Disk, and then save it as AgTech Status Report.

3. Divide the document into two sections. Insert a section break after the names of the task force members, and begin the executive summary on a new page.

4. Vertically align the first section of the document using the Justified alignment option in the Page Setup dialog box, and view the results in Print Preview.

5. Move the insertion point to section 2. Click View on the menu bar, and then click Header and Footer. Use the Word online Help system to learn the functions of the buttons on the Header and Footer toolbar. Then, on the Header and Footer toolbar, click the Switch Between Header and Footer button to move to the footer area of the document. Using the same techniques you used to create a header in the tutorial, create a footer for section 2 that reads "EverRipe Status Report" at the left margin, centers the page number preceded by the word "Page," and prints in 9-point bold Arial. (*Hint:* To center the page number, use the second tab stop.)

6. Create a header for this section that aligns your name at the left margin and the date at the right margin. (*Hint:* Use the Insert Date button on the Header and Footer toolbar to insert the date.) Close the Header and Footer toolbar.

7. Attach the Professional Report template to the document using the Style Gallery command on the Format menu, and preview how the report will look with sample text.

8. AutoFormat automatically formats selected text based on the options available in the attached template. Try using AutoFormat now by selecting the text of the title page, clicking Format on the menu bar, and then clicking AutoFormat on the Format menu. In the AutoFormat dialog box, make sure the AutoFormat now option button is selected, then click the OK button. Do you like the look of the formatted page? Why or why not?

9. Select the heading and text of the executive summary, and apply the Block Quotation style.

10. Apply the Heading 1 style to the heading "Introduction."

11. Apply the Heading 2 style to the headings "Loss of Profits for the EverRipe Crop," "Efforts to Improve Profitability," "Cost of the Improvements," and "Other Factors Influencing Profitability." Notice that the Heading 2 style does not insert space above the heading, so insert a return before each one.

12. Apply the Heading 3 style to the headings "Upgraded Packaging Plants," "Improved Distribution Methods," and "Improved Delivery." Insert a paragraph return before each Heading 3.

13. Save the document.

14. Preview and print the document, and then close it.

Open the file ZonReq from the TAssign folder for Tutorial 3 on your Student Disk, save the document as Zoning Request, and then complete the following:

15. Divide the document into two sections. End the first section after the words "Chicago, Illinois"; begin the second section on a new page.

16. Vertically align the first section of the document using the Top alignment option in the Page Setup dialog box.

17. Create a header for section 2 that prints "Zoning Request" at the left margin and has a right-aligned page number preceded by the word "Page."

18. On the Header and Footer toolbar, click the Switch Between Header and Footer button to move to the footer area of the document. Using the same techniques you used to create a header in the tutorial, create a footer for section 2 that aligns your name at the left margin and the date on the right margin.

19. Attach the Contemporary Report template to the document.

20. Using the styles you think most appropriate, format section 1. Preview the title page to make sure it fits on one page, and make any necessary adjustments.

21. Apply the Heading 1 style to the headings "Expansion Plans," "Benefits to the Community," and "Request for Zoning Changes." (*Hint:* After applying the style once, use the F4 key to apply it subsequent times.)

22. Apply the Heading 2 style to the headings "Plans to Expand Our Current Packaging Plant" and "Plans to Build a Distribution Center."

23. Apply the Block Quotation style to the "Summary" heading and paragraph text.

24. Save the document; then preview and print it.

Create a table before the Summary summarizing the Zoning Request report by completing the following:

25. Use the Insert Table button on the Standard toolbar to insert a 6-by-3 table. (In other words, a table with six rows and three columns.)

26. Type the headings "Project," "Cost" and "Jobs Added" in row 1.

27. In row 2, type "Expand Packaging Plant," "$1,200,000," and "150" in the appropriate cells.

28. In row 3, type "Build Distribution Center," "$1,300,000," and "150" in the appropriate cells.

29. Skip two rows, and then in the last row type "Total".

30. Use the AutoSum button on the Tables and Borders toolbar to total the Cost and Jobs Added column. Format the Cost total without decimal points using the Formula command on the Table menu.

31. Use the same techniques you learned for inserting rows to delete the blank row 4. Begin by selecting the row, and then right-clicking to open the Table shortcut menu. Then click Delete Rows. Repeat these steps to delete the remaining blank row.

32. Drag the right border of column B to the left until the border reaches 3 inches on the ruler. Drag the right border of column C (the Jobs Added column) to the left until the border reaches 4.25 inches on the ruler. Continue adjusting columns as necessary until the columns appear correctly formatted.

33. Right-align the numbers in the table and center the headings.

34. Format the heading row by adding a light gray shading and by bolding the headings as well. This time use the Tables and Borders toolbar. Click the Tables and Borders button to display the toolbar. Click the Shading Color arrow, and then click the light gray color of your choice.

35. Increase the height of the heading row, and then center the headings vertically in the row.

36. Center the table on the page by selecting all the table rows, and clicking the center button on the Formatting toolbar.

37. Preview, print and close the document.

Word will automatically convert text separated by commas, paragraph marks or tabs into a table. To try this feature now, open the file Members from the TAssign folder for Tutorial 3 on your Student Disk, and save it as Task Force Members. Then complete the following:

38. Select the list of task force members (including the heading), click Table on the menu bar, and then click Convert Text to Table. In the Convert Text to Table dialog box, make sure the settings indicate that the table should have 2 columns and that the text is currently separated by commas. Then click the OK button. Word automatically converts the list of task force members into a table.

39. Format the table appropriately, using the techniques you learned in the tutorial.

40. Save the document, and then preview and print it.

Case Problems

1. Ocean Breeze Bookstore Annual Report As manager of Ocean Breeze Bookstore in San Diego, California, Reed L. Paige must submit an annual report to the Board of Directors.

1. If necessary, start Word, make sure your Student Disk is in the appropriate drive, and check your screen to make sure your settings match those in the tutorials.

2. Open the file OceanRep from the Cases folder for Tutorial 3 on your Student Disk, and save it as Ocean Breeze Report. Then complete the following:

3. Divide the document into two sections. End the first section after the phrase "Ocean Breeze Bookstore"; begin section 2 on a new page.

4. Move the insertion point to section 2. Create a header for the entire document that aligns "Ocean Breeze Annual Report" on the left margin and the date on the right margin. To make the header appear in both sections, select the Same as Previous button on the Header and Footer toolbar.

5. Attach the Elegant Report template to the document.

6. Apply the Part Label style to the title page text, and then vertically align the first section of the document using the Center alignment option in the Page Setup dialog box.

7. Select the heading and text of the summary and apply the Block Quotation style.

8. Apply the Heading 2 style to the headings "Introduction," "Mission Statement," "Company Philosophy," and "Organization." (*Hint:* Use the F4 key to apply the style the second and subsequent times.)

9. Apply the Heading 1 style to the headings "Children's Story Hour," "Summer Reading Contest," and "Home Delivery."

10. Apply the Heading 3 style to the headings "Board of Directors," "Store Management and Personnel," and "Autograph Signings."

11. Preview and save the document.

12. Scroll to the end of the document and insert one blank line. Then insert a 2-column by 8-row table listing first the members of the board of directors and then the managers. Use the headings "Name" and "Title." You'll find the names and titles listed in the report.

13. Adjust the table column widths as necessary.

14. Increase the height of the heading row, center the column headings horizontally and vertically, and then bold them.

15. Insert a row and add your name to the list of board of directors members.

16. Format the heading row with a light gray shading.

17. Save, preview, print, and close the document.

2. Ultimate Travel's "Europe on a Budget" Report As director of Ultimate Travel's "Europe on a Budget" tour, Bronwyn Bates is required to write a report summarizing this year's tour.

1. If necessary, start Word, make sure your Student Disk is in the appropriate drive, and check your screen to make sure your settings match those in the tutorials.

2. Open the file Europe from the Cases folder for Tutorial 3 on your Student Disk, and save it as Europe Tour Report.

3. Divide the document into two sections. End the first section with the phrase "Tour Director"; begin the second section on a new page.

4. Vertically align the first section using the Center alignment option in the Page Setup dialog box.

5. Create a header for section 2 that contains the text "Ultimate Travel," centered. (*Hint:* To center text in the header, use the second tab stop.)

6. On the Header and Footer toolbar, click the Switch Between Header and Footer button to move to the footer area of the document. Using the same techniques you used to create a header in the tutorial, create a footer for section 2 that aligns "Evaluation Report" on the left margin and the date on the right margin.

7. Attach the Professional Report template to the document.

8. Apply the Heading 1 style to all the headings.

9. In the table, adjust column widths as necessary.

10. Bold the text in column A (the left-hand column) and then center it horizontally.

11. Use the same techniques you learned for inserting rows to delete the blank row 2: select the row, right-click to open the Table shortcut menu, and then click Delete Rows.

12. Format column A (the left-hand column) with a light gray shading.

13. Save, preview, print, and close the document.

3. Advisory Letter on a Tuition Increase Your school wants to raise tuition beginning next term. As head of the Student Advisory Board, you must submit a letter to the school's president about the increase.

1. If necessary, start Word, make sure your Student Disk is in the appropriate drive, and check your screen to make sure your settings match those in the tutorials.

2. Write a one-page letter explaining the following issues: what the current tuition or fees are at your school, what the new current tuition and fees will be, and three reasons why the school should wait for another year to increase tuition. Include a return address, inside address, date, salutation, and closing.

3. Save your document as Tuition Letter in the Cases folder for Tutorial 3 on your Student Disk.

4. Correct spelling and punctuation as necessary.

5. Attach the Professional Letter template.

6. AutoFormat automatically formats selected text based on the options available in the attached template. Try using AutoFormat now by clicking Format on the menu bar, and then clicking AutoFormat. In the AutoFormat dialog box, click the AutoFormat and review each change option button, and then click the OK button. Do you like the look of the formatted letter? Why or why not? Accept the AutoFormat changes, or reject them and choose another format.

7. What are the font and paragraph attributes for the inside address and closing for the Professional Letter template? Apply new styles as necessary.

8. Print your letter.

9. Attach the Contemporary Letter template.

10. Use the Style list on the Formatting toolbar to apply new styles to each part of your letter.

11. Print your letter with the Contemporary Letter template styles.

12. Attach the Elegant Letter template.

13. What are the font and paragraph attributes for the date and body text for the Elegant Letter template?

14. Use either the Style list box or AutoFormat to apply new styles to each part of your letter.

15. Print your letter with the Elegant Letter template styles.

16. Save the current version of your letter using the filename Tuition Letter 2, and then close the document.

4. Monthly Menu Deciding what to cook each night can be difficult when it's dinnertime and you're hungry. To avoid making spaghetti every night next month, you'll plan next month's dinner menu now.

1. If necessary, start Word, make sure your Student Disk is in the appropriate drive, and check your screen to make sure your settings match those in the tutorials.

2. Open a new document and create a table (7 rows by 7 columns).

3. In row 2 of the table, type the days of the week in 12-point font of your choice.

4. Adjust the right column borders so that the name of each day of the week is on one line.

5. Bold the days of the week headings and center them horizontally in the cells. Add a light gray shading. Adjust column widths as necessary.

6. Type the number of each day of the month in a cell, and press the Enter key to place the number on its own line; then press the Tab key to move to the next cell. For example, if September 1 is a Tuesday, type "1" in cell C3, press the Enter key, and then press the Tab key. Repeat for the remaining days of the month.

7. Type the name of a main dish in the second line of each cell of the table for the first two weeks of the month.

8. Use a variation of drag and drop to copy each menu item from the first two weeks into the cells of the second two weeks. Highlight the first menu item (not including the date), and then press and hold down the Ctrl key and drag the menu item to the first day of the third week.

9. Fill in the remaining cells by copying menu items for the rest of the month.

10. Save the menu document as Monthly Menu in the Cases folder for Tutorial 3 on your Student Disk.

11. Preview and print the document. Then close the document.

Desktop Publishing a Newsletter

Creating a Newsletter for FastFad Manufacturing Company

OBJECTIVES

In this tutorial you will:

- Identify desktop publishing features

- Create a title with WordArt

- Create newspaper-style columns

- Insert clip art

- Wrap text around a graphic

- Incorporate drop caps

- Use typographic characters

- Add a page border and shaded background

CASE

FastFad Manufacturing Company

Gerrit Polansky works for FastFad Manufacturing Company, which designs and manufactures plastic figures (action figures, vehicles, and other toys) for promotional sales and giveaways in the fast-food and cereal industries. It is Gerrit's job to keep FastFad's sales staff informed about new products. He does this by producing and distributing a monthly newsletter that contains brief descriptions of these new items and ideas for marketing them. Recently, FastFad added MiniMovers, which are small plastic cars, trucks, and other vehicles, to its line of plastic toys. Gerrit needs to get the information about these products to the sales staff quickly—so the company can market the toys to FastFad's clients while the toys are still the fad. He has asked you to help him create the newsletter.

The newsletter needs to be eye-catching because the sales reps get a lot of printed product material and it's sometimes difficult for them to focus on any one product. Gerrit also wants you to create a newsletter that is neat, organized, and professional-looking. He wants it to contain headings so the sales reps can scan it quickly for the major points, as well as graphics that will give the newsletter a distinctive "look" that the reps will remember. He wants you to include a picture that will reinforce the newsletter content and help the reps remember the product. All of these tasks are easy in Word, especially with the Microsoft Clip Gallery, which lets you choose from a large collection of predesigned images that you can insert in your documents.

In this tutorial, you'll plan the layout of the newsletter, keeping in mind the audience (the sales representatives). Then you'll get acquainted with the desktop publishing features and elements you'll need to use to create the newsletter you want, and you'll learn how desktop publishing differs from other word processing tasks. You'll format the title using an eye-catching design and divide the document into newspaper-like columns to make it easier for the sales reps to read. You'll include a piece of predesigned art that adds interest and focus to the text. You'll then fine-tune the newsletter layout, give it a more professional appearance with typographic characters, and put a border around the page and a shaded background behind the text to give the newsletter a finished look.

In this session, you will see how Gerrit planned his newsletter, and learn about desktop publishing features and elements. Then you will create the newsletter title using WordArt, modify the title's appearance, and then format the text of the newsletter into newspaper-style columns.

Planning the Document

The newsletter will provide a brief overview of the new FastFad products, followed by a short explanation of what the MiniMovers are and why children will like them. Like most newsletters, it will be written in an informal style that conveys information quickly. The newsletter title will be eye-catching and will help readers quickly identify the document. The newsletter text will be split into two columns to make it easier to read, and headings will help readers scan the information quickly. A picture will add interest and illustrate the newsletter content. Drop caps and other desktop publishing elements will help draw readers' attention to certain information, make the newsletter design attractive, and give it a professional appearance.

Features of Desktop Publishing

Desktop publishing is the production of commercial-quality printed material using a desktop computer system from which you can enter and edit text, create graphics, compose or lay out pages, and print documents. The following features are commonly associated with desktop publishing:

- **High-quality printing.** A laser printer or high-resolution inkjet printer produces high-quality final output.

- **Multiple fonts.** Two or three font types and sizes provide visual interest, guide the reader through the text, and convey the tone of the document.

- **Graphics.** Graphics, such as horizontal or vertical lines (called **rules**), boxes, electronic art, and digitized photographs help illustrate a concept or product, draw a reader's attention to the document, and make the text visually appealing.

- **Typographic characters.** Typographic characters such as typographic long dashes, called **em dashes** (—), in place of double hyphens (--) separate dependent clauses; typographic medium-width dashes, called **en dashes** (–), are used in place of hyphens (-) as minus signs and in ranges of numbers; and typographic bullets (•) signal items in a list to make the text professional-looking.

- **Columns and other formatting features.** Columns of text, **pull quotes** (small portions of text pulled out of the main text and enlarged), shaded areas and other special formatting features that you don't frequently see in letters and other documents distinguish desktop-published documents.

You'll incorporate many of these desktop publishing features into the FastFad newsletter for Gerrit.

Elements of a Desktop-Published Newsletter

Successful desktop publishing requires that you first know what elements professionals use to desktop publish a document. Figure 4-1 defines the desktop publishing elements that you have not yet used in the preceding tutorials. Gerrit wants you to incorporate these elements to produce the final copy of the newsletter shown in Figure 4-2. The newsletter includes some of the typical desktop publishing elements that you can add to a document using Word.

Figure 4-1 ◀
Desktop
publishing
elements

Element	Description
Columns	Two or more vertical blocks of text that fit on one page
WordArt	Text modified with special effects, such as rotated, curved, bent, shadowed, or shaded letters
Clip art	Prepared graphic images that are ready to be inserted into a document
Drop cap	Oversized first letter of word beginning a paragraph that extends vertically into two or more lines of the paragraph
Typographical symbols	Special characters that are not part of the standard keyboard, such as em dashes (—), copyright symbols (©), or curly quotation marks (")

Figure 4-2 ◀
FastFad
newsletter

title created in
WordArt

different font types,
sizes, and styles

typographic symbol

clip art graphic

drop cap

border

two columns

bullets

em dash

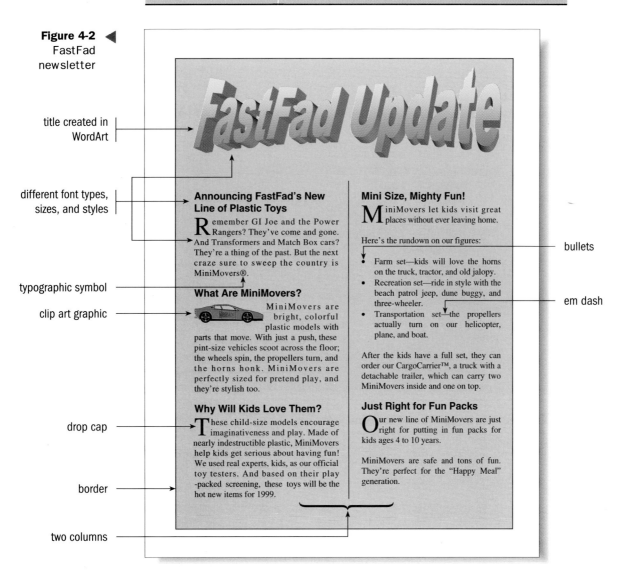

Announcing FastFad's New Line of Plastic Toys

Remember GI Joe and the Power Rangers? They've come and gone. And Transformers and Match Box cars? They're a thing of the past. But the next craze sure to sweep the country is MiniMovers®.

What Are MiniMovers?

MiniMovers are bright, colorful plastic models with parts that move. With just a push, these pint-size vehicles scoot across the floor; the wheels spin, the propellers turn, and the horns honk. MiniMovers are perfectly sized for pretend play, and they're stylish too.

Why Will Kids Love Them?

These child-size models encourage imaginativeness and play. Made of nearly indestructible plastic, MiniMovers help kids get serious about having fun! We used real experts, kids, as our official toy testers. And based on their play-packed screening, these toys will be the hot new items for 1999.

Mini Size, Mighty Fun!

MiniMovers let kids visit great places without ever leaving home.

Here's the rundown on our figures:

- Farm set—kids will love the horns on the truck, tractor, and old jalopy.
- Recreation set—ride in style with the beach patrol jeep, dune buggy, and three-wheeler.
- Transportation set—the propellers actually turn on our helicopter, plane, and boat.

After the kids have a full set, they can order our CargoCarrier™, a truck with a detachable trailer, which can carry two MiniMovers inside and one on top.

Just Right for Fun Packs

Our new line of MiniMovers are just right for putting in fun packs for kids ages 4 to 10 years.

MiniMovers are safe and tons of fun. They're perfect for the "Happy Meal" generation.

Your first step is to create the newsletter's title.

Using WordArt to Create the Newsletter Title

Gerrit wants the title of the newsletter, "FastFad Update," to be eye-catching and dramatic, as shown in Figure 4-2. The Microsoft Office WordArt feature, available from Word as well as from other Microsoft Office 97 programs, provides great flexibility in designing text with special effects that expresses the image or mood you want to convey in your printed documents. With WordArt you can apply color and shading, as well as alter the shape and size of the text. You can easily "wrap" the document text around WordArt shapes.

You begin creating a WordArt image by choosing a text design from the WordArt Gallery. Then you type in the text you want to enhance, and format it.

When you create a WordArt image, Word automatically switches to page layout view. When the document is in normal view, WordArt images are not visible. Page layout view is the most appropriate view to use when you are desktop publishing with Word, because it shows you exactly how the text and graphics fit on the page, and the vertical ruler that appears in page layout view helps you to position graphical elements more precisely.

CREATING SPECIAL TEXT EFFECTS USING WORDART

- Click the Drawing button on the Standard toolbar to display the Drawing toolbar.
- Click the Insert WordArt button on the Drawing toolbar.
- Click the style of text you want to insert, and then click the OK button.
- Type the text you want in the Edit WordArt Text dialog box.
- Click the Font and Size list arrows to select the font and font size you want.
- If you want, click the Bold or Italic button, or both.
- Click the OK button.
- With the WordArt selected, drag any handle to reshape and resize it. To keep the text in the same proportions as the original, press and hold down the Shift key while you drag a handle.

To begin, you'll open the file that contains Gerrit's text, often called **copy**, and then you'll use WordArt to create the newsletter title. Gerrit wants the title formatted in the Arial font, since the headings in the rest of the document are in Arial.

To create the title of the newsletter using WordArt:

1. Start Word, and insert your Student Disk in the appropriate drive. Make sure your screen matches the figures in this tutorial, and make sure you display the nonprinting characters so you can see more accurately where to insert text and graphics.

2. Open the file **MiniInfo** from the **Tutorial.04** folder on your Student Disk, and then save it as **FastFad Newsletter**.

3. With the insertion point at the beginning of the document, press the **Enter** key to insert a new, blank line, and press the ↑ key to return the insertion point to the new, blank line. Then apply the **Normal** style using the Style list on the Formatting toolbar.

4. With the insertion point at the beginning of the document, click the **Drawing** button 🖼 on the Standard toolbar to display the Drawing toolbar, which appears at the bottom of the screen.

5. Click the **Insert WordArt** button 🖼 on the Drawing toolbar. The WordArt Gallery dialog box opens, displaying the 30 WordArt styles available.

6. Click the **WordArt style** in the bottom row, the fourth column from the left, as shown in Figure 4-3.

Figure 4-3 ◀
WordArt
Gallery styles

click this style —

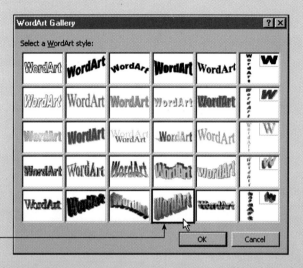

7. Click the **OK** button. The Edit WordArt Text dialog box opens, displaying "Your Text Here," the default text, which you will replace with Gerrit's newsletter title.

8. Type **FastFad Update**. Make sure you make "FastFad" one word, no space.

9. Click the **OK** button.

   The WordArt image appears as the newsletter title at the top of the newsletter, the WordArt toolbar appears on the screen, and the document changes to page layout view. Don't worry that the image partially covers the newsletter text or if it's below the first paragraph. You'll fix that later.

The WordArt image you have created is considered a Word **drawing object**. This means that you can modify its appearance (color, shape, size, alignment, etc.) using the buttons on the Drawing toolbar or the WordArt toolbar. Although the object looks like text, Word does not treat it like text. The object will not appear in normal view, and Word will not spell check it, as it does regular text. Think of it as a piece of art rather than as text.

The WordArt object is selected, indicated by the eight small squares called **resize handles** surrounding it, and the small yellow diamond called an **adjustment handle**. The resize and adjustment handles let you change the size and shape of the selected object. Before you change the size of the object, you'll first change its font size and formatting. The default font for this WordArt style is Impact, but Gerrit wants you to change it to match the font of the newsletter headings.

To change the font and formatting of the WordArt object:

1. Double-click the **WordArt object**. The Edit WordArt Text dialog box opens.

2. Click the Font list arrow, scroll to and then click **Arial Black**. The text in the preview box changes to Arial Black. Black indicates a thicker version of the Arial font, not its color. Now change the font size and style.

   TROUBLE? If you do not have Arial Black on your font menu, choose Arial or another sans serif font.

> **3.** Click the **Size** list arrow, scroll to and then click **40**, and then click the **Italic** button [*I*]. The text in the preview box enlarges to 40 points italic.
>
> **4.** Click the **OK** button. The newsletter title changes to 40-point, italic Arial Black.

The default shape of the WordArt style you selected is an upward slanting shape called Cascade Up. Gerrit wants something a little more symmetrical. In WordArt, you can easily change the shape of any object to any of the 40 shapes that Word supplies.

To change the shape of the WordArt object:

> **1.** Click the **WordArt Shape** button [Abc] on the WordArt toolbar. The palette of shapes appears, with the Cascade Up shape selected.
>
> **2.** Click the **Deflate** shape (fourth row, second column from the left), as shown in Figure 4-4.

Figure 4-4 ◀
WordArt
shapes

Deflate shape ————

WordArt toolbar ————

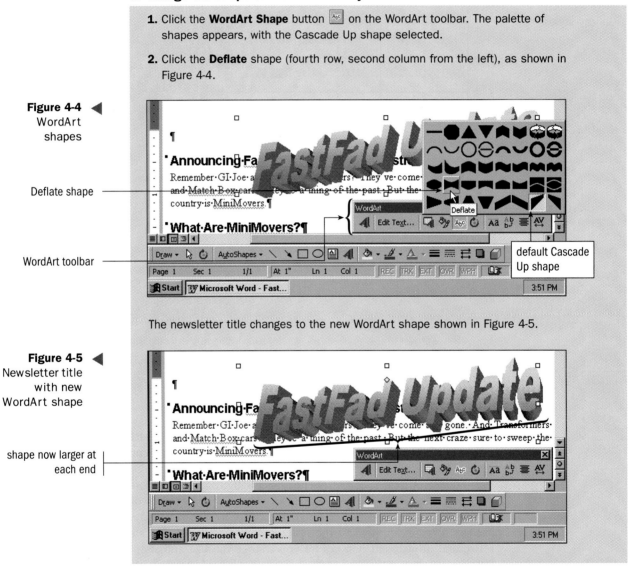

The newsletter title changes to the new WordArt shape shown in Figure 4-5.

Figure 4-5 ◀
Newsletter title
with new
WordArt shape

shape now larger at
each end

Editing a WordArt Object

Now that the newsletter title is the font and shape you want, you'll move the title above the text and insert space between the WordArt object and the newsletter text. You'll do this using the text wrapping feature in the Format WordArt dialog box. This dialog box gives you the option of changing many WordArt features at once. For now, however, you'll just use it to separate the object from the text.

To insert space between the WordArt object and the newsletter text:

1. With the WordArt object selected, click the **Format WordArt** button [icon] on the WordArt toolbar to open the Format WordArt dialog box.

2. Click the **Wrapping** tab.

3. In the Wrapping style section, click the **Top & bottom** icon. See Figure 4-6.

Figure 4-6
Settings to separate WordArt object from text

Wrapping tab

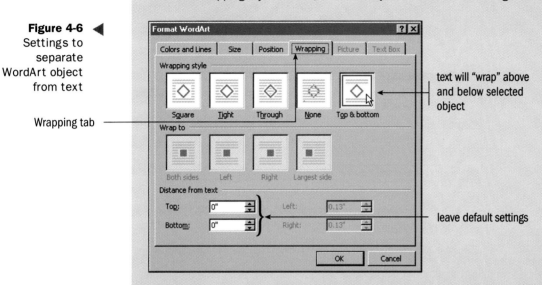

text will "wrap" above and below selected object

leave default settings

You could use the settings at the bottom of the dialog box to insert space between the object and the text, but the title object has enough space around it, so you don't need to change these settings now.

4. Click the **OK** button. The newsletter title is now above the text.

TROUBLE? If the title is not above the text, drag it there now.

Now you only need to position the title and widen it proportionally so it fits neatly within the newsletter margins. The position of the WordArt object in the text is indicated by a small anchor symbol in the left margin. You can widen any WordArt object by dragging its resize handle. To keep the object the same proportion as the original, you hold down the Shift key as you drag the resize handle, which will prevent "stretching" the object more in one direction than the other. Then you'll rotate it a little so it looks more balanced.

To position, enlarge, and rotate the WordArt object:

1. Drag the WordArt object to the left until the lower-left corner of the first "F" in the word "FastFad" is aligned with the left margin and then release the mouse button. Since you can only see the text outline (not the text itself) as you drag the object, you might need to repeat the procedure. Use the left edge of the text or the left margin in the ruler as a guide.

2. With the WordArt object still selected, position the pointer over its lower-right resize handle. The pointer changes to ↘.

3. Press and hold the **Shift** key and drag the resize handle to the right margin, using the horizontal ruler as a guide. See Figure 4-7. As you drag the handle, the pointer changes to +. If necessary, repeat the procedure to make the rightmost edge of the "e" in the word "Update" line up with the right margin. Now you'll lower the right side of the WordArt object.

Figure 4-7 ◀
Resizing the
WordArt object

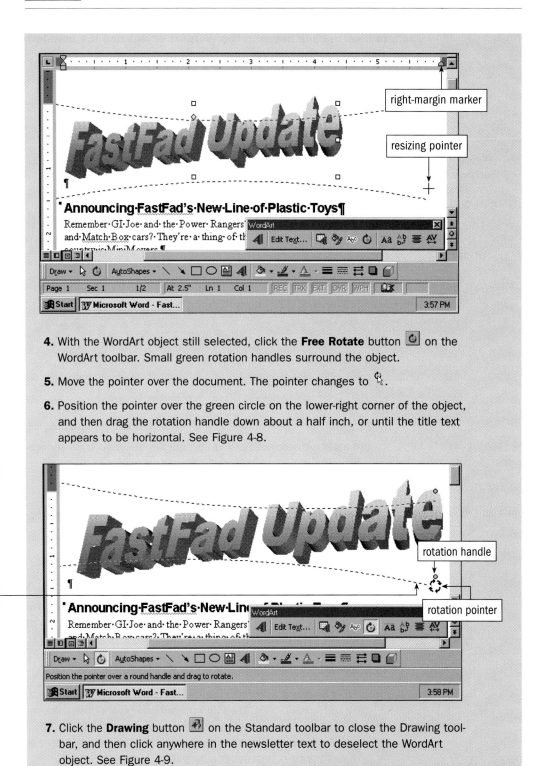

4. With the WordArt object still selected, click the **Free Rotate** button on the WordArt toolbar. Small green rotation handles surround the object.

5. Move the pointer over the document. The pointer changes to .

6. Position the pointer over the green circle on the lower-right corner of the object, and then drag the rotation handle down about a half inch, or until the title text appears to be horizontal. See Figure 4-8.

Figure 4-8 ◀
Rotating the
WordArt Object

lower the right side of
the image

7. Click the **Drawing** button on the Standard toolbar to close the Drawing toolbar, and then click anywhere in the newsletter text to deselect the WordArt object. See Figure 4-9.

Figure 4-9
Newsletter
after enlarging
and rotating
the WordArt
object

title aligned between
left and right margins

You have inserted and formatted a WordArt object that will draw the attention of the sales reps to the newsletter as they review this document among all the other product literature they have to read.

Formatting Text into Newspaper-Style Columns

Because newsletters are meant for quick reading, they usually are laid out in newspaper-style columns. In **newspaper-style columns**, a page is divided into two or more vertical blocks or columns. Text flows down one column, continues at the top of the next column, flows down that column, and so forth. Newspaper-style columns are easier to read because the columns tend to be narrow and the type size a bit smaller than the text in a letter. This enables the eye to see more text in one glance than when text is set in longer line lengths and in a larger font size.

If you want some of your text to be in columns and other text to be in full line lengths, you must insert section breaks into your document and apply the column format only to those sections you want in columns. In this case, Gerrit wants only the text below the title to be divided into two columns. You could select this text and use the Columns button on the Standard toolbar to automatically insert a section break and divide the text into columns, but Gerrit also wants you to add a vertical line between the columns. So you'll use the Columns command on the Format menu, which lets you both divide the text into columns with a line between them and insert a section break in the location you specify. Without the section break, the line between the columns would extend up through the title.

FORMATTING TEXT INTO NEWSPAPER-STYLE COLUMNS

REFERENCE window

- Select the text you want to divide into columns, or don't select any text if you want the entire document divided into columns.
- Click the Columns button on the Standard toolbar, and highlight the number of columns you want to divide the text into. or
- Move the insertion point to the location where you want the columns to begin.
- Click Format on the menu bar, and then click Columns to open the Columns dialog box.
- Select the column style in the Presets section, and type the number of columns you want in the Number of columns text box.
- If necessary, click the Equal column width check box to deselect it, and then set the width of each column in the Width and spacing section.
- Click the Apply to list arrow, and select the This point forward or Whole document option.
- If you want a vertical rule between the columns, click the Line between check box and click the OK button.

To apply newspaper-style columns to the body of the newsletter:

1. Position the insertion point to the left of the word "Announcing" just below the title.

2. Click **Format** on the menu bar, and then click **Columns**. The Columns dialog box opens.

3. In the Presets section, click the **Two** icon.

4. If necessary, click the **Line between** check box to select it. The text in the Preview box changes to a two-column format with a vertical rule between the columns.

   You want these changes to affect only the text after the title, so you'll need to insert a section break and apply the column formatting to the text after the insertion point.

5. Click the **Apply to** list arrow, and then click **This point forward** to have Word automatically insert a section break at the insertion point. See Figure 4-10.

Figure 4-10 ◀
Completed columns dialog box

creates two columns of the same width

adds section break at insertion point location

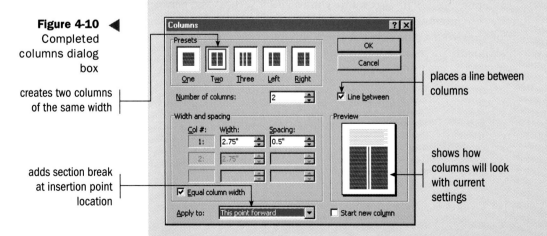

places a line between columns

shows how columns will look with current settings

6. Click the **OK** button to close the dialog box and return to the document window. A section break appears, and the insertion point is now positioned in section 2.

> **TROUBLE?** You might need to move the WordArt object so it is above the section break. If necessary, drag the WordArt object above the section break. The section break moves down and the two-column text begins just after it. If necessary, drag the WordArt object again to adjust its position. When an object is selected, you can also use the arrow keys on the keyboard to adjust its position.
>
> **7.** Click anywhere in the newsletter text to deselect the WordArt object.

Viewing the Whole Page

As you lay out a document for desktop publishing, you should periodically look at the whole page, so you can see how the layout looks. The best way to do this is in page layout view using Zoom Control.

To zoom out and view the whole page:

1. Click the **Zoom Control** list arrow [100% ▼] on the Standard toolbar, and then click **Whole Page**. Word displays the entire page of the newsletter so you can see how the two-column format looks on the page. See Figure 4-11.

Figure 4-11 ◀
Page layout view showing the two columns

section break between title and copy

line between columns

text arranged in two columns

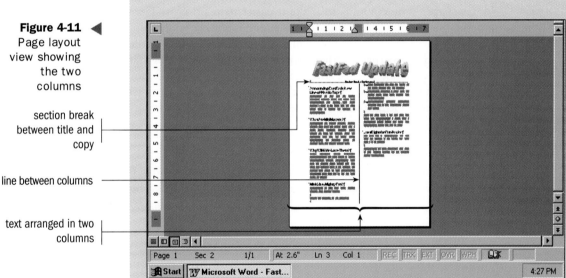

> **TROUBLE?** Your columns may break at a slightly different line than those shown in the figure. This is not a problem; just continue with the tutorial.

The newsletter title, now with a horizontal orientation, is centered on the page and the copy is in a two-column format. The text fills the left column but not the right column, and the top of the right column is higher than the left. You'll fix this later, after you add a graphic and format some of the text.

2. Click the **Zoom Control** list arrow again, and then click **100%**. Word returns to the full-size page layout view.

3. Save the document.

Quick Check

1 In your own words, explain three features commonly associated with desktop publishing.

2. In your own words, define the following terms:
   a. WordArt
   b. resize handle
   c. newspaper-style columns

3. List the steps for creating a WordArt object in a Word document.

4. How do you change the size of a WordArt object after you have inserted it into a Word document?

5. What is the purpose of the WordArt Shape button on the WordArt toolbar?

6. True or False: Normal view shows how text will fit into newspaper-style columns.

7. To format text into newspaper-like columns, you use the _____ command on the _____ menu.

8. If you want one part of your document to be in two columns and another part to be in full width, you must insert a _____ between the two sections.

9. True or False: Formatting a document into newspaper-like columns will automatically make the columns of equal length.

You have set up an eye-catching title for Gerrit's FastFad newsletter and formatted the text in newspaper style columns to make it easier to read. Now Gerrit wants you to insert a graphic that is appropriate to the newsletter content, possibly some type of car to represent the MiniMover product. As you will see, the Microsoft Clip Gallery, available from Word as well as other Microsoft Office programs, contains graphics that you can use with many different types of documents. After you add clip art, you'll add more graphic interest by formatting some of the text. Then you'll give the newsletter a finished look by making the columns equal in length, and give the page some depth by adding a shaded background.

SESSION

4.2

In this session you will insert, resize, and crop clip art, and change the way the text wraps around the clip art. Then you'll create drop caps, insert typographic symbols, balance columns, place a border around the newsletter, add a shaded background, and print the newsletter.

Inserting Clip Art

Graphics, which can include artwork, photographs, charts, tables, designs, or even designed text like WordArt, add variety to documents and are especially appropriate for newsletters. Word enables you to include many types of graphics in your documents. You can create a graphic in another Windows program and insert it into your document using the Picture command on the Insert menu. You can also insert a picture, as well as sounds and videos, from the Microsoft Clip Gallery, a collection of **clip art** images, or existing artwork that you can insert into documents, which is part of Microsoft Office 97. You will insert an existing piece of clip art into the newsletter. Gerrit wants you to use a graphic that reflects the newsletter content.

REFERENCE window

INSERTING CLIP ART

- Move the insertion point to the location in your document where you want the graphic image to appear.
- Click Insert on the menu bar, point to Picture, and then click Clip Art to open the Microsoft Clip Gallery 3.0 dialog box.
- Click the Clip Art tab.
- Click the category that best represents the type of art you need.
- Click the image you want to use.
- Click the Insert button.

To insert the clip art image of a car into the newsletter:

1. If you took a break after the last session, make sure Word is running, the FastFad Newsletter is open, the document is in page layout view, and the non-printing characters are displayed.

2. Position the insertion point to the left of the word "MiniMovers" in the second paragraph of the newsletter just below the heading.

3. Click **Insert** on the menu bar, point to **Picture**, and then click **Clip Art**. The Microsoft Clip Gallery 3.0 dialog box opens.

   TROUBLE? If you see a dialog box informing you that additional clips are available on the Microsoft Office CD-ROM, click the OK button.

4. If necessary, click the **Clip Art** tab to display the clip art options, and then click the **Transportation** category.

5. Click the **red sports car image** in the upper-left corner of the preview window. See Figure 4-12.

Figure 4-12 ◄
Clip Art tab of the Microsoft Clip Gallery 3.0 dialog box

selected sports car image will be inserted

only images in the transporation category are displayed

images shown here reflect selected category

click to insert selected image into document

click here to see enlarged preview

6. Click the **Insert** button to insert the image of the red sports car in the newsletter at the insertion point, and then save the newsletter.

   The sports car clip art extends across both columns. Like the WordArt object you worked with earlier, the clip art image is a graphic object with resize handles that you can use to change its size. Word inserts an anchor symbol in the left margin, indicating the object's position relative to the text. The Picture toolbar appears whenever the clip art object is selected. See Figure 4-13.

Figure 4-13
The newsletter with the clip art object inserted

resize handles

object inserted at insertion point between heading and text

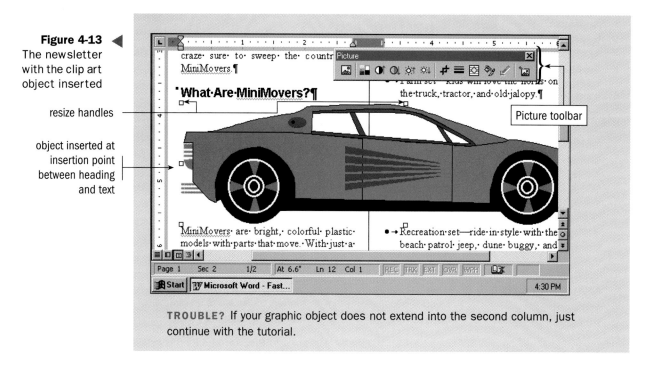

Picture toolbar

TROUBLE? If your graphic object does not extend into the second column, just continue with the tutorial.

Gerrit would like the image to be smaller so it doesn't distract attention from the text.

Resizing a Graphic

Often, you need to change the size of a graphic so that it fits into your document better. This is called **scaling** the image. You can resize a graphic by either dragging its resize handles or, for more precise control, by using the Format Picture dialog box.

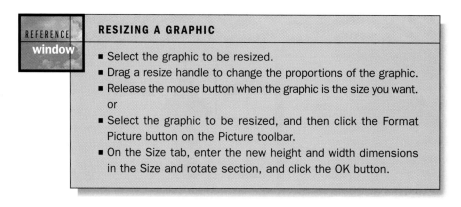

REFERENCE
window

RESIZING A GRAPHIC

- Select the graphic to be resized.
- Drag a resize handle to change the proportions of the graphic.
- Release the mouse button when the graphic is the size you want.
  or
- Select the graphic to be resized, and then click the Format Picture button on the Picture toolbar.
- On the Size tab, enter the new height and width dimensions in the Size and rotate section, and click the OK button.

For Gerrit's newsletter, the dragging technique will work fine.

To resize the clip art graphic:

1. Make sure the clip art graphic is selected, and scroll to the right so you can see the lower-right resize handle of the object.

2. Drag the lower-right resize handle up and to the left, so the front of the car extends only about halfway into the first column. You don't have to hold down the Shift key, as you do with WordArt, to resize it proportionally. See Figure 4-14.

Figure 4-14 ◄
Resizing the
sports car
graphic

anchor symbol
indicates position
relative to text

dotted line box
indicates new size

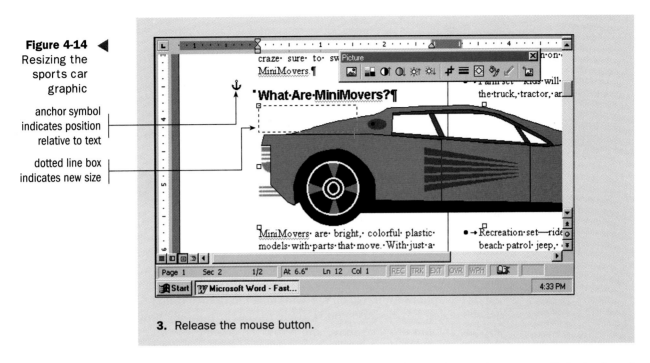

3. Release the mouse button.

Gerrit wonders if the sports car image would look better if you cut off the back end and showed only the front half.

Cropping a Graphic

You can **crop** the graphic, that is, cut off one or more of its edges, using either the Crop button on the Picture toolbar or the Format Picture dialog box. Once you crop a graphic, the part you crop off becomes hidden from view, but still remains a part of the graphic image, so you can always change your mind and restore a cropped graphic to it original form.

To crop the sports car graphic:

1. If necessary, click the clip art to select it. The resize handles appear.

2. Click the **Crop** button ⊞ on the Picture toolbar.

3. Position the pointer directly over the left-middle resize handle of the object. The pointer changes to ⍔ .

4. Press and hold down the mouse button and drag the handle to the right so that only the front door and hood are visible. and then release the mouse button. See Figure 4-15.

Figure 4-15 ◄
Cropping the
sports car
graphic

cropping tool

left half of image
hidden from view

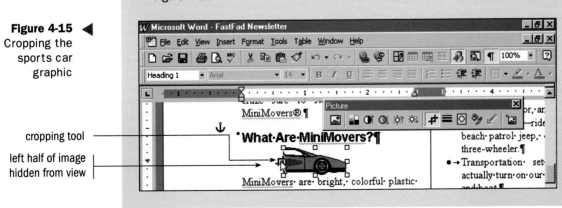

> Gerrit decides he prefers you to display the whole sports car, so he asks you to return to the original image.
>
> **5.** Click the **Undo** button 🔄 on the Standard toolbar. The cropping action is reversed, and the full image of the sports car reappears.

Now Gerrit wants you to make the text to wrap (or flow) to the right of the graphic, making the car look as if it's driving into the text.

Wrapping Text Around a Graphic

Text wrapping is often used in newsletters to add interest and to prevent excessive open areas, called **white space**, from appearing on the page. You can wrap text around objects many different ways in Word. You can have the text wrap above and below the graphic, through it, or wrap the text to follow the shape of the object, even if the graphic has an irregular shape. To wrap text you can use the Text Wrapping button on the Picture toolbar or the options available on the Wrapping tab of the Format Picture dialog box. You'll use the dialog box because you're going to change not only how the text will wrap, but also the amount of space above and below the graphic.

To wrap text around the car graphic:

1. If necessary, click the clip art to select it.

2. Click the **Format Picture** button 🖼 on the Picture toolbar. The Format Picture dialog box opens.

3. Click the **Wrapping** tab.

4. In the Wrapping style section, click the **Tight** icon, the second icon from the left.

5. In the Wrap to section, click the **Right** icon.

6. In the Distance from text section, click the **Right** up arrow once to display **.2"**. Don't worry about the Left setting, since the text will wrap only around the right side. Now you'll add space above the graphic so it is separated from the section heading.

7. Click the **Position** tab, and click the **Vertical** arrows until the text box displays **.5"**.

8. Click the **OK** button. The text wraps around the car, following its shape.

9. Click anywhere in the text to deselect the graphic, and then save the newsletter. Your screen should look similar to Figure 4-16.

Figure 4-16 ◀
Text wrapped
around graphic

graphic separated
from text above
and below

text fits around
irregular shape

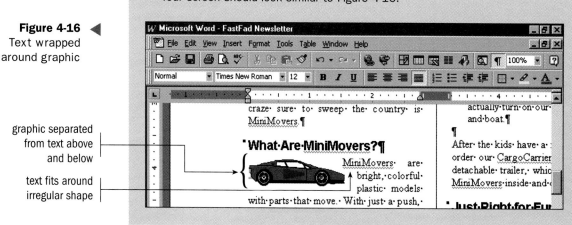

The image of the sports car draws the reader's attention to the beginning of the newsletter, but the rest of the text looks somewhat plain. Gerrit suggests adding a drop cap at the beginning of each section.

Inserting Drop Caps

A **drop cap** is a large, uppercase (capital) letter that highlights the beginning of the text of a newsletter, chapter, or some other document section. The drop cap usually extends from the top of the first line of the paragraph down two or three succeeding lines of the paragraph. The text of the paragraph wraps around the drop cap. Word allows you to create a drop cap for the first letter of the first word of a paragraph.

You will create a drop cap for the first paragraph following each heading in the newsletter (except for the first heading, where the clip art image is located). The drop cap will extend two lines into the paragraph.

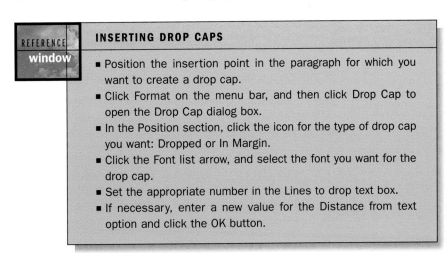

REFERENCE window

INSERTING DROP CAPS

- Position the insertion point in the paragraph for which you want to create a drop cap.
- Click Format on the menu bar, and then click Drop Cap to open the Drop Cap dialog box.
- In the Position section, click the icon for the type of drop cap you want: Dropped or In Margin.
- Click the Font list arrow, and select the font you want for the drop cap.
- Set the appropriate number in the Lines to drop text box.
- If necessary, enter a new value for the Distance from text option and click the OK button.

To insert drop caps in the newsletter:

1. Position the insertion point in the paragraph following the first heading, just to the left of the word "Remember."

2. Click **Format** on the menu bar, and then click **Drop Cap**. The Drop Cap dialog box opens.

3. In the Position section, click the **Dropped** icon.

4. Click the **Lines to drop** down arrow once to display **2**. You won't need to change the default distance from the text. See Figure 4-17.

Figure 4-17 ◀
Drop Cap
dialog box

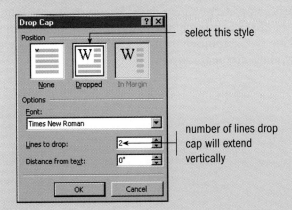

select this style

number of lines drop cap will extend vertically

5. Click the **OK** button to close the dialog box. Word automatically formats the first character of the paragraph as a drop cap. See Figure 4-18.

Figure 4-18 ◄
Drop cap
begins the
paragraph

text wraps around
drop cap

drop cap selected

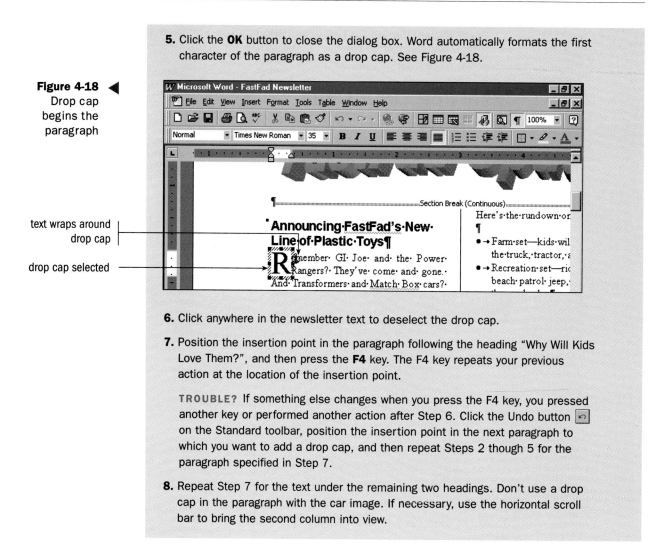

6. Click anywhere in the newsletter text to deselect the drop cap.

7. Position the insertion point in the paragraph following the heading "Why Will Kids Love Them?", and then press the **F4** key. The F4 key repeats your previous action at the location of the insertion point.

> **TROUBLE?** If something else changes when you press the F4 key, you pressed another key or performed another action after Step 6. Click the Undo button 🔄 on the Standard toolbar, position the insertion point in the next paragraph to which you want to add a drop cap, and then repeat Steps 2 though 5 for the paragraph specified in Step 7.

8. Repeat Step 7 for the text under the remaining two headings. Don't use a drop cap in the paragraph with the car image. If necessary, use the horizontal scroll bar to bring the second column into view.

The newsletter looks more lively with the drop caps. Next, you turn your attention to the issue of inserting a registered trademark symbol beside the trademark names.

Inserting Symbols and Special Characters

Gerrit used standard word-processing characters rather than **typographic characters** (special symbols and punctuation marks) when he typed the newsletter copy. For example, he typed straight quotation marks instead of curly quotation marks and he typed two dashes in place of an em dash. However, Word automatically converted some of the standard characters (such as the dashes and the quotation marks) into the more polished looking typographic characters. Figure 4-19 lists some the characters that Word converts to symbols automatically.

Figure 4-19 ◄
Common
typographical
symbols

To insert this symbol or character	Type	Word converts it to
em dash	word- -word	word—word
quotation marks	"word"	"word"
copyright symbol	(c)	©
registered trademark symbol	(r)	®
trademark symbol	(tm)	™
ordinal numbers	1st, 2nd, 3rd, etc.	1st, 2nd, 3rd, etc.
fractions	1/2, 1/4	½, ¼
arrows	--> or <--	→ or ←

To insert typographic characters into a finished document after you've finished typing it, it's easiest to use the Symbol command on the Insert menu. In order to make the newsletter look professionally formatted, you'll insert a special character now—namely, a registered trademark symbol—at the appropriate places.

FastFad protects the names of its products by registering the names as trademarks. You'll indicate that in the newsletter by inserting the registered trademark symbol (®) at the first occurrence of the trademark names "MiniMovers" and a trademark symbol (™) for the first occurrence of "CargoCarrier."

REFERENCE
window

INSERTING SYMBOLS AND SPECIAL CHARACTERS

- Move the insertion point to the location where you want to insert a particular symbol or special character.
- Click Insert on the menu bar, and then click Symbol to open the Symbol dialog box.
- Click the appropriate symbol from those shown in the symbol character set on the Symbols tab, or click the name from the list on the Special Characters tab.
- Click the Insert button.
- Click the Close button.

To insert the registered trademark symbol:

1. Position the insertion point at the end of the word "MiniMovers" in the first paragraph, just before the period.

2. Click **Insert** on the menu bar, and then click **Symbol** to open the Symbol dialog box.

3. If necessary, click the **Special Characters** tab. See Figure 4-20.

Figure 4-20 ◄
Special
Characters tab
in Symbol
dialog box

click to display
this tab

insert this symbol

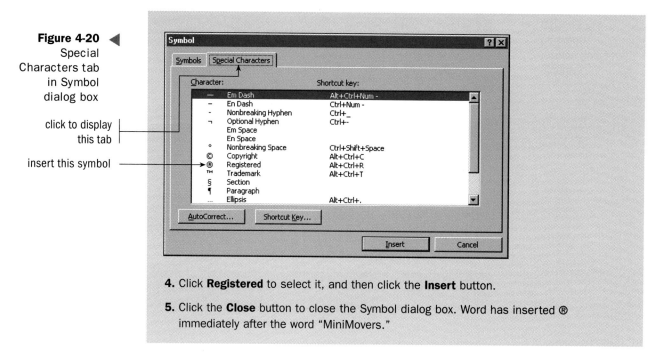

4. Click **Registered** to select it, and then click the **Insert** button.

5. Click the **Close** button to close the Symbol dialog box. Word has inserted ® immediately after the word "MiniMovers."

If you have to insert symbols repeatedly, or if you want to insert them quickly as you type, it's often easier to use the Word AutoCorrect feature to insert them. You'll use AutoCorrect now to insert the trademark symbol (™) after the first occurrence of CargoCarrier. First, you'll look in the AutoCorrect settings to make sure the correct entry is there.

To enter a symbol using AutoCorrect:

1. Click **Tools** on the menu bar, and then click **AutoCorrect**. In the Replace column on the left side of the dialog box, you see (tm), which means that any occurrence of (tm) in the document will automatically be corrected to the trademark symbol.

2. Click the **Cancel** button.

3. Position the insertion point just after the word "CargoCarrier" in the second column, in the paragraph above the heading "Just Right for Fun Packs."

4. Type **(tm)**. Word automatically converts your typed characters into the trademark symbol.

The trademark symbols help make the newsletter look more professional. Next, you decide to adjust the columns of text so they are approximately the same length.

Balancing the Columns

You could shift text from one column to another by adding blank paragraphs to move the text into the next column or by deleting blank paragraphs to shorten the text so it will fit into one column. Instead, Word can automatically **balance** the columns, or make them of equal length, for you.

To balance the columns:

1. Position the insertion point at the end of the text in the right column, just after period following the word "generation." Now change the zoom control to Whole Page so you can see the full effect of the change.

2. Click the **Zoom Control** list arrow on the Standard toolbar, and then click **Whole Page**.

3. Click **Insert** on the menu bar, and then click **Break**. The Break dialog box opens.

4. In the Section breaks section, click the **Continuous** option button.

5. Click the **OK** button. Word inserts a continuous section break at the end of the text, which, along with the first section break you inserted earlier, defines the area in which it should balance the columns.

As you can see, Word automatically balances the text between the two section breaks.

The balanced columns make the layout look much more professional. However, notice that the top margin is narrower than the bottom margin. The newsletter would look better if it had the same amount of space above and below the content. You can do this by enlarging the document's top margin.

To increase the top margin of the newsletter:

1. Click **File** on the menu bar, and then click **Page Setup**. The Page Setup dialog box opens.

2. If necessary, click the **Margins** tab to select it.

3. Click the **Top** up arrow four times to increase the setting to **1.4"**.

4. In the **Apply to** list box in the lower-right portion of the dialog box, select **Whole Document**.

5. Click the **OK** button. The entire content of the newsletter moves down, creating a similar amount of space above and below it. See Figure 4-21.

Figure 4-21 ◀
The newsletter with balanced columns and vertical placement

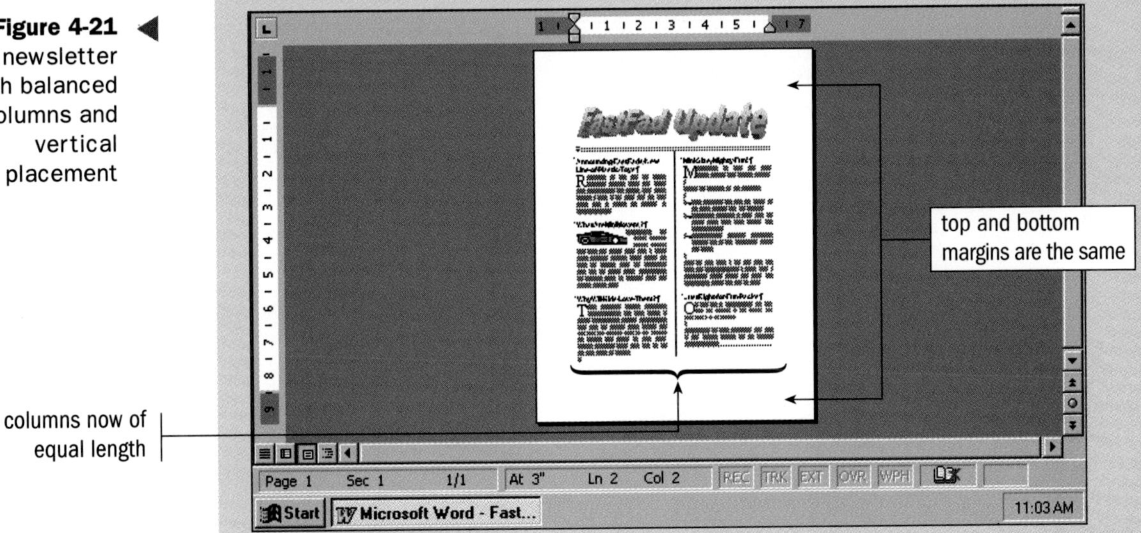

top and bottom margins are the same

columns now of equal length

TROUBLE? Depending on the size of the WordArt object, the placement of your newsletter content may differ from that shown in the figure. Adjust the size of the WordArt object and the top margin until the newsletter is centered vertically on the page.

Drawing a Border Around the Page

Gerrit wants to give the newsletter a little more pizzazz. He suggests adding a border around the newsletter, and adding a shaded background. In the steps that follow, you'll create a page border and background using the Word Drawing toolbar. You'll also learn how to move an object—in this case, a shaded box—behind text and other objects. In the Tutorial Assignments, you'll learn how to insert a page border using another, more automated method—the Page Border command.

To draw a border around the newsletter:

1. Make sure the document is in page layout view and that the zoom control setting is set to Whole Page, so you can see the entire newsletter.

2. Click the **Drawing** button 🔲 on the Standard toolbar. The Drawing toolbar appears at the bottom of the document window.

3. Click the **Rectangle** button 🔲 on the Drawing toolbar.

4. Position the pointer slightly higher than and to the left of the first "F" in the "FastFad" title near the upper-left corner of the newsletter. The pointer changes to + when positioned over the document.

5. Click and drag the pointer to the lower-right corner of the newsletter to surround the newsletter with a box. See Figure 4-22.

Figure 4-22 ◀
Drawing a
border around
the newsletter

drawing pointer

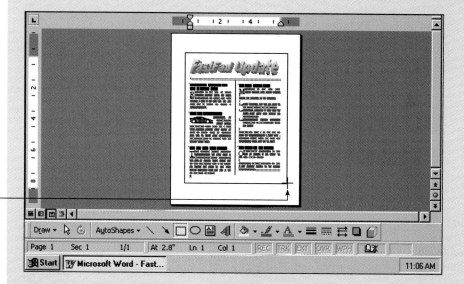

6. Release the mouse button.

    When you release the mouse button, a white rectangle covers the newsletter text. You'll fix this in a minute.

7. Click the **Line Style** button ▤ on the Drawing toolbar to display a list of line style options. See Figure 4-23.

Figure 4-23 ◀
Line styles on
the Drawing
toolbar

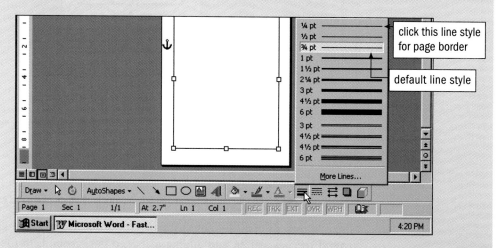

8. Click **1/4 pt** at the top of the list to select this line style option.

9. Click the list arrow next to the **Fill Color** button 🎨 on the Drawing toolbar, and then click More Fill Colors to open the Colors dialog box. Here you can select or customize the color you want for the shaded background.

10. Click the **first gray color tile** in the second row from the bottom. A preview of the color you have selected appears in the top half of the preview square on the right side of the dialog box. See Figure 4-24.

Figure 4-24 ◀
Selecting a
fill color

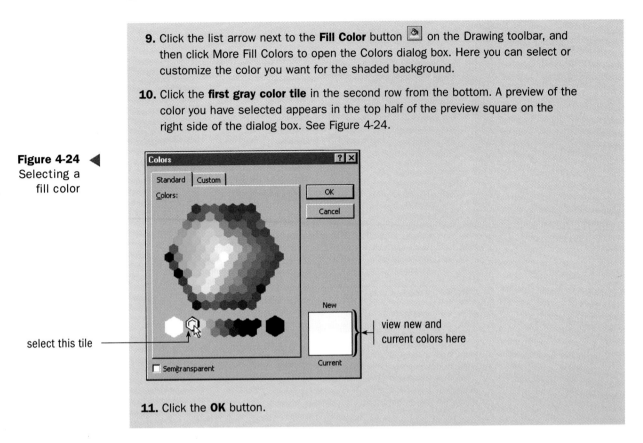

select this tile ———

view new and
current colors here

11. Click the **OK** button.

The fill color covers the text, but you want it to be a background shading. You'll need to send the filled rectangle to the back or bring the text to the front in order to see the text over the fill, which you'll do in the next section.

Document Layers

When you add shading or lines around text, you are creating layers. Think of printing your document on two sheets of clear plastic. One sheet contains the text of your document, the other sheet contains borders and shading. When you place one sheet on top of the other, or layer them, the sheets' contents combine to create the complete document. If you place the sheet with shading and borders over the text, you cannot see the text through it. If you place the sheet with the text over the shading and borders, the shading and borders are visible around the text.

Right now the background shading is positioned as the top layer of the document. You need to send that layer to the back of the text layer so the shading is visible behind the text instead of obscuring it.

To move the shading to the back and print the final newsletter:

1. Click the **Draw** button on the Drawing toolbar.

2. Point to **Order**, and then click **Send to Back**. The shaded box moves to the layer behind the WordArt and ClipArt objects.

3. Click the **Draw** button again, point to **Order**, and then click **Send Behind Text**. The shaded box moves to the layer behind the text.

4. Click anywhere in the newsletter text to deselect the border. The text layer and the graphics appear on top of the shading layer. See Figure 4-25.

Figure 4-25 ◀
Completed
newsletter

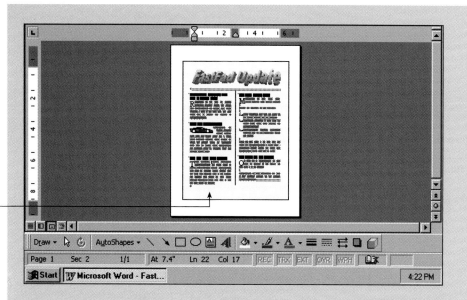

filled rectangle is now
behind newsletter
copy and graphics

TROUBLE? If the sports car disappears from the newsletter, you selected Send Behind Text, instead of Send to Back in Step 2. To correct this, select the shaded rectangle, and then repeat Steps 1 and 2, making sure you select Send to Back from the Order menu.

5. Save the completed newsletter.

6. Click the **Print Preview** button 🔍 on the Standard toolbar. Preview the newsletter.

7. Click the **Print** button 🖨 on the Print Preview toolbar to print the newsletter. If you have a black-and-white printer, the orange and yellow letters of the title and the red car appear in shades of gray.

TROUBLE? If you see an error message when you try to print, your printer might not have enough memory to print the newsletter with the background shading. Return to page layout view. Click the border to select it, click the Fill Color list arrow on the Drawing toolbar, click No Fill as the color to remove the background shading, and then try to print again. If you still have problems, ask your instructor or technical support person for assistance.

8. If necessary, click the **Close** button on the Print Preview toolbar to return to page layout view.

9. Close the newsletter and exit Word.

Quick Check

1. Define the following in your own words:
   a. clip art
   b. typographic characters
   c. drop cap
   d. crop

2. Describe the procedure for inserting a clip art graphic in Word.

3. In your own words, explain the difference between resizing and cropping a graphic.

4. Describe the procedure for creating a drop cap.

5. How do you insert the registered trademark symbol in a document? What are two other symbols or special characters that you can add to a document with Word?

6 Besides the Symbol command on the Insert menu, what is another way of entering typographic symbols?

7 Describe the process for drawing a border around text and adding background shading.

8 Describe the procedure for balancing columns in Word.

You give the printed newsletter to Gerrit, along with a copy on disk. He thinks it looks great and thanks you for your help. He'll print it later on a color printer (in order to make the most of the colors in the WordArt title and the sports car clip art) and distribute the newsletter to FastFad's sales staff.

Tutorial Assignments

Gerrit's FastFad newsletter was a success; the sales representatives all seemed to have good product knowledge, and the sales for MiniMovers were brisk. The sales reps themselves have asked Gerrit for a product information sheet, similar to the newsletter, about another product, FastFad Sports Figures. The sales reps want to be able to print it and send it directly to their clients. You'll produce that newsletter now.

1. If necessary, start Word and make sure your Student Disk is in the appropriate disk drive. Check your screen to make sure your settings match those in the tutorial and that the nonprinting characters and Drawing toolbar are displayed.

2. Open the file FigSpecs from the TAssign folder for Tutorial 4 on your Student Disk, and then save it as Sports Figures.

3. Insert a new, blank line at the top of the document, format in Normal style, and then click the Insert WordArt button on the Drawing toolbar.

4. Choose the WordArt style in the lower-left corner of the WordArt Gallery dialog box.

5. Type "FastFad Figures" in the Enter WordArt Text dialog box, click OK, and then drag the WordArt above the first heading.

6. Use the WordArt Shape button on the WordArt toolbar to apply the Deflate shape (fourth row, second column from left), and change the font to 24 point Arial bold.

7. Use the Format WordArt dialog box Wrapping tab to apply the Top & bottom wrapping style.

8. Drag the lower-right and then the lower-left resize handles to enlarge the image to the entire width between the left and right margins.

9. Save the document.

10. Position the insertion point to the left of the first word in the first heading, and then format the text into two columns using the Columns dialog box. Insert a section break so that the columns appear from this point forward. Do not insert a line between columns.

11. View the whole newsletter in page layout view, using the Whole Page zoom control setting, and make any necessary adjustments.

12. Return to 100% zoom control in page layout view, and then position the insertion point immediately after the first paragraph (on the same line). Click Insert on the menu bar, point to Picture, and then click **Clip Art** to open the Microsoft Clip Gallery dialog box.

13. Insert the tennis player clip art image from the Sports & Leisure category.

14. Select and resize the sports image so it fits in the left half of the first column.

15. Crop the graphic to remove the tennis racket from the left side of the image, and then move the graphic left using the keyboard arrow keys.

16. Select the clip art object, click the Format Picture button on the Picture toolbar, and click the Wrapping tab. Set the Wrapping style to Tight, and wrap the text around the right side of the image for the Dropped position.

17. Format a drop cap for the first paragraph following the "Five Sets of Figures" heading, using the default settings for the Dropped position.

18. Insert the trademark symbol after the first occurrence of "FastFad Sports Figures," using either of the techniques you used in the tutorial.

19. As you might have noticed, Word automatically justifies text in newspaper columns. To try changing the alignment now: Select both columns of text by clicking before the first word of text, pressing and holding down the Shift key, and then clicking at the end of the text. Use the Align Left button on the Formatting toolbar to change the columns' text alignment to left alignment.

20. Make the columns of equal length by balancing the columns. Position the insertion point at the end of the document, click Insert on the menu bar, and then click Break. In the Section breaks section, click the Continuous option button, and then click the OK button.

21. A pull quote is a phrase or quotation taken from the text that summarizes a key point. To insert a pull quote now: Select the words "FastFad: We take play seriously" (at the end of the second column) and then click the Cut button on the Standard toolbar. Click the Text Box button on the Drawing toolbar, and then below the two columns, drag the pointer to draw a text box that spans the width of the page. With the insertion point located in the text box, click the Paste button on the Standard toolbar. Select the text in the text box, and then use the Font command on the Format menu to format the text in the box as 16 point Arial italic. Click the Center button on the Formatting toolbar to center the text in the box. Use the Fill Color list arrow on the Drawing toolbar to fill the selected text box with a light turquoise color.

22. Sometimes you may want to use the Replace command to replace standard word processing characters with typographic characters. To replace every occurrence of -- (two dashes) with — (em dash): Position the insertion point at the beginning of the first paragraph of text. Click Edit on the menu bar, and then click Replace. In the Find what text box type "--" (two dashes), and then press the Tab key to move the insertion point to the Replace with text box. Click the More button to display more options, and then click the Special button at the bottom of the dialog box. Click Em Dash in the list to display Word's special code for em dashes in the Replace with text box. Click the Replace All button. When the operation is complete, click the OK button, and then click the Close button.

23. Add a border to the page using the Page Border command. Click Format on the menu bar, and then click Borders and Shading. In the Borders and Shading toolbox, click the Page Border tab. You can use this tab to customize the border type, line style, color, and width. Select the following options—Setting: Box, Width: 1pt., Apply to: Whole document—and then click OK.

24. Look at the newsletter border in page layout view, using the Whole Page zoom control setting. Center the newsletter contents vertically by adjusting the top margin for the whole document in the Page Layout dialog box.

25. Preview, save, and print the document.

Case Problems

1. City of San Antonio, Texas Blas Rodriguez is the manager of information systems for the city of San Antonio. He and his staff, along with the city manager, have just decided to convert all city computers from the DOS/Windows 3.1 operating system to Windows 95 and to standardize applications software on Microsoft Office 97. Blas writes a monthly newsletter on computer operations and training, so this month he decides to devote the newsletter to the conversion to Windows 95 and to Microsoft Office 97.

1. If necessary, start Word, make sure your Student Disk is in the appropriate drive, and check your screen to make sure your settings match those in the tutorials.

2. Open the file CityComp from the Cases folder for Tutorial 4 on your Student Disk, and then save the file as Computer.

3. Cut the text of the newsletter title, "Focus on Computers." Click the Insert WordArt button on the Drawing toolbar, and then choose the WordArt style in the fourth row, first column. Paste the text (using the Ctrl + V shortcut keys) into the Edit WordArt Text dialog box.

4. In Edit WordArt Text dialog box, set the font to 32 point Arial bold, and apply the Triangle Up shape (top row, third button from the left).

5. Drag the WordArt to the top of the newsletter, and set the wrapping style to Top & bottom in the Format WordArt dialog box.

6. Experiment with changing the shape of the WordArt object by dragging the yellow adjustment handle.

7. Resize the WordArt object so that it spans the width of the page from left margin to right margin and so that its maximum height is about 1 inch. (*Hint:* Use the resize handles while watching the horizontal and vertical rulers in page layout view to adjust the object to the appropriate size.)

8. Center and italicize the subtitle of the newsletter, "Newsletter from the Information Management Office."

9. Insert a continuous section break before the subtitle.

10. To highlight the paragraph with the city name, center the text and then insert a border around all four sides. (*Hint:* Use the Borders button on the Formatting toolbar.)

11. Format the body of the newsletter into two newspaper-style columns, and set the format of the columns so that no vertical rule appears between the columns.

12. Position the insertion point at the beginning of the first paragraph under the heading "Training on MS Office 97," and insert the clip art image from the People at Work category that shows a person talking in front of a group.

13. Resize the picture so that it is 35 percent of its normal size. Instead of dragging the resize handles as you did in the tutorial, use the Size tab in the Format Picture dialog box to scale the image. Adjust the Height and Width settings to 35 percent in the Scale section, and then make sure the Lock aspect ratio check box is selected.

14. Drag the graphic horizontally to the center of the newsletter, and in the Wrapping tab of the Format Picture dialog box, set the wrapping style to Tight, and Wrap to option to Both sides. Make the Left and Right Distance from text .2.

15. Replace any double hyphens with typographic em dashes.

16. Make sure the newsletter fits on one page; if necessary decrease the height of the WordArt title until the newsletter fits on one page.

17. Draw a rectangular border around the entire page of the newsletter. Fill it with a color of your choice, and then use the Draw button on the Drawing toolbar to layer it at the back.

18. If necessary, balance the columns and adjust the newsletter's position on the page.

19. Save and print the newsletter, and then close the file.

2. Federal Van Lines Corporation Martin Lott is the executive secretary to Whitney Kremer, director of personnel for Federal Van Lines (FVL) Corporation, a national moving company with headquarters in Minneapolis, Minnesota. Whitney assigned Martin the task of preparing the monthly newsletter People on the Move, which provides news about FVL employees. Although Martin and others before him have been preparing the newsletter for several years, Martin decides it's time to change the layout and wants to use Word's desktop publishing capabilities to design the newsletter. You will use text assembled by other FVL employees for the body of the newsletter.

1. If necessary, start Word, make sure your Student Disk is in the appropriate drive, and check your screen to make sure your settings match those in the tutorials.

2. Open the file FVL_News from the Cases folder for Tutorial 4 on your Student Disk, and then save it as FVL Newsletter.

3. Change the top and bottom margins to 0.75 inches, and the right and left margin to 1.0 inch. Then insert a blank line at the beginning of the newsletter and apply the normal style to it.

4. Create a WordArt title for the newsletter "People on the Move"; set the font to 24 point Arial bold. Apply the WordArt style in the third row, fourth column from the left, and set the shape of the text to Wave 2 (third row, sixth column from the left).

5. Drag the WordArt title to the top of the newsletter, and set the wrapping style to Top & bottom.

6. Resize the WordArt proportionally so that the title spans the width of the page from left margin to right margin and so that the height of the title is about 1 inch. (*Hint:* Use the resize handles while watching the horizontal and vertical rulers in page layout view to adjust the object to the appropriate size.)

7. Format the body of the newsletter into three newspaper-style columns of equal width and place a vertical rule between the columns. (Remember to use three columns, and not two as you did in the tutorial.) Make sure the rules do not extend through the title object.

8. Position the insertion point at the beginning of the paragraph below the heading "FLV Chess Team Takes Third," and insert the image called "Knight" from the Cases folder for Tutorial 4 on your Student Disk. (*Hint:* Use the same method as you would to insert a clip art image, except instead of selecting Clip Art from the Insert Picture menu, select From File. In the Insert Picture dialog box, go to the location of the file on your Student Disk, select the filename, and then click the Insert button.)

9. Scale the height and the width of the picture to 60 percent of its normal size. (*Hint:* To scale the size, use the Format Picture command, and then set the Scale values on the Size tab, making sure the Lock aspect ratio check box is selected.)

10. Crop 0.3, 0.4, 0.2, and 0.4 inches from the left, right, top, and bottom of the picture, respectively. Use the Picture tab in the Format Picture dialog box, and insert the values in the Crop from text boxes.

11. Drag the clip art to the right side of the center column about 2 inches below the heading. (*Hint:* Select the clip art, and then drag it from the center.)

12. Wrap the text around the clip art.

13. Format drop caps in the first paragraph after each heading. Use the default settings for number of lines, but change the font of the drop cap to Arial.

14. If necessary, decrease the height of the WordArt title until the entire newsletter fits onto one page and so each column starts with a heading.

 15. Add a rectangular border around the entire page of the newsletter using the Page Border command. See the Tutorial Assignments, step 23, for instructions.

16. Save the newsletter, preview, and then print the newsletter. Close the file.

3. Riverside Wellness Clinic The Riverside Wellness Clinic, located in Vicksburg, Mississippi, is a private company that contracts with small and large businesses to promote health and fitness among their employees. MaryAnne Logan, an exercise physiologist, is director of health and fitness at the clinic. As part of her job, she writes and desktop publishes a newsletter for the employees of the companies with which the clinic contracts. She's ready to prepare the newsletter for the October 1998 issue.

1. If necessary, start Word, make sure your Student Disk is in the appropriate drive, and check your screen to make sure your settings match those in the tutorials.

2. Open the file Wellness from the Cases folder for Tutorial 4 on your Student Disk, and then save it as Wellness Newsletter.

3. Change the top and bottom margins to 0.5 inches and the left and right margins to 0.75 inches.

4. At the beginning of the newsletter, create a WordArt title "To Your Health." Choose any WordArt style that you feel would be appropriate to the newsletter content, and set the font to Arial bold, 24 point.

5. Set the shape of the text to any option that looks appropriate to the subject matter.

6. Move the title to the top of the document.

 7. Add a shadow to the WordArt title (or adjust the existing one) by clicking the Shadow button on the Drawing toolbar. Select a Shadow option, and then use the Shadow Settings option on the Shadows menu to select a good color for the shadow. Close the Shadow settings menu. For the purpose of this exercise, choose a shadow style that is behind the text, not in front of it.

 8. Rotate the WordArt 90 degrees. (*Hint:* In the Format WordArt dialog box, click the Size tab and set the Rotation option to 90 degrees.)

 9. Resize the WordArt graphic box so that the WordArt object spans the height of the page from the top margin to the bottom margin, and so that the width of the object is about 1 inch. (*Hint:* Use the resize handles while watching the horizontal and vertical rulers in page layout view to adjust the object to the appropriate size.)

10. Drag the WordArt object to the left edge of the page.

 11. Set the Wrapping style to Square, set the Wrap to option to Right, and then change the Right setting under Distance from text to .2".

12. At the top of the page, to the right of the title, italicize the subtitle and the line that contains the issue volume and number of the newsletter.

13. Format the body of the newsletter into two newspaper-style columns with a vertical rule between the columns. (*Hint:* The columns' widths will be uneven because the WordArt title takes up part of the first column space.)

14. To the right of each of the words "NordicTrack" and "HealthRider," insert a registered trademark symbol (®), and then change the font size of the symbol to 8 points. (*Hint:* Highlight the symbol and change the font size.)

15. Balance the columns and if necessary adjust the top margin to center the newsletter vertically on the page.

16. Add a rectangular border around the page using the Page Border command. To do this, follow the instructions in the Tutorial Assignments, step 23.

17. Save the newsletter, preview, and then print it. Close the document.

4. Holiday Greetings Newsletter As a way of keeping in touch with family and friends, a friend suggests that you send out a New Year's greeting newsletter. In the one-page newsletter, you'll include articles about you and your family or friends, recent activities, favorite hobbies, movies, books, and future plans. You'll desktop publish the copy into a professional-looking newsletter.

1. If necessary, start Word, make sure your Student Disk is in the appropriate drive, and check your screen to make sure your settings match those in the tutorials.

2. Write two articles to include in the newsletter; save each article in a separate file.

3. Plan the general layout of your newsletter.

4. Create a title ("New Year's News") for your newsletter with WordArt.

5. Save the document as "New Years News."

6. Insert the current date and your name as editor below the title.

7. Insert the articles you wrote into your newsletter. Open the first article file, select all of the text, copy it, click in the newsletter file at the location where you want it to appear, then paste it. Repeat the procedure for the second article.

8. Format your newsletter with multiple columns.

9. Insert a clip art picture into your newsletter, and wrap text around it.

10. Format at least two drop caps in the newsletter.

11. Create a colored background for the newsletter. Center the contents vertically by adjusting the top margin.

12. Save and print the newsletter.

13. Close the document.

Answers to Quick Check Questions

SESSION 1.1

1   Determine what you want to write about; organize ideas logically; determine how you'll say what you want to say; create your document with Word; edit your document; format your document; print your document.

2   Click Start, point to Programs, click Microsoft Word on the Programs menu or point to Microsoft Office on the Programs menu and click Microsoft Word.

3   a. a ribbon of icons providing menu shortcuts;
    b. bar displaying grid marks every 1/4 inch;
    c. blinking vertical bar indicating where typed characters will appear;
    d. set of characters of a certain shape;
    e. set of standard format settings.

4   Click Format, click Font, select the desired font size, click Default, click Yes.

5   Click View, point to Toolbars, click Standard.

6   Click the Show/Hide ¶ button on the Standard toolbar.

SESSION 1.2

1   You should save a document several times so you don't lose your work in the event of a power failure or other computer problem.

2   Click the Save button on the Standard toolbar. Specify the correct folder and directory in the Save in list box, type the file name in the File name text box, click Save.

3   To display a portion of the document that has scrolled from sight, click the up or down scroll arrows on the vertical scroll bar.

4   Print Preview allows you to see what the printed document will look like. You should use it before printing a document that you have made changes to or when printing a document for the first time.

5   a. shifting or moving the text in the document window to see the entire document one screen at a time;
    b. automatic breaking of a line of text at the right margin;
    c. feature that automatically corrects common misspellings and typing errors;
    d. Help feature that answers questions about current tasks; sometimes appears automatically.

6   Click the Word window Close button.

SESSION 2.1

1 Click the Open button on the Standard toolbar, or click File, click Open, and double-click the file. Click File, click Save As, select the location, type the new filename, click OK.

2 a. Ctrl + End
   b. Ctrl + Home
   c. Ctrl + PageDown

3 Select the text to delete, press Delete.

4 a. The process of first selecting the text to be modified, and then performing operations such as moving, formatting, or deleting on it.
   b. The blank space in the left margin area of the document window, which allows you to easily select entire lines or large blocks of text.
   c. The process of moving text by first selecting the text, then pressing and holding the mouse button while moving the text to its new location in the document, and finally releasing the mouse button.

5 Position the pointer at the beginning of the phrase, press and hold down the mouse button, drag the mouse pointer to the end of the phrase, and then release the mouse button.

   Click in the selection bar next to the line of text you want to select.

6 The Undo command allows you to reverse the last action or set of actions you performed.

   The Redo command allows you to restore a change you reversed using Undo.

7 False.

8 When you use cut and paste, the text is removed from its original location and inserted at a new location in the document.

   When you use copy and paste, the text remains in its original location, and a copy of it is also inserted in a new location in the document.

9 The text will be inserted at the location of the dashed insertion point.

10 Click the Select Browse Object button, click the Find button, click the Replace tab, type the search text in the Find what text box, type the replacement text in the Replace with text box, click Find Next or click Replace All.

SESSION 2.2

1 Align left: each line flush left, ragged right; align right: each line flush right, ragged left; center: each line centered, both ends ragged; justify: each line flush left and flush right; select the text to be aligned or justified, click the appropriate button on the Formatting toolbar.

2 The Format Painter allows you to easily apply the formatting from one block of text to other text.

   Select the text whose format you want to copy, double-click the Format Painter button on the Standard toolbar, click in each paragraph you want to format. When you are done, click the Format Painter button to turn it off.

3 Make sure the insertion point is located in the paragraph you want to indent, and then click the Increase Indent button on the Formatting toolbar once for each half-inch you want to indent.

4 False.

5 Select all the items you wish to bullet, and then click the Bullets button on the Formatting toolbar.

6 Select the text you wish to make bold, and then click the Bold button on the Formatting toolbar.

7 Select the text whose font you wish to change, click the Font list arrow on the Formatting toolbar, and then click the name of the new font on the list.

8 Click the Select Browse Object button, click the Find button, click the Replace tab, type "strategy" in the Find what text box, type "plan" in the Replace with text box, click Replace All.

9 With no text selected, click File, click Page Setup, click the Margins tab, type the new values in the text boxes or click the spin arrows to change the settings. Make sure the Apply to text box displays Whole document, and then click OK.

SESSION 3.1

1 a. a set of formats that can include font, size, and attributes such as bold and italic;
b. a set of predefined styles designed for a specific type of document;
c. a list, accessible from the Formatting toolbar, that allows you to apply a style to selected text;
d. a unit or part of a document that can have its own page orientation, margins, headers, footers, and vertical alignment;
e. the position of the text between the top and bottom margins;
f. text that is printed at the top of every page

2 A section break allows you to format different parts of the document in different ways. In the tutorial, the section break you inserted allowed you to create a header that was printed only on pages 2 and 3, and it allowed you to vertically center the text on the first page only.

3 Insert a section break, move the insertion point within the section you want to align, click File, click Page Setup, click the Layout tab, select the center in the Vertical Alignment list box, make sure This section is selected in the Apply to list box, click OK.

4 A header appears at the top of a page, while a footer appears at the bottom of a page.

5 Click the Insert Page Number button on the Header and Footer toolbar.

6 First, attach the template to the document. Then apply the template's styles to the various parts of the document.

7 Click Format, click Style Gallery, click the template you want to preview, verify that you have selected the template you want, click OK.

8 You selected text, clicked the Style list arrow on the Formatting toolbar, clicked the name of the style to apply to the text.

SESSION 3.2

1 Click the place in the document where you want to insert the table. Click the Insert Table button on the Header and Footer toolbar, click and drag to select the numbers of rows and columns you want in your table, release the mouse button.

2 Position the pointer over the border between two columns, click and drag the pointer until the column is the width you want, release the mouse button.

3 d.

4 a. information arranged in horizontal rows and vertical columns; b. the area where a row and column intersect; c. a gray or colored background

5 Click cell A2 or press the Tab key; click cell B6 or press the ↑ key.

6 Click the cell below the column, click the Tables and Borders button on the Standard toolbar, and then click the AutoSum button on the Tables and Borders toolbar.

7 Click in the selection bar to select the row above which you want to insert a row, right-click the selected row, click Insert Rows.

SESSION 4.1

1 (list 3) The printing is high-quality; the document uses multiple fonts; the document incorporates graphics; the document uses typographic characters; the document makes use of columns and other special formatting features.

2 a. a Microsoft Office feature that allows you to design text with special effects;
   b. a square handle you can use to change the size of a graphic;
   c. an arrangement of text using narrow columns that read top to bottom and consecutively from left to right

3 Position the insertion point at the location where you want to create WordArt, click the Drawing button on the Standard toolbar, click the Insert WordArt button on the Drawing toolbar, click the style of text you want to insert, click OK, type the text you want and make formatting selections, click OK.

4 To resize a WordArt object, select the object, drag the resize handles; to resize proportionally, press and hold the Shift key while dragging a handle.

5 The WordArt Shape button allows you to choose the basic shape of a WordArt object.

6 True. Normal view shows each column in its own section; only page layout view, however, shows how the columns appear in the final document.

7 To format text into newspaper-like columns, you use the <u>Columns</u> command on the <u>Format</u> menu.

8 If you want one part of your document to be in two columns, and another part to be in full width, you must insert a <u>section break</u> between the two sections.

9 False. Column formatting will automatically justify the text on each line, but not the lengths of the columns.

SESSION 4.2

1 a. existing artwork that you can insert into your document;
   b. special symbols and punctuation marks that distinguish desktop-published documents;
   c. a large, uppercase letter that highlights the beginning of the text of a newsletter, chapter, or some other document section;
   d. to cut off one or more of the edges of a graphic

2 Position the insertion point at the location where you want to insert the image, click Insert, point to Picture, click Clip Art, click the Clip Art tab, click the category you want to use, click the image you want to insert, click Insert.

3 Resizing leaves the graphic intact but changes its dimensions. Cropping actually removes part of the graphic from view.

4 Click in the paragraph that you want to begin with a drop cap, click Format, click Drop Cap, click the icon for the type of drop cap to insert, select the font, set the appropriate number in the Lines to drop text box, click OK.

5 Click where you want to insert the symbol in the document, click Insert, click Symbol, select the symbol to insert, click Insert.

   ™, ©

6 Make sure that the AutoCorrect feature is set up to replace typing with special symbols; then type text that Word will convert to the symbol you want to insert.

7 Click the Drawing button on the Standard toolbar, click the Rectangle button on the Drawing toolbar, drag to create the rectangle you want to insert, click the Line Style button and select the appropriate style, click the Fill Color list arrow and select the fill color you want to use, click OK.

8 Position the insertion point at the end of the last column you want to balance, click the Zoom Control list arrow on the Standard toolbar, click Whole Page, click Insert, click Break, click the Continuous option button in the Section breaks section, click OK.

NEW
PERSPECTIVES
S E R I E S

Microsoft®
Word 97

LEVEL II

TUTORIALS

Read This **Before You Begin**

STUDENT DISKS

To complete Word 97 Tutorials 5–7 you need four Student Disks. Your instructor will either provide you with Student Disks or ask you to make your own.

If you are supposed to make your own Student Disks, you will need four blank, formatted high-density disks. You will need to copy a set of folders from a file server or standalone computer onto your disks. Your instructor will tell you which computer, drive letter, and folders contain the files you need. The following table shows you which folders go on each of your disks, so that you will have enough disk space to complete all the tutorials, Tutorial Assignments, and Case Problems:

Student Disk	Write this on the disk label	Put these folders on the disk
1	Student Disk 1: Tutorial 5	Tutorial.05
2	Student Disk 2: Tutorial 6	Tutorial.06
3	Student Disk 3: Tutorial 7 and Tutorial Assignments	Tutorial.07
4	Student Disk 4: Tutorial 7 Case Problems	Tutorial.07

When you begin each tutorial, be sure you are using the correct Student Disk. See the inside front or inside back cover of this book for more information on Student Disk files, or ask your instructor or technical support person for assistance.

COURSE LAB

Tutorial 7 features an interactive Course Lab to help you understand Internet and World Wide Web concepts. There are Lab Assignments at the end of the tutorial that relate to this Lab. To start the Lab, click the Start button on the Windows 95 taskbar, point to Programs, point to Course Labs, point to New Perspectives Applications, and click The Internet: World Wide Web.

USING YOUR OWN COMPUTER

If you are going to work through this book using your own computer, you need:

■ **Computer System** Microsoft Windows 95 or Microsoft Windows NT Workstation 4.0 (or a later version) and Microsoft Word 97 must be installed on your computer. This book assumes a typical installation of Microsoft Word that includes Web Page Authoring (HTML).

■ **Student Disks** Ask your instructor or technical support person for details on how to get the Student Disks. You will not be able to complete the tutorials or end-of-tutorial assignments in this book using your own computer until you have Student Disks. The Student Files may also be obtained electronically over the Internet. See the inside front or inside back cover of this book for more details.

■ **Course Lab** See your instructor or technical support person to obtain the Course Lab software for use on your own computer.

To complete Word 97 Tutorials 5–7 your students must use a set of files on four Student Disks. These files are included in the Instructor's Resource Kit, and they may also be obtained electronically over the Internet. See the inside front or inside back cover of this book for more details. Follow the instructions in the Readme file to copy the files to your server or standalone computer. You can view the Readme file using WordPad. Once the files are copied, you can make Student Disks for the students yourself, or you can tell students where to find the files so they can make their own Student Disks.

COURSE LAB SOFTWARE

The Course Lab software is distributed on a CD-ROM included in the Instructor's Resource Kit. Refer to the Readme file for essential technical notes related to running the Lab in a multi-user environment. Once you have installed the Course Lab software, your students can start the Lab from the Windows 95 desktop by following the instructions in the Course Lab section above.

COURSE TECHNOLOGY STUDENT FILES AND LAB SOFTWARE

You are granted a license to copy the Student Files and Course Lab software to any computer or computer network used by students who have purchased this book.

Creating Styles, Outlines, Tables, and Tables of Contents

Writing a Business Plan for EstimaTech

OBJECTIVES

In this tutorial you will:

- Use the Thesaurus and the Spelling and Grammar Checker
- Change fonts and adjust font sizes
- Create and modify paragraph and character styles
- Set tabs and align information with tabs
- Create and modify an outline
- Create, modify, and format tables
- Double-space and hyphenate the document
- Add footnotes and endnotes
- Create a table of contents

CASE

EstimaTech

Chiu Lee Hwang and Robert Camberlango, recent computer science graduates, earned their college tuition by working summers and vacations for a company that specializes in historically accurate renovations of older homes. Their employer asked them to use their computer skills to help him estimate the cost of restoring or renovating buildings and homes. They developed a computer program for the task that lets them easily create well-formatted documents they can present to potential customers. It has worked so well that they have decided to develop it into a commercial product and call it EstimaQuote. They hope to sell it to contractors, subcontractors, and individuals, as well as agencies and foundations.

To bring the product to market, they need to secure a $475,000 loan from Commercial Financial Bank of New England for the start-up of EstimaTech, the company that will let them fine-tune the product for commercial use and let them market the software. To obtain the necessary financing, Chiu Lee and Robert are writing a **business plan**, a report that details all aspects of starting a new business, including market, operations, financial information, and personnel. They have written a draft of the plan and have asked you to help them complete Chapter 2, "Industry Analysis," in time for their meeting with the bank. Specifically, they want you to edit the word usage, improve the format, organize the chapter sections more logically, summarize the results of recently completed market research in a table, and create front matter for the chapter.

SESSION

5.1

In this session, you'll see how Chiu Lee and Robert planned their report. You'll then open the report and use Microsoft Word's Thesaurus and Word's Spelling and Grammar Checker to edit the report. You'll learn about using fonts, and then learn how to modify, create, and apply styles to format the report. Finally, you'll set tabs to change the alignment of columns of information.

Planning the Document

A thorough business plan informs prospective investors about the purpose, organization, goals, and projected profits of the proposed business. It also analyzes the target industry, including available market research information. A business plan should convince readers that the venture is viable, well-thought-out, and worthy of funding. Chapter 2 of the EstimaTech business plan analyzes the industry and discusses the market research on potential customers for the new cost-estimating software.

Chiu Lee and Robert want to follow a standard business plan organization. The industry analysis begins by explaining how they performed the market research, followed by a summary of the results. Because numerical information is easier to understand when organized in columns and rows, Chiu Lee and Robert want to summarize the results of their market research in a table. They also want to include a table of contents for the chapter.

Chiu Lee and Robert use facts and statistics in their business plan to convince potential investors that the company would be profitable and the cost-estimating software would fill an existing need in the marketplace. They wrote in a formal business style.

Chiu Lee and Robert have begun to format the document but want you to check the fonts, margins, headers, and styles, and make sure the formatting is consistent. They also need you to add the table summarizing their market research and to create a table of contents.

Opening the Business Plan

Chiu Lee and Robert have written a draft of Chapter 2 of their business plan. You should read the draft before you reorganize it to check for correct word usage and grammar. You'll begin by opening a draft of Chapter 2. Robert wants you to create a new folder for this chapter. You'll create the folder and then save the document using a different filename into the new folder.

To open the document and save it into a new folder:

1. Start Word, if necessary, make sure your Student Disk is in the appropriate drive, and check the screen. For this tutorial, make sure the ruler appears below the Formatting toolbar and display the nonprinting characters so you can see the table markers.

2. Open the file **Industry** from the **Tutorial.05** folder on your Student Disk.

3. Click **File** on the menu bar, and then click **Save As** to display the Save As dialog box. You'll now create a new folder called Chapter 2 within the Tutorial.05 folder.

4. Click the **Create New Folder** button located near the top of the Save As dialog box. The New Folder dialog box opens.

5. Type **Chapter 2**, the name of the new folder, and then click the **OK** button.

6. Double-click the **Chapter 2** folder, and then save the document in that folder using the filename **Industry Analysis**.

Now Industry Analysis is in the Chapter 2 folder. Later, Robert will add folders for the other chapters of the business plan.

Using the Thesaurus

In the paragraph about market size on page 2 of the plan, the word "restore" occurs twice, and Robert has asked you to find another word that has the same meaning for the second occurrence. You can do this easily using the Thesaurus. The **Thesaurus** is a Word feature that contains a list of words and their synonyms and antonyms. Similar to a thesaurus reference book, Word's Thesaurus lets you look up a specific word, find its synonyms, antonyms, and related words. After you have found an appropriate replacement word, you can immediately replace the word you looked up with its synonym or antonym. The Thesaurus is a good editing tool to help make your word choices varied and exact.

REFERENCE window	**USING THE THESAURUS**
	■ Move the insertion point to the word that you want to replace with a synonym or an antonym.
	■ Click Tools on the menu bar, point to Language, and then click Thesaurus.
	■ If necessary, scroll the replacement word into view.
	■ Click the replacement word, and then click the Replace button.

You'll use the Thesaurus to find a synonym for the word "restore" in the "Size of Market" paragraph.

To find a synonym for "restore" using the Thesaurus:

1. Move the insertion point to the second occurrence of the word "restore," which appears in the paragraph below the heading "Size of Market" (page 2, about line 16). If necessary, you can use the Find command on the Edit menu to find the first occurrence, and then click the **Find Next** button to go to the second occurrence. The word you want to look up in the Thesaurus must be selected, or the insertion point must be within the word or immediately to its left or right.

2. Click **Tools** on the menu bar, point to **Language**, and then click **Thesaurus** to highlight "restore" and open the Thesaurus dialog box. The word "restore" appears in the Looked Up list box. Three words, each representing a related definition, appear in the Meanings list box, and several synonyms of "reinstate" appear in the Replace with Synonym list box.

    The meaning of "restore" closest to your meaning is "rebuild."

3. Click **rebuild (verb)** in the Meanings list box, and the synonyms for "rebuild" appear in the Replace with Synonyms list on the right. See Figure 5-1. Robert feels that "renovate" is the best synonym.

Figure 5-1
Thesaurus
dialog box with
word selected
in document

selected word
in document

selected meaning

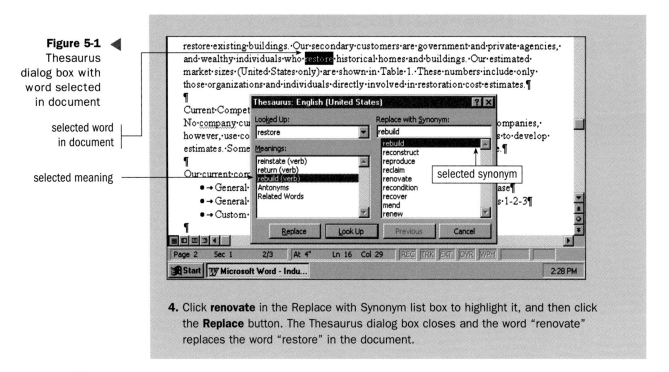

4. Click **renovate** in the Replace with Synonym list box to highlight it, and then click the **Replace** button. The Thesaurus dialog box closes and the word "renovate" replaces the word "restore" in the document.

As you can see, the Thesaurus helps you increase your word power as you write. Robert wants his business plan to be well-written, so he now asks you to use the Spelling and Grammar Checker to help improve the writing.

Using the Spelling and Grammar Checker

Word comes with automatic proofing tools that help you reduce the errors in your documents. The Spelling and Grammar Checker analyzes your document or selected text for common spelling, grammar, and style errors, such as incorrect subject-verb agreement. It explains the potential problem, and often suggests a correction. Although the Spelling and Grammar Checker can help you catch and fix spelling, grammatical and stylistic problems, it is by no means a cure-all. It can suggest changes that are appropriate for your document, but some suggested changes might not be applicable. You need to review each suggested change and determine whether to accept it or ignore it.

The changes that the Grammar Checker suggests might be appropriate for one document but not another. You can set the Grammar Checker to evaluate your document using a writing style that is appropriate for the type of document you're writing. These styles include Casual, Standard, Formal, Technical, and Custom. For example, in the Formal style, the Grammar Checker flags any contractions ("can't"), jargon and colloquialisms ("this is pretty good"), wordiness ("prior to" instead of "before"), whereas in the Casual style the Grammar Checker doesn't flag these items.

By default, Word uses the Standard style and automatically checks the grammar as you type. You can set Word to check spelling only, or spelling and grammar at the same time. You can have Word check as you type, or if you prefer to focus on spelling and grammar after you've written the document, you can check the document all at once. The Grammar Checker then goes through your document and marks words, phrases, and sentences that it detects as potential problems with a wavy green underline. The Spelling Checker marks words that it doesn't find in its dictionary with a wavy red underline.

REFERENCE window

CHANGING OPTIONS IN THE SPELLING AND GRAMMAR CHECKER

■ Click Tools on the menu bar, click Options, and then click the Spelling & Grammar tab.
■ Change the spelling and grammar options as desired.
■ Click the OK button.

For this business plan, you'll make sure the Grammar Checker is turned on and the writing style is set to Formal.

To turn on the Grammar Checker and set the writing style:

1. With the insertion point anywhere in the document, click **Tools** on the menu bar, click **Options** to open the Options dialog box, and then click the **Spelling & Grammar** tab. See Figure 5-2.

Figure 5-2 ◀
Options
dialog box

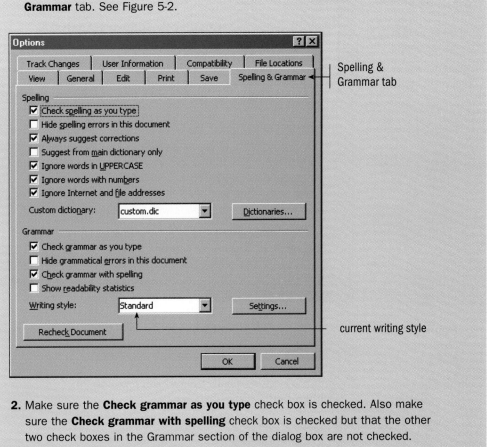

2. Make sure the **Check grammar as you type** check box is checked. Also make sure the **Check grammar with spelling** check box is checked but that the other two check boxes in the Grammar section of the dialog box are not checked.

3. Click the **Writing Style** list arrow, and then click **Formal**. Now Word will check your grammar and writing style at a formal level.

4. Click the **OK** button to close the dialog box and return to the document window.

5. Press **Ctrl + Home** to move the insertion point is at the beginning of the document.

Word now has marked potential grammar and style problems with a wavy green underline, if it hadn't done so before. Now you're ready to respond to these potential problems. The first marked text is in the title, "Chapter 2." You can see a description of the potential problem by right-clicking on the marked text.

To see the potential problem with the marked text:

1. Right-click anywhere in the marked phrase "Chapter 2" at the beginning of the document. The Grammar shortcut menu appears. See Figure 5-3. The description of the potential problem is "Fragment (no suggestions)," meaning that the marked text is a sentence fragment rather than a complete sentence. If you wanted more information at this point, you would click Grammar at the bottom of the shortcut menu. Because you understand the potential problem (sentence fragments) and want to tell Word to ignore this problem, you don't need to click Grammar for more explanation.

Figure 5-3 ◄
Text marked by
Grammar
Checker and
Grammar
pop-up menu

insertion point in
marked phrase

green marking by
Grammar Checker

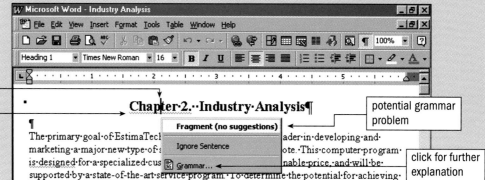

2. Click **Ignore Sentence**. Word removes the wavy green underline from the title. The next potential grammar problem is the phrase "is designed" in the first paragraph. This is an example of passive voice, which you'll ignore throughout the document. The Grammar Checker has also marked the phrase "Prior to," located below the first heading "Market Research." Suppose you're not sure what the potential problem is with this phrase.

3. Right-click the phrase "Prior to." The shortcut menu suggests replacing "Prior to" with "Before." To find out why Word would suggest this replacement, click **Grammar** on the shortcut menu. The Grammar: English (United States) dialog box opens. See Figure 5-4. "Prior to" is an example of jargon that is usually inappropriate for formal writing. The preferred usage is "before."

Figure 5-4 ◄
Grammar
dialog box

type of grammar
problem

explanation of
problem

suggested
replacement for
marked phrase

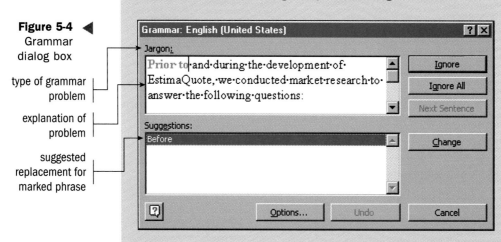

4. Click the **Change** button. Word replaces "Prior to" with "Before."

5. Right-click the next phrase Word has marked, "Who are our potential customers and how many are there?" and then click **Grammar** to get an explanation of the potential grammar or style problem. When the Grammar dialog box appears, however, you're still not sure what the problem is, except that it deals with sentence structure. To get a fuller explanation, you can consult the Office Assistant.

Word

6. Click the **Office Assistant** button 🔲 on the dialog box. The Office Assistant appears on the screen with an explanation of the sentence structure problem. See Figure 5-5.

Figure 5-5 ◄
Office
Assistant with
explanation of
grammar
problem

marked sentence

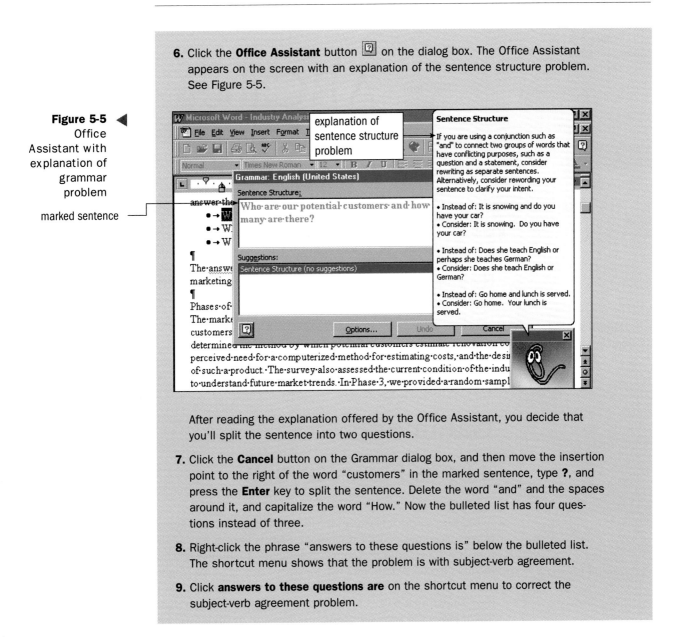

After reading the explanation offered by the Office Assistant, you decide that you'll split the sentence into two questions.

7. Click the **Cancel** button on the Grammar dialog box, and then move the insertion point to the right of the word "customers" in the marked sentence, type **?**, and press the **Enter** key to split the sentence. Delete the word "and" and the spaces around it, and capitalize the word "How." Now the bulleted list has four questions instead of three.

8. Right-click the phrase "answers to these questions is" below the bulleted list. The shortcut menu shows that the problem is with subject-verb agreement.

9. Click **answers to these questions are** on the shortcut menu to correct the subject-verb agreement problem.

The Grammar Checker has marked several other phrases in the document, but you decide to ignore them because none are serious grammatical or stylistic problems. Now that you have dealt with the proposal's grammar, style, and spelling issues, you can turn your attention to its design and appearance.

Choosing Fonts

Although Word's default font is Times New Roman, this is not the best font for many documents. In fact, Times New Roman was specifically designed for narrow-column newspaper text. For books, manuals, and other documents that have wider columns, a wider font is more readable. Here are some general principles that might help you decide which fonts to use in your documents:

■ Use a serif font as the main text of your documents. A **serif** is a small embellishment at the tips of the lines of a character, as shown in Figure 5-6.

Figure 5-6 ◄
Serif and sans
serif fonts

serifs

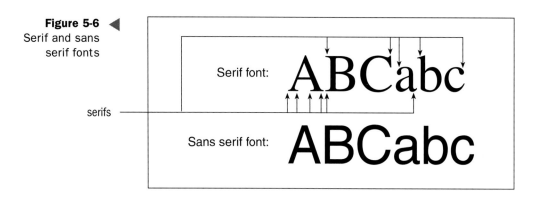

- Common serif fonts include Baskerville Old Face, Book Antiqua, Century Schoolbook (also called New Century Schoolbook), Courier, Garamond, Goudy Old Style, Rockwell, and Times New Roman, some of which are shown in Figure 5-7. Because serif fonts are highly readable, they are appropriate not only for the main text but also for titles and headings.

Figure 5-7 ◄
Sample serif
fonts

Century Schoolbook
Courier
Garamond
Times New Roman

- Avoid sans serif fonts except in titles, headings, headers and footers, captions, and other special parts of the document. **Sans** is French for "without"; thus a **sans serif** font is a font without the embellishments. Examples of common sans serif fonts include Arial, Arial Narrow, Century Gothic, Eras Light, Eurostile, Franklin Gothic Book, and Lucida Sans, some of which are shown in Figure 5-8. Studies have shown that large blocks of text in sans serif font are harder to read than serif fonts. However, sans serif fonts in titles and headings are attractive and readable.

Figure 5-8 ◄
Sample sans
serif fonts

Arial
Arial Narrow
Century Gothic
Franklin Gothic Book

- Avoid all-uppercase sans serif text. It is difficult to read. All-uppercase serif font is more readable, but mixed uppercase and lowercase text in any font is more readable still.

- Avoid unusual or fancy fonts except for certificates, invitations, advertisements, and other specialty documents. Examples of fonts that might be appropriate in these specialty documents include Brush Script, Braggadocio, French Script, Lucida Blackletter, Monotype Corsiva, and Stencil, as shown in Figure 5-9.

Figure 5-9
Sample
specialty fonts

Brush Script

French Script

Monotype Corsiva

STENCIL

- Avoid excessive changes in fonts and font attributes. Normally, the text of a document should include only one or two fonts—one for the main paragraphs and another one for the titles and headings. Excessive boldface and italics makes documents look cluttered and sloppy, and detracts attention from the content.

Robert wants you to use appropriate fonts and apply them properly to the business plan. The most efficient way to apply the correct font is to change the fonts within the styles. The existing styles don't have the fonts you want, so you'll change the style definitions.

Modifying and Defining Styles

As they wrote this chapter of the business plan, Chiu Lee and Robert applied the Heading 1 style to the chapter title, but didn't apply styles to the other headings. They want you to apply the heading styles, modify the styles to make the document more attractive and readable, and create a new style for this document and for other chapters in their business plan.

The predefined styles that are available in your document depend on the template that Chiu Lee and Robert selected when they started the new document. By using a template, you can match the overall design of the current document with the design in existing documents. As you know, Word provides templates for formatting reports, brochures, memos, letters, or resumes, among others. Word's default Normal template is appropriate for many documents. It contains the Normal paragraph style, which is the default style for document text, and other paragraph styles, such as those for titles, headings, lists, and envelopes.

You're already familiar with using the set of styles in a template as they are, but you can also modify the styles, create your own styles to add to a template, or create a new template for which you define all the styles. You can open a new document using any of the Word templates, or you can create a document using the Normal template and then attach a template after you've completed the document. Word updates the styles in the Styles list box to match the current template. Word uses some of the same style names from template to template, so that when you attach a template, these styles in your document are updated automatically to the new definition.

Applying Styles

You're familiar with applying styles using the Style drop-down list on the Formatting toolbar, so you'll apply styles to the business plan headings.

To apply styles to the headings:

1. Move the insertion point anywhere within the heading "Market Research" near the beginning of the document, click the **Style** list arrow on the Formatting toolbar, and click **Heading 2**. Because the heading style includes spacing above and below the text, you can delete the blank line above the heading. (You'll learn more about adding space above and below text later in this tutorial.)

2. Move the insertion point to the blank line above the heading, and press the **Delete** key to delete the blank line.

3. Repeat Steps 1 and 2 for all the other headings in the document: "Phases of the Market Research," "Market Definition," "Demographic Description of Target Users," "Size of the Market," "Current Competition," "Customer Needs," and "Market Trends." Remember that you can use the F4 key to repeat a previous action.

Now all the headings have a style applied to them. Normally, you should apply heading styles to all the headings in a document as you prepare the first draft. This will save time and effort as you format and edit your documents.

Modifying a Predefined Style

Having applied the heading styles, you're now ready to modify them. Robert suggests that you change the headings to a sans serif font. You'll change the font of the Heading 1, Heading 2, and Heading 3 styles to Arial. To do this, you change the **style definition**, which is the particular font, size, style, and format for that style. Once you change the style definition, all the headings with that style applied to them will automatically be reformatted with the new, modified style. You don't have to go back and reapply any of the styles with new definitions. This automatic updating capability makes styles one of the most flexible and helpful Word tools.

To modify the font in a style from serif to sans serif:

1. Click **Format** on the menu bar, and then click **Style** to display the Style dialog box.

2. Click **Heading 1** in the Style list box, click the **Modify** button to display the Modify Style dialog box, click the **Format** button, and then click **Font**. The Font dialog box opens. See Figure 5-10. The name of the current font, Times New Roman, is highlighted in the Font text box.

Figure 5-10 ◀
Font dialog box

type new font name here

current font (selected)

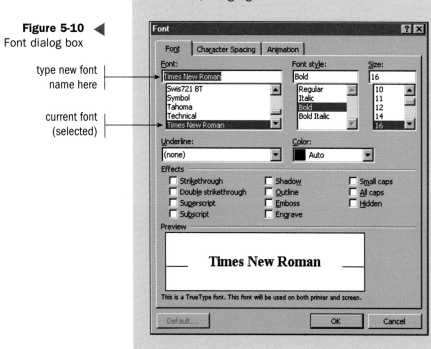

3. Type the font name **Arial**, so the font name becomes highlighted in the font list, and then click the **OK** button. Typing all or part of a font name is a fast way to locate a particular font in a long list. The Modify Style dialog box now shows the Heading 1 text in 16-point Arial bold, as shown in the Preview box and in the Description.

4. Click the **OK** button. The Style dialog box should still appear on the screen.

5. Repeat Steps 2 through 4, except modify the Heading 2 and Heading 3 styles. Now all three style definitions should include the sans serif font Arial.

   Now you'll change the font of the Normal (default) style from Times New Roman to Century Schoolbook (or to New Century Schoolbook), a better font for documents with wide columns.

6. Repeat Steps 2 through 4, except modify the Normal style so that the font is Century Schoolbook or New Century Schoolbook.

7. Click the **Close** button on the Style dialog box to return to the normal document window. Move the insertion point to the beginning of the document. See Figure 5-11.

Figure 5-11
Document window with modified styles

Heading 1 style (Arial font)

Normal style (Century Schoolbook font)

Heading 2 style (Arial font)

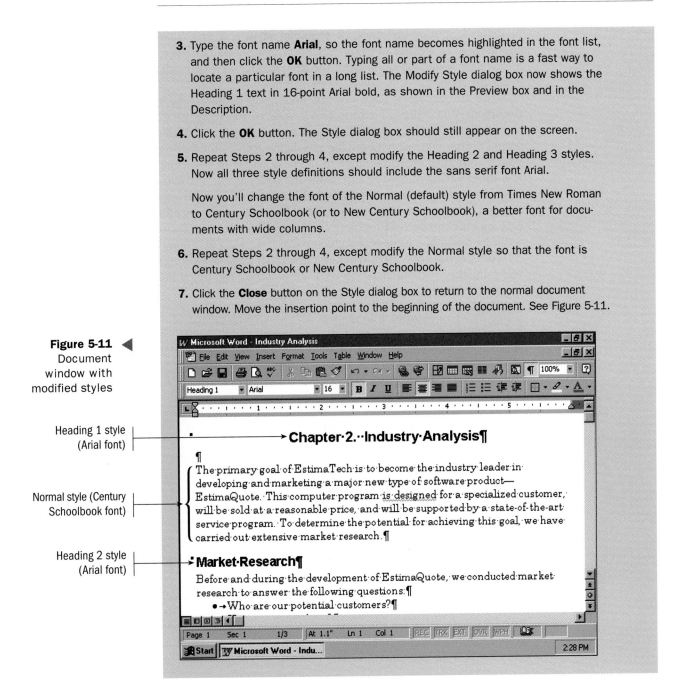

The Heading 1 and Heading 2 styles in the document now appear in the Arial font, and the main text appears in Century Schoolbook font. When you apply Heading 3 in the document, it also will be in the Arial font.

Defining New Styles with the Style Command

To add interest and improve appearance of each chapter in their business plan, Robert asks you to define a new style for the introductory (first) paragraph of each chapter. **Defining**, or creating, a new style is very similar to modifying an existing style. To define a new style, you specify a style type (paragraph or character), provide it a new style name, and give it a new style definition. A **paragraph style** is a style that you apply to complete paragraphs, including short paragraphs such as titles and headings. To apply a paragraph style to a particular paragraph, you can select the paragraph or simply move the insertion point to any location within the paragraph, and then apply the style just as you apply any predefined or modified style. A **character style** is a style that you apply to a single character or to a range of characters, such as a phrase, sentence, or paragraph. To apply a character style, you must select the desired character or range of characters, and then apply the style.

Word automatically adds any new styles you define to the style list of your current document, but it doesn't attach a new style to the template unless you specify that it should. For example, you could save the style list from a recommendation report to a new template after you finish modifying and defining styles for that report. Later, Robert could attach your customized template to the next report he's working on and quickly format it without having to modify and define the styles again. You can also define all your own styles for a document, and then save the styles in a customized document template that you can use again for similar documents. Regardless of the method you use, styles are an easy way for companies to achieve a consistent look to their documents, without excessive work by individual writers in the company.

Word provides two ways to define a new style: using an existing paragraph as an example and using the Style command on the Format menu. You'll first use the Style command.

REFERENCE window	**DEFINING A STYLE**
	■ Format a paragraph with the font, margins, alignment, spacing, and so forth, that you want for the style, and then select the paragraph.
	■ Click in the Style text box on the Formatting toolbar.
	■ Type the name of the new style (replacing the current style name), and then press the Enter key.
	or
	■ Select the text for which you want to define a style.
	■ Click Format on the menu bar, click Style, click the New button, and type the name of the new style in the Name text box.
	■ Click Format on the menu bar, and then specify the formatting options you want for the style.
	■ Click the OK button, and then click the Apply button.

Now Robert wants you to define a new style to apply to the first paragraph of each chapter in their business plan. They want the first paragraph to present the major topic and set the direction for the entire chapter. Because of this, they want the first paragraph to be indented and justified, and to appear in Arial font. You'll now define a style, called First Paragraph, that contains these formatting features.

To define the new style:

   1. Move the insertion point anywhere within the first paragraph of the document, below the chapter title. You could also select the paragraph. You'll now define the style.

   2. Click **Format** on the menu bar, and then click **Style**. The Style dialog box opens. Click the **List** list arrow, and then click **Styles in use**, to indicate that you only want to display styles that are currently being used in the document. See Figure 5-12.

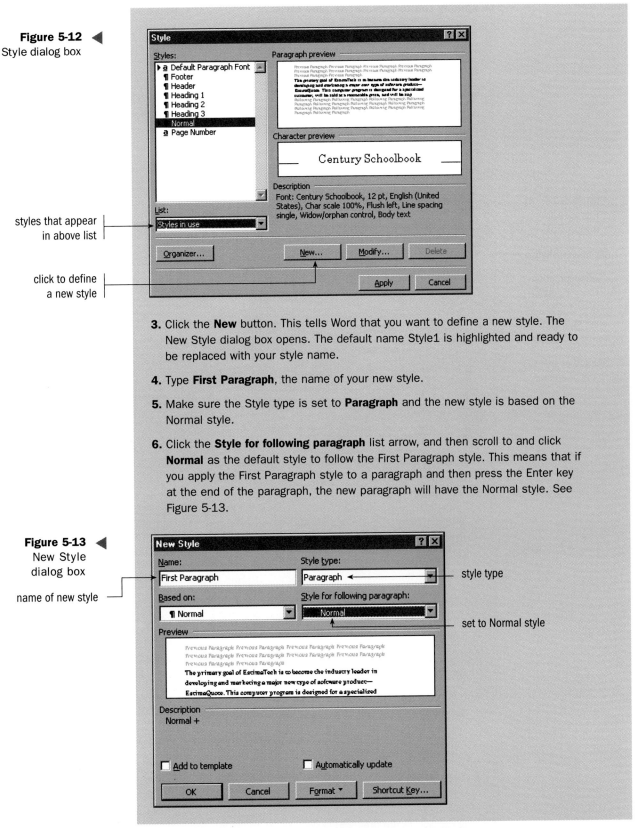

Figure 5-12 ◀
Style dialog box

styles that appear
in above list

click to define
a new style

3. Click the **New** button. This tells Word that you want to define a new style. The New Style dialog box opens. The default name Style1 is highlighted and ready to be replaced with your style name.

4. Type **First Paragraph**, the name of your new style.

5. Make sure the Style type is set to **Paragraph** and the new style is based on the Normal style.

6. Click the **Style for following paragraph** list arrow, and then scroll to and click **Normal** as the default style to follow the First Paragraph style. This means that if you apply the First Paragraph style to a paragraph and then press the Enter key at the end of the paragraph, the new paragraph will have the Normal style. See Figure 5-13.

Figure 5-13 ◀
New Style
dialog box

name of new style

style type

set to Normal style

You have told Word the name and type of the new style, and have specified the style that should apply to any paragraph after it when you press the Enter key in your document. Now you're ready to specify the format of the new style.

To specify the format of the new style:

1. Click the **Format** button and then click **Paragraph**. The Paragraph dialog box opens. If necessary, click the **Indents and Spacing** tab.

2. Change the Alignment to **Justified**.

3. Change the Spacing Before to **12 pt** and the Spacing After to **6 pt**. This will add white space above and below the paragraph so it stands out from the text surrounding it. Later, you'll add a border around the paragraph to make it stand out even more.

4. In the Indentation section of the dialog box, change Left to **0.5"**. See Figure 5-14.

Figure 5-14 ◄
Paragraph
dialog box

alignment setting ——

left indentation
setting ——

amount of space
above the paragraph ——

amount of space
below the paragraph ——

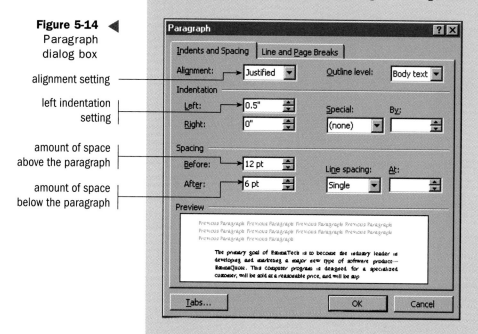

This completes the paragraph formatting. Next you'll change the font of the style from Times New Roman to Arial.

5. Click the **OK** button on the Paragraph dialog box, click the **Format** button, and then click **Font** on the shortcut menu. The Font dialog box opens.

6. Change the font to **Arial**. Leave the font style as Regular and the font size as 12 point. Click the **OK** button. The Font dialog box closes. Now you'll add a border around the paragraph.

7. Click the **Format** button, and then click **Border** on the shortcut menu. The Borders and Shading dialog box opens. If necessary, click the **Borders** tab.

8. In the Setting section of the dialog box, click the **Box** icon to place a box border around the paragraph, and then click the **OK** button.

Look over the New Style dialog box, especially the Description, to make sure you have defined the style as you would like it.

9. Click the **OK** button to close the New Style dialog box. With the First Paragraph style highlighted in the Styles list box of the Style dialog box, click the **Apply** button. The dialog box closes and, because the insertion point was in the first paragraph at the time you clicked Apply, the new paragraph style is applied to it. See Figure 5-15.

Figure 5-15 ◀
Newly defined
style

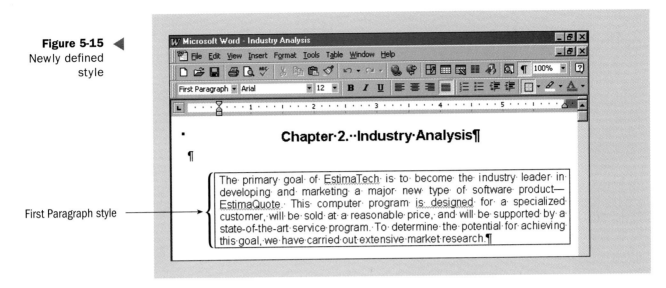

First Paragraph style ──────▶

You have defined and applied the new paragraph style called First Paragraph. Robert has also asked you to create a character style formatted with 10-point, bold, italic, Arial font. You'll create this style by example.

Robert wants you to use this style whenever the business plan lists phases of action, so you'll name the style "Phase." Instead of defining the style characteristics in the Style dialog box, this time you'll create the new style by example.

To create a character style by example:

1. Scroll down until you see the phrase "Phase 1. Analysis of potential customers," below the heading "Phases of the Market Research" and above the heading "Market Definition."

2. Select the phrase "Phase 1" (not including the period that follows the phrase).

3. Using the Formatting toolbar, set the font of the selected text to 10-point, bold, italic Arial.

4. Click **Format** on the menu bar, click **Style** to display the Style dialog box, and click the **New** button to display the New Style dialog box.

5. Type **Phase**, the name of the new style, and then change the Style type to **Character**. See Figure 5-16.

Figure 5-16 ◀
New Style
dialog box

style name ──────▶

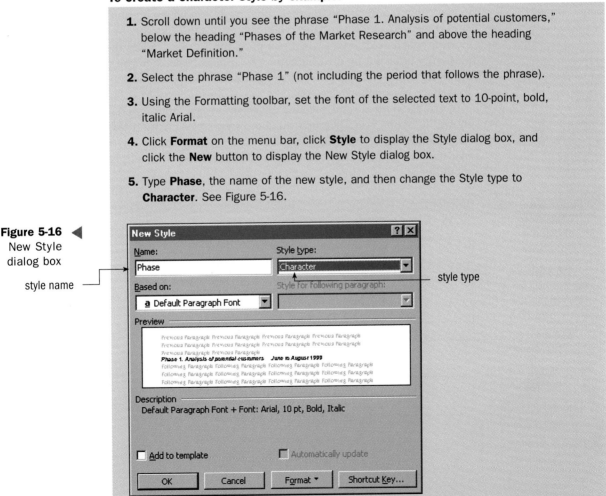

← style type

6. Click the **OK** button to return to the Style dialog box, and then click the **Apply** button.

This creates the new character style called "Phase." You'll now apply this style to text in the next two lines.

To apply a character style:

1. Select the phrase "Phase 2" on the line below the current location of the insertion point.

2. Click the **Style** list arrow on the Formatting toolbar, and then click **Phase**. The selected text becomes formatted in bold, italic, Arial font.

3. Apply the Phase style to the phrase "Phase 3" on the next line.

You have now created and applied two new styles, one paragraph style and one character style. When you give Chiu Lee and Robert your file for this chapter, they will save the styles you have created and modified into a new template, which they will attach to existing future chapters of their business plan.

Setting Tab Stops

Tabs are useful for indenting paragraphs and for vertically aligning text or numerical data in columns. A **tab** adds space between the margin and text in a column, or between text in one column and text in another column. (If you were creating several long columns of data, however, you'd probably want to use a table instead of tabs.) A **tab stop** is the location where text moves when you press the Tab key. When the Show/Hide ¶ button is pressed, a nonprinting tab character ➡ appears wherever you press the Tab key. A tab character is just like any other screen character you type; you can delete it by pressing the Backspace key or the Delete key.

Word provides several **tab stop alignment styles**: left, centered, right, and decimal, as shown in Figure 5-17. The first three tab stop styles position text in a similar way to the Align Left, Center, and Align Right buttons on the Formatting toolbar. The difference is that with a tab, you can determine line by line, where the left, center, or right alignment should occur.

Figure 5-17 ◄
Tab stop
alignment
styles

tab alignment
selector (with left-
aligned tab stop
marker)

left-aligned tab
stop marker

center-aligned tab
stop marker

right-aligned tab
stop marker

decimal-aligned tab
stop marker

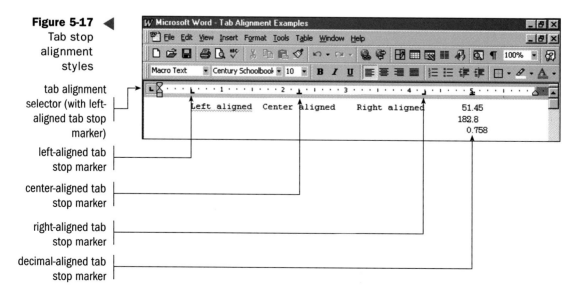

The default tab stops on the ruler are **left-aligned tab stops**, which position the left edge of text at the tab stop, and extend the text to the right. **Centered tab stops** position text so that it's centered evenly on both sides of the tab stop. **Right-aligned tab stops** position the right edge of text at the tab stop, and extend the text to the left. **Decimal-aligned tab stops** position numbers so that their decimal points are aligned at the tab stop.

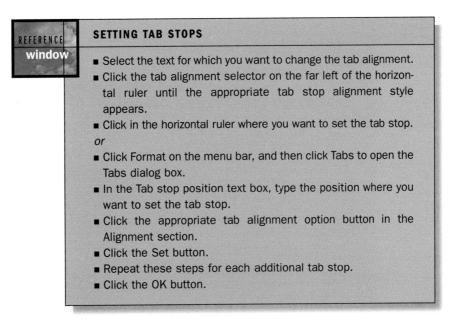

REFERENCE window

SETTING TAB STOPS

- Select the text for which you want to change the tab alignment.
- Click the tab alignment selector on the far left of the horizontal ruler until the appropriate tab stop alignment style appears.
- Click in the horizontal ruler where you want to set the tab stop.

or

- Click Format on the menu bar, and then click Tabs to open the Tabs dialog box.
- In the Tab stop position text box, type the position where you want to set the tab stop.
- Click the appropriate tab alignment option button in the Alignment section.
- Click the Set button.
- Repeat these steps for each additional tab stop.
- Click the OK button.

Word's default tab stop settings are every one-half inch, as indicated by the small gray ticks at the bottom of the ruler shown in Figure 5-18. You set a new tab stop by selecting a tab stop alignment style (from the tab alignment selector at the left end of the horizontal ruler) and then clicking on the horizontal ruler to insert the tab stop. You can remove a tab stop from the ruler by clicking it and dragging the tab stop off the ruler.

Figure 5-18
Ruler with
tab stops

ruler →

tab stops every
0.5 inch

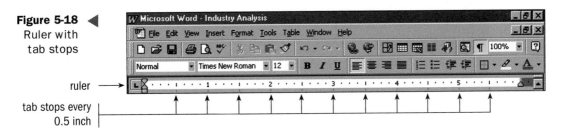

You should never try to align columns of text by adding extra spaces with the spacebar. Although the text might seem precisely aligned in the document window, it might not be aligned when you print the document. Furthermore, if you edit the text aligned with extra spaces, the alignment is disturbed, whereas if you edit text aligned with tabs, the alignment usually remains intact. If you are going to add a lot of text, however, it is better to use a table.

All the main paragraphs in the document are formatted with the correct indentation and alignment. Robert indicated that the second column of the two-column list of the Phases of the Market Research (to which you just applied the character style) should be aligned to make the information more attractive and readable. Robert pressed the Tab key between the first and second columns of text when he wrote the first draft of the business plan, but he didn't set the tab stop on the ruler. You'll set a new tab stop.

You can add new tab stops by clicking the bottom of the ruler. When you click that part of the ruler, Word removes the default tab stops, indicated by small tick marks, and adds a new tab stop marker.

To add a new tab stop on the ruler:

1. Make sure the current tab stop alignment style is ⌊L⌋, as shown in Figure 5-18. If ⌊L⌋ doesn't appear at that location, click the tab alignment selector one or more times until ⌊L⌋ does appear.

2. Select the three paragraphs of text that begin with the Phase character style.

3. Change the font size to 10 points, so that each paragraph in the list of phases will fit on one line of text when you set the new tab stop.

4. Click the pointer on the tab stop that occurs at 4.0 inches. Word automatically inserts a left tab stop at that location and removes the tab stop ticks to its left. The second column of text shifts the location of the new tab stop.

5. Deselect the highlighted text and then move the insertion point anywhere in the list of phases. See Figure 5-19.

Figure 5-19
Left tab stop
on ruler

new tab stop

aligned second
column

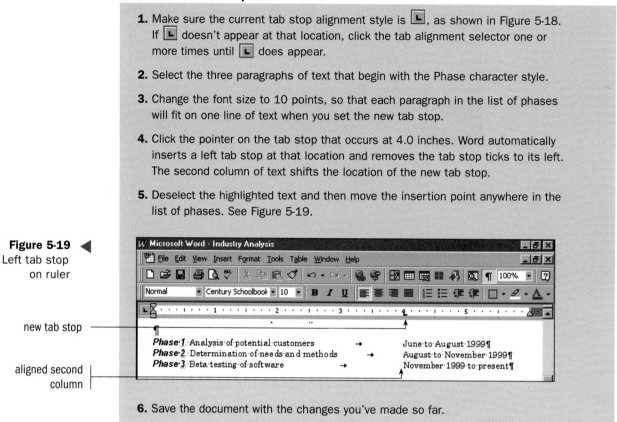

6. Save the document with the changes you've made so far.

The two columns of information are now aligned, as Robert requested. Notice that Word changed the tab stops only for the selected paragraphs, not for all the paragraphs in the document.

Quick Check

1. What is the Thesaurus?

2. List at least four synonyms that the Thesaurus provides for the word "placed."

3. How do you find an explanation of the grammar rule for a potential grammar error that Word flags in your document?

4. Define serif and sans serif font. When would you use each of these types of fonts? Give two examples of each.

5. How do you modify a predefined style?

6. Describe the two methods for defining a new style.

7. Explain the difference between a paragraph style and a character style.

8. How do you set the location of a tab stop using the ruler?

You have improved the EstimaTech business plan chapter by modifying the word choice and writing style, by selecting proper fonts, and by using styles to give the plan a consistent look. You've also used tabs to make the project timetable more attractive and readable. Next you'll change the business plan's organization using outline view, and then draw a table that summarizes EstimaTech's research on market size.

SESSION

5.2

In this session, you'll learn how to rearrange the document using outline view. You'll also learn how to insert a table using the Draw Table command, sort the data within the table, change the existing table structure, change the weight of rules (lines) within the table, and add a caption to the table.

Creating and Editing an Outline

Chiu Lee and Robert created an outline of their business plan with the Word Outline feature. An **outline** is a list of the basic points of a document and the order in which to present them. You can create an outline before typing any other text of a document, or you can view and edit the outline of an existing document created in normal view or in page layout view. When you create an outline when you first create a document, you open a blank document and change to outline view. Word then automatically applies heading styles (Heading 1, Heading 2, and so forth) to the outline paragraphs that you type. To create an outline as you type the text of a document in normal view or page layout view, you must apply heading styles (Heading 1, Heading 2, and so forth) to all the headings in your document. Chiu Lee and Robert used this latter method as they wrote their business plan. You'll change to outline view to modify and reorganize the outline.

In outline view, you can see and edit as many as nine levels of headings in a document. As with any outline, the broadest or most general topic is the first-level heading (in Heading 1 style) and the remaining topics become increasingly narrow or more specific with second-level headings (in Heading 2 style) and in subsequent headings (in Heading 3 style, and so on).

After reviewing the organization of the business plan, you realize that the market research explanation should appear before the results. That means the topic "Current Competition" should appear after the topic "Market Trends." Also the topic "Size of the Market" should appear before "Demographic Description of Target Users." Because you have applied the predefined heading styles to the headings, you can easily reorder the text in outline view.

In outline view, the Outline toolbar replaces the ruler. As you reorder the headings, the text below the headings will move as well.

REFERENCE window	**CREATING AND EDITING OUTLINES**
	■ Click the Outline View button, or click View on the menu bar, and then click Outline.
	■ Enter new heading text or edit existing headings.
	■ Click the appropriate Show Heading button to show only that number of headings in your document.
	■ Click the Move Up button or the Move Down button to reorder text.
	■ Click the Promote button or the Demote button to increase or decrease the levels of headings.
	■ Click the Normal View button, or click View on the menu bar, and then click Normal.

Next, you'll reorganize the order of topics in outline view.

To use outline view:

1. If you took a break after the last session, make sure Word is running, check your screen, and make sure the Industry Analysis document is open. For this session, you should display nonprinting characters.

2. Make sure the insertion point is at the beginning of the document, and then click the **Outline View** button. The Outline toolbar replaces the ruler.

3. Click the **Show Heading 3** button on the Outline toolbar to display three levels of headings. The document has only two levels of headings now, but later it will have three. The gray underlining below each heading indicates that text follows the heading. Notice that the space above and below each heading disappears and the headings are realigned in an outline format with each level of headings indented more than the previous level. See Figure 5-20.

Figure 5-20
Document in outline view

Level-1 outline heading

Level-2 outline heading

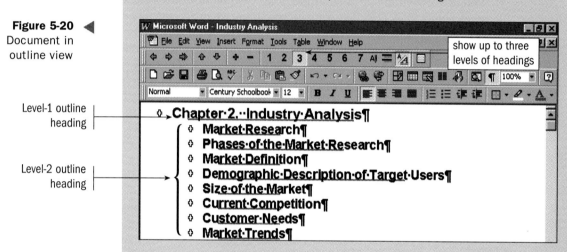

TROUBLE? If all the text changes to the same font type, style, and size, then click the Show Formatting button to show the styles formats.

TROUBLE? Depending on how your machine is set up, your outline toolbar may be in a different location.

Now that you see only the headings of the business plan, it is easier to edit the organization by reordering some headings and by changing the levels of some headings.

Moving Headings Up and Down in an Outline

You can rearrange the order of topics in an outline by moving the headings up and down in outline view. When you move a heading in outline view, any text below that heading (indicated by the underline) moves with it. Earlier you decided to move "Current Competition" (and its accompanying text) to follow the section "Market Trends."

To move headings in outline view:

1. Place the insertion point anywhere in the heading "Current Competition," and then click the **Move Down** button on the Outline toolbar. The heading and the text below it move down one line to follow the heading "Customer Needs," which does not move.

2. Click again to move the "Current Competition" heading to the end of the chapter, after "Market Trends."

Now you'll move the heading "Size of the Market" before "Demographic Description of Target Users."

3. Place the insertion point anywhere in the heading "Size of the Market," and then click the **Move Up** button 🔼 on the Outline toolbar. The heading and the text below it move up one line to appear just below "Market Definition."

Now that the topics of the outline are in a better order, you realize that some second-level headings (text in Heading 2 style) need to be third-level headings (in Heading 3 style).

Promoting and Demoting Headings in an Outline

You can easily change the levels of headings in outline view. To **promote** a heading means to increase the level of a heading—for example, to change an item from a third-level heading to a second-level heading. To **demote** a heading means to decrease the level, for example, to change a first-level heading to a second-level heading. Any changes you make in the heading levels in Outline view will automatically be reflected in other views.

While reviewing Chapter 2 of the business plan, you realize that the heading "Size of the Market" and "Demographic Description of Target Users" should actually be sub-headings below the heading "Market Definition." You'll now demote these two headings.

To demote headings:

1. While still in outline view, make sure the insertion point is in the heading "Size of the Market" or the heading is still selected, and then click the **Demote** button ⏩ on the Outline toolbar. The heading moves right and becomes a third-level heading with the Heading 3 style.

2. Place the insertion point anywhere in the heading "Demographic Description of Target Users," and then click the **Demote** button ⏩. Again, the heading moves right and becomes a third-level heading. See Figure 5-21.

Figure 5-21 ◀
Promoting and demoting headings

click to promote heading

click to demote heading

demoted headings

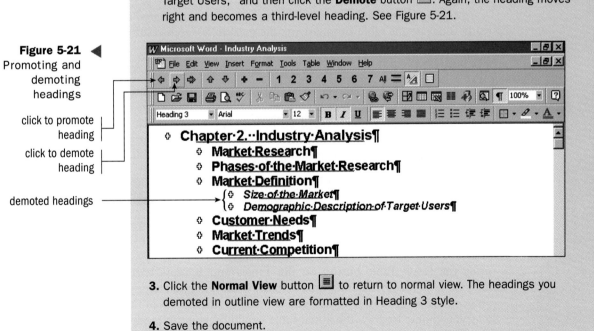

3. Click the **Normal View** button 📄 to return to normal view. The headings you demoted in outline view are formatted in Heading 3 style.

4. Save the document.

Promoting a heading in outline view is just as easy as demoting. You place the insertion point in the desired heading and click the Promote button.

Printing the Outline

If you print the document in outline view, only the text in the document window (in our case, only the outline itself) will print.

To print the outline:

1. Click the **Outline View** button 🔲.

2. Click the **Show Formatting** button 🔳 on the Outline toolbar to deselect it. Word converts the outline to plain text (whatever text is the Normal style).

3. Click the **Print** button 🖨 on the Standard toolbar to print the outline. See Figure 5-22.

Chapter 2. Industry Analysis
    Market Research
    Phases of the Market Research
    Market Definition
        Size of the Market
        Demographic Description of Target Users
    Customer Needs
    Market Trends
    Current Competition

4. Click 🔳 again to show the formatting of the outline text.

5. Click the **Page Layout View** button 🔲. You'll want to be in page layout view when you draw a table in the next section.

You have reorganized Chapter 2 of the business plan, printed the outline, and are now ready to create the table summarizing the market research results.

Drawing and Editing Tables

In the first session, you learned how to align text in columns using tabs. Tabs work well if you have only two or three columns with three or four rows of information, but tabs and columns become tedious and difficult to work with when you need to organize a larger amount of more complex information. Word's Table feature allows you to quickly organize data, and to place text and graphics in a more readable format.

Creating a Table Using the Draw Table Command

As you know, a table is information arranged in horizontal rows and vertical columns to form a grid of cells. Earlier, you created a table using the Insert Table button on the Standard toolbar. You can also create a table by using the new Draw Table feature. By using the Draw Table button on the Tables and Borders toolbar, you can then drag diagonally in the document window to draw the size and shape of the entire table. Then you can draw (or erase) vertical and horizontal lines to fill in the table structure. Either way you choose to draw the initial table structure, you can modify it by using commands on the Table menu.

Robert wants you to create a table that summarizes the information on EstimaTech's potential customers. You'll use the Draw Table command to create that table.

To create a blank table using the Draw Table command:

1. Scroll until you see the paragraph entitled "Size of the Market" near the top of page 2. Position the insertion point after the phrase "... in restoration cost estimates" and before the paragraph mark at the end of the paragraph.

2. Press the **Enter** key to insert a blank line into the document. The insertion point is now at the location where you want the table.

3. Click the **Tables and Borders** button 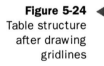 on the Standard toolbar. The Tables and Borders toolbar opens, the document window automatically switches to page layout view, if it wasn't in that view already, and the pointer changes to ∥.

4. Scroll the document window, if necessary, so that the paragraph mark at the insertion point is in the top half of the screen but not obscured by the Tables and Borders toolbar. Move ∥ to the location of the insertion point, press and hold the mouse button, drag the pointer down and to the right to form a rectangle the size and shape of the table you want, about 4.0 inches wide by 2.0 inches high. See Figure 5-23. Then release the mouse button. Word draws the rectangle border for a table with only one cell. You'll next create additional cells drawing row and column boundaries within the rectangle.

Figure 5-23 ◀
Drawing a table

Tables and Borders
toolbar

upper-left corner
of table

pointer at lower-right
corner of table

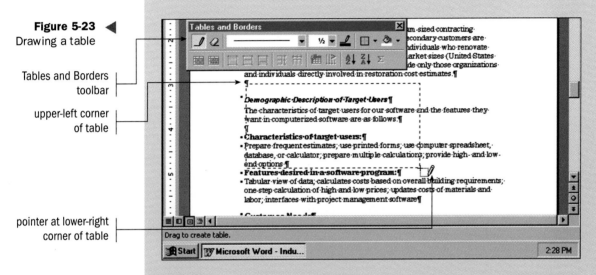

TROUBLE? If your rectangle isn't exactly the same size and shape as the one in Figure 5-23, don't worry; you can change the dimensions later.

5. Draw six horizontal border lines within the rectangle to create a total of seven rows in the table, and then draw two vertical border lines, one at about 1.5 inches and the other at about 2.75 inches, to create three columns. See Figure 5-24.

Figure 5-24 ◀
Table structure
after drawing
gridlines

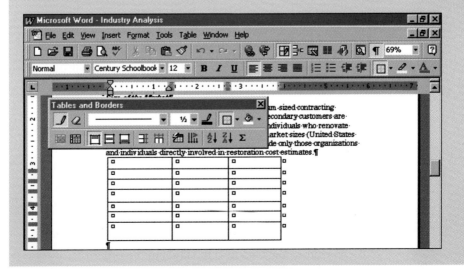

As you can see in Figure 5-24, the row heights and column widths don't have to be the same, because you can easily adjust them later. You'll begin by adjusting the row heights.

6. Click **Table** on the menu bar, and then click **Select Table**. The entire table becomes selected. This allows you to adjust the heights of all the rows at once.

7. Click the **Distribute Rows Evenly** button ⊞ on the Tables and Borders toolbar. The vertical borders move so that all the row heights are the same. The overall size of the table stays the same.

   As you look at the table, however, you realize that you don't necessarily want the row heights that appear on your screen. Instead, you would like Word to automatically adjust the row heights to fit the font of the text that you'll type into the table.

8. With the entire table still selected, click **Table** on the menu bar, click **Cell Height and Width** to display the Cell Height and Width dialog box, click the **Row** tab (if necessary), click the **Height of row** list arrow, click **Auto**, and then click the **OK** button. Deselect the table, but leave the insertion point inside the table.

Now that you've created the table, you're ready to enter the customer data Robert gave you. You can enter text in a table by moving the insertion point to a cell and typing. If the text takes up more than one line in the cell, Word automatically wraps the text to the next line and increases the height of that cell and all the cells in that row.

To enter text into the table:

1. Move the insertion point to cell A1 (the cell in the upper-left corner of the table), and type **Potential Customers**, press the **Tab** key, type **Percent**, press the **Tab** key, type **Number**, and press the **Tab** key to move to cell A2, the first cell on the second row.

2. Continue inserting text into the table until it looks like Figure 5-25.

Figure 5-25 ◀
Table with
completed
information

heading row

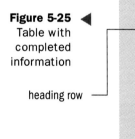

Potential Customers□	Percent□	Number□	□
Contractors□	40%□	14,400□	□
Government Agencies□	3%□	1,080□	□
Private Foundations□	1%□	360□	□
Subcontractors□	47%□	16,900□	□
Individuals□	9%□	3,200□	□
Miscellaneous□	0.1%□	36□	□

TROUBLE? If a new row (row 8) appeared in your table, you pressed the Tab key after entering text in cell A7, the last cell in the table. Click the Undo button ↰ on the Standard toolbar to remove row 8 from the table.

TROUBLE? If the text in some cells wraps down to make two lines of text in the cell, don't worry. You'll adjust the cell widths later.

3. Save the document with the new table.

You entered the data into the table in the order that Robert provided. You decide that you want to reorder the data in a more logical manner. You can manually cut and paste rows in the table, but it is much easier to reorganize the table by sorting the rows.

Sorting Rows in a Table

Word allows you to **sort**, automatically rearrange information, in alphabetical, numerical, or chronological order. The most common use for sorting is to rearrange rows in a table, but you can use the Sort feature to sort any list of information. For example, in the table you just created (Table 1), you could sort the list of potential customers alphabetically in ascending alphabetical order (from A to Z) or in descending alphabetical order (from Z to A). Alternatively, you could sort the table numerically in descending numerical order (highest to lowest) or in ascending numerical order (lowest to highest). When you sort table data, Word does not sort the heading row into the other information, but instead leaves the heading row at the top of the table as long as you indicate that you have used a heading row.

Robert feels that arranging the potential customers in the table in ascending numerical order, from the lowest percentage to the highest percentage, best emphasizes who will most likely purchase EstimaQuote.

To sort the information in the table:

1. Place the insertion point anywhere within the table.

2. Click **Table** on the menu bar, and then click **Sort**. The entire table is selected, and the Sort dialog box opens showing column 1, "Potential Customers," as the Sort by column. You want to sort by the Percent column, so you'll need to change the Sort By column.

3. Click the **Sort by** list arrow, and then click **Percent** from the list of column headings.

4. Make sure **Number** appears in the Type list box as the sort type.

5. If necessary, click the **Ascending** option button to select the sort order.

6. If necessary, click the **Header row** option button. This ensures that Word won't include the row containing the column headings in the sort. The dialog box should match Figure 5-26.

Figure 5-26 ◀
Sort dialog box

heading of
sort column

indicates header row
(not to be sorted)

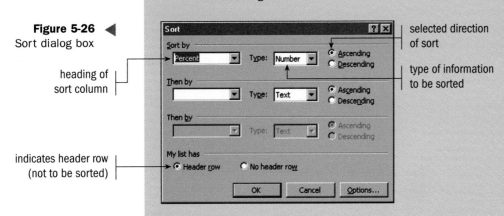

selected direction
of sort

type of information
to be sorted

7. Click the **OK** button to perform the sort, and then deselect the highlighted rows by clicking anywhere in the table. Rows 2 through 7 of the table are now arranged numerically from the lowest to the highest percentage in the Percent column. See Figure 5-27.

Figure 5-27 ◀
Table after
being sorted

values sorted in
ascending order

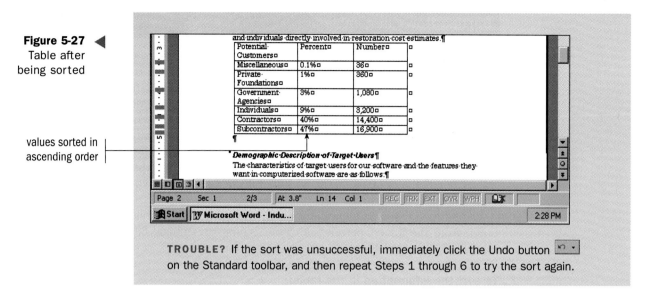

and·individuals·directly·involved·in·restoration·cost·estimates.¶

Potential· Customers□	Percent□	Number□	□
Miscellaneous□	0.1%□	36□	□
Private· Foundations□	1%□	360□	□
Government· Agencies□	3%□	1,080□	□
Individuals□	9%□	3,200□	□
Contractors□	40%□	14,400□	□
Subcontractors□	47%□	16,900□	□

¶

Demographic·Description·of·Target·Users¶
The·characteristics·of·target·users·for·our·software·and·the·features·they·
want·in·computerized·software·are·as·follows:¶

Page 2   Sec 1   2/3   At 3.8"   Ln 14   Col 1   REC TRK EXT OVR WPH 🗅🗷   Σ

Start | 🝚 Microsoft Word - Indu...   2:28 PM

TROUBLE? If the sort was unsuccessful, immediately click the Undo button 🔄 ▾
on the Standard toolbar, and then repeat Steps 1 through 6 to try the sort again.

You have just finished sorting the information in the table, when Robert stops by and asks you to total columns B and C. You'll need to modify the structure of the table so you can show totals for the data in the table.

Modifying an Existing Table Structure

Often when you create a table, you're unsure how many rows or columns you'll actually need. You might need to delete extra rows and columns, or, as in this case, you might need to add them. Either way, you can easily modify or change an existing table's structure.

Inserting Additional Rows in a Table

Word allows you to insert additional rows within the table or at the end of a table. You can insert a row or rows within the table with the Insert Rows command on the Table menu. To insert a row at the end of the table, you simply place the insertion point in the last cell of the last row and press the Tab key.

Within the table in the business plan, you need to insert a row for totals at the bottom of the table.

To insert a row at the bottom of the table:

1. Click cell **C7**, the last cell of the last row in the table, which contains the number "16,900."

2. Press the **Tab** key. A blank row is added to the bottom of the table similar to the rows above it. You might need to scroll the document window to see the entire table.

   TROUBLE? If a blank row is not added to the bottom of the table, click the Undo button 🔄 ▾ on the Standard toolbar. Check to make sure the insertion point is in the last cell of the last row, and then press the Tab key.

3. Type **Totals** in cell A8, press the **Tab** key, click the **AutoSum** button Σ on the Tables and Borders toolbar, press the **Tab** key, and then click Σ again. The column sums appear in the Totals row.

You now decide to delete row 2 from the table because the numbers in the Miscellaneous customers category are so small, and therefore an insignificant portion of EstimaQuote's potential customers.

Word

Deleting Rows and Columns in a Table

With Word, you can delete either the contents of the cells or the structure of the cells. To delete the contents of the cells in a selected row, you press the Delete key. However, to delete both the contents and structure of a selected row or column from the table entirely, you must choose the Delete Rows or Delete Columns command from the Table menu.

You'll delete the row using the Table shortcut menu, which contains frequently used table commands.

To delete a row using the Table shortcut menu:

1. Click the selection bar next to row 2 to select the row that contains the Miscellaneous item.

2. With the pointer ⤢ anywhere over the selected text, click the right mouse button. The Table shortcut menu opens.

3. Click **Delete Rows**. The selected row is deleted from the table structure.

   TROUBLE? If the Table shortcut menu displays Delete Cells, you have right-clicked without first selecting the row. Repeat Steps 1 through 4, making sure you select row 2 before right-clicking within the row.

4. Select the two cells containing the sums at the bottom of the table, and then press the **F9** key (which in Word is the Update key). The totals are updated to include only the rows now in the table.

5. Deselect the cells. See Figure 5-28.

Figure 5-28 ◀
Table after
deleting row

"Miscellaneous"
row deleted

totals updated

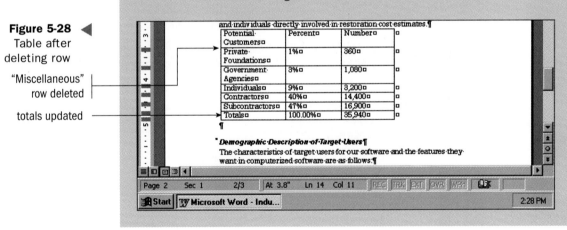

You have modified the structure of the table in the business plan by inserting and deleting rows. Now you'll complete the formatting of the table by adjusting the column widths and changing the thickness of the borders between rows.

Changing Column Width with the Alt Key

The appearance and readability of the table will improve significantly if you change the column widths to fit the data better. You're already familiar with dragging the table gridlines to adjust the column widths. Here you'll use the same procedures, except you'll hold down the Alt key so that you can read the column width in inches on the ruler.

To change the width of the columns by dragging the gridlines:

1. Place the insertion point anywhere in the table. Make sure you do not select any cells.

2. Move the pointer over the gridline between columns A and B. The pointer changes to ⊹.

3. Press and hold down the **Alt** key (to display the column widths on the ruler), drag the boundary gridline to the right, until the first column width is about 1.75 inches, and then release the mouse button and the Alt key.

4. Again while holding down the **Alt** key, click and drag the gridline between columns B and C to the left, until the second column width is about 0.85 inch.

5. Now, again holding down the **Alt** key, click and drag the gridline on the right side of the table (to the right of column C) until the third column is also about 0.85 inch in width.

The table now appears as it should. Now you'll right-align the numeric data in the table to make it more readable.

Selecting Columns and Aligning Text

The percentages and numbers of potential customers in the table would be much easier to read if they were right-aligned. The headings of columns B and C would also look better if they were right-aligned.

To select an entire column and right-align text and data:

1. Make sure the insertion point is in one of the cells in the table.

2. Move the pointer to the top of column B, so that the pointer changes to ↓, and then click the top of the column to select the entire column. Now that you've selected the column, you can align the text within it.

3. Click the **Align Right** button 🔳 on the Formatting toolbar. The highlighted text right-aligns.

4. Using the same procedure, align the text and numbers in column C. See Figure 5-29.

Figure 5-29 ◀
Columns of text
right-aligned

gray selection
indicates formulas

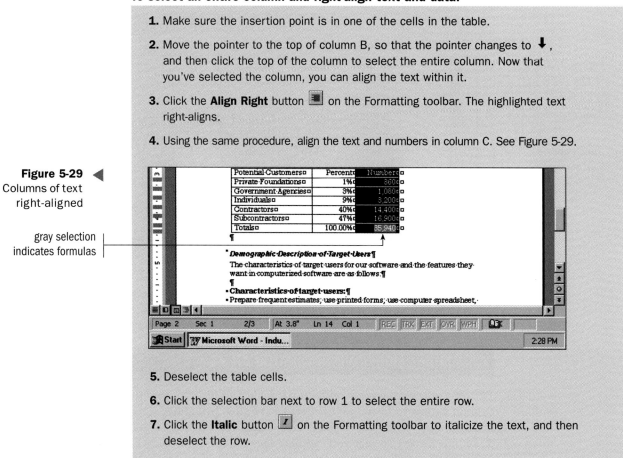

5. Deselect the table cells.

6. Click the selection bar next to row 1 to select the entire row.

7. Click the **Italic** button 🔳 on the Formatting toolbar to italicize the text, and then deselect the row.

You now decide to make the tables more attractive and more readable by changing the table's borders and rules.

Changing Borders and Rules with Draw Table

Word allows you to add or modify a table's borders and rules. The **border** is the box that frames tables and table cells, text, or graphics; it is made up of four rules. A **rule** is a horizontal or vertical line that you use to set off a portion of your document to enhance its appearance or improve its readability. Rules can be placed to the right, left, top, or bottom of table cells, text, or graphics.

You can modify the existing borders and rules (or even create new ones) using the Tables and Borders toolbar.

To modify the rules of the table:

1. Make sure the insertion point is anywhere within the table.

2. Click the **Line Weight** list arrow on the Tables and Borders toolbar, and then click **1 1/2 pt** so that the current line weight becomes 1.5 points.

3. Move ⌀ to the upper-left corner of the table, drag the pointer along the top border of the table to the upper-right corner, and then release the mouse button. The top border becomes a thicker line.

   TROUBLE? If you can't see any change in the line weights, you'll be able to see the change once you switch to normal view.

4. Repeat Step 3 to draw a thicker line below the heading row, above the Totals row, and at the bottom of the table.

   Now you'll use a similar method to remove rules (without removing the gridlines) between rows of the table.

5. Click the **Line Style** list arrow on the Tables and Borders toolbar, and then click **No Border**.

6. Drag ⌀ along the rule between rows 2 and 3 (that is, between the first and second row of data). Only the light gray gridline remains.

   TROUBLE? If you don't see the light gray gridline, click Table on the menu bar and then click Show Gridlines.

7. Repeat Step 6 to remove the horizontal rules between all the rows of data.

8. Close the Tables and Borders toolbar. The mouse pointer returns to I. Then switch to normal view. See Figure 5-30.

Figure 5-30 ◀
Table after changing line weights and styles

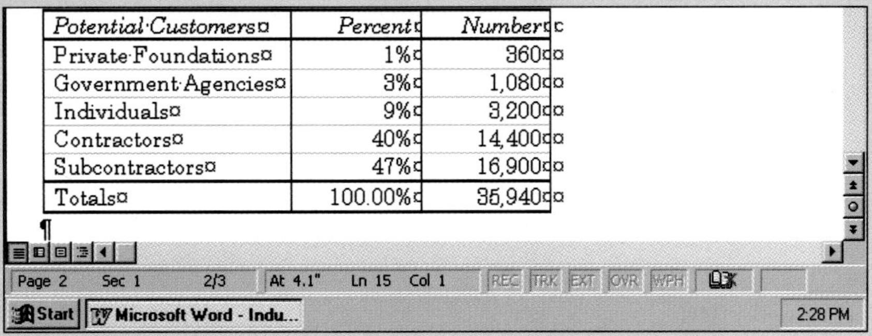

Potential·Customers¤	Percent¤	Number¤	¤
Private·Foundations¤	1%¤	360¤	¤
Government·Agencies¤	3%¤	1,080¤	¤
Individuals¤	9%¤	3,200¤	¤
Contractors¤	40%¤	14,400¤	¤
Subcontractors¤	47%¤	16,900¤	¤
Totals¤	100.00%¤	35,940¤	¤

Page 2   Sec 1   2/3 | At 4.1"   Ln 15   Col 1 | REC   TRK   EXT   OVR   WPH   ⬛

🔳Start | 📄 Microsoft Word - Indu... | 2:28 PM

Changing the rules on the table has made the table more readable and attractive.

Centering a Table

If a table doesn't fill the entire page width, you can center it between the left and right margins. The Center button on the Formatting toolbar centers only text within each selected cell, not the table across the page. To center a table across the page (between the left and right margins), you need to use the Table Cell Height and Width command.

The market size table will stand out more and look better if it is centered between the left and right margins.

To center the table across the page:

1. Place the insertion point anywhere within the table, click **Table** on the menu bar, and then click **Cell Height and Width**. The Cell Height and Width dialog box opens.

2. Click the **Row** tab, if necessary, to display row information.

3. In the Alignment section, click the **Center** option button. This will center the table between the left and right margins.

    You also want to make sure that a page break doesn't occur within rows in a table in the Cell Height and Width dialog box.

4. Click the **Allow row to break across pages** check box to deselect this option. Now if the table happens to span more than one page, all the contents of any row will always appear on one page or another, but not split between pages. See Figure 5-31. Your value for indent from left might be different.

Figure 5-31 ◀
Cell Height
and Width
dialog box

Row tab —

check box
deselected

select to center table
across page

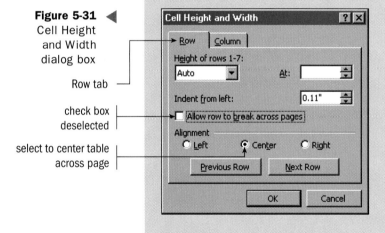

5. Click the **OK** button. The table centers between the left and right margins.

Now that you have completed formatting the table, you'll add a caption to it.

Adding a Caption to a Table

Robert likes the table format, but because the other chapters of the business plan will have numerous tables, he wants you to make them easier to understand and reference by adding captions. A **caption,** text that identifies a table or figure with a number and name, allows a reader to quickly determine the content of tabular material or other figures. You could just type captions for each table right in the document, but Word's Caption feature formats the captions with bold type and adds space above and below the caption. It even updates the table number in the caption automatically if you add, delete, or move tables. You can place the caption above or below the table or anywhere else you want.

Word

REFERENCE window

ADDING A CAPTION

- Place the insertion point on a blank line above or below the table or figure.
- Click Insert on the menu bar, and then click Caption.
- Click the Label list arrow, and then choose a label type.
- Type the caption in the Caption text box.
- Click the Numbering button, click the Format list arrow, and choose a numbering type format you want to use.
- Click the OK button in both the Numbering and the Caption dialog boxes.

For the business plan, Chiu Lee and Robert have been placing captions below the tables. You'll add a caption below Table 1.

To add a caption:

1. Move the insertion point to the blank line immediately below the table, the location where you want to insert the caption.

2. Click **Insert** on the menu bar, and then click **Caption**. The Caption dialog box opens with "Figure 1" or "Figure 1.1" in the Caption text box.

3. Click the **Label** list arrow to show a list of possible label names.

4. Click **Table** as the label name. The Caption text box changes to "Table 1."

5. Place the insertion point in the Caption text box following the phrase "Table 1," delete any spaces after the phrase, type a period (.), press the **spacebar** twice, and then type **Number of Potential Customers** as the title of Table 1. See Figure 5-32.

Figure 5-32 ◄
Caption
dialog box

text of caption ─

type of label ─

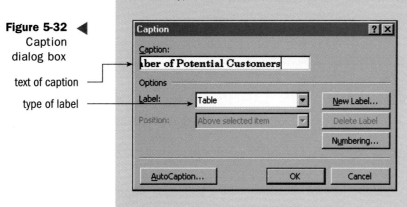

6. Click the **OK** button to close the Caption dialog box. Word inserts the caption into the document. The caption is now left-aligned beneath the table.

7. With the insertion point still at the end of the caption, click the **Center** button 🔲 on the Formatting toolbar. The caption centers below the table.

8. Save the document with the completed Table 1.

The caption emphasizes the purpose of the table, and makes it consistent with the other chapters of the business plan.

Quick Check

1 What is the purpose of moving headings up and down in an outline?

2 What does it mean to promote a heading? To demote a heading? Explain how to promote or demote a heading in a Word outline.

3 True or False: You can use outline view only if you have applied Word's predefined heading styles in normal view.

4 In what order would the following numbers appear in a table if you sorted them in ascending numerical order: 25, 10, 75, 45?

5 Define or describe the following:
a. border
b. rule

6 How do you center a table between the left and right margins?

7 What is the purpose of a table caption?

You have rearranged text in the EstimaTech business plan using outline view, and inserted and edited a table summarizing their market size research. Next you'll give the plan a more professional look by double-spacing and hyphenating the document, and help readers find related information by adding footnotes and a table of contents.

SESSION

5.3

In this session, you'll learn how to double-space the report, how to automatically hyphenate appropriate words at the end of lines, how to add footnotes and endnotes, and how to create a table of contents for a document. You'll also browse through the document by quickly jumping from one heading to another.

Double-Spacing the Lines in a Document

Robert informs you that he and Chiu Lee would like the text of the report double-spaced.

REFERENCE
window

DOUBLE-SPACING LINES OF TEXT

- Click Format on the menu bar, click Style, and click Normal (if necessary) in the Styles list, and then click the Modify button. The Modify Style dialog box opens.
- Click the Format button, and then click Paragraph on the shortcut menu.
- Click the Line Spacing list arrow, and then click Double.
- Click the OK button on the Paragraph dialog box, click the OK button on the Modify Style dialog box, and then click the Close button or the Apply button on the Style dialog box.

You'll now double-space the report by changing the paragraph format of the Normal style.

To double-space the document:

1. If you took a break after the last session, start Word, check your screen, and make sure the Industry Analysis document is open. For this session, you should display nonprinting characters and be in page layout view.

2. Move the insertion point to a paragraph to which the Normal style is applied.

3. Click **Format** on the menu bar, click **Style**, and make sure Normal is selected in the Styles list.

4. Click the **Modify** button. The Modify Style dialog box opens.

5. Click the **Format** button, and then click **Paragraph** on the shortcut menu. The Paragraph dialog box opens.

6. Click the **Line Spacing** list arrow, and then click **Double**. Notice that the Line Spacing list includes Single, Double, 1.5, and other types of spacing.

   Normally, with double-spacing, you don't want a blank, double-spaced line between each paragraph, but instead want to indent the first line of each paragraph. You'll fix the paragraph indentation now.

7. Click the **Special** list arrow in the Indentation section of the dialog box, and then click **First line**. Word sets the amount of indentation of the first line to 0.5 inch. See Figure 5-33.

Figure 5-33 ◀
Paragraph
dialog box

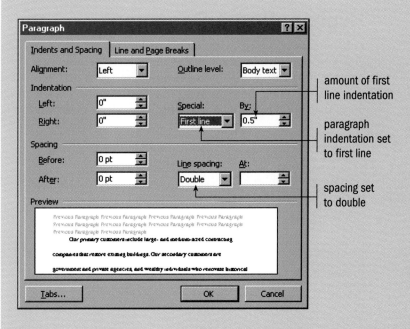

8. Click the **OK** button on the Paragraph dialog box, click the **OK** button on the Modify Style dialog box, and click the **Close** button on the Style dialog box.

The text of the report is double-spaced. You now must go through the document and fix formatting problems caused by changing to double-spacing.

To modify the business plan format:

1. Move the insertion point to the paragraph "Here is the time frame for the three phases," near the bottom of page 2.

2. Delete the blank lines above and below this paragraph.

3. Move the insertion point to the table, select the entire table, click **Format** on the menu bar, click **Paragraph**, and in the Paragraph dialog box, set the Line spacing back to **Single** and set the Special Indentation back to **(none)**.

4. Click the **Line and Page Breaks** tab, and click the **Keep lines together** and **Keep with next** check boxes to ensure that the entire table stays on the same page.

5. Click the **OK** button.

6. Move the insertion point about 3 lines below the table, and then delete the blank line above "Characteristics of Target Users," located below the next heading.

7. Move the insertion point anywhere within "Characteristics of Target Users," and set the paragraph format so that the paragraph is not indented. Repeat this for the next bolded text, "Features desired in a software program."

8. Delete all the other blank lines of text from the current location of the insertion point to the end of the document.

9. Modify the Heading 1, Heading 2, Heading 3, and Header styles so that they are not indented.

The document is now formatted well for double-spaced text.

Hyphenating a Document

One potential problem with left-aligned text is excessive raggedness along the right margin. You can solve the problem of raggedness by justifying the text, but that introduces another problem: Word inserts extra white space between words to stretch the lines of text to align along the right margin. Sometimes this causes unsightly **rivers**, that is, blank areas that run down a page and distract readers, as shown in Figure 5-34.

Figure 5-34 ◀
Rivers within a
justified column
of text

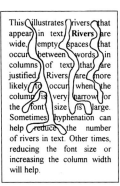

Hyphenating the text can sometimes reduce the raggedness in left-aligned text or reduce the rivers in justified text. The Hyphenation feature allows you to hyphenate a document either automatically, in which case Word decides the exact point at which to divide a word, or manually, in which case you can accept, reject, or change the suggested hyphenation.

To determine which words to hyphenate, Word uses a **hyphenation zone**, the amount of space at the right margin within which a word will be hyphenated. To increase the number of hyphenated words and thus reduce the amount of white space inserted between words, you can decrease the size of the hyphenation zone. To decrease the number of hyphenated words, which you might want to do so that only long words are hyphenated, you can increase the size of the hyphenation zone. You can also set how many successive lines can end with hyphenated words. If too many lines in a row end in a hyphen, this can be distracting and more difficult to read.

Robert asks you to hyphenate the business plan to eliminate as much raggedness as possible.

To set the hyphenation zone and to hyphenate the newsletter:

1. With the insertion point anywhere in the document, click **Tools** on the menu bar, point to **Language**, and then click **Hyphenation**. The Hyphenation dialog box opens.

2. Change the Hyphenation zone to **0.4"**. This decreases the amount of hyphenating by increasing the size of the zone that accepts words without hyphenation.

3. Set the Limit consecutive hyphens to **3**. This prevents Word from hyphenating words at the end of more than three lines in a row.

4. Click the **Automatically hyphenate document** check box. See Figure 5-35.

Figure 5-35
Hyphenation
dialog box

check box selected

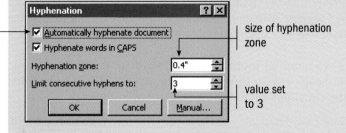

size of hyphenation
zone

value set
to 3

5. Click the **OK** button. Word goes through the document and hyphenates words as needed. For example, scroll the document so that the heading "Phases of Market Research" is at the top of the document window. You can now see several hyphenated words in Figure 5-36.

Figure 5-36
Document with
automatic
hyphenation

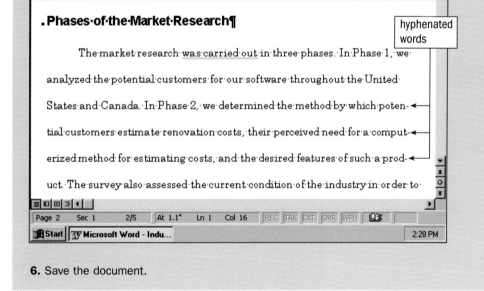

hyphenated
words

6. Save the document.

You should look through your document to make sure you like how Word has hyphenated it. For example, just below the heading "Market Definition," Word has hyphenated the word "After." If you don't like such hyphenations, then you should not set hyphenation to automatic but rather perform a manual hyphenation. You would make sure the Automatically hyphenate document check box is unchecked, and click the Manual button. Then Word stops at each word before it is hyphenated to let you accept or reject the suggested hyphenation or change the location of the hyphen. In this case, Robert is satisfied with the automatic hyphenation.

Adding Footnotes and Endnotes

As you read through the chapter, you realize that under the heading "Customer Needs," the text refers to the results of a survey. Robert wants to include the survey results in an appendix at the end of the business plan, and wants you to insert a cross-reference to this fact in a footnote. A **footnote** is a line of text that appears at the bottom of the printed page, and often includes an explanation, the name of a source, or a cross-reference to another place in the document. When all notes for a document are gathered together and printed at the end of the document, instead of at the bottom of each page, they are called **endnotes**. Usually a document will contain footnotes or endnotes, but not both. You can insert footnotes and endnotes into a Word document quickly and easily with the Footnote command on the Insert menu.

The Footnote feature provides several benefits over just typing notes at the bottom of a page or end of a document:

- Word numbers footnotes or endnotes automatically. If you add a note anywhere in the document, delete a note, or move a note, Word automatically renumbers all the remaining footnotes or endnotes consecutively.

- Word automatically formats the footnote text at the bottom of the page or the endnote text at the end of the document.

- You can edit a footnote or endnote at any time. To modify the text, select Footnote from the View menu and use the same editing commands you use in the document window.

- If you add or delete text that moves the footnote reference onto a different page, the footnote will also move to that page. The reference in the text and the footnote at the bottom of the page will always be on the same page.

REFERENCE window

INSERTING FOOTNOTES OR ENDNOTES

- Position the insertion point where you want the footnote or endnote number to appear.
- Click Insert on the menu bar, and then click Footnote to open the Footnote and Endnote dialog box.
- Select the option button to indicate where you want the note to appear: the Bottom of the page (Footnote) or the End of the document (Endnote).
- Select the method of numbering the note, and then click the OK button.
- Type the text in the footnote or endnote window.
- Click the Close button on the Footnote or Endnote toolbar to close the footnote or endnote window and return to the document window.

Now you'll insert a footnote in the business plan that refers the reader to the survey information in the appendix.

To insert a footnote:

1. Make sure the document is in normal view, scroll down until you can see the heading "Customer Needs," and then position the insertion point after the period at the end of the first sentence, which ends "such as EstimaQuote." This is where you want to add the first footnote number.

Word

2. Click **Insert** on the menu bar, and then click **Footnote**. The Footnote and Endnote dialog box opens.

3. Make sure the Footnote option button is selected, make sure the AutoNumber option button is selected, and then click the **OK** button. The footnote number appears in the text and the insertion point appears in a blank footnote window at the bottom of the page. See Figure 5-37.

Figure 5-37 ◀
Creating a
footnote

footnote number
in text

Footnote toolbar

footnote window

insertion point

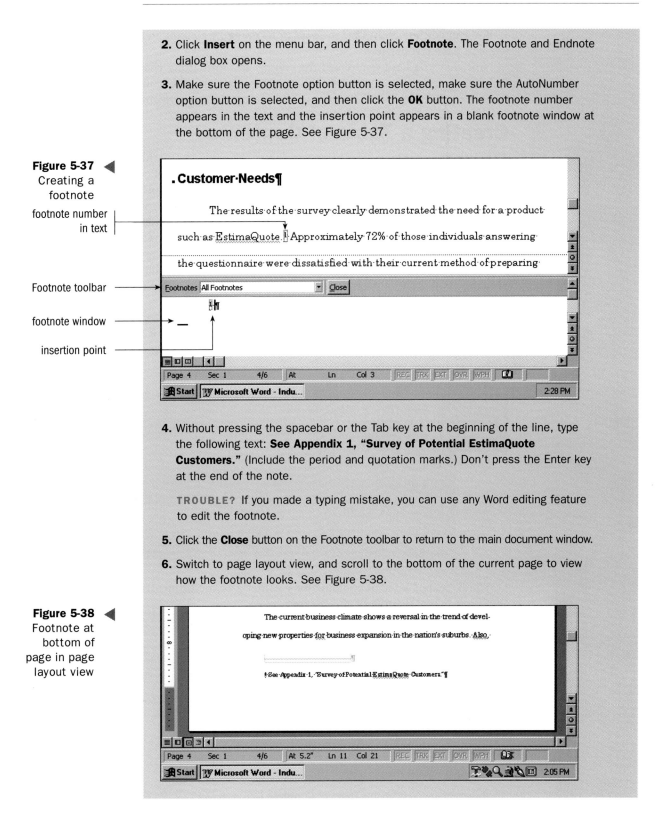

4. Without pressing the spacebar or the Tab key at the beginning of the line, type the following text: **See Appendix 1, "Survey of Potential EstimaQuote Customers."** (Include the period and quotation marks.) Don't press the Enter key at the end of the note.

   TROUBLE? If you made a typing mistake, you can use any Word editing feature to edit the footnote.

5. Click the **Close** button on the Footnote toolbar to return to the main document window.

6. Switch to page layout view, and scroll to the bottom of the current page to view how the footnote looks. See Figure 5-38.

Figure 5-38 ◀
Footnote at
bottom of
page in page
layout view

You can delete a note just as easily as you added it. To delete a footnote or endnote, just highlight the footnote or endnote number in the document and press the Delete key. When you delete the number, Word automatically deletes the text of the footnote or endnote and renumbers the remaining notes consecutively.

You can move a footnote or endnote using the cut-and-paste method. Just highlight and cut the note number from the document, and then paste it anywhere in your document. Again, Word automatically renumbers the notes consecutively and places the footnote on the same page as its reference number.

You can edit the text of an endnote or footnote by clicking in the footnote or endnote while in page layout view.

Now that you have completed the editing and formatting changes that Chiu Lee and Robert wanted you to make to the business plan chapter, you can create a Table of Contents, which should always be one of the last tasks you perform in creating a document.

Creating a Table of Contents

Although this chapter of the business plan is relatively short, the entire business plan is quite lengthy, so Chiu Lee and Robert want to include a table of contents at the beginning of each chapter. Eventually, they will create a table of contents for the entire business plan.

Word will create a table of contents for any document if you have applied heading styles in the form of Heading 1, Heading 2, Heading 3, and so forth. Word quickly creates a table of contents in the style you choose and inserts the page numbers based on the page breaks of your document at that time. If you add or delete text so that one or more headings move to a new page, the table of contents will not be automatically updated. However, you can easily update the table of contents by clicking anywhere in the table of contents and pressing the F9 key.

Once you create a table of contents, it becomes an object. You can delete it by selecting it and pressing the Delete key. To modify the appearance of a table of contents, you modify the styles that were used to build it, rather than trying to format the table of contents text directly on the screen.

REFERENCE window

CREATING A TABLE OF CONTENTS

- Make sure you have applied heading styles Heading 1, Heading 2, Heading 3, etc.
- Click Insert on the menu bar, and then click Index and Tables.
- Click the Table of Contents tab in the Index and Tables dialog box.
- Select a predefined style in the Formats list box, set the show levels number to the number of heading levels you want to show, and then click the OK button.

You'll create a table of contents for Chapter 2 of the EstimaTech business plan, inserting it just below the title of the chapter.

To insert the table of contents for Chapter 2:

1. Move the insertion point to the blank line immediately below the chapter title on page 1. Switch to normal view. You'll first type the heading for the table of contents.

2. Click the **Bold** button on the Formatting toolbar, type **Contents**, click **B** again to turn off bolding, and then press the **Enter** key. The insertion point is now located where you want to insert the table of contents.

3. Click **Insert** on the menu bar, and then click **Index and Tables**. The Index and Tables dialog box opens.

4. If necessary, click the **Table of Contents** tab.

   Word provides a variety of formats for the Table of Contents page, but Chiu Lee and Robert have been using the From template style. This means that Word will format the table of contents using the Normal style from the template you are using.

5. Make sure the From template style is selected in the Formats list box. The Preview box shows a sample of the format. See Figure 5-39.

Figure 5-39
Index and
Tables
dialog box

Table of
Contents tab

selected style

Preview box

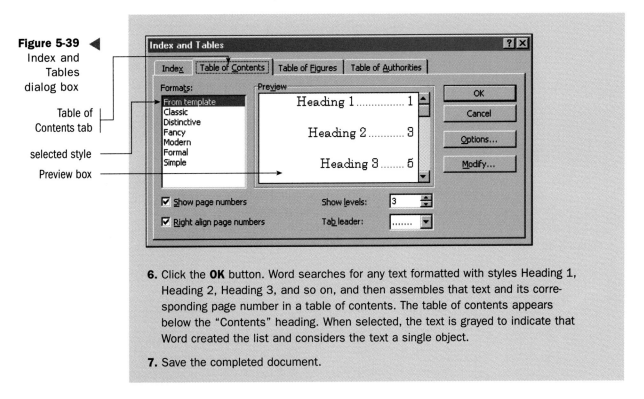

6. Click the **OK** button. Word searches for any text formatted with styles Heading 1, Heading 2, Heading 3, and so on, and then assembles that text and its corresponding page number in a table of contents. The table of contents appears below the "Contents" heading. When selected, the text is grayed to indicate that Word created the list and considers the text a single object.

7. Save the completed document.

With the table of contents at the beginning of the chapter, you are almost ready to print the document. Before you print, however, it's a good idea to review the document on screen first. In the next section, you browse through the document by heading.

Browsing by Heading

Now that you have finished working on Chapter 2 of the business plan, you can print it for Robert and Chiu Lee. Before you print the business plan, however, you should browse through it to double-check its appearance and organization. Word provides various ways for you to browse through a document, such as browse by headings (in which you can easily move from one heading to another) and browse by page (in which you can easily move from one page to another). You'll browse through the chapter by heading.

To browse by heading:

1. Click the **Select Browse Object** button ⊙ located near the bottom of the vertical scroll bar. A palette of objects you can browse opens.

2. Click the **Browse by Heading** button ▤. The Previous Page button ▲ and Next Page button ▼ change to the Previous and Next Heading buttons, which are blue. Now when you click one of these buttons, Word will move the insertion point to the next heading.

3. Move the insertion point to the beginning of the document, within the chapter title, and then click the **Next Heading** button ▼. Word moves the insertion point to the next heading, "Phases of the Market Research."

   TROUBLE? If Word goes to the "Contents" heading instead, the program might have automatically assigned a heading to it. Just continue browsing.

4. Click the **Next Heading** button ▼ several times, pausing after each time to read the heading and view the format of the document.

5. Click the **Previous Heading** button ▲ several times, again pausing each time to read the heading.

This demonstrates that power of browsing by heading. You can now change the browsing object back to pages.

6. Click the **Select Browse Object** button ⊙, and then click the **Browse by Page** button. The Previous and Next buttons become black, indicating that your browse object is now set back to Page.

7. Preview and then print Chapter 2 of the business plan. If Word displays a message about updating the table of contents, then click the OK button in the message dialog box(es). Your completed document should look like Figure 5-40.

Your page breaks might be at different locations, depending on your fonts. Don't be concerned about this. Just scroll through your document and add return characters as necessary so that the lines of text are well-grouped.

Figure 5-40 ◀

Chapter 2. Industry Analysis

Contents

The primary goal of EstimaTech is to become the industry leader in developing and marketing a major new type of software product—EstimaQuote. This computer program is designed for a specialized customer, will be sold at a reasonable price, and will be supported by a state-of-the-art service program. To determine the potential for achieving this goal, we have carried out extensive market research.

EstimaTech Business Plan   Industry Analysis page 2

Market Research

Before and during the development of EstimaQuote, we conducted market research to answer the following questions:

- Who are our potential customers?
- How many are there?
- What features do these potential customers want in estimating software?
- Would these potential customers purchase our product?

The answers to these questions are crucial to the continued development and the future marketing of EstimaQuote.

Phases of the Market Research

The market research was carried out in three phases. In Phase 1, we analyzed the potential customers for our software throughout the United States and Canada. In Phase 2, we determined the method by which potential customers estimate renovation costs, their perceived need for a computerized method for estimating costs, and the desired features of such a product. The survey also assessed the current condition of the industry in order to understand future market trends. In Phase 3, we provided a random sample of our potential customers with a pre-release beta copy (version 0.5) of EstimaQuote. We observed these customers as they installed and used this software, making particular note of the problems and difficulties they encountered. We are continuing with Phase 3 as we develop a new pre-release ver-

---

EstimaTech Business Plan   Industry Analysis page 3

sion of the software and improve our customer-support methods. As of this writing, we have almost completed, but not yet released, version 1 of the EstimaQuote, and have begun to develop version 2.

Here is the time frame for the three phases:

Phase 1. Analysis of potential customers   June to August 1999

Phase 2. Determination of needs and methods   August to November 1999

Phase 3. Beta testing of software   November 1999 to present

Market Definition

EstimaTech will operate in the national and international market. After completing version 2 of EstimaQuote in English, we plan to expand to Spanish, French, German, and Japanese versions over the next four years. We will continue to improve our software in all languages.

Size of the Market

Our primary customers include large- and medium-sized contracting companies that restore existing buildings. Our secondary customers are government and private agencies, and wealthy individuals who renovate historical homes and buildings. Our estimated market sizes (United States only) are shown in Table 1. These numbers include only those organizations and individuals directly involved in restoration cost estimates.

EstimaTech Business Plan   Industry Analysis page 4

Potential Customers	Percent	Number
Private Foundations	1%	360
Government Agencies	3%	1,080
Individuals	9%	3,200
Contractors	40%	14,400
Subcontractors	47%	16,900
Totals	100.00%	35,940

Table 1. Number of Potential Customers

Demographic Description of Target Users

The characteristics of target users for our software and the features they want in computerized software are as follows:

Characteristics of target users:

Prepare frequent estimates; use printed forms; use computer spreadsheet, database, or calculator; prepare multiple calculations; provide high-and low-end options

Features desired in a software program:

Tabular view of data; calculates costs based on overall building requirements; one-step calculation of high and low prices; updates costs of materials and labor; interfaces with project management software

Customer Needs

The results of the survey clearly demonstrated the need for a product such as EstimaQuote.[1] Approximately 72% of those individuals answering the

---

[1] See Appendix 1, "Survey of Potential EstimaQuote Customers."

Figure 5-40
continued

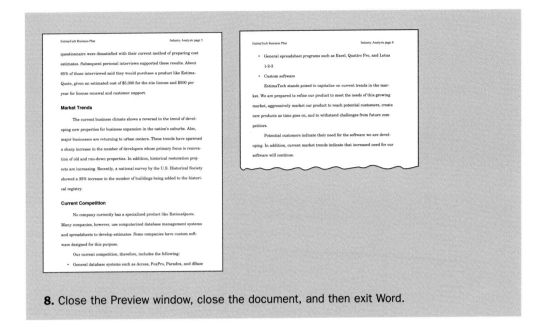

8. Close the Preview window, close the document, and then exit Word.

You now have a hard copy of the final Chapter 2 of the business plan, which you take to Robert and Chiu Lee. They are pleased with its appearance.

Quick Check

1 How do you double-space a document?

2 Define or describe a river in justified text.

3 What is the hyphenation zone? If you increase its size, how will the number of hyphenated words be affected?

4 What are the advantages of using the Footnote feature to insert footnotes into a document?

5 True or False: You must apply Word's built-in Heading styles to the various levels of headings in a document in order for Word to create a table of contents automatically.

6 How do you browse through a document by heading?

In this tutorial, you have edited the business plan content with the Word Spelling and Grammar Checker, and improved its appearance using fonts and styles. You have reorganized the document in outline view and drawn, edited, and formatted a table, and added a caption to the table. To improve itsreadability, you double-spaced and hyphenated the document. You also added a footnote and a table of contents to make the chapter information easier to read. Chiu Lee and Robert combine it with the rest of their business plan for EstimaTech, and rush off to meet with a loan officer at the bank.

Tutorial Assignments

Chiu Lee and Robert have received the startup funding they wanted, and are almost ready to begin marketing their software. They have written a summary of their customer training and support policies. They've asked you to help edit and format the document.

1. Start Word, if necessary, and make sure that nonprinting characters and the ruler are displayed. Open the file Training from the TAssign folder for Tutorial 5 on your Student Disk, and then save it as Training Courses.

2. Use the Thesaurus to replace "periodic" (in the first line of the first paragraph under the heading "Training") with a simpler word that means about the same thing.

3. Check each word or phrase flagged by the Spelling and Grammar checker. Set the Grammar checker to the Formal writing style. Make any necessary grammar or stylistic corrections. (You can ignore passive voice problems, but eliminate any contractions.)

4. Modify the Title and Heading 1 styles so that the font is a sans serif font. Keep the font size and style the same. Change the Heading 2 style so that the font is boldface and italic sans serif.

5. Change the font of the Normal style to Century Schoolbook (or New Century Schoolbook). If you don't have this font available, select some other serif font except Times New Roman.

6. Double-space the document. Make any necessary modification to the Normal style to make the document readable and attractive. Change the company name, address, and phone numbers back to single spacing.

7. Using outline view, reorganize the document so the introduction section is the first section of the document.

8. Promote the section "Using Technical Support" to make it a first-level heading, and then switch to normal view.

9. Using tabs, indent by one-half inch the two columns of text that begin with "Bronze" and end with "1.2 min" below the first paragraph under "Average Wait Times."

10. With the columns still selected, insert a decimal-aligned tab stop at 2.5 inches on the ruler. (*Hint:* Click the tab alignment selector on the far left edge of the ruler until the decimal-aligned tab stop icon appears, and then click at 2.5 inches on the bottom of the ruler.)

11. Using the Draw Table feature, create a table (three rows by three columns) after the first paragraph below the "Training" heading. Insert a blank line between the text and the top of the table. Single-space the text in the table.

12. Enter the data shown in Figure 5-41 into the table.

Figure 5-41 ◀

EstimaQuote Beginners	Installation, How to Get Started, Making Estimates, Printing Reports	January 21-23, 1999
EstimaQuote Intermediate	Making On-Site Estimates, EstimaQuote Tips and Tricks	February 26-27, 1999
EstimaQuote Advanced	Styles, Script Files, Interfacing with Project Management Programs	March 26-27, 1999

13. Insert one row at the top of the table. (*Hint:* With the insertion point in the top row, use the Insert Rows command.)

14. Type the text for the cells in the new row in the following order: "Class," "Topics," "Dates."

15. Increase the weight of the horizontal rules at the top and bottom of the table and below the heading row, so that the line weight is 1.5 points.

16. Insert the following boldface caption immediately below the table: "Table 1. Schedule of Training Courses."

17. Change the width of column A to about 1.5 inches, column B to 2.5 inches, and column C to 1.5 inches.

Word

18. Center the table across the page, and center the caption below the figure. If any part of the table or caption splits onto a second page, insert a hard page break above the table.

19. Insert a table (four rows by four columns) under the heading "Technical Support Plans," directly above the note explaining the cost per year of the Gold and Platinum plans. Leave a blank line above the table. Enter the text shown in Figure 5-42 into the table. Type the information in the order shown, and include any apparent errors. Single-space the text in the table.

Figure 5-42 ◄

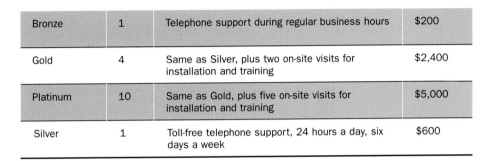

Bronze	1	Telephone support during regular business hours	$200
Gold	4	Same as Silver, plus two on-site visits for installation and training	$2,400
Platinum	10	Same as Gold, plus five on-site visits for installation and training	$5,000
Silver	1	Toll-free telephone support, 24 hours a day, six days a week	$600

20. Insert an additional row at the top of the table, and then type the headings for the first row in the following order: "Name," "Minimum Licenses," "Description," "Cost Per Year."

 EXPLORE

21. Sort the rows in the table in ascending numerical order, from Bronze $200 to Platinum $5,000. Make sure you mark the Header row option so the heading row is not included in the sort operation.

22. Set the first column width to about .80 inch, the second column width to about .80 inch, the third column width to about 3 inches, and the fourth column width to about 1 inch.

23. Center the number of minimum licenses within the cells; right-align the cost per year numbers within the cells.

24. Change weight of appropriate horizontal rules to make the table more attractive.

25. Insert the following boldface caption immediately below the table: "Table 2. Technical Support Plans."

26. Insert a boldface heading, "Contents," immediately following the title and company address and phone numbers. (Don't apply a heading style to this heading; if you do, it will appear as part of the table of contents.) Below the "Contents" heading, create a table of contents for the document; use the From template format style. Specify the number of heading levels necessary to include all headings in the Table of Contents.

27. Below the heading, "Technical Support Plans," after the period at the end of the sentence, insert a footnote. Type the following text for the footnote: "As the needs and resources of your company change, you can change your technical support plan. Changes can be made only at the expiration of the current contract period."

 EXPLORE

28. Below the table of contents, insert a blank line and the boldface heading, "List of Tables" (with no heading style). Below that heading, create a list of tables; use the From template format style. (*Hint:* Creating a table of figures is similar to creating a table of contents; click Insert on the menu bar, click Index and Tables, click the Table of Figures tab, and proceed from there.)

 EXPLORE

29. Hyphenate the document using manual hyphenation. When Word stops to let you choose if and where to hyphenate a word, don't hyphenate words in which only two letters appear alone on a line.

30. Save and preview your document. If a row in the table spans two pages, fix it so it automatically stays together on one page.

31. When the formatting is correct, save and print the document, and then close the file.

Case Problems

1. Mountainland Nursery Raynal Stubbs is the sales manager of Mountainland Nursery in Steamboat Springs, Colorado. Twice each year he provides sales representatives with guidelines for helping customers with their planting needs. Raynal has asked you to help him prepare this year's list of spring-blooming perennials.

1. Start Word, if necessary, and then open the file Flowers from the Cases folder for Tutorial 5 on your Student Disk and save it as Mountainland Flowers.

2. Using outline view, reorder the document so the introduction section is the first section of the document.

3. Promote the section "Guidelines for Helping Customers" to a first-level heading. (*Hint:* Show all text by clicking the All button, so you can see the sentence to promote.)

4. Make "Guidelines for Helping Customers" the last section in the document.

5. Print the outline, without showing the formatting of the headings.

6. Change the font of the Title style and the Heading 1 style to sans serif.

7. Change the font of the Normal style to some serif font other than Times New Roman.

8. In the last item of the bulleted list, change "shoppers" to one of its synonyms in the Thesaurus.

9. Check for any grammatical errors using the Grammar Checker (with the writing style set to Formal). Correct any errors. Edit the passive voice sentence to make it active voice, with the subject "gardeners" and the verb "should plant." If necessary, consult the Grammar Checker for an explanation of passive and active voice.

10. Insert an additional row for headings at the top of the existing table.

11. Type the following column headings (in boldface) in the cells of the new row: "Common Name," "Name," "yellow," "red," "blue," "white." If necessary, widen the columns so the text remains on one line.

12. Use Help to learn about moving columns in a table, and then move the Name column to the first column in the table.

13. Sort the table alphabetically by Name (the new first column). Remember to specify that the table contains a header row.

14. Insert a row following the flower Aurinia saxatilis, and type the words "Bellis perennis" in the first cell and "English Daisy" in the second cell.

15. Delete the row containing the flower Cynoglossum amabile.

16. Insert another row at the top of the table. Highlight the blank cells above the flower colors and merge them into one cell. (*Hint:* Use the Merge Cells command on the Table menu.)

17. Type the following heading (in sans serif boldface) in the newly created cell above the flower colors: "Blossom Color."

18. Center the text in the top two rows (all the headings) and bold the text in row 2.

19. Remove the top and left border lines from cells A1 and B1, as shown in Figure 5-46. (*Hint:* Use the Erase button on the Tables and Borders toolbar, and drag the erase tool along the border lines.)

20. Add 30% shading to the cells, as shown in Figure 5-43. Use the F4 key to repeat the shading step.

Figure 5-43 ◀

Name	Common Name	Blossom Color			
		yellow	red	blue	white
Aquilegia	Columbine	■	■	■	■
Aster	Aster		■	■	■
Aurinia saxatilis	Basket-of-Gold	■			
Bellis perennis	English Daisy	■		■	■
Cymbidium	Terrestrial Orchids	■	■	■	■
Digitalis	Foxglove	■		■	
Iberis sempervirens	Evergreen Candytuft	■			■
Viola cornuta	Tufted pansy	■	■	■	■
Viola odorata	Sweet violet		■	■	■

21. After the word "perennials" in the first sentence below the heading "Suggested Spring Blooming Perennials," insert a footnote reference. Type the following text for the footnote: "Information taken from Andrea Macula's "Gardening in the West," published by Gladstone Press, Flagstaff, Arizona."

22. Double-space and hyphenate the document. Use automatic hyphenation. Convert the first six lines of the document back to single spacing. Convert the table back to single spacing.

23. Insert a table of contents for the document above the introduction. Use the Formal format style for the table of contents.

24. Save your changes. Preview the document for problems, such as the table splitting between two pages, fix any problems, and then print the document. Close the document.

2. Classical CD Sales at The Master's Touch   Austin Cornelius is the purchasing agent for The Master's Touch, a music store in Little Rock, Arkansas. Each month Austin publishes a list of the classical CDs that are on sale at The Master's Touch. He has asked you to create a table showing this month's list of sale items.

1. Open the file Classics from the Cases folder for Tutorial 5 on your Student Disk, and save it as Classical Music CDs.

2. Correct any grammatical errors marked by the Grammar Checker.

3. Highlight the list of CDs—Chopin Nocturnes through The Nine Symphonies—separated by commas, and convert it into a table (right rows by five columns). (*Hint:* Click Table on the menu bar, click Convert Text to Table. In the dialog box, select Commas as the Separate text at option.)

4. Move the right column boundary location (not column width) to 1.5 inches for the first column, 3.0 inches for the second column, 4.5 inches for the third column, and 5.25 inches for the fourth column.

5. Insert an additional row for headings at the top of the table.

6. Add the following headings (in a sans serif boldface font) in the order given: "Title," "Artist," "Label," "#CDs," and "Price."

7. Insert a row after "The Best of Chopin," and then type the following in the cells: "Beethoven Piano Sonatas," "Alfred Brendel," "Vox," "2," "18.95."

8. Sort the rows in the table in ascending alphabetical order of the titles. Make sure you mark the Header row option so the header row is not included in the sort operation.

9. Center the number of CDs within the cells.

10. Right-align the price within the cells.

11. Draw 1.5-point horizontal rules along appropriate row boundaries to improve readability of the table.

12. In the final sentence of the document, change the word "accepted" to one of its synonyms found in the Thesaurus, to avoid the strange sounding phrase "accepted except."

13. Indent and format the two columns of information on the discounts on certain labels. The percent discount numbers should be right-aligned.

14. Change the Normal style to 11-point sans serif.

15. If necessary, adjust the table's column widths so that the column widths aren't too big for the text.

16. Create a new style for the final paragraph of the document. Name the style "NoticeToCustomers." Make the font of the style 10-point, italics Century Schoolbook. Set the paragraph indentation to 0.5 on the left and on the right. Then apply the style to the paragraph.

17. Save your document; then preview and print it. Close the document.

3. The Business of Basketball As part of the requirements for your advanced writing class, your writing group has written a term paper on "The Business of Basketball." Your assignment is to edit the preliminary outline and create a table for the final paper.

1. Start Word, if necessary, and check your screen, making sure that nonprinting characters are displayed. Open the file Business from the Cases folder for Tutorial 5 on your Student Disk, and then save it as "Business of Basketball."

2. Using outline view, reorder the outline at the end of the paper so that "Team Philosophy" follows "Management Style."

3. Demote the section "Marketing" to make it a second-level heading.

4. Print the completed outline of the document, with the Show Formatting feature turned off.

5. Switch to page layout view, and then check for any grammatical errors using the Spelling and Grammar checker (with the writing style set to Casual). Correct any errors. Don't break up the long sentence into shorter ones. For other potential errors, consult the Grammar Checker for an explanation, and then decide if you have to edit the text or not. Don't make changes just because the Grammar Checker suggests them. (*Note:* The green marking of several flagged words and characters is hard to see. You might want to run the Spelling and Grammar tool by clicking Tools on the menu bar, and then clicking Spelling and Grammar.)

6. Use the Thesaurus to find a synonym to replace "lucrative" in the first sentence under the heading "Introduction."

7. Scroll to the table in the document, and then at the end of the table title, add the footnote with the text, "Data taken from *Financial World*, May 25, 1997, page 29."

8. Change the Heading 1 style so that the font is sans serif.

9. Create a new paragraph style called Abstract. In this style, modify the font to Arial and the line spacing to single. Add a box border around the paragraph. Apply the style to the paragraph under the heading "Abstract."

10. Set the heading row for the table. (*Hint:* Select the top row, click Table on the menu bar, and then click Headings. By setting the heading row, Word will print the heading row on every page of the table if it spans two or more pages, and will not sort the row when you perform an automatic sort.)

11. Sort the table by franchise value in descending numerical order.

12. Insert a row at the top of the table.

13. Change the line weight below the new row 2 to 1½ points.

14. Remove the border above row 2. (*Hint:* With the Tables and Borders toolbar on the screen, change the line style to No Border, and then drag the pointer along the border.)

15. Merge all the cells in row 1 except the cell above the NBA Team column. (*Hint:* To merge cells, select the cells and then use the Merge Cells command.)

16. Type the heading "Millions of Dollars" in the merged cell, and then center it horizontally and vertically.

17. Center the text of all the headings in the second row of the table.

18. Right-align all of the numbers in the cells.

19. Add a ¾-point rule below each cell of rows 2 through 10.

20. Add your name to the list of authors.

21. Insert a section break following the date on the title page, so that the Table of Contents begins a new page.

22. Create a table of contents for the report to appear on its own page following the title page. Use the Formal template format style for the table of contents.

23. To improve the document's appearance, insert a hard page break above the heading "Abstract" and, if necessary, above the table title. (*Hint:* To insert a hard page break, move the insertion point to the desired location, and press Ctrl + Enter.)

24. Save the changes to your report; then preview and print it. Close the file.

4. Report on Median Family Income Arlene Littlefield is an economic analyst for a consulting firm that helps minority businesses market their products. She is preparing a short report on the median family income of American families, from 1980 to 1991, based upon the ethnicity of the head of household. She has obtained a government report that contains two tables of data, which she gives to you as unformatted Word tables, and asks you to help her analyze the information and write her report.

1. Start Word, if necessary, making sure that nonprinting characters are displayed. Open the file Income from the Cases folder for Tutorial 5 on your Student Disk and print the document. Analyze the two tables. On scratch paper (or in a Word document window), jot down your observations, ideas, and conclusions about the data in the two tables. As you analyze the data, you might be interested in noting that the average family income for all families in the U.S. in 1950, 1960, and 1970 was $3,319, $5,630, and $9,867 in current dollars and $18,757, $25,850, and $34,636 in constant dollars. (Data for minorities during those time periods is scarce or not available.)

2. Start a new document, switch to outline view, and create an outline of your report. Your headings might be the following, not listed in any particular order of organization or importance): "Introduction" (which explains the purpose of your report), "Income Increases During the 1980s" (with subheadings "Income Increase for Whites," "Income Increases for Blacks," and "Income Increases for Hispanics"), "Comparison of Incomes Based on Ethnicity," "Are Minorities Catching Up in Income with Whites?," and "Economic Progress during the 1980s: Did We Get Richer?," "Four Decades of Economic Progress in the U.S." You might want to use some of these sample headings or none of them. Organize your headings (outline) in a logical manner. Make sure your final heading is "Summary" or "Conclusion."

3. Print the outline, without formatting.

4. Switch to page layout view, set the document to double-spacing, and write your report. One or two paragraphs under each heading is sufficient.

5. At the appropriate places in your document, copy the tables from the document Income into your document.

6. Format your tables to be attractive and readable. Make sure they are single-spaced and each table appears in its entirety on one page rather than spanning two pages.

7. Add appropriate captions for the tables.

8. At the end of each caption, insert a footnote with the citation for the table: U.S. Department of Commerce, Bureau of the Census, Current Population Reports, Series P-60, *Money Income of Families and Persons in the United States*, nos. 105 and 107. Use this same citation for both tables.

9. Change the fonts of the Normal and the heading styles as desired.

10. Hyphenate your document as desired.

11. Create a table of contents at the appropriate location in your document.

12. Save your report as Median Family Income then preview and print it. Close the documents.

Creating Form Letters and Mailing Labels

Writing a Sales Letter for The Pet Shoppe

OBJECTIVES

In this tutorial you will:

- Create, edit, and format a mail merge main document

- Create, edit, and format a mail merge data source

- Sort records in a data source

- Merge files to create personalized form letters

- Create, format, and print mailing labels

- Create a telephone list from a data source

CASE

The Pet Shoppe

Alicia Robles is vice president of sales for The Pet Shoppe, a chain of 15 superstores based in Colorado Springs, Colorado. The Pet Shoppe, which has customers throughout the state, sells a wide variety of pets, pet food, supplies, and services. As part of her job, Alicia sends information about The Pet Shoppe's products and services to customers who request to be on the company mailing list. Alicia needs to send the same information to many customers, but because of the large number of Pet Shoppe customers, she and her staff don't have the time to write a personal letter to each one. Instead, she can create a **form letter** that contains the content she wants to send all customers and then she can add personal information for each customer, such as the name, address, type of pet, and so on, in specific places. To do this manually would be very time-consuming. Fortunately, Microsoft Word provides a timesaving method that makes Alicia's job easier. By using Word's Mail Merge feature, Alicia can produce multiple copies of the same letter yet personalize each copy with customer-specific information in about the same amount of time it takes to personalize just one letter. She could also use this feature to create such documents as catalogs, directories, and contracts.

The Pet Shoppe is celebrating its tenth anniversary. As a promotional tool, Alicia wants to send out a form letter to all customers on the mailing list telling them about the chain's 10th Anniversary Celebration and offering them a discount if they purchase a product or service anytime during the store's anniversary month. Alicia has already written the letter she wants to send, but she needs to add the personal information for each customer. She asks you to create the form letters and the mailing labels for the envelopes.

In this tutorial, you'll help Alicia create a form letter and mailing labels using Word's Mail Merge feature. First, you'll open the letter that will serve as the main document. Next, you'll create a data source document that contains the name and address of each customer who will receive the customized letter.

Then you'll have Word merge the main document with the data source, which creates the customized letters, and sort them in zip code order. You'll also send a special version of the letter offering special savings on surplus inventory to customers in a particular zip code. Finally, you'll use the data source document to create mailing labels Alicia can put on the envelopes, and to create a telephone list so Alicia can have the sales representatives follow up the mailing with a phone call to each customer.

In this session you'll see how Alicia planned her letter. Then you'll open the form letter and create a document containing the specific customer information that will be inserted into the form letter using Word's Mail Merge feature.

Planning the Document

Alicia hopes to generate increased sales for The Pet Shoppe chain by announcing a 10 percent discount on the purchase of any product or service as part of the company's 10th Anniversary Celebration.

An effective sales letter convinces customers to purchase a product or service. Alicia's sales letter will inform current customers about The Pet Shoppe's 10th Anniversary Celebration and offer them a special discount on products and services during the month of November. She has organized her letter to capture the reader's attention. First she cites a few examples of the need The Pet Shoppe fills, then she briefly describes The Pet Shoppe's services and products, and finally she offers a discount to encourage readers to visit their local stores.

Alicia writes in a persuasive style, using informal language. She illustrates the need and quality of The Pet Shoppe's services by including personal experiences of current customers. Alicia wants to send a professional-looking, personalized letter to each customer on The Pet Shoppe's mailing list. She uses a standard business letter format and will print the letters on stationery that is preprinted with the company letterhead.

The Merge Process

Alicia asks you to use Word's Mail Merge feature to create the form letters. In general, a **merge** combines information from two separate documents to create many final documents, each of which contains customized information that makes it slightly different from the others. In Word, the two separate documents are called a main document and a data source.

A **main document** is a document (such as a letter or a contract) that, in addition to text, contains areas of placeholder text (called merge fields) to mark where variable information (such as a name or an address) will be inserted. Alicia's main document is a letter that looks like Figure 6-1, except that merge fields to mark the locations of the customer's name, address, and other data will replace the red text.

Figure 6-1 ◀
Alicia's form
letter

The Pet Shoppe

121 Stilltoe Avenue ■ Colorado Springs, CO 80901
Phone: (719) 555-5555 ■ Fax: (719) 555-5556

[Date]

[FirstName] [LastName]
[Address1]
[City,] CO [PostalCode]

Dear [FirstName:]

Ten years ago, Stephen Mueller was unable to find suitable grooming facilities for his dog, Rusty. Maria Fuentes drove 100 miles to buy food for her cat, Sneakers. And Carole Cochran only dreamed of owning an armadillo lizard. Today, Stephen, Maria, and Carole are among The Pet Shoppe's loyal customers.

Established in 1988, The Pet Shoppe chain provides a complete line of high quality yet affordable pet supplies and services for customers throughout Colorado. We're committed to helping you meet the needs of your [PetKind] in a caring manner.

We invite you and your pet to join us in our 10th Anniversary Celebration. Just bring this letter to The Pet Shoppe in the [Branch] anytime during the month of November and you'll receive a 10% discount on the purchase of any product or service. And remember to register [PetName] for our month-long "Purrfect Pet" drawing. We'll be giving away over $1,000 worth of prizes and services each week.

We look forward to seeing you at The Pet Shoppe.

Sincerely yours,

Alicia Robles
Vice President, Sales

A **data source** is a document that contains information, such as customers' names and addresses that will be merged into the main document. Alicia's data source is a name and address list of The Pet Shoppe customers.

Inserting information from a data source into a main document produces a final document, called a **merged document**. Figure 6-2 illustrates how the data source and main document combine to form a merged document.

Figure 6-2 ◄
Merging a main
document with
a data source
to create a
merged
document

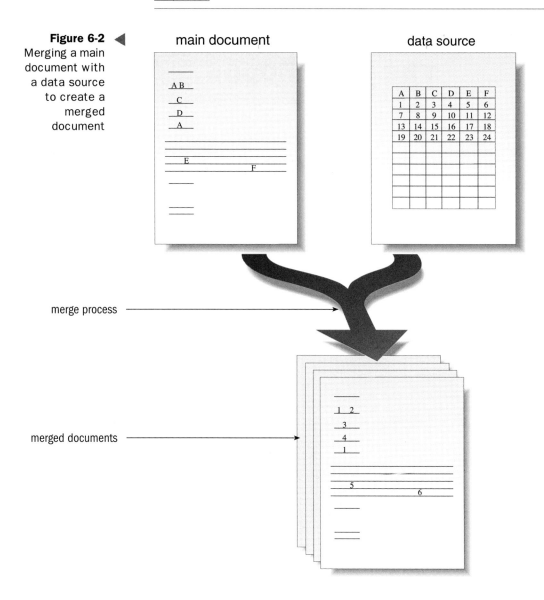

merge process

merged documents

Mail Merge Fields

During a mail merge, the **merge fields** (the placeholders for text that changes in the main document) instruct Word to retrieve specific information from the data source. For example, one merge field in the main document might retrieve a name from the data source, while another merge field might retrieve an address. For each complete set of data (in this instance, a name and address) in the data source, Word will create a new, separate page in the merged document. Thus, if Alicia has five sets of customer names and addresses in her data source, the merge will produce five versions of the main document, each one containing a different customer name and address in the appropriate places.

In addition to merge fields, a main document can also contain Word fields, which retrieve information from sources other than the data source. For example, a Word field might insert the current date into a main document, prompt you to input text from the keyboard, or print information only if certain, specified conditions are met. Figure 6-3 lists some of the most common Word and merge fields.

Figure 6-3 ◀
Common fields
used in mail
merge

Word Fields	Action
DATE	Inserts current date
FILLIN	Displays a prompt during merge; response is inserted into the merged document
IF	Prints information only if a specified condition is met
MERGEFIELD	Extracts information from the data source document and inserts it into the merged document

You can distinguish merge fields from the other text of the main document because each merge field name is enclosed by pairs of angled brackets << >>. You don't actually type the merge field into your main document; instead you use the Insert Merge Field command to place the merge fields into your main document, and Word automatically inserts the brackets.

Data Fields and Records

The data source for a mail merge consists of data fields and records organized into a Word table, as shown in Figure 6-4. The **header row**, the first row of the table, contains the name of each merge field used in a main document in a separate cell. Every other cell of the table contains a **data field**, or the specific information that replaces the merge field in the main document. As in Figure 6-4, one data field might be the first name of a customer, another data field the customer's address, another data field the customer's city, and so forth. Each row of data fields in the table make up a complete **record**, or all the information about one individual or object. For a mail merge to work properly, every record in the data source must have the same set of merge fields.

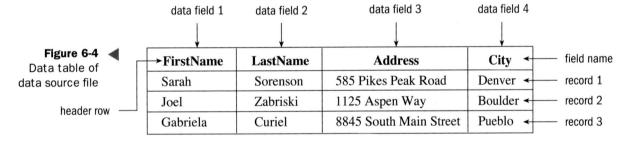

Figure 6-4 ◀
Data table of
data source file

header row

Data sources are not limited to records about customers. You could create data sources with inventory records, records of suppliers, or records of equipment. After you understand how to manage and manipulate the records in a data source, you'll be able to use them for many applications.

Creating a Main Document

The main document contains the text that will appear in all the letters, as well as the merge fields that tell Word where to insert the information from the data source. In the first step of the merge process, you must indicate which document you intend to use as the main document. You can either create a new document or use an existing document as the main document.

Alicia has already written the letter she wants to send out to all Pet Shoppe customers, so you don't need to create a new document. Instead, you'll modify an existing document to create the main document.

CREATING A MAIN DOCUMENT

- Click Tools on the menu bar, and then click Mail Merge to display the Mail Merge Helper dialog box.
- Click the Create button in the Main document section of the dialog box, and then click the type of main document that you want to create (such as Form Letters).
- Click the Active Window button to use the active, open document as the main document. Click the New Main Document button if you want to open a new, blank document as the main document.
- Click the Edit button on the Mail Merge Helper dialog box. If necessary, click the appropriate filename.
- Edit (or create) the text of the main document; add merge fields into the main document by clicking the Insert Merge Field button on the Mail Merge toolbar.

To start Word and create the main document:

1. Start Word as usual and insert your Student Disk in the appropriate drive, open the **PetShopp** file from the **Tutorial.06** folder on your Student Disk, and then save the document on the disk as **Pet Shoppe Form Letter**. This is the text of the letter that Alicia wrote to send to Pet Shoppe customers and will become the main document of your form letter. You won't need to display nonprinting characters for this tutorial.

2. Click **Tools** on the menu bar, and then click **Mail Merge**. The Mail Merge Helper dialog box opens. See Figure 6-5. The Mail Merge Helper dialog box contains a checklist to help you create merged documents.

Figure 6-5 ◀
Mail Merge
Helper dialog
box

click to create main
document (form
letter)

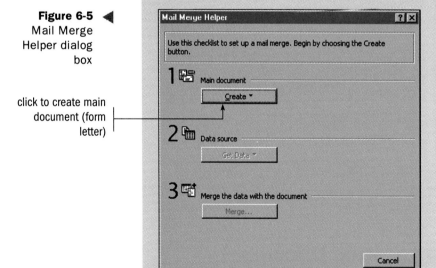

3. Click the **Create** button in the Main document section. A list of main document types appears.

4. Click **Form Letters**. A message dialog box opens, prompting you to select the document you want to use as the main document. You'll use the document in the active window (the letter you just opened) as the main document.

5. Click the **Active Window** button. The Main document section of the dialog box shows the type of merge (Form Letters) and the name of the main document (the active document Pet Shoppe Form Letter). See Figure 6-6.

Figure 6-6 ◄
Mail Merge
Helper dialog
box after
selecting a
main document

type of main
document

click to create data
source

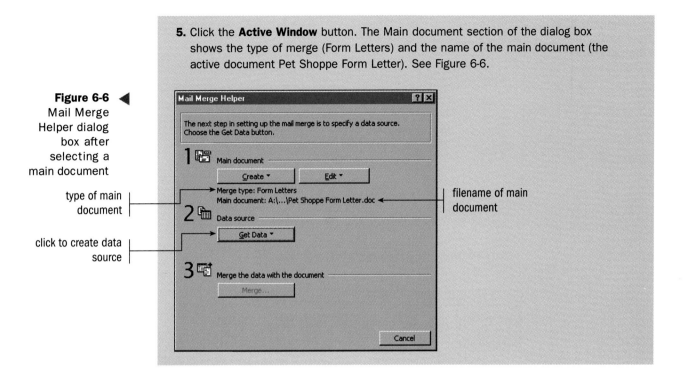

filename of main
document

You'll add the merge instructions to the main document later, after you create the data source.

Creating a Data Source

The data source document is a Word table with a header row that contains the merge fields (the names of the data fields). Each field name is a label for a different type of information in the records. For example, you'll use the field name FirstName to label the data field that contains the first name of Pet Shoppe customers. You must follow several conventions when choosing field names:

■ Each field name in the header row must be unique; that is, you can't have two fields with the same name.

■ Names of data fields can contain underscores, but not spaces.

■ Names of data fields must begin with a letter.

■ Names of data fields can be as long as 40 characters (including numbers and letters).

In mail merge, you link the data source document to the main document so that Word will know in which file to find the information you want inserted into the main document.

You need to create the data source that contains all the information about The Pet Shoppe's customers. Alicia has given you a list of the type of information you'll merge into the letter and the field names you should use, as shown in Figure 6-7.

Figure 6-7
Field names for
the records in
the data source

Data Field Name	Description
FirstName	Customer's first name
LastName	Customer's last name
Address1	Customer's street address
City	Customer's city (in Colorado)
PostalCode	Customer's zip code
HomePhone	Customer's phone number
Branch	Location of The Pet Shoppe branch
PetKind	The kind of pet owned by the customer
PetName	The name of the customer's pet

REFERENCE
window

CREATING A DATA SOURCE

- Click Tools on the menu bar, click Mail Merge to open the Mail Merge Helper dialog box, and then select the main document.
- In the Data source section of the Mail Merge Helper dialog box, click the Get Data button, and then click Create Data Source to attach the data source to the main document. The Create Data Source dialog box opens.
- Add or delete field names in the Field names in header row list, and then click the OK button. The Save As dialog box opens.
- In the Save As dialog box, save the new data source file to your disk. A message dialog box opens, asking you what document you want to edit: the data source or the main document.
- Click the Edit Data Source button. The Data Form dialog box opens.
- Enter the information into the data fields for each record of the data source, and then click the OK button.

Attaching the Data Source and Creating the Header Row

The first step in creating a data source document is to attach the data source to the main document. In this context, **attach** means to associate or link the data source to the main document so that Word knows where to find the specific information (data fields) that replace the merge fields in the main document. Although the order of field names in the data source doesn't affect their placement in the main document, you'll want to arrange them in a logical order. This way, you can enter information quickly and efficiently. For example, you probably want first and last name fields adjacent or city, state, and zip code fields adjacent.

Just as you did with the main document, you can either open an existing data source document and attach it to the main document, or you can create a new data source document and attach it to the main document. Alicia doesn't have an existing data source document, so you'll create a new one.

To attach the data source to the main document:

1. Click the **Get Data** button in the Data source section of the Mail Merge Helper dialog box. The Get Data list box opens. The data source document will be attached to the file listed in the Main document section of the dialog box. See Figure 6-8. Alicia determined the field names for the data fields based on the information cards that customers complete to join the mailing list. You'll use these field names to create the header row of the table in the data source.

Figure 6-8 ◄
Mail Merge Helper dialog box with Get Data list box

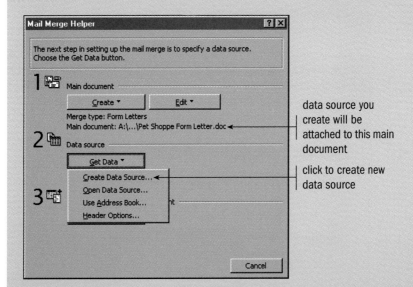

data source you create will be attached to this main document

click to create new data source

2. Click **Create Data Source** in the Get Data list box. The Create Data Source dialog box opens. See Figure 6-9. The Field names in the header row list box provide a list of commonly used field names, which you can add to and remove from as needed.

Figure 6-9 ◄
Create Data Source dialog box

enter new field names here

current list of field names

click to delete a field name

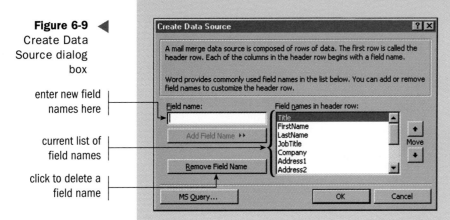

3. Scroll through the list of field names in the Field names in header row list box. The form letter will include some of these field names—FirstName, LastName, Address1, City, PostalCode, and HomePhone—but you need to create field names for the store branch, the type of pet, and the name of the pet.

4. If necessary, place the insertion point in the Field name text box, type **Branch**, and then click the **Add Field Name** button to add "Branch" to the list of field names in the Field names in header row list box. This tells Word that one data field in each record will contain the name of the Pet Shoppe store nearest the customer.

5. Repeat Step 4 to add the field names **PetKind** and **PetName** to the Field names in header row list box. Now each customer record will contain fields with the kind of pet the customer owns and the name of that pet.

TROUBLE? If the Add Field Name button is dimmed, you might have entered "PetKind" or "PetName" as two separate words. Word will not accept field names that contain spaces. Delete the space between the words, and then click the Add Field Name button.

Some of the field names in the Field names in header row list box aren't applicable to The Pet Shoppe, so you'll remove those field names.

6. Scroll to the top of the Field names in header row list, and then click **Title** and click the **Remove Field Name** button. The field name "Title" disappears from the list.

7. Repeat Step 6 to remove the following field names: **JobTitle**, **Company**, **Address2**, **State**, **Country**, and **WorkPhone**. See Figure 6-10. Check the Field names in header row list in the Create Data Source dialog box carefully to make sure it contains the following: FirstName, LastName, Address1, City, PostalCode, HomePhone, Branch, PetKind, and PetName.

Figure 6-10 ◀
Completed
Create Data
Source dialog
box

field name that has
been removed
from list

completed list of
field names

scroll to see PetKind
and PetName

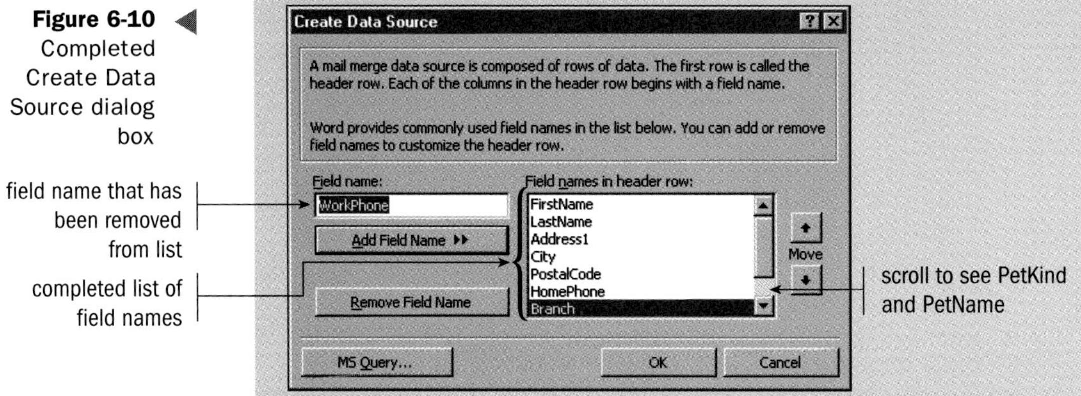

TROUBLE? If your list of field names doesn't match the list in Figure 6-10 exactly, you need to edit the list. Remove any extra or incorrect field names and add the correct ones.

8. Click the **OK** button in the Create Data Source dialog box to accept the field name list. The Save As dialog box opens, allowing you to save the data source document and attach it to the letter.

9. Make sure the Tutorial.06 folder of your Student Disk is selected, type **Pet Shoppe Data** in the File name text box, and then click the **Save** button. The data source document Pet Shoppe Data is now attached to the main document Pet Shoppe Form Letter.

Word now displays a message dialog box, noting that the data source you just created contains no records. You have the option to edit either the data source or the main document. First you'll edit the data source by entering the data for each customer record; in the next session, you'll edit the main document by adding the merge fields to it.

Entering Data into a Data Source

The Pet Shoppe staff uses customer information cards to collect data from their customers, as shown in Figure 6-11. The data source will contain a field for each piece of information on the card. You'll add the information for three customers (the first three records) into the data source document.

Word

Figure 6-11 ◀
Sample card
gathering
customer
information to
make records
in data source

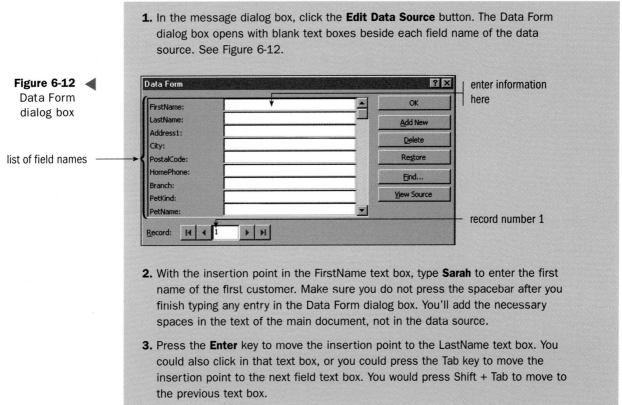

The Pet Shoppe

First Name *Sarah*   Last Name *Sorenson*

Address   *585 Pikes Peak Road*

City   *Denver*   , Colorado

ZIP   *80207*   Home Phone   *303-555-8976*

Store Branch   *High Prairie Mall*

Kind of Pet: **Name of Pet**:

☒ dog   ☐ armadillo   *Rascal*
☐ cat   ☐ Gila monster
☐ parrot   ☐ fish
☐ parakeet   ☐ lizard
☐ turtle   ☐ Other_____
☐ pigeon

Word provides two methods for adding records to the data source: entering data directly into a data source table, just as you would enter information into any other Word table, or using the Data Form dialog box, in which you can enter, edit, or delete records. You'll use the data form to enter information about three of The Pet Shoppe's customers into the data source.

To enter data into a record using the data form:

1. In the message dialog box, click the **Edit Data Source** button. The Data Form dialog box opens with blank text boxes beside each field name of the data source. See Figure 6-12.

Figure 6-12 ◀
Data Form
dialog box

list of field names →

enter information here

record number 1

2. With the insertion point in the FirstName text box, type **Sarah** to enter the first name of the first customer. Make sure you do not press the spacebar after you finish typing any entry in the Data Form dialog box. You'll add the necessary spaces in the text of the main document, not in the data source.

3. Press the **Enter** key to move the insertion point to the LastName text box. You could also click in that text box, or you could press the Tab key to move the insertion point to the next field text box. You would press Shift + Tab to move to the previous text box.

4. Type **Sorenson** and then press the **Enter** key to insert the customer's last name and move the insertion point to the next field name.

5. Type **585 Pikes Peak Road**, and then press the **Enter** key to insert the customer's street address and move the insertion point to the next field name.

6. Type **Denver** and then press the **Enter** key to insert the city where the customer lives and move the insertion point to the next field name.

7. Type **80207** and then press the **Enter** key to insert the customer's zip code (or postal code) and move to the next field name.

8. Type **303-555-8976** and press **Enter**, type **High Prairie Mall** and press **Enter**, and then type **dog** and press **Enter**. You have inserted the customer's home phone number, the branch location of The Pet Shoppe, and the kind of pet the customer owns. The insertion point is now in the text box of the last field, PetName.

9. Type **Rascal** *but do not press the Enter key yet.* Your Data Form dialog box should match Figure 6-13.

Figure 6-13 ◄
Data Form
dialog box with
completed
record 1

Data Form	? ✕
FirstName:	Sarah
LastName:	Sorenson
Address1:	585 Pikes Peak Road
City:	Denver
PostalCode:	80207
HomePhone:	303-555-8976
Branch:	High Prairie Mall
PetKind:	dog
PetName:	Rascal

OK • Add New • Delete • Restore • Find... • View Source

Record: |◄ ◄ 1 ► ►|

You have completed the information for the first record of the data source document. Now you are ready to enter the information for the remaining two records.

To create additional records in the data source:

1. With the insertion point still at the end of the last field of the first record, press the **Enter** key. This creates a new, blank record. Notice that the Record text box at the bottom of the data form displays "2," indicating that you are editing the second record.

2. Enter the information for the second record, as shown in Figure 6-14.

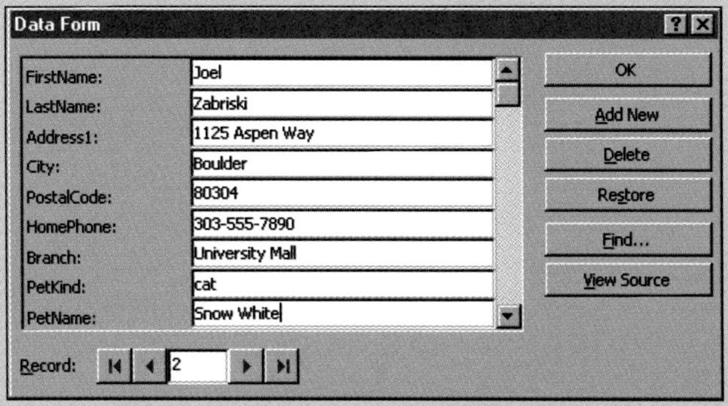

Figure 6-14 ◄
Completed
record 2

Data Form	? ✕
FirstName:	Joel
LastName:	Zabriski
Address1:	1125 Aspen Way
City:	Boulder
PostalCode:	80304
HomePhone:	303-555-7890
Branch:	University Mall
PetKind:	cat
PetName:	Snow White

OK • Add New • Delete • Restore • Find... • View Source

Record: |◄ ◄ 2 ► ►|

3. After entering data into the last field, click the **Add New** button to open another blank record. Notice that you can press the Enter key or click the Add New button to create a blank record.

4. Enter the information for the third record, as shown in Figure 6-15, *but do not press the Enter key after the last field.* If you were to press Enter or click the Add New button, you would add a blank record as the fourth record.

Figure 6-15 ◀
Completed
record 3

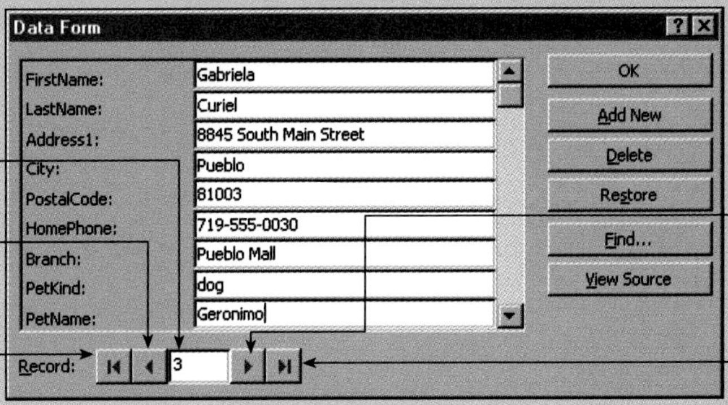

current record
number

click to move to
previous record

click to jump to
first record

click to move to
next record

click to jump to
last record

TROUBLE? If a new, blank record opens, you pressed the Enter key at the end of the third record or you clicked the Add New button in the Data Form dialog box. Click the Delete button in the Data Form dialog box to remove the unneeded fourth record.

You have entered the records for three customers. You should proofread each record to make sure you typed the information correctly. Any misspelled names or other typos will print in the final letters and reflect poorly on The Pet Shoppe. You can move among individual records within the data source by using the Record arrow buttons. You'll begin by proofreading the first data record.

To move to the first record within the data source:

1. Click the **First Record** button 🖽 at the bottom of the Data Form dialog box to move to the first record. The record number changes to 1, and the first record appears in the data form with the data you entered.

2. Proofread the data by comparing your information with Figure 6-13. Make any necessary corrections by selecting the text and retyping it.

3. Click the **Forward** button ▶ at the bottom of the Data Form dialog box to move to the next record. The record number changes to 2 and the information for the second data record appears. Compare your record with Figure 6-14.

4. Click ▶ to review the third record. Compare your record with Figure 6-15. Make corrections where necessary.

You have entered and edited the three records using the data form. You can also add and edit records in the data source while viewing the records as a Word table.

Krishan, a Pet Shoppe employee, created a Word table with the other records you need to add to the data source. You'll view the data source as a table and add those records.

To view the data source as a table and add new records to the data form:

1. Click the **View Source** button in the Data Form dialog box. The data source table appears in the document window and the Database toolbar appears above the document window. See Figure 6-16. Some contents of the cells are hard to read because they wrap onto one or more lines and break between words. Don't worry about this. You aren't going to print the table, and the data within the table will be formatted when they are merged into the main document. However, you could edit, format, or print the data source table just as you would any other Word table.

Figure 6-16 ◄
Data source
table

Database toolbar ──►

word wraps in table
will not show in final
merged letter

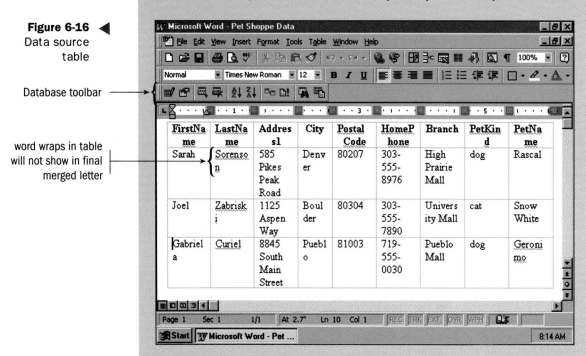

TROUBLE? If your data source table does not show the gridlines shown in Figure 6-16, display them by clicking Table on the menu bar and then clicking Show Gridlines.

2. Move the insertion point to the end of the document, onto the blank line below the table.

3. Click **Insert** on the menu bar, and then click **File**. The Insert File dialog box opens.

4. Make sure the Tutorial.06 folder on your Student Disk is selected, click the file-name **ShopDat**, and then click the **OK** button. Word automatically adds the 11 records in the ShopDat data source table to the three records of the Pet Shoppe Data source table.

5. Scroll up to view all 14 records in the data source table.

   Now that you have entered and edited records using the data form and inserted additional customer records, you should save the data source document.

6. Save the document. Word saves the file using the current filename Pet Shoppe Data.

Alicia's data source eventually will contain hundreds of records for all Pet Shoppe customers. The current data source, however, contains only the records Alicia wants to work with now.

Quick Check

1 Define the following in your own words:
a. form letter
b. main document
c. data source
d. merge field
e. record
f. data field

2 Which of the following are valid field names?
a. Number of Years on the Job
b. PayGrade
c. 3rdQuarterProfits
d. StudentIdentificationNumber
e. ThePetShoppeCompanyEmployeeSocialSecurityNumber
f. Birth Date

3 All the information about one individual or object in a data source is called a _____.

4 True or False: For a mail merge to work properly, every record in the data source must have the same set of fields.

5 Suppose you want to insert information for a field named "Gender" into the data source. How would you do it?

6 What is the purpose of the data form?

7 How do you move to individual records within the data source?

You have opened the main document for the form letter and created the data source that will supply the customer-specific information for Alicia's mailings. In the next session, you'll insert merge fields into the main document and merge the main document with the data source. Then you'll sort the data source by zip code and repeat the merge using the sorted data with the main document.

SESSION

6.2

In this session you'll return to the form letter main document and insert merge fields into it, and then you'll create the merged document. You'll also sort the data source and merge it with the main document. Then you'll filter the data source, edit the main document, and merge the two.

Editing a Main Document

You opened Alicia's sales letter earlier, but didn't enter any of the merge instructions. Now that the data source contains all the records you need to use, you are ready to edit the sales letter.

Alicia wants the date to print below the company letterhead. Instead of just typing today's date, you'll insert a date field. By entering the date field, you won't have to modify the main document each time you send it; the date field will automatically insert the current date when you print the document.

To insert the date field:

1. If you took a break after the last session, make sure Word is running and the Pet Shoppe Form Letter and Pet Shoppe Data are open.

2. If you're viewing the data source document, click the **Mail Merge Main Document** button 📑 on the Database toolbar to switch from the data source document to the main document, Pet Shoppe Form Letter. You should now be viewing Alicia's form letter. Notice that the Mail Merge toolbar appears below the Formatting toolbar. See Figure 6-17.

Figure 6-17 ◀
Main document
before inserting
merge fields

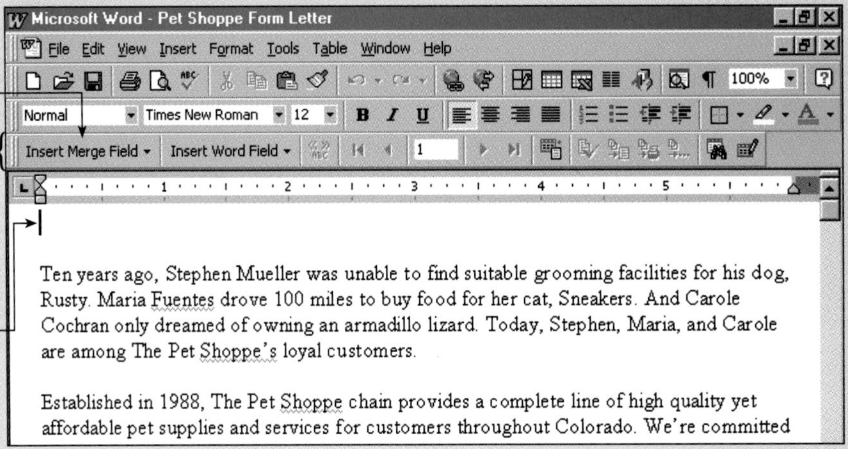

click to insert a
merge field

Mail Merge toolbar

insertion point at
beginning of form
letter

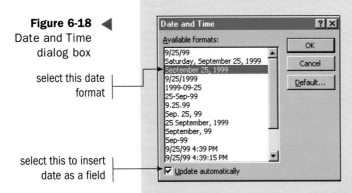

TROUBLE? If the main document, Pet Shoppe Form Letter, is already in the document window, your document window should match Figure 6-17. Just continue with Step 3.

3. Make sure the insertion point is at the very beginning of the form letter, on the first blank line, and then press the **Enter** key six times to position the insertion point where you want the date, leaving enough space for the company letterhead that is preprinted on the company stationery.

Now, rather than typing today's date, you'll insert the Word date field, so that no matter when you print the document, the current date will appear.

4. Click **Insert** on the menu bar, and then click **Date and Time**. The Date and Time dialog box opens.

5. Click the month-day-year format from the list of available formats. If necessary, click the **Update automatically** check box to select it. See Figure 6-18.

Figure 6-18 ◀
Date and Time
dialog box

select this date
format

select this to insert
date as a field

TROUBLE? The date that shows in your dialog box will differ. Just click the format that lists the month, the day, and then the year.

Word

6. Click the **OK** button. The current date appears in the document. Now, whenever you or Alicia print the merged document letter for Pet Shoppe's customers, the current date will print.

> **TROUBLE?** If you see {TIME \@ "MMMM d, yyyy"} instead of the date, then your system is set to view field codes. To view the date, click Tools on the menu bar, click Options, click the View tab, click the Field codes check box in the Show section of the View tab to deselect that option, and then click the OK button.

You are now ready to insert the merge fields for the inside address of the form letter.

Inserting Merge Fields

The sales letter is a standard business letter, so you'll place the customer's name and address below the date. You'll use merge fields for the customer's first name, last name, address, city, and zip code to create the inside address of the form letter. As you insert these merge fields into the main document, you must enter proper spacing and punctuation around the fields so that the information in the merged document will be formatted correctly.

To insert a merge field:

1. Press the **Enter** key four times to leave three blank lines between the date and the first line of the inside address.

2. Click the **Insert Merge Field** button on the Mail Merge toolbar. A list appears with all the field names that you created earlier in the data source. See Figure 6-19.

Figure 6-19 ◀
Insert Merge
Field list

list of field names ──────→

3. Click **FirstName** in the list of field names. Word inserts the merge code for the field name, FirstName, in the form letter at the location of the insertion point.

Word places angled brackets << >>, also called **chevrons**, around the merge field to distinguish it from normal text.

> **TROUBLE?** If you make a mistake and insert the wrong merge field, select the entire merge field, including the chevrons, press the Delete key, and then insert the correct merge field.

Later, when you merge the main document with the data source, Word will retrieve the first name from the data source and insert it into the letter at that location. Now you're ready to insert the merge fields for the rest of the inside address. You'll add the spacing and punctuation to the main document as well.

To insert the remaining merge fields for the inside address:

1. Press the **spacebar** to insert a space after the FirstName field, click the **Insert Merge Field** button on the Mail Merge toolbar, and then click **LastName** in the Insert Merge Field list. Word inserts the LastName merge field into the form letter.

2. Press the **Enter** key to move the insertion point to the next line, click the **Insert Merge Field** button, and then click **Address1** in the Insert Merge Field list. Word inserts the Address1 merge field into the form letter.

3. Press the **Enter** key to move the insertion point to the next line, click the **Insert Merge Field** button, and then click **City** in the Insert Merge Field list. Word inserts the City merge field into the form letter.

4. Type **,** (a comma), press the **spacebar** to insert a space after the comma, and then type **CO** to insert the abbreviation for the state of Colorado. If The Pet Shoppe had a significant number of customers outside Colorado, you would use the State field name in the data source and here in the main document form letter. Because all of the customers live in Colorado, you can make the state name part of the main document, where it will be the same for every letter.

5. Press the **spacebar** to insert a space after the state abbreviation, click the **Insert Merge Field** button, and then click **PostalCode** in the list of fields. Word inserts the PostalCode merge field into the form letter. See Figure 6-20.

Figure 6-20 ◀
Form letter with merge fields

blank space for letterhead

date field

fields for the inside address

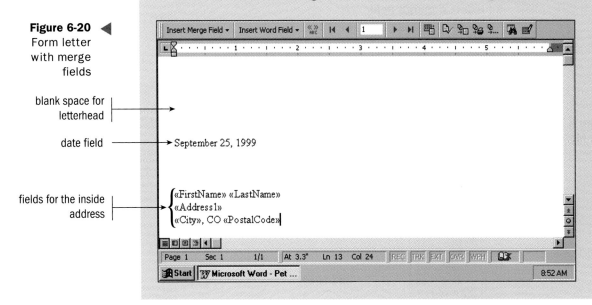

The inside address is set up to match the form for a standard business letter. You can now add the salutation of the letter, which will contain each customer's first name.

To insert the merge field for the salutation:

1. Press the **Enter** key twice to leave a line between the inside address and the salutation, and then type **Dear** and press the **spacebar**.

2. Click the **Insert Merge Field** button on the Mail Merge toolbar, and then click **FirstName**. Word inserts the FirstName merge field into the form letter.

3. Type **:** (a colon). This completes the salutation.

   TROUBLE? If the Office Assistant asks if you want help writing the letter, click Just type the letter without help.

Word

Alicia wants each customer to know that The Pet Shoppe values its customers and remembers them and their pets. You'll personalize the letter even further by including the kind of pet each customer owns and the pet's name.

To finish personalizing the letter:

1. Select the placeholder **[kind of pet]** (including the brackets) in the second paragraph of the form letter. You'll replace this phrase with a merge field.

2. Click the **Insert Merge Field** button on the Mail Merge toolbar, and then click **PetKind**. Word replaces your placeholder with the PetKind merge field into the form letter. If necessary, press the **spacebar** to make sure there is a space between the field and the next word, "in."

3. Select **[branch]** in the third paragraph of the form letter, click the **Insert Merge Field** button, and then click **Branch**. Word inserts the Branch merge field into the form letter. Press the **spacebar** if necessary to make sure there is a space between the field and the next word, "anytime."

4. Similarly, replace **[pet's name]** in the third sentence of the third paragraph of the form letter with the **PetName** field, and make sure there is a space between the merge field and the next word, "for." Your document should look like Figure 6-21.

Figure 6-21
Form letter after inserting merge fields

click to view data merged into main document

fields inserted into text

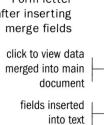

5. Carefully check your document to make sure all the field names and spacing are correct.

   TROUBLE? If you see errors, use Word's editing commands to delete the error, and then insert the correct merge field or spacing.

   You can use the View Merged Data button on the Mail Merge toolbar to see how the letter will look when the merge fields are replaced by actual data.

6. Click the **View Merged Data** button [ ] on the Mail Merge toolbar. The data for the first record replaces the merge fields in the form letter. See Figure 6-22. Scroll to the top of the document so you can see the inside address and salutation. Carefully check over the letter to make sure the text and format are correct. In particular, check to make sure that the spaces before and after the merged data are correct because it is easy to omit spaces or add extraneous spaces around merge fields.

Figure 6-22
Form letter
with merged
data

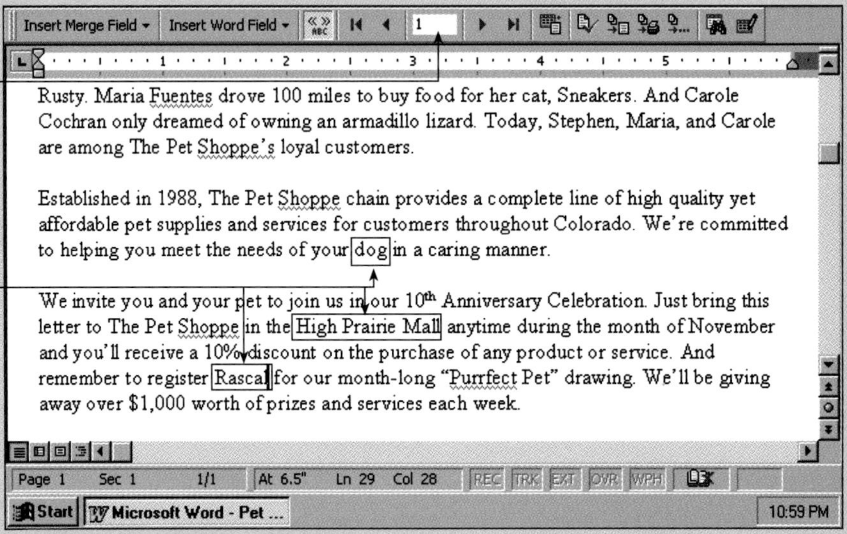

record number

merged data

Insert Merge Field ▼   Insert Word Field ▼

Rusty. Maria Fuentes drove 100 miles to buy food for her cat, Sneakers. And Carole
Cochran only dreamed of owning an armadillo lizard. Today, Stephen, Maria, and Carole
are among The Pet Shoppe's loyal customers.

Established in 1988, The Pet Shoppe chain provides a complete line of high quality yet
affordable pet supplies and services for customers throughout Colorado. We're committed
to helping you meet the needs of your dog in a caring manner.

We invite you and your pet to join us in our 10th Anniversary Celebration. Just bring this
letter to The Pet Shoppe in the High Prairie Mall anytime during the month of November
and you'll receive a 10% discount on the purchase of any product or service. And
remember to register Rascal for our month-long "Purrfect Pet" drawing. We'll be giving
away over $1,000 worth of prizes and services each week.

Page 1   Sec 1   1/1   At 6.5"   Ln 29   Col 28   REC   TRK   EXT   OVR   WPH

Start   Microsoft Word - Pet ...   10:59 PM

7. Click 🔲 again to deselect it. The merge fields reappear.

8. Save the form letter.

The form letter (main document) of the mail merge is complete. As you saw while creating the main document, merge fields are easy to use and very flexible:

■ You can use merge fields anywhere in the main document. For example, in Alicia's form letter, you inserted fields for the inside address and you inserted fields within the body of the letter.

■ You can use the same merge field more than once. For example, Alicia's form letter uses the FirstName field in the inside address and in the salutation.

■ You don't have to use all the fields from the data source in your main document. For example, Alicia's form letter doesn't use the HomePhone field.

Merging the Main Document and Data Source

Now that you have created the form letter (main document) and the list of customer information (data source), you are ready to merge the two files and create personalized letters to send to The Pet Shoppe's customers. Because the data source consists of 14 records, you'll create a merged document with 14 pages, one letter per page.

REFERENCE window

MERGING A MAIN DOCUMENT AND DATA SOURCE TO A NEW DOCUMENT

- Make sure the mail merge main document is in the document window with the Mail Merge toolbar above it.
- Click the Merge to New Document button on the Mail Merge toolbar.

You could merge the data source and main document directly to the printer using the Merge to Printer button on the Mail Merge toolbar, which is often quicker and doesn't require disk space. However, Alicia wants to keep a copy of the merged document on disk for her records. So you'll merge the data source and main document to a new document on disk.

To merge to a new document:

1. Click the **Merge to New Document** button on the Mail Merge toolbar. Word creates a new document called Form Letters1, which contains 14 pages, one for each record in the data source. The Mail Merge toolbar closes.

2. Save the merged document to the Tutorial.06 folder with the filename **Pet Shoppe Form Letters1**.

3. Click the **Print Preview** button on the Standard toolbar to switch to Print Preview, click the **Zoom Control** list arrow on the Print Preview toolbar, and then click **Page Width** so the text is large enough to read. Click the **Previous Page** button or **Next Page** button below the vertical scroll bar to move to the beginning of each letter. Notice that each letter is addressed to a different customer and the branch location, kind of pet, and pet name are different in each letter.

    TROUBLE? If the Next and Previous Page buttons are blue and don't display the beginning of each letter, click the Select Browse Object button and click the Browse by Page button.

4. Click the **Close** button on the Print Preview toolbar to return to the normal view.

5. Press **Ctrl + End** to move the insertion point to the end of the document. Notice on the status bar that you are viewing page 14, the final letter in the merged document.

6. Click **File** on the menu bar, and then click **Print** to open the Print dialog box.

7. Click the **Current page** option button in the Page range section of the dialog box so Word will print only the current page (the last letter) of the merged document, and then click the **OK** button to print the document. Figure 6-23 shows what the letter will look like when Alicia prints it on company letterhead.

Figure 6-23 ◀
Last page of
merged
document

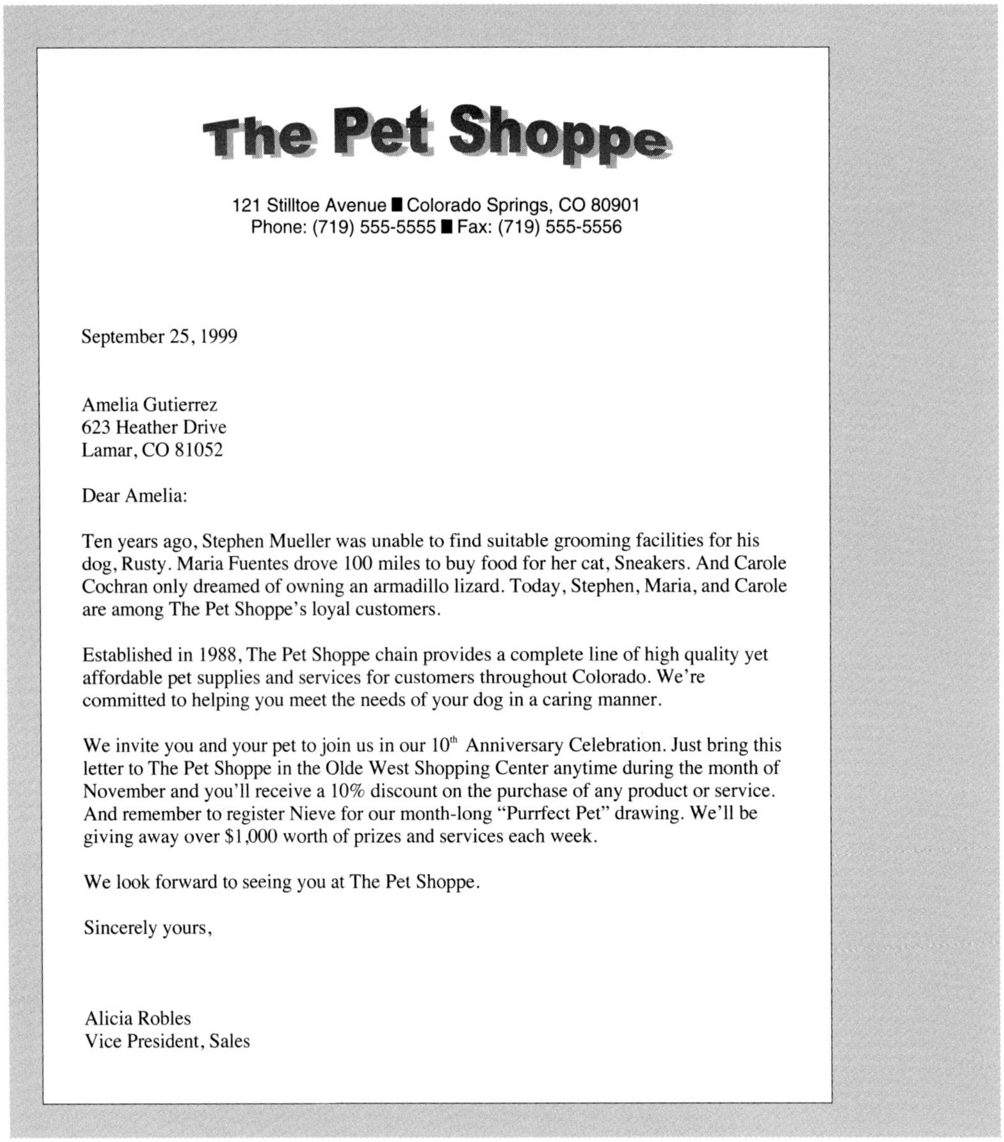

The Pet Shoppe

121 Stilltoe Avenue ■ Colorado Springs, CO 80901
Phone: (719) 555-5555 ■ Fax: (719) 555-5556

September 25, 1999

Amelia Gutierrez
623 Heather Drive
Lamar, CO 81052

Dear Amelia:

Ten years ago, Stephen Mueller was unable to find suitable grooming facilities for his dog, Rusty. Maria Fuentes drove 100 miles to buy food for her cat, Sneakers. And Carole Cochran only dreamed of owning an armadillo lizard. Today, Stephen, Maria, and Carole are among The Pet Shoppe's loyal customers.

Established in 1988, The Pet Shoppe chain provides a complete line of high quality yet affordable pet supplies and services for customers throughout Colorado. We're committed to helping you meet the needs of your dog in a caring manner.

We invite you and your pet to join us in our 10th Anniversary Celebration. Just bring this letter to The Pet Shoppe in the Olde West Shopping Center anytime during the month of November and you'll receive a 10% discount on the purchase of any product or service. And remember to register Nieve for our month-long "Purrfect Pet" drawing. We'll be giving away over $1,000 worth of prizes and services each week.

We look forward to seeing you at The Pet Shoppe.

Sincerely yours,

Alicia Robles
Vice President, Sales

You have completed the mail merge and generated a merged document. Alicia stops by to see how the letters are coming.

Sorting Records

As Alicia looks through the letters to Pet Shoppe customers in the merged document, she notices one problem—the letters are not grouped by zip codes. Currently, the letters are in the order in which customers were added to the data source file. She is going to use bulk mailing rates to send her letters, but the U.S. Postal Service requires bulk mailings to be separated into groups according to zip code. She asks you to sort the data file by zip code (the PostalCode field) and perform another merge, this time merging the main document with sorted data source.

You can sort information in a data source table just as you sort information in any other table. Recall that to sort means to rearrange a list or a document in alphabetical, numerical, or chronological order. You can sort information in ascending order (A to Z, lowest to highest, or earliest to latest) or in descending order (Z to A, highest to lowest, or latest to earliest) using the Sort Ascending button or the Sort Descending button on the Database toolbar.

SORTING A DATA SOURCE

REFERENCE window

- Make sure the data source is in the document window and the Database toolbar is visible.
- Move the insertion point to the field name in the header row whose data you want to sort. For example, if you want to sort by LastName, move the insertion point to the header cell containing the LastName.
- Click the Sort Ascending button or the Sort Descending button on the Database toolbar.

You'll sort the records in ascending order of the PostalCode field in Pet Shoppe Data.

To sort the data source file by zip code:

1. With the merged file still in the document window, click **File** on the menu bar, and then click **Close** to close the file. If you are prompted to save your changes, click Yes.

2. Click the **Edit Data Source** button 📝 on the Mail Merge toolbar to open the Data Form dialog box, and then click the **View Source** button. The data source table appears in the document window.

3. Position the insertion point in the **PostalCode** cell in the header row of the data table. The exact location of the insertion point in the cell doesn't matter.

4. Click the **Sort Ascending** button ⬇ on the Database toolbar. Word sorts the rows of the data table from lowest zip code number to highest. See Figure 6-24.

Figure 6-24
Data source table after sorting by PostalCode

click to sort records in ascending order

record with the lowest zip code is now first

records are sorted by the data in this column

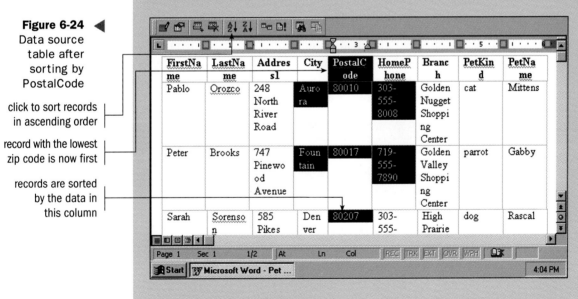

Now when you merge the data source with the form letter, the letters will appear in the merged document in order of the zip codes.

5. Click the **Mail Merge Main Document** button 📑 on the Database toolbar to switch to the Pet Shoppe Form Letter.

6. Click the **Merge to New Document** button 🗐 on the Mail Merge toolbar. Word generates the new merged document with 14 letters, one letter per page, as before, but this time the first letter is to Pablo Orozco, who has the lowest zip code (80010). See Figure 6-25.

Figure 6-25 ◀
Letter of
customer with
lowest zip code

zip code of first
record after sort

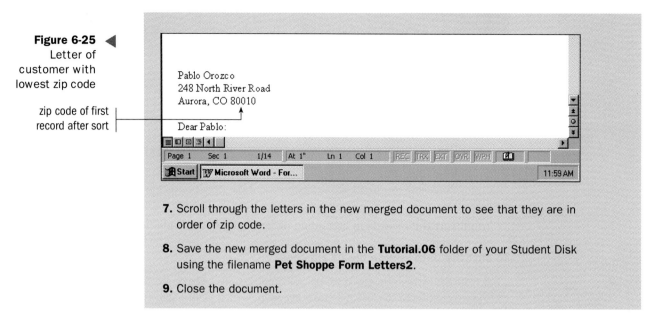

7. Scroll through the letters in the new merged document to see that they are in order of zip code.

8. Save the new merged document in the **Tutorial.06** folder of your Student Disk using the filename **Pet Shoppe Form Letters2**.

9. Close the document.

As Alicia requested, you have created a merged document with the letters to Pet Shoppe customers sorted by zip code. She stops back to tell you that the letters to customers who frequent one branch of The Pet Shoppe need additional information.

Selecting Records to Merge

The Pet Shoppe is going to offer additional savings on certain surplus items at the High Prairie Mall in Denver. Alicia wants to modify the form letter slightly, and then merge it with only those records of customers of The Pet Shoppe in the High Prairie Mall.

You can select specific records from the data source, or **filter** records, to merge with the main document by specifying values for one or more fields with a filtering operation. A **filtering operator** is a mathematical or logical expression (such as Equal to, Not Equal to, or Less than) that you use to include certain records and exclude others. Figure 6-26 shows the filtering operators available for a mail merge.

Figure 6-26 ◀
Filtering
operators
available in
Word

Operator	Retrieves a record if data field
Equal to	Matches value of Compare to text box
Not Equal to	Does not match value of Compare to text box
Less than	Is less than the value of Compare to text box
Greater than	Is greater than the value of Compare to text box
Less than or Equal	Is less than or equal to the value of the Compare to text box
Greater than or Equal	Is greater than or equal to the value of the Compare to text box
Is Blank	Is blank or empty
Is Not Blank	Contains any value

A complete expression is called a **query**. An example of a query is "PostalCode Greater than 80010," which tells Word to filter the records in a data source by the PostalCode field and select any records that include a zip code that is higher than 80010. In the steps below, you'll set the Branch field so that it is equal to "High Prairie Mall." That way, Word will select only records of customers who shop at the High Prairie Mall branch of The Pet Shoppe and filter out all other records. But first, you'll modify the form letter.

To edit the form letter:

1. In the Pet Shoppe Form Letter, position the insertion point to the right of the phrase "10% discount on the purchase of any product or service" in the third paragraph of the form letter, just before the period.

2. Press the **spacebar** and type **and a 25% discount on the purchase of selected items**. See Figure 6-27.

Figure 6-27 ◀
Form letter
with inserted
text

added phrase ⟶

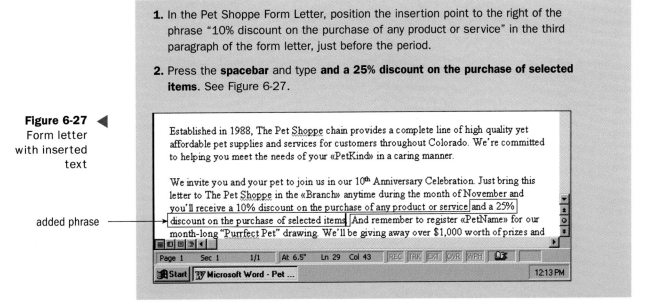

Alicia wants to send this version of the letter only to customers of the High Prairie Mall store. You'll use the Equal to filtering operator to select only those records for High Prairie Mall, and then you'll merge the revised form letter with the records in the data source that match the query.

To filter records for a merge:

1. Make sure the main document appears in the document window, and then click the **Mail Merge** button [icon] on the Mail Merge toolbar. The Merge dialog box opens.

2. Click the **Query Options** button on the dialog box. The Query Options dialog box opens. If necessary, click the **Filter Records** tab. See Figure 6-28. This is where you'll specify the query using a filtering operator.

Figure 6-28 ◀
Query Options
dialog box

select this tab

click to select field
name

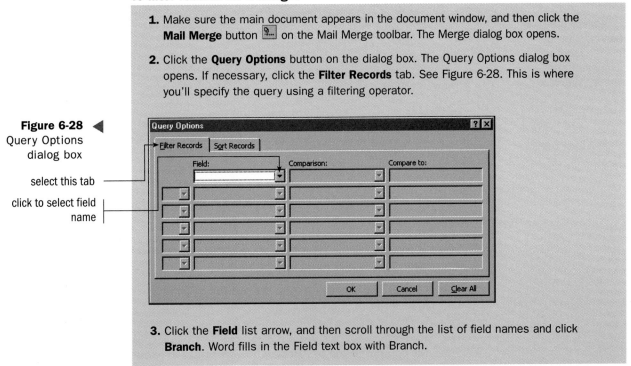

3. Click the **Field** list arrow, and then scroll through the list of field names and click **Branch**. Word fills in the Field text box with Branch.

4. If necessary, click the **Comparison** list arrow, and then click **Equal to** to select the filtering (comparison) operator. This tells Word that you want the value of the Branch field to be equal to something.

Next you'll specify what you want the Branch field to equal.

5. Position the insertion point in the Compare to text box, and type **High Prairie Mall**. Be careful to spell it exactly as shown. If any character or space differs, Word will fail to find any records that match. The completed Query Options dialog box should look like Figure 6-29. This is the only condition that Alicia needs to select customers who shop at High Prairie Mall.

Figure 6-29 ◀
Completed query in Query Options dialog box

filtering operator ─────────

name of Branch field to match ─────

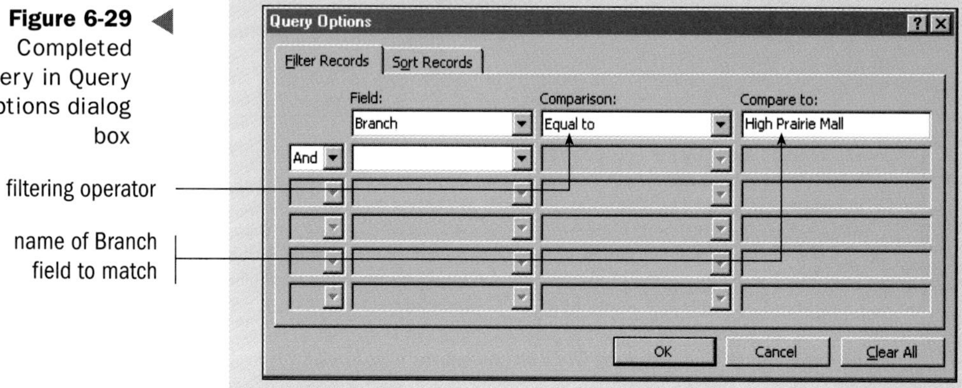

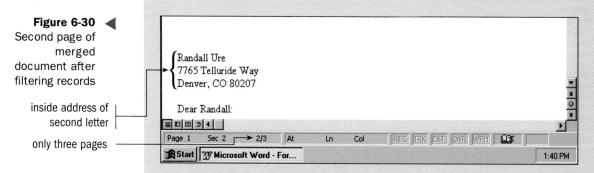

6. Click the **OK** button to accept the query options and return to the Merge dialog box. Notice that the phrase "Query Options have been set" appears at the bottom of the dialog box.

7. Make sure the Merge to text box displays **New Document**, and then click the **Merge** button. Word performs the merge and creates a new document that merges the modified form letter with all the records that match the query. Notice that the document is only three pages because only three records list High Prairie Mall in the Branch field. Scroll through the merged document to see the three letters. See Figure 6-30.

Figure 6-30 ◀
Second page of merged document after filtering records

inside address of second letter ─────

only three pages ─────

As you can see, this merged document consists of only three letters, those to Sarah Sorenson, Randall Ure, and Julia Akin—customers of The Pet Shoppe in the High Prairie Mall.

8. Save the document in the **Tutorial.06** folder on your Student Disk as **Pet Shoppe Form Letters3** and close the document.

9. Close the form letter but do not save the changes of the revised version, and then save and close Pet Shoppe Data, the data source file.

You give the completed file to Alicia, who will print the letters on letterhead.

Quick Check

1 What is the purpose of a date merge in a main document?

2 How do you insert a merge field into a main document?

3 How can you distinguish the merge field from the rest of the text in a main document?

4 Define the following in your own words:
a. merged document
b. sort
c. query
d. filtering operator

5 Suppose one of the data fields contains the zip code of your customers. How would you select only those customers with a certain zip code?

6 How can you preview how the main document will look when the merge fields are replaced by actual data?

7 If your main document is a form letter and you have 23 records in your data source, how many letters will the merged document create?

8 Do you have to print every letter in a merged form letter document?

You have created merged documents for a sorted data source file, filtered records in a data source, and an edited main document. In the next session, you'll create mailing labels and a phone list for Alicia to use when she has the sales reps make her follow-up phone calls.

SESSION

6.3

In this session you'll create and print mailing labels for the form letter envelopes and create a telephone list, both using the mail merge feature.

Creating Mailing Labels

Now that you have created and printed the personalized sales letters, Alicia is ready to prepare envelopes in which to mail the letters. She could print the names and addresses directly onto envelopes or she could create mailing labels to attach to the envelopes. The latter method is easier because 14 labels come on each sheet, and you don't have to feed envelopes through the printer one by one. Alicia asks you to create the mailing labels.

She has purchased Avery® Laser Printer Labels, product number 5162™ - Address. These labels, which are available in most office supply stores, come in 8½-×-11-inch sheets designed to feed through a laser printer. Each label measures 4 × 1.33 inches, and each sheet has seven rows of labels with two labels in each row, for a total of 14 labels per sheet, as shown in Figure 6-31. Word supports most of the Avery label formats.

Figure 6-31
Layout of a
sheet of Avery
5162 labels

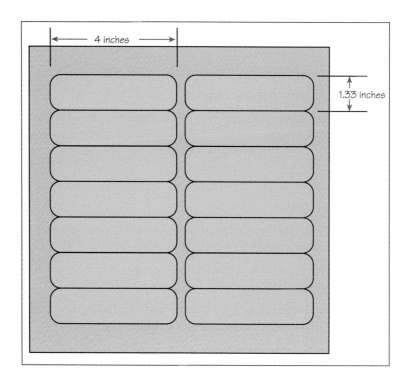

You can use the same data source file (Pet Shoppe Data) as you did earlier, but you'll have to create a new main document. The main document will be of type Mailing Labels instead of type Form Letters.

REFERENCE window

CREATING MAILING LABELS

- Create a main document of type Mailing Labels. (Refer to the Reference Window "Creating a Main Document," except select Mailing Labels when you set up the main document). The Labels Options dialog box opens.
- In the Labels Options dialog box, select the options for your printer type and tray location.
- In the Label products text box, select Avery Standard to print to letter-sized label sheets.
- In the Product number list, select the specific product number for the type of Avery labels that you have, and then click the OK button.

You'll begin creating the mailing labels by specifying the main document and data source.

To specify the main document and data source for creating mailing labels:

1. If you took a break after the last session, make sure Word is running and that your Student Disk is in the appropriate drive.

2. Click the **New** button 🗅 on the Standard toolbar to open a new, blank document.

   TROUBLE? If you already have a new, blank document open, just continue with Step 2.

3. Click **Tools** on the menu bar, and then click **Mail Merge** to open the Mail Merge Helper dialog box.

4. Click the **Create** button in the Main document section of the dialog box, and then click **Mailing Labels**. Word displays a message asking if you want to use the current document or a new one.

5. Click the **Active Window** button so that the current blank document window is the mailing label main document.

6. Click the **Get Data** button on the Mail Merge Helper dialog box, and then click **Open Data Source** because you'll use an existing data source—the table that contains Pet Shoppe customer information you created earlier. The Open Data Source dialog box opens.

7. Make sure the Tutorial.06 folder on your Student Disk is selected, click the filename **Pet Shoppe Data** (if necessary), and then click the **Open** button. Word displays a message advising that you need to set up your main document.

8. Click the **Set Up Main Document** button on the message dialog box. The Label Options dialog box opens.

You have specified the main document, which is the blank document in the document window, and the data source, which is the file Pet Shoppe Data. You're ready to select the type of labels and create the merged document of labels.

To create the mailing labels:

1. In the Printer information section of the dialog box, select the type of printer you'll use—dot matrix or laser and ink jet. If you print to a laser or ink jet printer, you might also have the option of specifying the printer tray that will contain the mailing-label sheets. For example, if you have a LaserJet 4L printer, the printer type is a laser printer and the tray might be the upper tray. You should select the options that are appropriate for your printer.

   TROUBLE? If you're not sure which options to choose for your printer, consult your instructor or technical support person.

2. Make sure **Avery standard** displays in the Label products text box. Even if you don't have Avery labels, you can print the merged document in the format of an Avery label sheet on an 8½-×-11-inch letter-sized sheet of paper.

3. Scroll down the Product number list box and click **5162 - Address**. Your dialog box should look like Figure 6-32, except your printer specifications might be different.

Figure 6-32 ◀
Label Options
dialog box

select this label
format

4. Click the **OK** button. Word opens the Create Labels dialog box, which contains an area where you can insert the merge fields in a sample label.

5. Click the **Insert Merge Field** button on the dialog box and click **FirstName** to insert the field, press the **spacebar** to insert a space between the first and last names, and then click the **Insert Merge Field** button and click **LastName** to insert the field.

6. Press the **Enter** key to move to the next line; use the same method as in Step 5 to insert the **Address1** field, press the **Enter** key, insert the **City** field, type **,** (a comma), press the **spacebar**, type **CO** (the abbreviation for Colorado), press the **spacebar**, and insert the **PostalCode** field. The completed Create Labels dialog box should look like Figure 6-33.

Figure 6-33 ◀
Create Labels
dialog box

inserted merge fields ──────▶

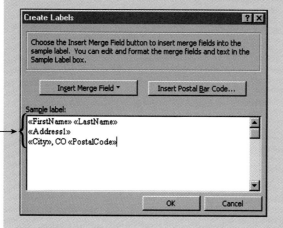

7. Click the **OK** button. The Mail Merge Helper dialog box is still open and you are ready to merge the data source into the mailing labels document.

8. Click the **Merge** button in the Merge the data with the document section. The Merge dialog box opens.

9. Make sure that the Merge to option is set to New Document and that the Records to be merged option is set to **All**, and then click the **Merge** button. Word creates a new merged document formatted for the Avery 5162 - Address mailing-label sheets. See Figure 6-34.

Figure 6-34 ◀
Merged
document with
mailing labels

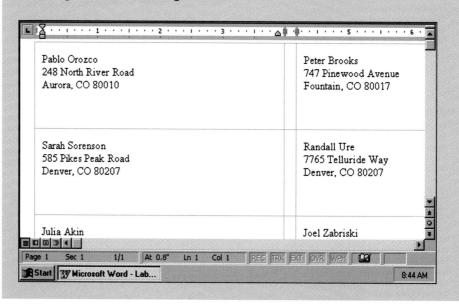

The labels are all set up. All you need to do is save the document and print the labels. For now, you'll just print the labels on an 8½-×-11-inch sheet of paper so you can see what they look like. Later, Alicia will print them again on the sheet of labels.

To save and print the labels:

1. Save the merged document to the **Tutorial.06** folder of your Student Disk with the filename **Pet Shoppe Labels**.

2. Scroll through the document to preview the labels.

3. Print the merged document of labels just as you would print any other document.

   TROUBLE? If you want to print on a sheet of labels, consult your instructor or technical support person about how to feed the sheet into the printer. If you're using a printer that you share with other users, you may need to make special arrangements so other users' documents aren't accidentally printed on your label sheets.

4. Close the merged document.

5. Save the main document to the **Tutorial.06** folder on your Student Disk with the filename **Pet Shop Labels Form**, and then close the document.

6. If necessary, close the data source file, but do not exit Word.

If Alicia wanted you to print envelopes instead of mailing labels, you would have created a new main document similar to the one for creating mailing labels, except you would choose Envelopes as the type of main document rather than Mailing Labels.

Creating a Telephone List

As your final task, Alicia wants you to create a telephone list for all the customers in the data source table. She asked some of the sales personnel to call customers and remind them of The Pet Shoppe's anniversary sale; the sales reps will call all the customers on the phone list you create.

You'll begin by setting up a mail merge as before, except this time you'll use a Catalog type of main document rather than a Form Letter. Even though you aren't actually creating a catalog, you'll use the Catalog type because in Form Letter, Word automatically inserts a section break, which forces a page break, after each merged record. In a Catalog type of main document, all the entries (records) in the telephone list will print on one page rather than each record printing on its own page.

To prepare for creating the telephone list:

1. Click the **New** button on the Standard toolbar to open a new, blank document window.

2. Click **Tools** on the menu bar, and then click **Mail Merge**. The Mail Merge Helper dialog box opens.

3. Click the **Create** button in the Main document section of the dialog box. A list of main document types appears.

4. Click **Catalog**.

5. Click the **Active Window** button.

6. Click the **Get Data** button, and then click **Open Data Source** and open **Pet Shoppe Data** from the **Tutorial.06** folder of your Student Disk.

7. Click the **Edit Main Document** button in the message dialog box.

You are ready to create the main document for the telephone list and merge the main document with the data source. The format of the telephone list is the customer's name (last name first) at the left margin of the page and the phone number at the right margin.

You'll set up the main document so that the phone number is preceded by a dot leader. A **dot leader** is a dotted line that extends from the last letter of text on the left margin to the beginning of text aligned at a tab stop.

To create the main document:

1. With the insertion point in a blank document window, insert the **LastName** merge field, type **,** (a comma), press the **spacebar**, and insert the **FirstName** merge field.

   Now you'll set a tab stop at the right margin (position 6 inches) with a dot leader.

2. Click **Format** on the menu bar, and then click **Tabs** to open the Tabs dialog box.

3. Type **6** in the Tab stop position text box, click the **Right** option button in the Alignment section, and then click **2 ....** in the Leader section to create a dot leader. See Figure 6-35.

Figure 6-35 ◀
Tabs dialog box

set tab stops to 6 inches

set alignment to right

select this dot leader

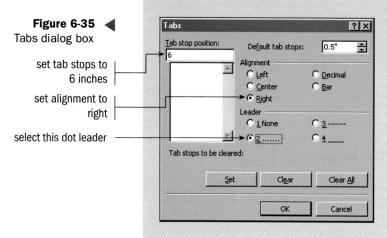

4. Click the **OK** button. Word clears the current tab stops and inserts a right-aligned tab stop at position 6 inches, the right margin of the page.

5. Press the **Tab** key to move the insertion point to the new tab stop. A dot leader appears in the document from the end of the FirstName field to the tab stop.

6. Insert the **HomePhone** merge field at the location of the insertion point, and then press the **Enter** key. You inserted a hard return here so that each name and telephone number will appear on a separate line. Notice that the dot leader shortened to accommodate the inserted text. The completed main document looks like Figure 6-36.

Figure 6-36 ◀
Completed main document for telephone list

dot leader

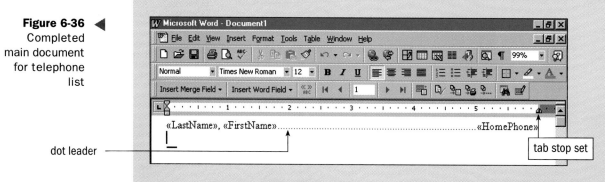

7. Save the document to the **Tutorial.06** folder on your Student Disk with the file-name **Pet Shoppe Phone Form**.

You are almost ready to merge this file with the data source, except that you want the name and phone numbers list to be alphabetized by the customers' last names. First you'll sort the data source, and then you'll merge the files.

To sort the data source by last name and merge the files:

1. Click the **Edit Data Source** button on the Mail Merge toolbar, and then click the **View Source** button to display the data table.

2. Move the insertion point to the **LastName** cell in the header row, and then click the **Sort Ascending** button on the Database toolbar. Word sorts the records by customer last name. You're ready to perform the merge.

3. Click **Window** on the menu bar, and then click **Pet Shoppe Phone Form** to switch to the Pet Shoppe Phone Form.

4. Click the **Merge to New Document** button on the Mail Merge toolbar. Word generates the telephone list. See Figure 6-37.

Figure 6-37 ◀
Merged
document of
telephone list

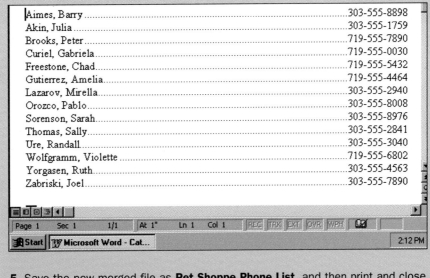

Aimes, Barry	303-555-8898
Akin, Julia	303-555-1759
Brooks, Peter	719-555-7890
Curiel, Gabriela	719-555-0030
Freestone, Chad	719-555-5432
Gutierrez, Amelia	719-555-4464
Lazarov, Mirella	303-555-2940
Orozco, Pablo	303-555-8008
Sorenson, Sarah	303-555-8976
Thomas, Sally	303-555-2841
Ure, Randall	303-555-3040
Wolfgramm, Violette	719-555-6802
Yorgasen, Ruth	303-555-4563
Zabriski, Joel	303-555-7890

Page 1   Sec 1   1/1   At 1"   Ln 1   Col 1   REC TRK EXT OVR WPH

Start   Microsoft Word - Cat...   2:12 PM

5. Save the new merged file as **Pet Shoppe Phone List**, and then print and close the file.

6. Save and close the Pet Shoppe Phone form.

7. Exit Word without saving the sorted data source file.

You have created the telephone list. Alicia will have it copied and distributed to the appropriate sales personnel. She thinks that The Pet Shoppe's 10th Anniversary Celebration will be a great success.

Quick Check

1. Which of the following are not a type of main document:
   a. mailing labels
   b. merge fields
   c. envelopes
   d. telephone list
   e. form letters

2. True or False: To create mailing labels you can use the same data source file you used for a form letter.

3. Describe the general process for creating and printing an address list that will print directly to envelopes.

4. True or False: Word automatically inserts an end of section break, which forces a page break, after each merged record in a Catalog type of main document.

5   What is a dot leader? (The telephone list you created in this tutorial used a dot leader.)

6   How do you display a data table?

7   How do you sort a data source using the LastName field so that all the customers are arranged in reverse alphabetical order (Z to A)?

In this tutorial, you have created a form letter and merged it with a data source to create a personalized mailing to Pet Shoppe customers. You have also created mailing labels and a telephone list to help in their marketing efforts. Alicia thanks you for your help and prepares the letters for mailing to Pet Shoppe's customers.

Tutorial Assignments

The Pet Shoppe's 10th Anniversary Celebration was a great success, and Alicia was pleased with how convenient it was to send out form letters with the Word mail merge feature. She decides to use it to remind customers about the pet vaccines that the shop offers, using the services of a visiting veterinarian. She asks you to help her with a mailing.

1. If necessary, start Word and make sure your Student Disk is in the appropriate drive. Open the file PetVacc from the TAssign folder in the Tutorial.06 folder on your Student Disk, and then save it on your Student Disk as Pet Shoppe Vaccines.

2. In mail merge, create a form letter main document using Pet Shoppe Vaccines as the main document.

3. Create a data source document, using the filename Pet Vaccine Data, with the following eight field names: FirstName, LastName, Address1, City, PostalCode, Branch, PetKind, and PetName.

4. Create records using the following information:
   Elmo Zoulek, 1771 Levan Drive, Boulder, CO 80307, University Mall, dog, Ringo
   AnnaClair Smuin, 927 S. Crestview, Cortez, CO 81321, Cortez, dog, Charity
   Percy Burnside, 1037 Wilderness Ave., Greeley, CO 80631, Rocky Mountain Mall, cat, Buffy
   Armand Walborsky, 21 Parkway Circle #202, Denver, CO 80204, High Prairie Mall, cat, Zorba

5. Sort the data source by postal code from the lowest to the highest postal code.

6. Save the data source document Pet Vaccine Data to your Student Disk.

7. Switch to the main document and replace the text of the field names in brackets with actual merge fields.

8. Save the changes to the main document, and then view the document as it will appear when it is merged, and check for any mistakes in the records you have added.

9. Print only those records for customers who own a dog.

10. Close all documents, saving changes as needed.

Open the file Payroll from the TAssign folder in the Tutorial.06 folder on your Student Disk, and then save it as Payroll Memo. Complete the following:

11. Create a form letter main document using Payroll Memo as the active file.

12. Create a data source with the following field names: FirstName, LastName, Address1, WorkPhone, and Exemptions.

13. Save the data source document as Payroll Data.

14. Create a record for each of the following Pet Shoppe employees working at company headquarters:
Leslie Knecht, B-141, 552-1121, 3
Mei-Young Soh, B-333, 552-1818, 2
Cesar Velarde, B-353, 552-1811, 2
Scott Coe, B-147, 552-1135, 1

Edit the main document by doing the following:

15. To the right of "TO:," press the Tab key and insert the FirstName field (for the employee's first name), press the spacebar, and then insert the LastName field (for the employee's last name).

16. To the right of "DATE:" in the memo, press the Tab key and insert the Word date field. Select the Word date field and turn off bolding.

17. In the body of the memo, immediately before the word "exemptions," insert the Exemptions field followed by a space.

18. Save the main document with the changes, and then view the memo as it will appear when merged and check each record for any mistakes.

 19. Print only the records of employees with two exemptions.

20. Close all documents, saving any changes. If Word asks if you want to save changes to a template, click No. Create a new main document of the Envelopes type.

 21. Insert the FirstName, LastName, and Address1 fields into the Envelope Address dialog box, using Payroll Data as the data source.

22. Save the envelopes main document as Payroll Envelope Form.

23. Merge the envelopes main document and data source Payroll Data, and then save the merged document as Payroll Envelopes. Use the default return address, or substitute your own.

24. Print the last employee address on an 8½-×-11-inch sheet of paper, and then close all documents.

25. Open a new, blank document window and create a main document for generating a one-page telephone list. Use Payroll Data as the data source.

26. Create an employee telephone list by inserting the LastName and FirstName fields at the left margin. Insert the WorkPhone field at the right margin with a dot leader.

27. Format the main document so that each telephone number appears on a separate line, and then sort the data source alphabetically by last name in ascending order.

28. Generate the telephone list and save the new merged document as Employee Phone List.

29. Print the telephone list, and then close all documents, saving changes as needed.

Case Problems

1. DeeDee Sandau for Mayor DeeDee Sandau is preparing to run for the office of mayor of Jefferson City, Missouri. DeeDee's campaign staff is creating a data file of prospective supporters of her campaign, and she asks you to help her.

1. If necessary, start Word and make sure your Student Disk is in the appropriate drive. Open the file Campaign from the Cases folder in the Tutorial.06 folder on your Student Disk, and then save it as Campaign Form Letter.

2. Create a data source document with the following field names: FullName, NickName, Title, Company, Address, Phone, and Party.

3. Save the data source document as Supporters Data.

4. Enter the following four records into the data source. Each line is one record. The fields in each record are separated by commas. (Don't include the commas in the records.)

    Maria De Jesus, Maria, Chief Medical Officer, Jefferson Medical Center, 1577 Lancelot Drive, 552-7740, Republican

    Randall Dakota, Randy, President, Dakota Appraisal Services, 633 Wentworth, 552-1095, Democrat

    Leilani Kinikini, Lani, Business Manager, Nolan and Ash Architects, 4424 Bedford, 552-9850, Independent

    David Bezzant, Dave, Chief Financial Officer, Midtown Missouri State Bank, 844 Heatherton Rd, 552-0180, Republican

Edit the Campaign Form Letter as follows:

5. At the beginning of the document, insert the Word date field, and then leave two blank lines between the date and the inside address.

6. Insert merge fields for the complete inside address. Include fields for each person's name, title, company, and address. All the inside addresses should include the city (Jefferson City), the abbreviation for the state (MO), and the zip code (65101).

7. Insert a blank line below the fields for the inside address and create the salutation of the letter. Use the field name NickName in the salutation. Make sure there is a blank line between the salutation and the body of the letter.

8. In the third paragraph, replace the words in brackets with the actual field names.

9. Save the edited main document.

10. Merge the files to create a set of letters to prospective contributors.

11. Save the merged letters document as Campaign Letters.

12. Print the first two letters.

13. Create a main document to print envelopes for the letters, and save the document as Campaign Envelope Form.

14. Merge the envelopes main document with the Supporters Data data source, and save the merged document as Campaign Envelopes.

15. Print the first page of the envelope file on an 8½-×-11-inch sheet of paper.

16. Sort the data source in descending order by phone numbers.

17. Create a telephone list of prospective contributors. Use a dot leader to separate the name on left from the phone number on right.

18. Save the main document for the telephone list as Campaign Phone Form.

19. Save the merged document of the telephone list as Campaign Phone List.

20. Print the telephone list on a sheet of paper.

21. Close the documents.

2. Gina's Gems Gina Lujan owns a small jewelry store in White Plains, New York. She frequently notifies her regular customers of upcoming sales. She decides to prepare personalized form letters to mail to all her regular customers one month before their birthdays. She'll mail the letters in manila envelopes along with a two-page color catalog and a gift certificate. She asks you to help her perform a mail merge using Word.

1. If necessary, start Word and make sure your Student Disk is in the appropriate drive. Open the file Gems from the Cases folder in the Tutorial.06 folder of your Student Disk, and then save it as Gems Form Letter.

2. Create a data source document with the following field names: FirstName, LastName, Address1, City, State, PostalCode, BirthDay, BirthMonth, BirthStone.

3. Save the data source document as Gems Data.

4. Enter the following five records into the data source. Each line is one record. The fields in each record are separated by commas. (Don't include the commas in the records.) Enter months by numbers (1, 2, 3) not names (January, February, March) so you can sort in chronological order.

   John, Pataki, 426 Hudson Way, White Plains, NY, 10602, 23, January, garnet

   Allison, Mandelkern, 11812 Westbrook Way, Croton-on-Hudson, NY, 10520, 31, August, sapphire

   Susan, Gardner, 804 Lake Placid Road, West Haven, CT, 06156, 14, June, pearl

   Garth, Poduska, 77 Catskill Circle, Lake Carmel, NY, 10512, 7, January, garnet
   Donald, Truong, 4055 Empire Road, Scarsdale, NY, 10583, 22, August, sapphire

5. At the beginning of the main document, Gems Form Letter, insert the date field and data fields for the inside address and salutation. Use the customer's first name in the salutation.

6. In the body of the letter, insert the fields BirthMonth, BirthDay, and BirthStone at the locations indicated by the bracketed words. Put a slash (/) between the BirthDay and BirthMonth.

7. Sort the data source alphabetically by the customer's last name.

8. Save the main document using its current filename.

9. Using Query Options, select those records for customers whose birthdays are in January, and then merge the main document with the data source.

10. Save the merged document as Gems Letters.

11. Print the letters that result from the merge.

12. Create a main document for generating mailing labels on sheets of Avery 5162 - Address Labels.

13. Save the document as Gems Labels Form.

14. Print the labels on an 8½-×-11-inch sheet of paper, and save the labels as Gems Labels.

15. Create a main document for generating a list of customers. Use the following example to format your merge fields, put a blank line after the last line, and bold the first line:

Name: Garth Poduska
Address: 77 Catskill Circle, Lake Carmel, NY 10512
Birth date: 1/7
Birthstone: garnet

16. Save the main document as Gems Customer List Form.

17. Sort the data source in ascending order by birth month, then by birth day. (*Hint:* Click the Query Options button on the Mail Merge Helper dialog box, use the Sort Records tab, set the Sort by text box to BirthMonth and the Then by text box to BirthDay.)

18. Merge the customer list form with the data source.

19. Save the merged document as Gems Customer List.

20. Print the list.

21. Close the files.

3. Heritage Auto Sales Joe Whitlock is the customer relations manager for Heritage Auto Sales in Cadillac, Michigan. After a customer purchases a new car, Joe sends out a Sales Satisfaction Survey accompanied by a personalized letter. He would like you to help him use the Word mail merge feature to perform this task.

1. If necessary, start Word and make sure your Student Disk is in the appropriate drive. Open the file AutoSale from the Cases folder in the Tutorial.06 folder on your Student Disk, and then save it as Auto Sale Form Letter.

2. Create a data source with the following field names: FirstName, LastName, Address1, City, PostalCode, CarMake, CarModel, SalesRep.

3. Save the data source document as Auto Sale Data.

4. Enter the following five records into the data source. Each line is one record. Commas separate the fields in each record. (Don't include the commas in the records.)
   Patty, Muelstein, 4102 Apple Avenue, Detroit, 48235, Honda, Civic, Carl
   Delbert, Greene, 875 Gunnison Road, Ecorse, 48229, Toyota, Camry, Audrey
   Li, Du, 2221 Wolverine Drive, Kentwood, 49508, Honda, Accord, Michael
   Art, Zupan, 301 Maple Avenue, Walker, 49504, Toyota, Corolla, Carl
   Dina, Webb, 772 West University Drive, Detroit, 48238, Honda, Civic, Michael

5. Edit the main document to include the following in the letter: date, inside address, and salutation. (*Hint:* You'll need to add the state as text.)

6. Edit the body of the form letter to replace words in brackets with their corresponding merge field names.

7. Save the form letter. If Word asks if you want to save changes to a template, click No.

8. Sort the data source alphabetically by the last name.

9. Use the Query Option to select only those records whose sales representative was Michael.

10. Merge the form letter with the data source.

11. Save the merged document as Auto Letters.

12. Print letters in the merged document.

13. Create a main document for printing envelopes for the letters that you printed.

14. Save the new main document as Auto Envelopes Form.

15. Merge the main document with the data to generate a file for printing envelopes.

16. Save the merged document as Auto Envelopes.

17. Print the envelopes in the file on 8½-×-11-inch sheets of paper.

18. Close all the files, saving any changes as needed.

4. Special Event Announcements Mailing List At some point, you might want to send announcements to your friends and family telling them about a special event—a graduation, marriage, move to a new city, etc. You can do this easily with Word's Mail Merge feature. Do the following:

1. If necessary, start Word and make sure your Student Disk is in the appropriate drive.

2. Create a data source containing the names and addresses of at least five people. You can use real or fictitious names and addresses.

3. Save the data source document as Special Event Data in the Tutorial.06 folder on your Student Disk.

4. Write a brief form letter telling your friends and family about the special event. Include the following in the letter:

   a. Word field for the current date

   b. merge fields for the inside address and salutation of the letter

   c. at least one merge field within the body of the letter

   d. information to your friends and family about the time, date, and location of your special event

5. Save the main document as Special Event Form Letter.

6. Sort the data source in ascending order by last name.

7. Merge the main document and data source.

8. Save the merged document as Special Event Merge. If your documents are long, you may need to save it to a separate disk.

9. Print the first two pages (letters) of the merged document.

10. Create a labels main document. You can use any printer label type you like, as long as each name and address fits on one label and all the labels fit on one page.

11. Save the labels main document as Special Event Labels Form.

12. Merge the files, and save the merged document of labels as Special Event Labels.

13. Print the labels on a plain sheet of paper.

Integrating Word with Other Programs and with the World Wide Web

Writing a Proposal to Open a New Branch of Family Style, Inc.

LAB

The Internet
World Wide Web

CASE

Family Style, Inc.

Nalani Tui is one of the founders and owners of Family Style, Inc., a retail company with six outlets in the central and southern regions of Indiana. When she and her partners founded Family Style in 1988, their concept was simple. They would buy high-quality used home merchandise—clothing, sports equipment, appliances, furniture, televisions, personal computers, and so forth—and resell it at a profit, but still for far less than consumers would pay for similar new merchandise.

The concept was immediately popular. Customers who have items for sale can receive immediate cash, and customers who want to buy items can purchase them at very low prices. Family Style is successful because the outlets readily attract sellers and buyers and because the management has kept administrative, marketing, and overhead expenses low.

Nalani thinks that Family Style is ready to expand to cities in northern Indiana. She is preparing a written proposal for the other owners and investors of Family Style on the advantages and disadvantages of opening new outlet stores. The proposal will include an overview of the company's current financial picture, the rationale for expanding, possible sites for new outlets, and Nalani's recommendations for the first new branch site and manager. She wants you to help organize this information in the proposal document.

Nalani needs to make her proposal available to three different groups of people:

- current owners and stockholders of the company, who live in different parts of the country
- the Family Style management team, who work in the Bloomington office
- potential investors in the company, who could reside anywhere

Nalani can simply mail a printed copy of her proposal to the current owners and stockholders. For the company's management team, she can make the proposal available to the company's network. For potential investors, she can reach a world-wide audience by placing her proposal on the company's World Wide Web site.

In this tutorial, you'll combine the text that Nalani has already written in Word with a worksheet file and a chart that other Family Style employees prepared using different software. Then you'll optimize the document for online viewing on the company's network. Your modifications will enable online viewers to easily navigate around the document and view additional, more detailed information. Finally, you'll save the document in a special format that is readable by Web browsers like Internet Explorer or Netscape Navigator, and you'll enhance the Web document's appearance.

SESSION

7.1

In this session you'll see how Nalani planned the proposal. Then you'll embed a worksheet file that was created in Microsoft Excel and modify it from within Word. Next, you'll insert a link to an Excel chart. You'll modify the chart from Excel, and learn how to update it in Word to see the effect of the modifications you made.

Planning the Document

Nalani has written the text of the proposal in Word. She has asked you to add two other components to her proposal: a worksheet and a chart, both from Excel. Together, the text, data, and chart will show the company's current financial state and the possible sites for new branches (retail outlets). The proposal also presents Nalani's recommendations for a new site and branch manager. Nalani gives you two files to combine with the Word document: a Microsoft Excel spreadsheet of financial data created by one of the store managers, and an Excel chart created by the Accounting department. Figure 7-1 shows how Nalani wants to combine these segments into a complete proposal.

The proposal begins with an executive summary, and then reviews the company objectives, explains the current situation and future expansion ideas, suggests some location options, and gives a final recommendation.

Your immediate task is to place the Excel worksheet and chart into the Word proposal document.

Figure 7-1 ◄
Proposal Nalani
envisions

Nalani's
proposal in
Word

Nalani wants
the Excel chart
placed here

Nalani wants
the Excel
worksheet
placed here

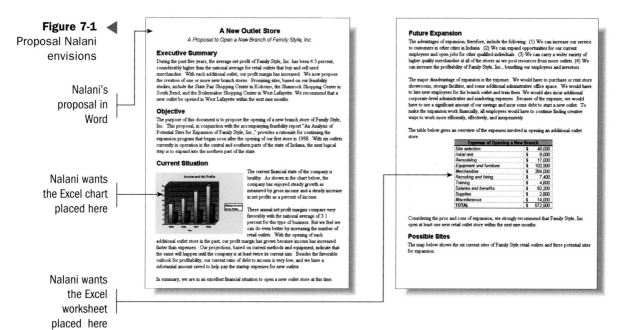

Integrating Objects from Other Programs

Every software program is designed to accomplish a set of specific tasks. As you've seen with Microsoft Word, you can use a word-processing program to create, edit, and format documents such as letters, reports, newsletters, and proposals. A spreadsheet program, on the other hand, allows you to organize, calculate, and analyze numerical data. For example, one of Family Style's managers used the Microsoft Excel spreadsheet program to prepare a breakdown of expenses involved in opening a new branch. The Accounting department created an Excel chart that provides a visual representation of income and profit data.

Both the worksheet and the chart are Excel objects. An **object** in Office 97 and other Windows programs is an item such as a graphic image, clip art, a WordArt image, a chart, or a section of text, that you can modify and move from one document to another. Nalani wants you to place the worksheet and chart objects into her proposal, but she also wants to be able to modify the Excel objects after they are in her document. A technology called **object linking and embedding**, or **OLE** (pronounced "oh-lay"), allows you to integrate information created in one program into a document created in another, and then to modify the object using the tools that created it.

The program used to create the original version of the object is called the **source program** (in this case, Excel). The program into which the object is integrated is called the **destination program** (in this case, Word). Similarly, the original file is called the **source file** and the file into which you insert the object is called the **destination file**.

Word supports three important methods for inserting an object from a source program into a destination program: importing, embedding and linking. This tutorial will help you learn about embedding and linking.

Embedding

Embedding allows you to place an existing object into (or create an object in) a destination document, and edit the object by double-clicking it to bring up the tools of the source program. Any changes you make to the embedded object are not made in the original file, and vice versa.

Figure 7-2 illustrates how you can use embedding to place the Excel worksheet into Nalani's Word proposal.

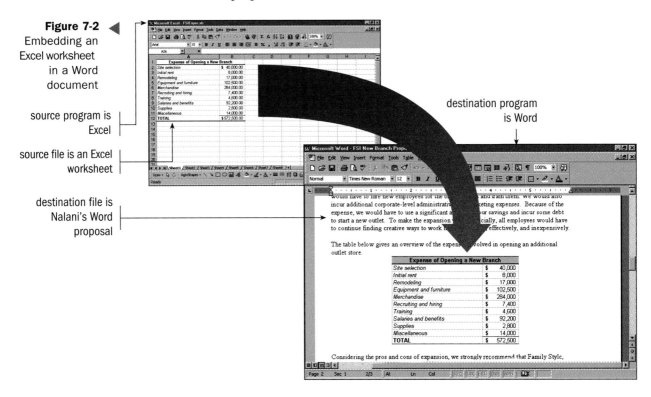

Figure 7-2
Embedding an Excel worksheet in a Word document

source program is Excel

source file is an Excel worksheet

destination file is Nalani's Word proposal

destination program is Word

Once an object is embedded, you can edit it using the source program's editing tools. You simply double-click the embedded Excel chart, and the Excel menus and toolbars appear without your having to leave Word. Excel must be installed on the computer you are using if you want to edit the Excel worksheet while you are still in Word.

Any edits you make to the embedded worksheet appear only in the worksheet copy in Word, not in the original Excel worksheet file. Similarly, after you embed the file, any changes you make to the original worksheet from Excel do not appear in the embedded worksheet in Word. The embedded worksheet retains a connection to the source program, Excel, but not to the source worksheet.

Linking

Linking is similar to embedding, except that the linked object maintains a two-way connection between the source program and destination program. If you want to edit the linked object, you can open the source program from within the destination program and make changes that will also appear in the original file. Likewise, if you edit the original file in the source program, the changes will appear in the linked object. As long as the source program is installed on your computer, you can edit a linked file. The linked object you see in the destination document is not a copy; it is only a representation that is linked back to the original object in the source file. So a document that contains a linked object usually takes up less space on a disk than a document containing an embedded version of the same object. Figure 7-3 illustrates how you can use linking to place the Excel chart into Nalani's Word document proposal.

Figure 7-3
Linking an Excel chart to a Word document

source program is Excel

source file is an Excel chart

destination program is Word

destination file is Nalani's Word proposal

linked chart represents the original

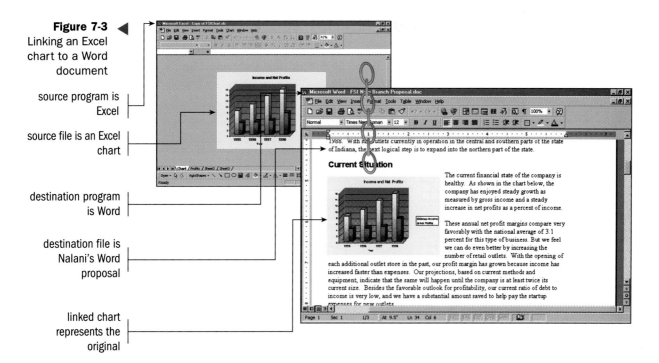

You can modify the chart in Excel, the source program. The changes you make to the chart in Excel appear in the linked representation in Word the next time you open the file.

Not all software programs allow you to embed or link objects. Only those programs that support OLE let you embed or link objects from one program to another. Fortunately, Windows 95 programs like Word, Excel, and PowerPoint, all are OLE-enabled programs and fully support object linking and embedding.

Choosing Between Embedding and Linking

When you want to integrate information created in another program (the source program) into Word (the destination program), and maintain a connection between the two files, which method should you choose—embedding, or linking?

Embed a file whenever the information in it is not likely to change over time, but when you still want to use the source program commands to modify it without affecting the source file. For example, if you want to integrate an Excel worksheet into your Word document and Excel is installed on your computer, you should embed the worksheet so you can access Excel commands if you ever need to modify formatting or data. The original Excel worksheet (the source file) remains unchanged, and you could even delete it from your disk without affecting the copy embedded in your Word document.

Link a file whenever you have dynamic data that might change over time, and want to update both the source and destination files from within either Word or the source program. For example, suppose you want to integrate an Excel worksheet into your Word document, but the information in the source document might change over time. In this case, you should link the worksheet file so you can update both the original worksheet and the copy in your Word document from either Word or Excel.

The advantage to linking is that the data in both the Excel worksheet and the Word document can reflect the latest revisions. The disadvantages to linking are that you must have access to both Excel and the linked file on your computer. If you don't want to modify the original Excel worksheet because it contains information and formatting you'll need later, you should embed the worksheet rather than link it.

Embedding an Excel Worksheet

Nalani prepared the new branch proposal using Word. Before you embed and link objects, you'll first open Nalani's Word document (the destination file).

To open the destination file:

1. Start Word, and insert your Student Disk in the appropriate drive. For this tutorial, you don't need to display the nonprinting characters.

2. Open the file **FSIProp** from the **Tutorial.07** folder on your Student Disk, and then save it as **FSI New Branch Proposal**.

3. Read the document to get an idea of its content.

   Because this tutorial will use many files, you'll want to make efficient use of your available disk space, especially if you are using floppy disks. You'll turn off the Word Fast Save feature to save disk space.

4. Click **Tools** on the menu bar, click **Options**, click the **Save** tab, click to remove the check mark from the Allow fast saves check box and click the **OK** button.

The proposal begins with an Executive Summary that quickly summarizes the main points of the document. Notice that in the "Current Situation" section, there is the placeholder [insert chart] where you'll insert the Excel chart that illustrates the company's growth in income and profits. In the "Future Expansion" section, there is the placeholder [insert spreadsheet] where you'll insert the worksheet outlining the expenses involved in opening a new retail outlet. Under Possible Sites, there is a map, originally created in Microsoft Paint, a graphics program included with Microsoft Windows, that has been inserted into the document. At the end of the proposal, Nalani has also inserted a photograph of Virgil Jackson, the proposed manager for the new location.

You'll start by embedding the Excel worksheet into the "Future Expansion" section of the proposal, in place of the [insert spreadsheet] placeholder. By embedding the worksheet, you can maintain a one-way connection between Excel and the worksheet in Word. You'll use the Object command on the Insert menu to embed the existing Excel worksheet into the proposal.

REFERENCE window

EMBEDDING AN EXISTING FILE

- Move the insertion point to the location in your document where you want the embedded file to appear.
- Click Insert on the menu bar, and then click Object to open the Object dialog box.
- Click the Create from File tab.
- Click the Browse button, select the file you want to embed, and then click the OK button twice.

Once the expense worksheet is embedded in the proposal document, you'll be able to modify its contents and appearance using Excel commands from within Word, as long as Excel is installed on your computer.

To embed the Excel worksheet:

1. Scroll until you see the bracketed phrase "[insert spreadsheet]" a few lines above the "Possible Sites" heading.

2. Select the entire line, and then delete the placeholder **[insert spreadsheet]** and the line on which it was located. The insertion point should appear on the blank line between the two paragraphs. This is where you want to embed the Excel worksheet.

   TROUBLE? If the insertion point is not on a blank line, or if two blank lines appear between the paragraphs, edit the proposal so that only one blank line appears between the paragraphs and that the insertion point blinks on that line.

3. Click **Insert** on the menu bar, and then click **Object** to open the Object dialog box, which has two tabs—Create New and Create from File.

4. Click the **Create from File** tab on the Object dialog box. You'll use the Browse feature to find the Excel worksheet file on your Student Disk.

5. Click the **Browse** button to open the Browse dialog box, and then, if necessary, change the Look in folder to Tutorial.07 so that a list of files in the Tutorial.07 folder on your Student Disk appears.

6. Click **FSIExpns** (which stands for FSI Expenses), and then click the **OK** button. The Browse dialog box closes and the filename FSIExpns.xls appears in the File name text box in the Object dialog box. See Figure 7-4.

Figure 7-4 ◄
Object dialog
box

name of file that will
be embedded

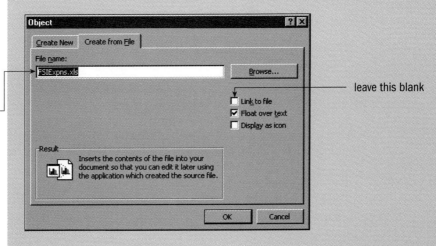

leave this blank

7. Make sure the Link to file check box is *not* selected. You don't want to link the worksheet, only embed it. Then click the **OK** button. The Excel worksheet appears in the document. See Figure 7-5.

Figure 7-5 ◀
Document with
embedded
Excel worksheet

embedded Excel |
worksheet |

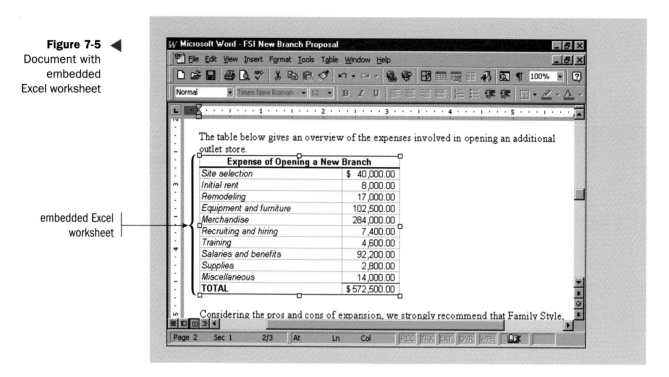

The table below gives an overview of the expenses involved in opening an additional outlet store.

Expense of Opening a New Branch	
Site selection	$ 40,000.00
Initial rent	8,000.00
Remodeling	17,000.00
Equipment and furniture	102,500.00
Merchandise	284,000.00
Recruiting and hiring	7,400.00
Training	4,600.00
Salaries and benefits	92,200.00
Supplies	2,800.00
Miscellaneous	14,000.00
TOTAL	$ 572,500.00

Considering the pros and cons of expansion, we strongly recommend that Family Style,

Once you have embedded an object in a Word document, you can adjust its placement on the page so it matches the overall look of your document.

Centering the Embedded Worksheet

You have embedded the worksheet in the proposal. It would look better, however, centered between the left and right margins rather than positioned at the left margin.

To center the worksheet:

1. With the worksheet still selected, click **Format** on the menu bar, and then click **Object**. The Format Object dialog box opens.

2. Click the **Position** tab, and in the Position on page section, set the Horizontal setting to **1.5"**.

3. In the From list box, select the **Margin** option.

4. Make sure the Move object with text check box is selected, and then click the **OK** button.

5. The Excel worksheet is centered horizontally in Nalani's proposal document. See Figure 7-6.

Figure 7-6
Embedded
Excel worksheet
centered
horizontally

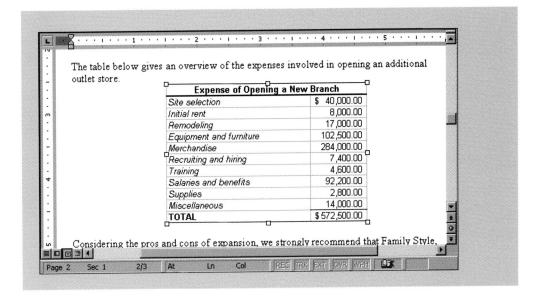

Once you have embedded an object, you might want to change the information it contains. It would be inconvenient to go back to the original Excel spreadsheet, make changes, and then embed it in your document again. Since the spreadsheet object is embedded, you can make changes to the object from within Word, which you'll do in the next section.

Modifying the Embedded Worksheet

Because the worksheet is embedded, and as long as the source program (Excel) is installed on your computer, you can edit the worksheet by double-clicking it and using Excel commands and tools. After you modify the worksheet, you can click anywhere else in the Word document to deselect the worksheet and redisplay the usual Word editing commands and tools. Any changes that you make in the embedded worksheet will affect only the copy in Word and will not affect the original FSIExpns file.

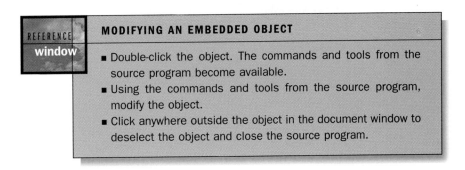

REFERENCE
window

MODIFYING AN EMBEDDED OBJECT

- Double-click the object. The commands and tools from the source program become available.
- Using the commands and tools from the source program, modify the object.
- Click anywhere outside the object in the document window to deselect the object and close the source program.

Nalani wants you to make two changes to the embedded worksheet. Since all the cost figures are large and are all rounded to the nearest $100 increment, she wants you to remove the decimal points and trailing zeroes. She also wants you to format the table heading to make it more prominent.

To eliminate the decimal places in the embedded worksheet:

1. Double-click the worksheet. After a moment, the menu bar and toolbars display Excel commands and tools, although the title bar retains the title of the Word program and document. See Figure 7-7.

   TROUBLE? If the Excel commands and toolbar don't appear or a message tells you it can't find the source program, ask your instructor or technical support person for assistance. Excel might not be installed on your computer.

Figure 7-7 ◀
Editing the
worksheet in
Word using
Excel
commands and
tools

Word title bar

Excel menu bar and
toolbars

frame indicates
worksheet is active

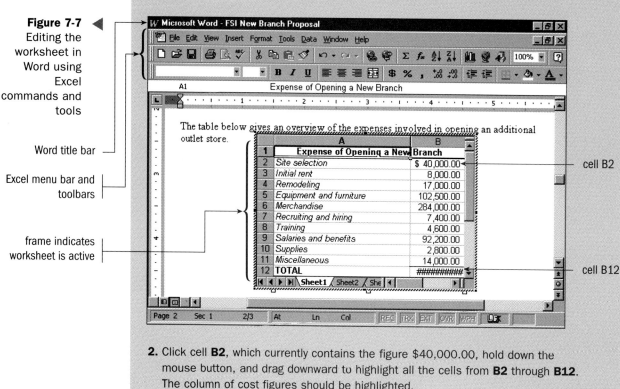

cell B2

cell B12

2. Click cell **B2**, which currently contains the figure $40,000.00, hold down the mouse button, and drag downward to highlight all the cells from **B2** through **B12**. The column of cost figures should be highlighted.

3. Click the **Decrease Decimal** button 🔢 on the Excel Formatting toolbar twice. The numbers change to whole dollar amounts.

Now you'll use the Excel tools to format the heading row of the worksheet with a shade of gray, to make it more prominent.

To add shading to the heading row of the embedded worksheet:

1. Click cell **A1** and drag to the right to cell **B1** to select the worksheet heading in cells A1 and B1, "Expenses of Opening a New Branch."

2. Click the **Fill Color** list arrow 🔲 on the Excel Formatting toolbar, and on the fill color palette click the **Gray - 25%** color tile (4ᵗʰ row, far right column). The heading row is now shaded with the gray color you selected.

3. Click anywhere on the proposal document outside of the embedded worksheet. The Excel commands and toolbars are replaced by the Word commands and toolbars, and the embedded worksheet displays the newly formatted figures and heading row. See Figure 7-8.

Figure 7-8
Edited and
formatted
worksheet
embedded in
the proposal

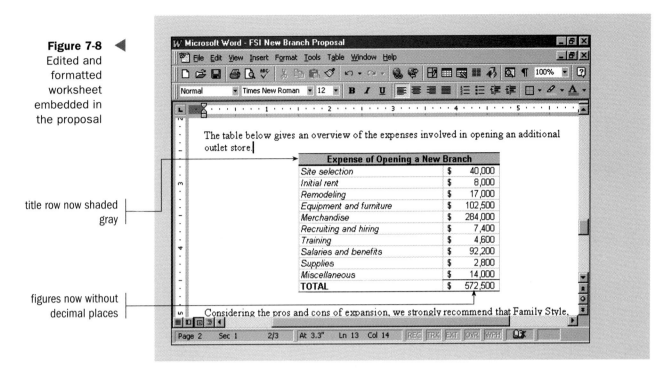

title row now shaded gray

figures now without decimal places

The table below gives an overview of the expenses involved in opening an additional outlet store.

Expense of Opening a New Branch	
Site selection	$ 40,000
Initial rent	$ 8,000
Remodeling	$ 17,000
Equipment and furniture	$ 102,500
Merchandise	$ 284,000
Recruiting and hiring	$ 7,400
Training	$ 4,600
Salaries and benefits	$ 92,200
Supplies	$ 2,800
Miscellaneous	$ 14,000
TOTAL	$ 572,500

The original Excel worksheet, FSIExps, remains in its original form on your disk, with the two decimal places and the unshaded heading row. You have only modified the embedded copy in Nalani's proposal.

Linking an Excel Chart

Nalani wants you to incorporate the financial chart that shows the increase in gross income and net profit of Family Styles for the previous four years, because she thinks this information will help convince others to open a new outlet. However, the Accounting department is currently auditing the sales and profit figures, and might have to modify the chart they have given her. Because the source document might change over time, and Nalani wants her proposal to display the most current information at the time it is printed or viewed online, she recommends that you link the chart to the proposal.

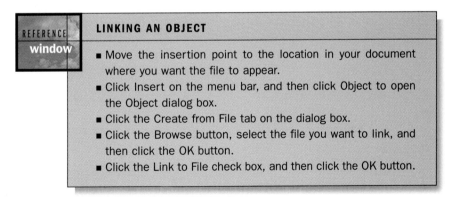

REFERENCE window

LINKING AN OBJECT

- Move the insertion point to the location in your document where you want the file to appear.
- Click Insert on the menu bar, and then click Object to open the Object dialog box.
- Click the Create from File tab on the dialog box.
- Click the Browse button, select the file you want to link, and then click the OK button.
- Click the Link to File check box, and then click the OK button.

Nalani's chart is located on a hard disk that contains company information that all employees can access. You'll link your proposal document to the FSIChart file on your Student Disk. Because you'll make changes to the chart after you link it, you'll make a copy of the chart as you link it, and leave the original file on your Student Disk unchanged in case you want to repeat the tutorial steps later.

To link an Excel chart to the proposal document:

1. Scroll up to the middle of page 1, until you see the "Current Situation" heading and the bracketed phrase "[insert chart]" at the beginning of the second paragraph under the heading.

2. Delete the placeholder **[insert chart]**. The insertion point blinks just to the left of the word "These," the place where you want to insert the linked chart.

3. Click **Insert** on the menu bar, and then click **Object** to open the Object dialog box. You used this same dialog box earlier to embed the Excel worksheet in the proposal. This time, you'll use it to link to a file.

4. Click the **Create from File** tab.

5. Click the **Browse** button to open the Browse dialog box, and then, if necessary, change the Look in folder to Tutorial.07. The dialog box displays a list of files in the Tutorial.07 folder on your Student Disk. Because you want to leave the original file unchanged on your Student Disk, you'll make a copy of it now.

6. Right-click the filename **FSIChart** and on the shortcut menu, click **Copy**. Press **Ctrl + V** to paste the copy in the file list.

7. Make sure the filename Copy of FSIChart is selected, and click the **OK** button. The chart name appears in the File name text box. Now you need to specify that you want the chart file to be linked, not embedded, in the proposal document.

8. Click the **Link to file** check box to select it. See Figure 7-9.

Figure 7-9 ◀
Completed
Create from File
tab in the
Object dialog
box

copy being linked to
keep original intact

select this check box
to link a file

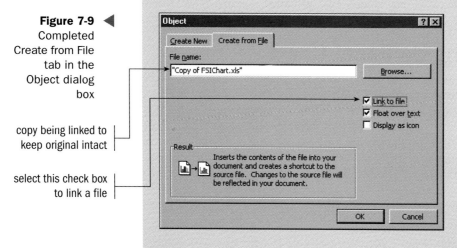

9. Click the **OK** button. After a moment, the chart image appears in the proposal, displaying income and profit numbers for the last four years.

The figure is too large for the document, but you can change its size easily.

To resize the chart and wrap text around it:

1. With the chart still selected, click **Format** on the menu bar, and then click **Object**.

2. Click the **Size** tab, and in the Scale section, click the **Height** down arrow to decrease the Height and Width settings to **30%**. Both the height and width of the selected object will be reduced by the same percentage, because the Lock aspect option is selected. This will reduce the chart to 30% of its original size both horizontally and vertically. Now you'll wrap text around the chart.

3. Click the **Wrapping** tab, and in the Wrapping style section, click the **Tight** icon, and in the Wrap to section, click the **Right** icon, and then click the **OK** button. The chart appears in its reduced size.

TROUBLE? If you have trouble placing the chart in the correct place, open the Format Object dialog box and on the Position tab, change the Horizontal position to 0" from margin and the Vertical position to 0" from paragraph.

4. If necessary, drag the chart to the left margin under the "Current Situation" heading. See Figure 7-10.

Figure 7-10 ◀
Linked Excel
chart in Word
proposal

slight increase in
profits over prior year

chart reduced 30% of
original size

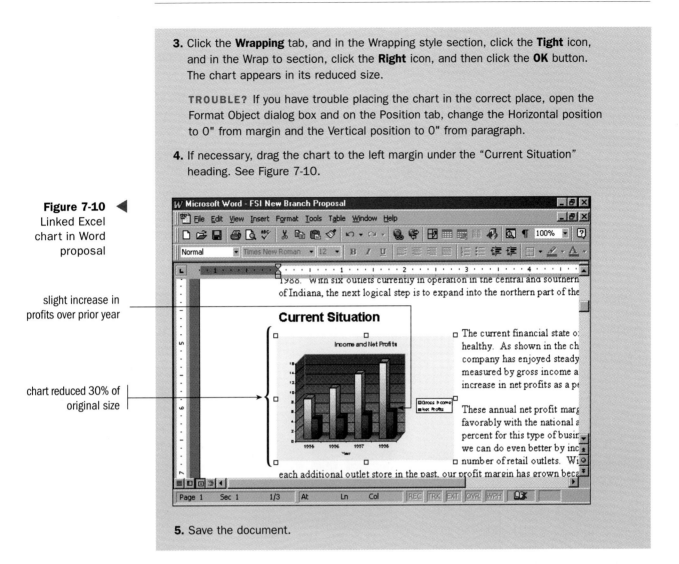

5. Save the document.

Because you have linked the file, you have not inserted a copy of the file in the proposal, but merely a visual reference to the original. The size of the proposal file on disk has not increased significantly as a result of the link. If you double-clicked the chart, Excel would start and display the original source file. Instead of seeing the Word title bar at the top of the screen, you would see the Excel title bar. Since Nalani wants to leave Accounting's chart intact, she will not modify it now. However, when Accounting updates the figures, the changes will be reflected in the linked chart in the proposal. You'll see how this works in the next set of steps.

Modifying the Linked Chart

The advantage of linking a file over embedding it is that the destination file is updated whenever you modify the source file, which you can do from within the source program or from within the destination program. That way, you can use the original object not only in your current document but also in future documents, and your documents will always display the latest version of the object.

You'll simulate what would happen if the Accounting department modified the file in Excel. You'll open the chart in Excel, the source program, change some figures, and then view the updated information in the Word proposal.

To modify the chart in the source program:

1. Click the **Start** button on the taskbar, point to **Programs**, and then click **Microsoft Excel**. The Excel program window opens.

   TROUBLE? You must have the Microsoft Excel 97 program installed to complete this section. If you do not see Microsoft Excel on your Programs menu, see your instructor or technical support person.

   TROUBLE? If the Office Assistant opens asking if you want help, click the Start Using Excel button.

2. Click the **Open** button 🖻 on the Standard toolbar to display the Open dialog box.

3. Click the **Look in** list arrow, open the **Tutorial.07** folder, and double-click **Copy of FSIChart**. The chart showing Family Style's income and profits opens. The profit figure for 1998 is somewhat higher than for 1997, indicating a modest growth in profit. See Figure 7-11.

Figure 7-11 ◀
Chart in source program, Excel

Excel title bar and toolbars

Profits tab holds figures that chart is based on

Chart tab

Excel active

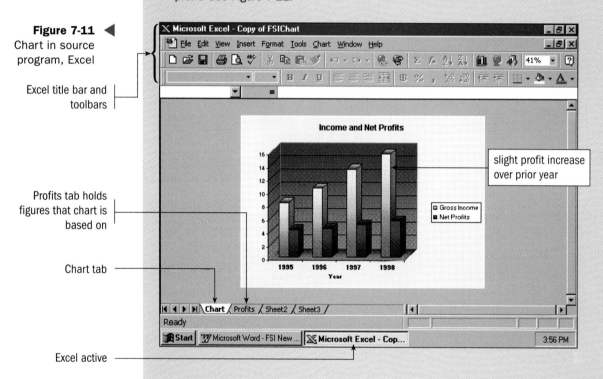

At the bottom of the window are four tabs. The Chart tab contains the chart, and the Profits tab contains the figures from which the chart was created. Any changes you make to the figures on the Profits tab will automatically be reflected in the chart. Now assume Accounting has audited its figures and has found that the profit as a percent of sales is actually higher than their original figure. You'll enter the new figure next.

4. Click the **Profits** tab. The worksheet containing the profits information appears. You'll change the profit figure for 1998.

5. Click cell **E4**, type **7.5**, and press the **Enter** key. Now you'll look at the chart in Excel and see the effect of the change.

6. Click the **Chart** tab, and see that the Net Profits bar for 1998 is now higher, reflecting the new figure you entered. See Figure 7-12.

Figure 7-12
Excel chart
reflecting higher
profit figure

1998 Net Profits bar
reflects higher figure

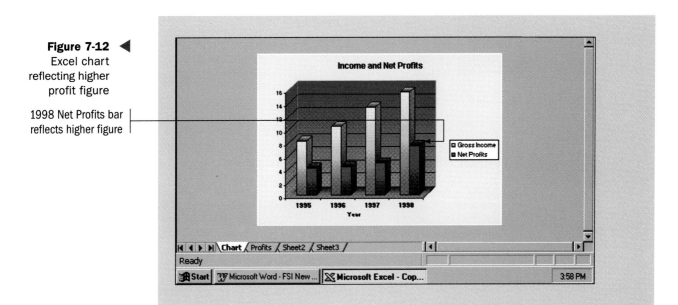

7. Save the Chart worksheet.

Now you'll return to the proposal and view the linked version.

To view the linked chart in the proposal:

1. Close Excel. The Word program window redisplays, with the linked version of the chart displayed in the FSI New Branch Proposal file.

You notice that the linked version of the chart still has the 1998 Net Profits bar that represents the older figure. Why doesn't it reflect the change you made in the source program? You must perform one more step to make sure the changes are carried to the linked version: updating the link.

Updating the Link

To **update** a link means to make sure the linked object in the destination file reflects the latest version of the source file. If you modify a linked object in the source program and the Word document to which it's linked is closed, the next time you open the file, in this case the proposal, Word will automatically update the link (or it might ask if you want to update the link). But if you modify a linked object in the source program and the Word document is still open, you'll have to tell Word to update the link.

UPDATING A LINK

- From within Word, click Edit on the menu bar, then click Links.
- Select the filename of the linked file, and then click the Update Now button.
- Click the OK button.

Once the linked chart is updated, it will reflect the change you made in Excel.

To update a linked file:

1. Make sure Microsoft Word appears in the title bar, and that you still see the linked chart in the document window. You should be looking at the original version of the chart, not the one with the higher profits bar.

2. Click **Edit** on the menu bar, and then click **Links** to open the Links dialog box. See Figure 7-13. Two linked files are listed: Copy of FSI Chart and Indiana.bmp, the graphic image of the state of Indiana.

Figure 7-13 ◀
Links dialog box

the two source files
linked to this
document

click to display
modified chart in
Word version

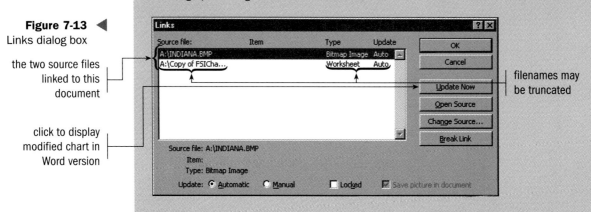

filenames may
be truncated

3. Click **Copy of FSICha...**, and then click the **Update Now** button. Word momentarily switches back to the document window, retrieves the latest version of the linked file, and then returns to the Links dialog box.

4. Click the **OK** button in the Links dialog box to close it.

5. If necessary, deselect the chart. The updated version of the chart appears in Word; the bar representing Net Profits for 1998 reflects the higher number you entered in Excel. See Figure 7-14.

Figure 7-14
Linked copy of
chart reflecting
higher Net
Profits figure

higher figure now
reflected in linked
copy

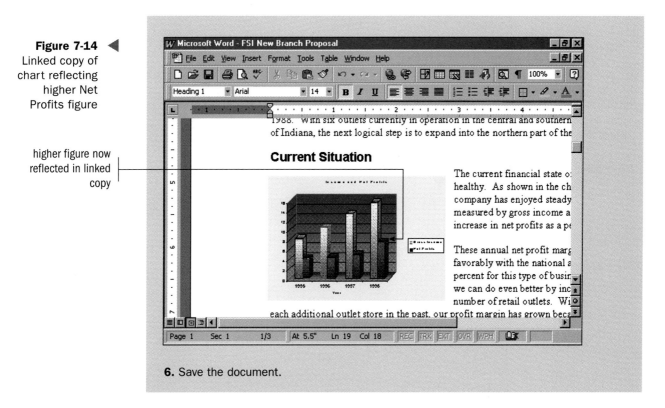

6. Save the document.

Now you can be assured that with the link in place, any updates that Accounting makes to the chart will be reflected any time the proposal is opened.

Although you just edited the source file by opening it in the source program (Excel), you could just as easily edit the source file in the destination program. You would double-click the linked object in the destination document window. The source program would start and the source file would open. After editing the source file, you would simply close the source program. The linked object in the destination file would update automatically.

Your document is finished. You are ready to print it for distribution to the owners and stockholders of Family Style.

To print and then close the document:

1. Preview, and then print the document. If necessary, drag the map to the top of the third page. Your three-page document should look like Figure 7-15.

Figure 7-15 ◀
Printed
document,
ready for
distribution to
owners and
stockholders

linked chart →

embedded worksheet →

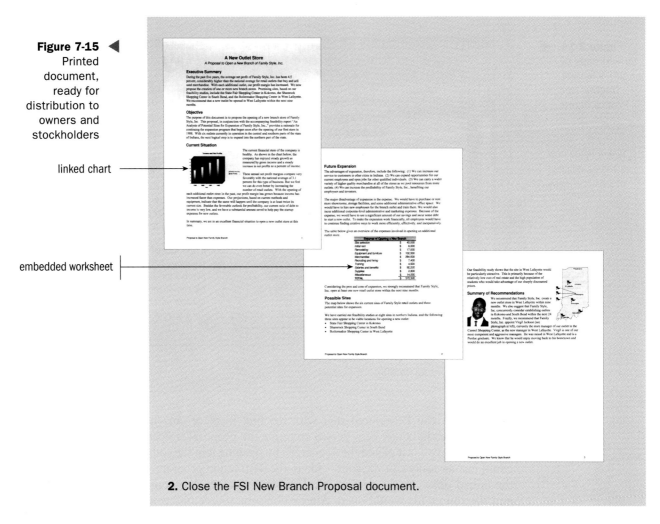

2. Close the FSI New Branch Proposal document.

You give the completed proposal to Nalani, who is pleased with your work. She distributes the proposal to the owners and stockholders who are considering the proposed expansion. She now wants you to focus on the task of distributing the document electronically, which you'll do in the next session.

Quick Check

1. Define the following in your own words:
   a. object
   b. source program
   c. destination program

2. What is embedding? What is linking? How do embedding and linking differ? In what situations would you choose linking over embedding?

3. What does OLE stand for? What does it mean to be an OLE-enabled program?

4. How do you embed an Excel worksheet into a Word document? How do you link an Excel chart into a Word document?

5. From within the Browse dialog box, how do you copy a file into the same folder?

6. How do you modify an embedded object from the destination program?

7. True or False: When you modify an embedded object, your changes are also made to the source file.

You've learned how to combine information created in different source programs into a single document. The OLE technology that makes this integration of information possible allows users of ordinary word processing programs to create highly informative, interesting, and well-illustrated documents. In the next session, you'll create the electronic document that Nalani will distribute to company employees.

SESSION

7.2

In this session you'll modify the proposal so that it is better suited to online viewing by Family Style management, who will access it over the company's network. You'll begin by creating hyperlinks that allow users to navigate through the document more easily and to access additional information. Then you'll see how the document looks in online layout view. Finally, you'll modify the document's appearance to make it more interesting for online viewers.

Creating and Navigating Hyperlinks

In addition to printing the proposal for company owners and investors, Nalani wants to place her proposal in a shared folder on the company's network so that other company employees will be able to read it. She wants you to modify the document so people can read it **online**, which means they will read it on the computer screen rather than on a printed page. Because people can't efficiently "flip through pages" when they read online, you should add navigational aids to the online document.

One such navigational aid is a **hyperlink** (short for "hypertext link" and also called a "hot link" or just "link"), which is a word, phrase, or graphic image that users click to "jump to" (or display) another location, called the **target**. Text hyperlinks are usually underlined and appear in a different color than the rest of the document. The target of a hyperlink can be to a location within the document, to a different document, or to a page on the World Wide Web. Figure 7-16 shows a hyperlink pointing to a different document, a resume.

Figure 7-16
Example of
hyperlink
pointing to a
target (in this
case, a
different
document)

Word document
containing hyperlink

Hyperlink is blue and
underlined; click it to
jump to target

target of hyperlink is
another Word
document

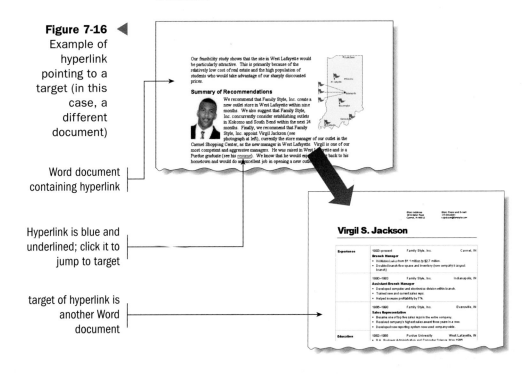

All Office 97 programs support hyperlinking. If you have many Office 97 documents that are related to each other, you can create a useful system of hyperlinks that allow users to retrieve and view related material. Nalani wants you to add two hyperlinks to the proposal document, one that targets a location within the proposal and one that targets a different document.

Inserting a Hyperlink to a Bookmark in the Same Document

Nalani wants users to be able to jump directly to the proposal's conclusions without having to scroll through topics sequentially. You can add a hyperlink at the beginning of the proposal that users can click to jump to the summary of recommendations at the end of the document. Creating a hyperlink to a location in the same document requires two steps. First, you insert an electronic marker called a **bookmark** at the location you want Word to target. Second, you enter the text that you want users to click, and format it as a hyperlink. Figure 7-17 illustrates this process.

Figure 7-17
Hyperlink that targets a bookmark

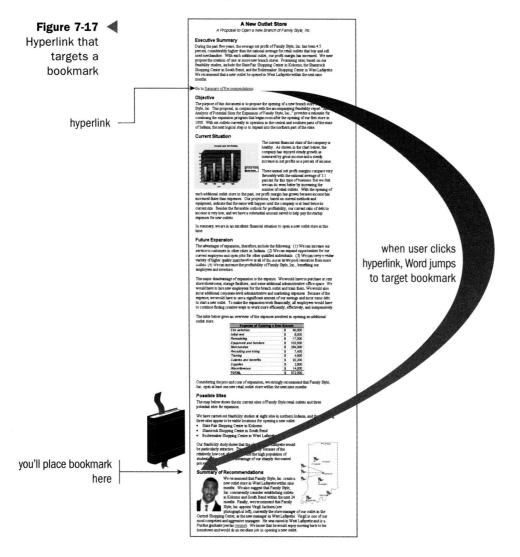

hyperlink

when user clicks hyperlink, Word jumps to target bookmark

you'll place bookmark here

INSERTING A HYPERLINK TO A TARGET IN THE SAME DOCUMENT

REFERENCE window

- Insert a bookmark at the target location.
- Select the text or graphic image you want to use as the hyperlink.
- Click the Insert Hyperlink button.
- Click the Named location in the file text box, click the Browse button, click the bookmark you want to link to, and then click the OK button. Leave the Link the file or URL text box blank.
- Click the OK button.

First, you'll open the document you saved at the end of the previous session. Then you'll insert the hyperlink to the Summary of Recommendations just below the Executive Summary.

To insert a hyperlink to a location within the same document:

1. If you took a break after the last session, make sure Word is running and that the FSI New Branch Proposal document is open.

2. Move the insertion point to the beginning of the heading "Summary of Recommendations," near the end of the document. This is where you'll insert a bookmark required for the hypertext link.

3. Click **Insert** on the menu bar, and then click **Bookmark**. The Bookmark dialog box opens. You can now type the bookmark name, which must be one word, without spaces.

4. Type **Recommendations** and click the **Add** button. Word inserts a bookmark named "Recommendations" at the location of the insertion point (you can't see it, but it's there). This will be the target of the hyperlink, that is, the location to which the insertion point jumps when you click the hyperlink.

5. Move the insertion point to the end of the "Executive Summary" paragraph, near the beginning of the document. The insertion point should immediately follow the phrase, "within the next nine months."

6. Press the **Enter** key twice to insert two new blank lines into your document, and type **Go to Summary of Recommendations**. You'll now create the hyperlink in this line of text.

7. Select the phrase **Summary of Recommendations** that you just typed, and then click the **Insert Hyperlink** button 🔘 on the Standard toolbar. The Insert Hyperlink dialog box opens. See Figure 7-18. You'll leave the Link to file or URL text box blank, because this hyperlink doesn't go to another file but to a bookmark within your current file.

Figure 7-18 ◀
Insert
Hyperlink
dialog box

indicate the "jump to"
location in the same
document

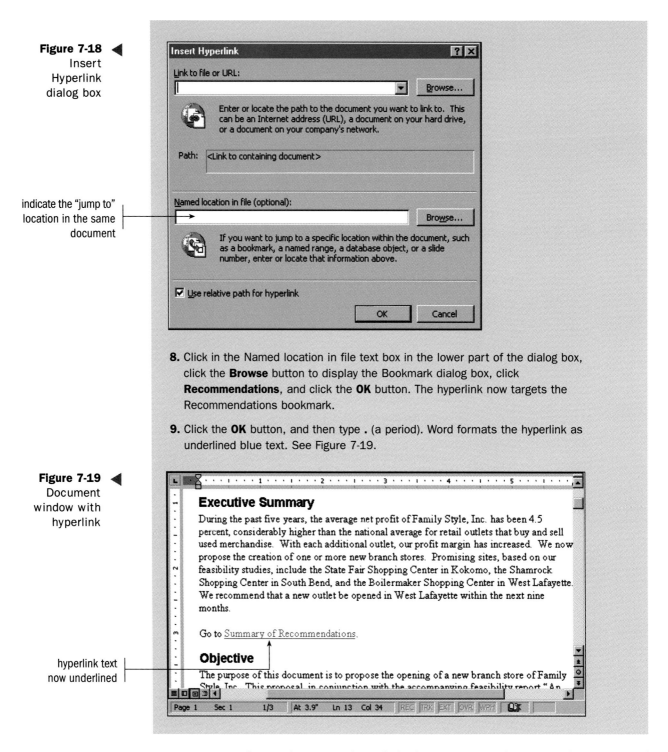

8. Click in the Named location in file text box in the lower part of the dialog box, click the **Browse** button to display the Bookmark dialog box, click **Recommendations**, and click the **OK** button. The hyperlink now targets the Recommendations bookmark.

9. Click the **OK** button, and then type **.** (a period). Word formats the hyperlink as underlined blue text. See Figure 7-19.

Figure 7-19 ◀
Document
window with
hyperlink

hyperlink text
now underlined

Your proposal now features a hyperlink that points to the proposal summary of recommendations.

Navigating Hyperlinks and the Web Toolbar

Now that you have inserted a hyperlink into the document, you should test it to make sure that it targets the correct location. When you click a hyperlink in a document, Word automatically displays the **Web toolbar**, a toolbar with buttons that let you access and navigate your document and the World Wide Web, a global information-sharing system you'll learn about in the next session. The Back button, for example, returns you to the previously-viewed document.

To test the hyperlink in your document:

1. Move the insertion point to the blue underlined text (the hyperlink). Notice that the pointer changes to 🖑. If you leave the pointer on the hyperlink for a moment, Word displays a ScreenTip (yellow rectangle) with the name of the bookmark.

2. Click the hyperlink. The insertion point jumps to the Recommendations bookmark and the "Summary of Recommendations" section appears. The Web toolbar appears above the document. See Figure 7-20. You'll use one of the Web toolbar buttons to return to the beginning of the document.

Figure 7-20 ◀
Hyperlink
destination and
Web toolbar

Web toolbar

Back button

destination for
the hyperlink

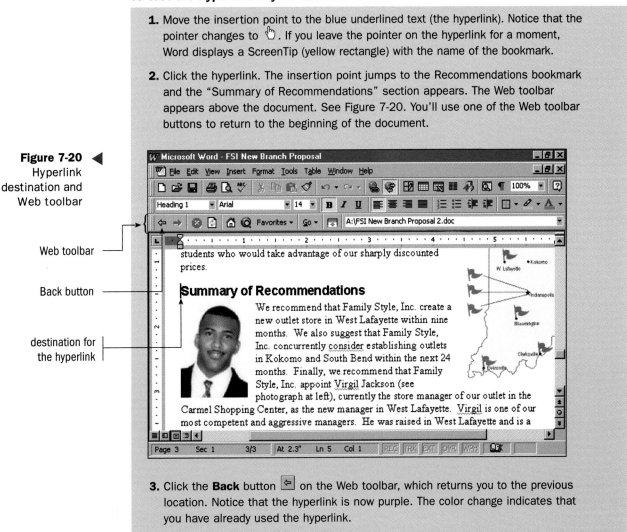

3. Click the **Back** button ⇐ on the Web toolbar, which returns you to the previous location. Notice that the hyperlink is now purple. The color change indicates that you have already used the hyperlink.

4. Save the document.

The fact that the hyperlink changes color after you use it doesn't have much significance in this document. However, hyperlinks can also point to other documents, including Web documents on the World Wide Web. In that environment, it's helpful to know which links you've already tried. If you were to close and then reopen the document, the hyperlink would still be blue until it is clicked again.

Creating Hyperlinks to Other Documents

The greatest power of hyperlinks is not in jumping to another location within the same document, but in jumping to other documents. These documents can be located on the World Wide Web, on your computer's hard drive, or on your company's network. When you add a hyperlink to another document, you don't necessarily target a bookmark as you do for hyperlinks pointing to a location within the same document. Instead, you target either a Web document address, called a **URL**, or a path and filename of a file on your computer or network.

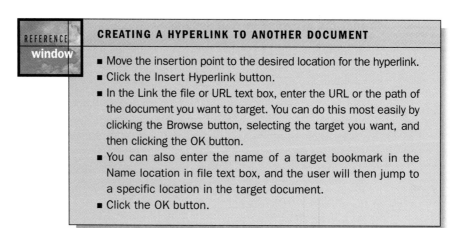

REFERENCE window

CREATING A HYPERLINK TO ANOTHER DOCUMENT

- Move the insertion point to the desired location for the hyperlink.
- Click the Insert Hyperlink button.
- In the Link the file or URL text box, enter the URL or the path of the document you want to target. You can do this most easily by clicking the Browse button, selecting the target you want, and then clicking the OK button.
- You can also enter the name of a target bookmark in the Name location in file text box, and the user will then jump to a specific location in the target document.
- Click the OK button.

Nalani's proposal recommends Virgil Jackson as the manager for the new Family Style branch. She has a Word file containing his resume, VJResume.doc, and she would like to make it available to interested Family Style employees so they can evaluate his skills. You can add a hyperlink that targets Virgil's resume. Because this hyperlink will take users to a different document, you don't need to insert a bookmark as the target. Instead, you use the name of the target document.

To create a hyperlink to another document:

1. Move the insertion point to the next-to-the-last sentence of the last paragraph of the document, after the phrase "a Purdue graduate," but before the period. This is where you'll insert text, some of which will become the hyperlink.

2. Press the spacebar and type **(see his resume)** (make sure you include the parentheses), and then select the word "resume" in the text you just typed. See Figure 7-21.

Figure 7-21 ◀
Document after typing new text and selecting a word

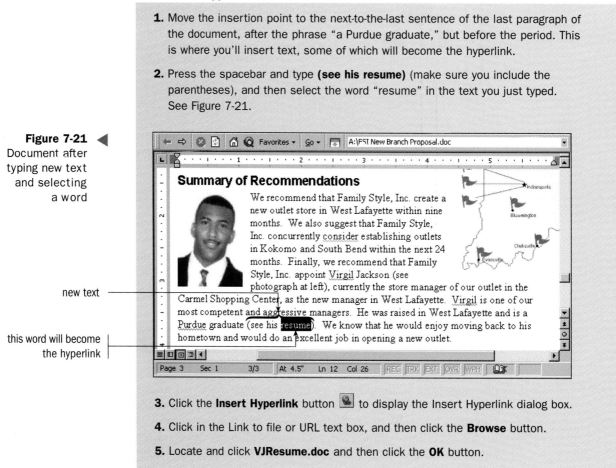

new text

this word will become the hyperlink

3. Click the **Insert Hyperlink** button 🖼 to display the Insert Hyperlink dialog box.

4. Click in the Link to file or URL text box, and then click the **Browse** button.

5. Locate and click **VJResume.doc** and then click the **OK** button.

6. Make sure the Use relative path for hyperlink check box at the bottom of the dialog box is selected. This ensures that Word will look in the same folder as the current document.

7. Click the **OK** button. The word "resume" now appears as a hyperlink. It looks the same as the first hyperlink you created, even though the target is another file, not a location within the same document.

When your documents include hyperlinks to other documents, you need to pay special attention to where you store those target documents. In this example, you told Word to use a relative path, so when a user clicks the hyperlink you just created, Word will start looking for the target document in the same folder that contains the proposal. Nalani needs to make sure that the FSI New Branch Proposal and VJResume documents are always together in the same folder. Now you're ready to test the hyperlink you just created.

To use a hyperlink to jump to another file:

1. Move the pointer to the hyperlink "resume." Again, the pointer changes to 🖑.

2. Click the hyperlink. Word opens the file VJResume.

3. Read through the resume, and then click the **Back** button ⬅ on the Web toolbar to return to the Proposal document. Notice that the hyperlink color is now purple, indicating that you have used the hyperlink.

4. Save the proposal. The hyperlinks are now in place.

Viewing a Document in Online Layout View

Because the version of the proposal you are working on now is intended for an online audience, Nalani suggests that you place it in online layout view. Online layout view offers several advantages for online viewers:

■ Text appears larger in online layout view.

■ Text wraps to the window, not to the printed page.

■ Documents can be displayed with different background effects.

■ Page setup elements, such as footers, headers, and breaks, are not displayed. Because users don't view the document as printed pages, these page elements aren't necessary.

If you switch to online layout view and then save the document in that view, it will open that way automatically. Online layout view also displays the **Document Map**, a list of the headings in your document. The Document Map is more than just a table of contents because you can use it as a navigational aid. If you want to move immediately to a certain section of your document, you click its heading in the Document Map. For this reason, the Document Map is an especially useful tool for online viewers, who might not want to scroll through an entire document. They can simply jump to the sections they are interested in.

To place a document in online layout view:

1. Click the **Online Layout View** button 📄. Your document appears on the right; the Document Map is on the left. Notice that the text now wraps to the width of the right window pane—not to the printed page boundaries.

TROUBLE? If the Document Map does not appear, click the Document Map button 📄 on the Standard toolbar.

2. Click the **Summary of Recommendations** heading in the Document Map. You jump to that heading. See Figure 7-22.

Figure 7-22 ◄
Online layout
view and
Document Map

Document Map
lists headings
in document

drag border to widen
or narrow Document
Map window

document wraps
to window

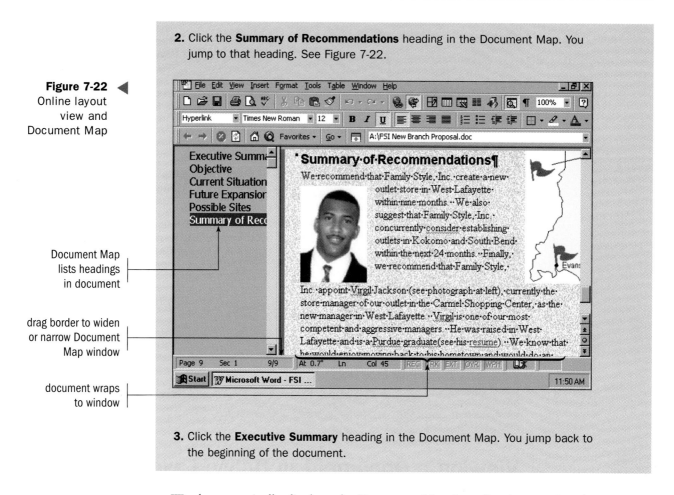

3. Click the **Executive Summary** heading in the Document Map. You jump back to the beginning of the document.

Word automatically displays the Document Map in online layout view, but you can display it in any view. You can also change the width of the Document Map by dragging its right border to the left or to the right. Now that you have inserted a hyperlink, and have seen how to navigate the document with the document map, you'll improve its appearance for online viewing.

Improving the Appearance of an Online Document

Nalani suggests you use two features to make the online version of the proposal more visually interesting for online viewers: animated text and a textured background.

Animating Text

Animated text is text that "comes alive," like a cartoon animation, because the text blinks, sparkles, shimmers, or displays a moving border. Word offers several animation formats. Nalani suggests you try animating the subtitle of the proposal, "A Proposal to Open a New Branch of Family Style, Inc.", with a moving border.

To animate the subtitle of the proposal:

1. Scroll to the beginning of the document.

2. Select the subtitle text **A Proposal to Open a New Branch of Family Style, Inc.**

3. Click **Format** on the menu bar, click **Font**, and then click the **Animation** tab.

4. Click **Marching Black Ants**. Notice the Preview box displays the sample text with a moving black border. See Figure 7-23.

Figure 7-23 ◀
Previewing
animated text

select this animation ──→

preview of
animated text

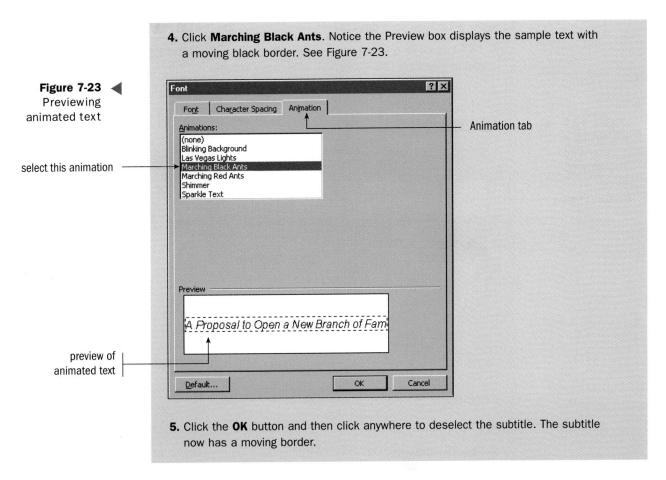

Animation tab

5. Click the **OK** button and then click anywhere to deselect the subtitle. The subtitle now has a moving border.

Animation draws an online viewer's eyes immediately to the animated text, so use this feature only for your most important words or phrases. Overusing animated text makes your document difficult to view. Animation effects don't appear in printed documents.

Applying a Textured Background

You can make an online document more visually appealing by applying background effects. Backgrounds appear only in online layout view, and they do not appear in printed documents. You can apply one of the following background effects:

- Solid color

- Gradient—a color or combination of colors that fades from one side of the screen to the other

- Texture—choose from a collection of textures; more are available on the installation CD-ROM

- Pattern—choose from a collection of interesting patterns; you designate the colors in the pattern

- Picture—a graphic image

In choosing a background color or texture, make sure your text is still readable. In poorly designed online documents, the background might be so dark or the pattern so obtrusive that the text is illegible. In addition, a background that contains a complicated background pattern will increase the file size and take longer to appear on a user's screen. Nalani suggests you use a Newsprint texture to give the background a professional, but not distracting, appearance.

To apply a texture to a document:

1. Click **Format** on the menu bar, point to **Background**, click **Fill Effects**, and then click the **Texture** tab. A selection of textures appears.

2. Click **Newsprint**, the first box in the top row. See Figure 7-24.

Figure 7-24 ◀
Selecting a
textured
background

Newsprint texture ————

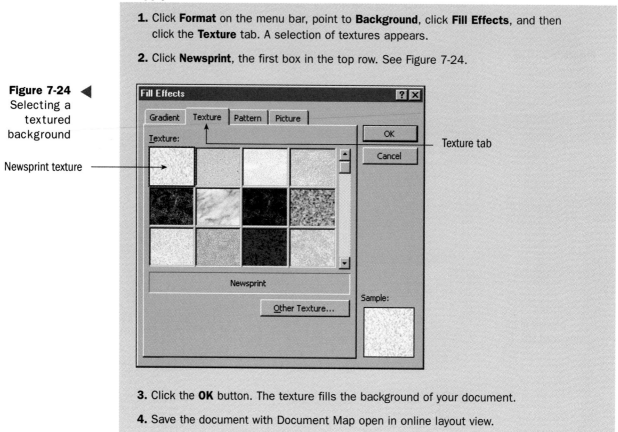

Texture tab

3. Click the **OK** button. The texture fills the background of your document.

4. Save the document with Document Map open in online layout view.

The background texture is light in color and attractive, and leaves the black text easy to read. Nalani agrees that the Newsprint background enhances the look of the online document.

Quick Check

1. What is a hyperlink?

2. True or False: A hyperlink always takes a user to another document.

3. True or False: You use a bookmark to link to another document.

4. Which name is an invalid bookmark name? a) Recommendations, b) Executive Summary, c) README

5. What does it mean when a hyperlink changes color?

6. When a hyperlink targets a different document and you use the relative path option, what are you telling Word about the location of the target document?

7. Name three differences between normal view and online layout view.

8. What happens when you click a Document Map heading?

You have finished preparing the proposal document for online viewing. Nalani places the document and its linked files in a shared folder on the company network and e-mails her colleagues that it is available for viewing. Any employee who opens it in Word has the immediate benefit of easy viewing in online layout view. The hyperlink you added, as well as the Document Map, make it easy to navigate, and your visual enhancements make it a pleasure to view.

SESSION	*In this session you'll convert Nalani's proposal into an HTML (HyperText Markup Language) document for placement on the World Wide Web, and then format the HTML document to make it more readable from a Web browser. Finally, you'll insert and edit hyperlinks that link the proposal and resume HTML documents.*
7.3	

The Internet World Wide Web

Publishing Documents on the World Wide Web

Nalani now wants you to prepare the final version of her proposal, which she will make available on the World Wide Web. Then, investors anywhere in the world can easily read the proposal over the **Internet**, a structure made up of millions of interconnected computers. The **World Wide Web** (also called the "Web" or "WWW") is a global information-sharing system that allows you to find and view electronic documents, called **Web pages**. Organizations and individuals make their Web pages available by placing them on high-capacity hard disks called **Web servers**, which users can access electronically by specifying the address in a **Web browser**, software that retrieves and displays Web pages on a computer screen. The electronic location of a Web page is called a **Web site**. Most companies and many private computer users operate their own Web sites.

Most Web sites contain a **home page**, a Web page that contains general information about the site. Home pages are like "home base"—they are a starting point for online viewers. They usually contain hyperlinks targeting other documents or Web pages that online viewers can click to locate the information they need. Nalani wants to include a hyperlink on the Family Style home page that targets her proposal. Potential investors can click that hyperlink to view the proposal.

To distribute a Word document on the World Wide Web so that any browser can read it, you have to convert it to a special format that is readable on the Web. The hyperlinks you already added remain intact during the conversion, but often you'll want to add more hyperlinks to other documents or back to the company's home page. You can do so before or after you convert the document.

Saving a Word Document as an HTML Document

To view a document on the World Wide Web, you use a Web browser such as Netscape Navigator™ or Microsoft Internet Explorer. The browser allows you to find, view, and interact with Web pages. Web browsers read documents formatted in **HTML (HyperText Markup Language)**, a special language for describing the format of a Web page to Web browsers. The HTML markings in a file tell the browser how to format the text. Fortunately, you don't have to learn the Hypertext Markup Language to create HTML documents; Word does the work for you. You can simply save any Word document as an HTML document, and Word will create the necessary markings (called "tags") for the desired format.

Some Word formatting features will not "translate" into HTML format, so when you save your document in HTML format, some of your document formatting might be lost. Once you save a document in HTML format, you'll probably want to modify it to make it more attractive and readable for users of the World Wide Web. This is because formatting that you use in a printed document doesn't always look good on screen, and because HTML documents support formatting features not always available in printed documents, such as color and animation.

REFERENCE window

CONVERTING A WORD DOCUMENT TO AN HTML DOCUMENT

- Click File on the menu bar, and then click Save as HTML.
- If desired, give the file a new filename. Word will automatically add the file extension .html at the end of the document.
- Click the Save button.
- If Word warns you that the document has formatting not supported by HTML, click the Yes button.

To prepare Nalani's proposal for viewing on the Web, you'll begin by saving the current document as an HTML file.

To save a document as an HTML file:

1. If you took a break after the last session, make sure Word is running and the FSI New Branch Proposal document is open.

2. Click **File** on the menu bar, and then click **Save as HTML**. The Save As HTML dialog box opens, with the Save as type given as HTML Document.

   TROUBLE? If the "Save As" appears in the title bar of the dialog box, and the file type does not read HTML Document, you probably clicked Save As instead of Save As HTML. Click the Cancel button, and try again.

3. Enter a space and type a **2** after the filename, so it reads FSI New Branch Proposal 2. See Figure 7-25.

Figure 7-25 ◄
Save As HTML
dialog box

file format will
be HTML

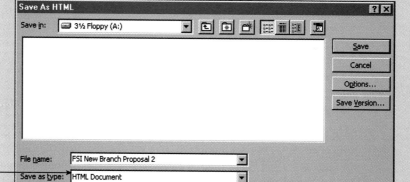

4. Click the **Save** button. Word saves the document using the filename FSI New Branch Proposal 2.html.

   TROUBLE? Word displays a warning message that some of the formatting features will be lost when you save the document as an HTML file, and asks if you want to continue saving; click the Yes button.

   TROUBLE? If you feel that Word is taking a long time to convert and save the file in HTML format, don't worry. Depending upon the speed of your system, it could take several minutes.

   TROUBLE? If a dialog box asks if you want to check the Internet for new versions of Web Authoring tools, click No.

5. If the Web toolbar doesn't appear automatically below the formatting toolbar, click **View** on the menu bar, point to **Toolbars**, and click **Web**. Your proposal appears in HTML format. See Figure 7-26.

   TROUBLE? If you see a dialog box saying that the dimensions after resizing are too small or too large, click the OK button.

Figure 7-26 ◀
Document in
HTML format

document name
is not filename

Web toolbar

margins no longer
visible

extra space added

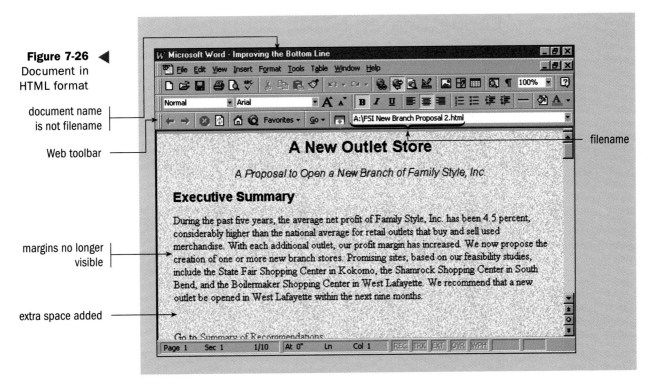

As you look through the document, you'll notice several differences between this HTML file and the original document:

- The document name on the title bar is "Improving the Bottom Line." Even though the filename is FSI New Branch Proposal 2.html (as shown on the Web toolbar), the document name for HTML documents is the title given in the Document Properties dialog box, not necessarily the filename.

- The margin settings are no longer the same. In fact, HTML documents don't have margin settings. The lines of text wrap so that the text fits within the width of the browser (or in this case, the document window), whatever size it might be.

- The embedded or linked objects are now simple graphic images. You can no longer edit the files by double-clicking them. In fact, Word has converted the four embedded or linked objects into GIF images. A **GIF** (Graphic Image Format) is a common format for graphics used in Web pages and is compatible with all Web browsers.

- The position and wrapping properties of the graphic images have been lost; all are treated as a single text character that begins a line of text.

- Spacing between paragraphs has increased. HTML documents automatically include blank space between paragraphs.

- Curly quotation marks have been converted to straight quotation marks, because HTML doesn't support these special characters.

- The subtitle animation no longer appears.

You might notice other differences as well. One of the major differences, in fact, is not apparent by viewing the document: The file size has decreased from about 500 KB to only 7 KB (plus about 90 KB of GIF image files). This is a tremendous advantage for Web pages that have to be transferred electronically over long distances and often through slow modems. The smaller file size allows them to appear more quickly in the document window of the Web browsers.

Formatting an HTML Document

You're now ready to format the HTML document to give it the look and feel of a typical Web page and to correct some of the problems that occur when you convert a file from a normal Word document to an HTML document. You'll begin by changing the document title.

Changing the Document Title

An HTML document title should describe the content of the document, because users will see the title on the title bar of their browser when they open the HTML document.

To change the HTML document title:

1. Click **File** on the menu bar, and then click **Properties** to display the Document Properties dialog box.

2. With the current title selected, type **FSI New Branch Proposal**, and click the **OK** button.

Now the title bar displays the more meaningful title. Next, you'll correct the text formatting.

Moving and Editing Text and Graphics

You can edit and format an HTML document the same way you would edit and format a normal Word document. You'll now edit some text and position the graphics to adjust for changes that occurred in the document when you saved it as an HTML document.

To move and edit text in the HTML document:

1. Scroll down until you can see the Income and Net Profits chart in the "Current Situations" section of the proposal. You want to move the text below the graphic and then center the graphic.

2. Move the insertion point between the graphic and the paragraph, and then press the **Enter** key. This moves the text down below the graphic. Now, to improve appearance of the document, you'll center the graphic.

3. Click the **Income and Net Profits chart** to select it, and then click the **Center** button ▤ on the Formatting toolbar. The graphic is centered between the left and right edges of the document. The Picture toolbar appears while the graphic is selected. See Figure 7-27.

Figure 7-27 ◀
Centering the
chart in HTML
document

Picture toolbar

chart now centered

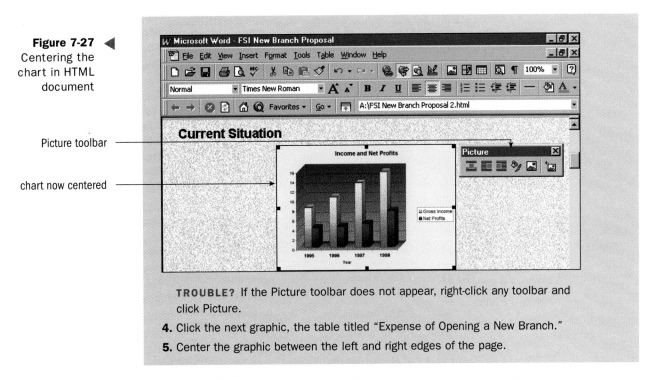

TROUBLE? If the Picture toolbar does not appear, right-click any toolbar and click Picture.

4. Click the next graphic, the table titled "Expense of Opening a New Branch."

5. Center the graphic between the left and right edges of the page.

Next you'll change the text wrapping around the last two graphic images.

To change the text wrapping around graphics:

1. Scroll so you can see the Map of Indiana, click the graphic to select it, click **Format** on the menu bar, and then click **Picture**. If necessary, click the **Position** tab of the Picture dialog box.

2. In the Text wrapping section of the dialog box, click the **Left** icon, so that the text will wrap around to the left of the map, and the map will move to the right side of the page. See Figure 7-28.

Figure 7-28 ◀
Picture
dialog box

Position tab

click to wrap
text around left
side of map

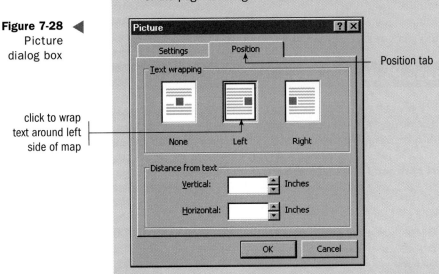

3. Click the **OK** button. The picture moves to the right, with the text to its left.

4. Drag the map up so its top is to the right of the bullets. You may need to reduce the size of the map. Now you'll position the picture of Virgil Jackson so it is located to the left of the text of the last paragraph.

5. Drag the last graphic, the picture of Virgil Jackson, so it is positioned immediately to the left of the last paragraph of the document, below the heading "Summary of Recommendations." Now you'll wrap the text around the right side of the graphic.

6. With the picture still selected, click the **Right Wrapping** button ▦ on the Picture toolbar, then click the text to deselect the graphic. Your screen should now look like Figure 7-29.

TROUBLE? If the Picture toolbar isn't available, click View on the menu bar, point to Toolbars, and then click Picture.

TROUBLE? If any of the text in the paragraph about Virgil wraps under the picture, enlarge the picture slightly by dragging its lower-right corner so all the text is to the right of the picture. Adjust the size and placement of the map so it does not extend into the Summary of Recommendations paragraph.

Figure 7-29 ◀
HTML document after changing text wrapping around graphic images

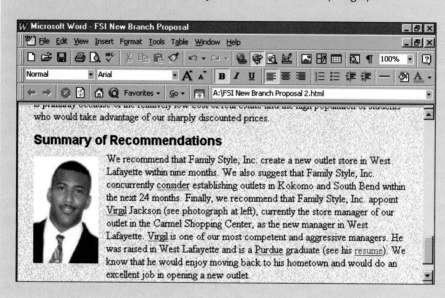

Now that you've corrected the placement of the text and graphics in Nalani's proposal, you'll add some rules (horizontal lines) to the online document.

Inserting Horizontal Lines

Many Web pages have horizontal lines that separate sections of document to make it easier to read and navigate, since on most computer screens you can only see a portion of the document. You'll add a horizontal line below the subtitle of the document and at the end of the document.

To insert horizontal lines into the HTML document:

1. Move the insertion point to the left of the "E" in "Executive Summary" near the beginning of the document.

2. Click the **Horizontal Line** button ▭ on the Formatting toolbar. After a moment, Word inserts a horizontal line above the heading. The line is a simple gray line. Nalani wants something with more color.

3. Select the grey line, and then press the **Delete** key.

4. Click **Insert** on the menu bar, and then click **Horizontal Line**.

5. Click the **second line** (the red one) and then click the **OK** button.

6. Move the insertion point to the end of the document, insert another horizontal red line, delete any extra return characters around the lines you inserted, and then scroll back to the top of the document. See Figure 7-30.

Figure 7-30
Document after
inserting
horizontal line

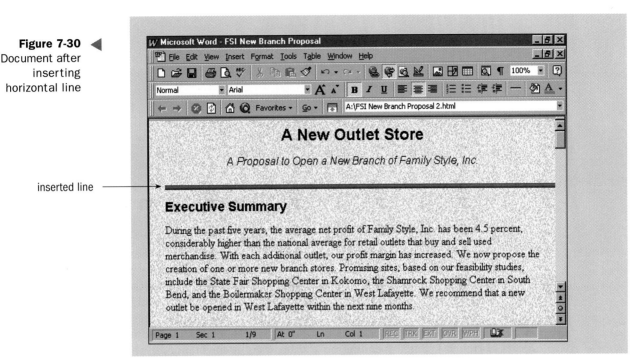

inserted line

Now that you've given shape to the document with horizontal lines, you decide to improve the appearance of the document's text.

Modifying Text Size and Color

Computer monitors that display color are more common than ever, so Web pages usually use colored text to enhance the appearance of the page and to call attention to important information. You use font size on a Web page the same as you would on a printed document. However, HTML supports only a limited number of font sizes: 9, 10, 12, 14, 18, 24, and 36 points in height. To improve the proposal's readability and appearance, Nalani wants you to increase the font size of the title text and to change its color to red.

To change the size and color of text:

1. Select the title **A New Outlet Store** at the beginning of the HTML document.
2. Click the **Increase Font Size** button [A] on the Formatting toolbar. The font size increases from 18 point to 24 point.
3. Click the **Font Color** list arrow [A] on the Formatting toolbar, click the **red** tile, the one on the second row and third column, and then deselect the text. The title now appears in red. See Figure 7-31.

Figure 7-31
Font changes
to title

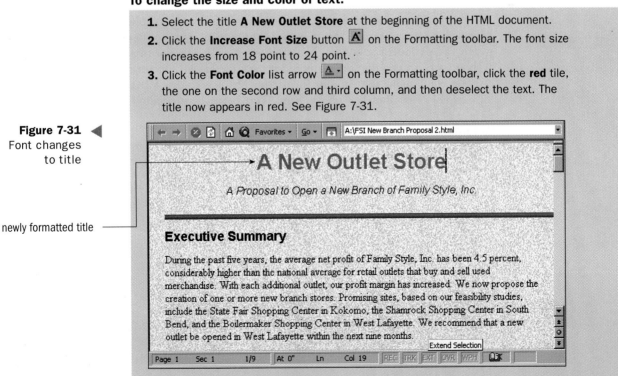

newly formatted title

4. Save the document.

> **TROUBLE?** If it seems like Word takes an excessively long time to save an HTML document, don't worry. Saving an HTML document can take longer than saving a document in Word format.

You've now formatted Nalani's proposal document so that it will be visually appealing on screen. Next, you'll create some additional hypertext links and edit one of the existing ones.

Creating and Editing Hyperlinks in an HTML Document

After you convert a Word document to HTML format, any hyperlinks you created in the Word document will still be present. If, however, you want any Web browser to be able to display the resume document, you should save it in HTML format. As you looked through the HTML version of the proposal, you probably noticed that the blue underlined hyperlink text is still present. A Web browser could successfully display the target of the first hyperlink (the one that links to the Summary of Recommendations in the same document), but, depending on the browser, it might not be able to display the Virgil Jackson resume (VJResume.doc) unless you convert it to HTML format. You'll need to convert the resume to an HTML document, create a new link from the resume back to the proposal, and then modify the hyperlink in the proposal so that browsers can easily view and jump between the two documents.

To convert the resume to an HTML document:

> **1.** Open the file **VJResume.doc** from the **Tutorial.07** folder on your Student Disk, and save it as the HTML document **VJResume 2.html**, using the procedure you learned earlier.
>
> > **TROUBLE?** If the word "Private" appears in the first cell of the table, just delete it.

After you save the document, notice that Virgil's address, phone number, and e-mail address have disappeared. This is because those items were located in separate text boxes, which HTML doesn't support. Nalani doesn't want this information on the Word Wide Web anyway, so you don't need to add it back the HTML document.

Now you'll make some minor formatting changes so that VJResume.html has the same look as FSI New Branch Proposal.html. You'll use the procedures you learned earlier.

To format Virgil's HTML resume document:

> **1.** Click **File** on the menu bar, click **Properties**, and change the document title in the Document Properties dialog box to read **Resume: Virgil Jackson**, and then click the **OK** button. Now you'll apply the Newsprint texture to the background, but you'll use a slightly different procedure than you did when creating the network version of the document.
>
> **2.** Click the **Background** button ⧉ on the Formatting toolbar, click **Fill Effects**, click the **Newsprint** pattern, and then click the **OK** button.
>
> **3.** Select the text **Virgil S. Jackson** at the top of the page, click the **Font Color** list arrow ⧉ on the Formatting toolbar, and select the **blue** tile (second row, second tile from the right) and deselect the text.
>
> **4.** Click the **Spelling and Grammar** button ⧉ on the Standard toolbar, click the **Ignore** button to remove any red or green underlinings and click **OK**.

5. Change the font color of "Experience," "Education," and "Interests" to **red**. Now you'll insert the same horizontal line you used in the proposal.

6. Move the insertion point to the end of the document, click **Insert** on the menu bar, click **Horizontal Line**, and then click the **red line** (second line down), and click the **OK** button.

The resume and the proposal now have a similar appearance.

Inserting a Hyperlink to an HTML Document

Users who read Virgil's resume will most likely want to return to the proposal, so you decide to insert a hyperlink that targets the proposal. You insert hyperlinks in HTML documents in the same way you do Word documents.

To insert a hyperlink:

1. Make sure the insertion point is below the horizontal line at the end of the document, and then type **Return to FSI New Branch Proposal**.

2. Select the text "FSI New Branch Proposal" in the phrase you just typed, click the **Insert Hyperlink** button 🔖 on the Standard toolbar, click in the Link to File or URL text box if necessary, click the **Browse** button, click the **FSI New Branch Proposal 2** HTML document, and click the **OK** button twice. Word inserts the hyperlink to the proposal.

3. Save and close the resume document. You return to the proposal.

The resume now contains a hyperlink that takes users back to the proposal.

Editing a Hyperlink

Recall that the proposal itself still contains the hyperlink that targets the resume in its Word document format. You need to edit the hyperlink so that it targets the resume in its HTML format. Rather than deleting the hyperlink and reinserting a new one, you can just edit the existing hyperlink and indicate the new target path. You want to target VJResume.html.

To edit a hyperlink:

1. Scroll to the end of the proposal, and *right*-click the **resume** hyperlink. Word displays a shortcut menu.

2. Point to **Hyperlink** and then click **Edit Hyperlink**. The Edit Hyperlink dialog box opens.

3. Edit the filename in the Link to file or URL text box so that it is **VJResume 2.html**, and then click the **OK** button.

4. Save the document.

The edited hyperlink in the proposal HTML document now correctly targets the resume HTML document. You're now ready to view the HTML document in a Web browser and to test the hyperlinks.

Viewing the HTML Document in a Web Browser

While you're editing an HTML document in Word, the document window shows how the document will look when viewed from a Web browser. But it's always a good idea to view your HTML documents with a Web browser so you'll see exactly how they will look and so you can test the hyperlinks. Before attempting to display your document in a browser, however, make sure you save any changes first. Also, if your browser is open at the time you make and save changes, you might need to update or reload the document in your browser to display the latest updates to the HTML file.

To view the HTML documents in a Web browser:

1. Click the **Web Page Preview** button 🔲 on the Standard toolbar. Word opens your Web browser and displays the FSI New Branch Proposal in its document window. See Figure 7-32. Your browser might be Netscape Navigator or some other browser, but the view of the FSI New Branch Proposal should be similar.

Figure 7-32 ◄
Viewing HTML
document in
Internet
Explorer

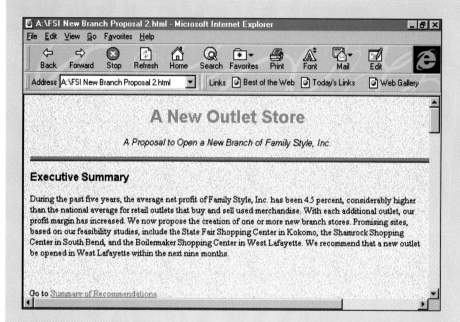

TROUBLE? If a message appears informing you that you have to save the document first, click the Yes button to save the document and display it in the Web browser.

TROUBLE? If you get a warning message informing you that the browser may not be able to view the document with the .html filename extension and then the browser fails to open your document, close the browser, click the OK button on the warning message, and try again to display the HTML document in the browser. It should work the second time; you just need to give Word time to finish saving your HTML document.

TROUBLE? If you get a message informing you that Internet Explorer is not your default browser, and asking you if you want to make it your browser, click the No button.

2. Scroll through the document so you can see how it looks in the browser.

3. Move the insertion point to the beginning of the document and click the **Summary of Recommendations** hyperlink. The view of the HTML document immediately changes so that the heading "Summary of Recommendations" is at the top of the document window.

4. Click the **resume** hyperlink in the last paragraph of the document. The browser opens VJResume.html. See Figure 7-33.

Figure 7-33
Browser
showing
resume
document

table information
rearranged

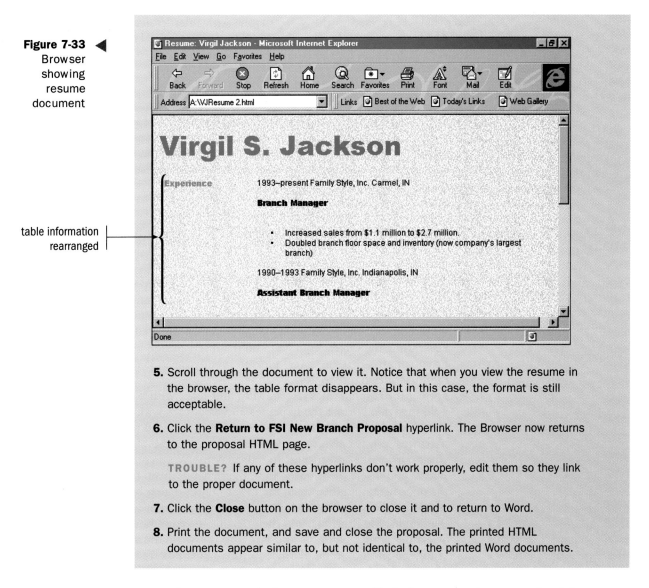

5. Scroll through the document to view it. Notice that when you view the resume in the browser, the table format disappears. But in this case, the format is still acceptable.

6. Click the **Return to FSI New Branch Proposal** hyperlink. The Browser now returns to the proposal HTML page.

   TROUBLE? If any of these hyperlinks don't work properly, edit them so they link to the proper document.

7. Click the **Close** button on the browser to close it and to return to Word.

8. Print the document, and save and close the proposal. The printed HTML documents appear similar to, but not identical to, the printed Word documents.

You have now finished preparing two HTML documents, the proposal and the resume, for online viewing.

Quick Check

1. Define the following terms:
   a. Web browser
   b. server
   c. HTML
   d. GIF format

2. Name three changes that can occur to your document when you save it in HTML format.

3. True or False: The title you see in the title bar of the Word window containing your HTML document is its filename.

4. Explain the difference between changing font size in a Word document and changing font size in an HTML document.

5. When you convert a document to HTML so that you can post it on the Web, what should you do if there are hyperlinks pointing to other Office documents?

You show your documents to Nalani, who tests them and sends them to the company's Internet service provider that manages the Web site for Family Style. Once the documents and all their related graphics files are placed in the appropriate hard disk folder on the computer that's connected to the Web, anyone with Internet access and a Web browser can view the documents. Nalani hopes that posting the proposal on the World Wide Web will attract new investors for the Family Style expansion.

Tutorial Assignments

Marina Leavitt is the director of sales for Family Style, Inc. She is preparing a quarterly sales report to give to each of the company's sales representatives. The main purpose of the short report is to show sales, income, and expenses over the last three months, but it will also include new policies for purchasing used merchandise. Marina has written the body of the report in Word and wants you to embed a spreadsheet of sales figures in the report, and then modify one of the figures. She also wants you to link a Paint graphics file showing the quarterly profits for each branch outlet, and then modify the file. Finally, she wants you to save the report in HTML format for publication on the World Wide Web, and create appropriate hyperlinks to related documents, including a URL for a Web page that contains additional information on Family Style procedures.

1. Make sure that Word is running, open the file SalesRep from the TAssign folder for Tutorial 7 on your Student Disk, and save it as Family Style Sales Report.
2. Delete the [insert worksheet here] placeholder, and in its place, embed the worksheet 2QSales from the TAssign folder for Tutorial 7 on your Student Disk, using the Object command on the Insert menu.
3. From within Word, use Excel tools to modify the 2QSales worksheet. Change the June sales figure to 1.42.
4. Format the column titles (April, May, and June) with a bright yellow fill and bold the type. Format the Expenses and Sales cells with boldface type only.
5. Double-click the borderline between columns A and B to make column A narrower so it is only as wide as the text it contains.
6. Click outside the spreadsheet to redisplay the Word commands and tools.
7. Locate and delete the phrase "[link figure here]" from the second paragraph of the document, and then open the Insert Object dialog box.
8. After you click the Browse button on the Create from File tab, make a copy of the graphic file BrnchSls, and then rename the copy Branch Sales.
9. Select the Branch Sales file and link it to the Word document.
10. Using the Size tab in the Format Picture dialog box, reduce the map graphic to 70% of its original size. Use the Position tab to place the map horizontally on the page four inches from the margin. Set the text wrapping style to Tight, and wrap the text to the left of the map. (You may need to change the Vertical setting to 0" from the margin.)

11. Change the color of the star at Indianapolis to red: Open the Paint program from the Start menu by clicking the Start button, pointing to Programs, pointing to Accessories, and then clicking Paint. Open the source file Branch Sales, and fill the star at Indianapolis with the bright red color. Save the revised file and then close Paint. (*Hint:* To color the star, click the Fill With Color button on the Paint tool box, click the red square in the palette of colors at the bottom of the window, and then click within the borders of the star.)
12. Return to Word, and update the link so that the red star shows in the Word representation of the graphic.

13. Now modify the linked graphic from within Word: Double-click the map to open Paint, and then apply the red color to each of the circles representing the cities. Close Paint, saving your changes, and save your Sales Report document with the updated map. Notice that the map updated automatically when you changed the linked representation from within the destination program.
14. Insert a hyperlink at the end of the document that reads "Return to Sales Report", and place the bookmark for it at the beginning of the document. (*Hint:* A bookmark title cannot have any spaces.)

15. View the document in Online Layout View.
16. Format the background with the Stationery texture.
17. Format the subtitle with the Las Vegas Lights animation. Remove any Spelling and Grammar markings and save the document.
18. Save the report as an HTML document under the name Family Style Sales Report 2. In the Document Properties dialog box, change the name that shows in the title bar to Family Style Sales Report.
19. Center the Sales spreadsheet.
20. Use the Format Picture command to position the map so the text wraps to its left. Make sure the text "The figure at right..." is correctly placed so the map is to its right.
21. Add or delete return characters to improve the layout of the document.
22. Enlarge the title one size, bold the subheading, and apply the color blue to the title, subtitle, and the "New Policies" heading.
23. Insert a red line below the subtitle and another line at the end of the document. Save the document, and leave it open.
24. Open the file FSIAds in the TAssign folder for Tutorial 7 of your Student Disk, and save it as an HTML document with the name FSIAds 2. Change the name that appears in the title bar to Family Style Q1 Ads.
25. Format the FSIAds document with the Stationery texture, and enlarge the "Family Styles Inc." title four sizes and color the title blue. Enlarge the "Advertising Summary" subhead three sizes. Put a red line under Q1 1999, and delete the extra return character above the red line. Save the document.
26. In the sales report document, locate the text in the first paragraph that reads "advertising efforts in the first quarter", and hyperlink that text to the FSIAds 2 HTML document. Test the hyperlink.
27. At the end of the FSIAds 2 document, insert the text "Return to Sales Report" and enlarge it one size. Then hyperlink it to the Family Style Sales Report 2 HTML document and test the link.

28. Now create the hyperlink to the URL for a related Family Style Web page. Scroll to the bottom of the Family Style Sales Report 2 document, press the Enter key to add a new blank line, and then type "Click to see more information on Family Style purchasing procedures for new merchandise". Highlight the line you just typed. Open the Insert Hyperlink dialog box, click the Link to file or URL box, and then type the following URL: http://www2.coursetools.com/cti/NewPerspectives/office97/famstyle.html
29. Click the OK button. Save the document and then use the Web Page Preview button to view it in your Web browser. Test the hyperlinks you added, including the one at the bottom of the document.
30. Save and close your documents.

Case Problems

1. Office Location for Workman Insurance Company John Rowley works for the Workman Insurance Company, a new insurance company that is growing rapidly. Arlene Herlevi, vice president of operations for the company, has proposed that Workman open a new downtown office and has assigned John the responsibility of finding a good location. John has contacted local real estate agencies through the World Wide Web, and he has located an available office building that seems to be satisfactory. He has downloaded an image of the office building. He asks you to prepare a memo to Arlene describing the office site. He'd like you to include the image in the memo. When you've finished, he wants you to e-mail the memo to Arlene for online viewing. Arlene won't be viewing the memo in her browser; she'll just open it directly in Word.

1. If necessary, start Word and make sure your Student Disk is in the appropriate drive. Open the file NewOffic from the Cases folder for Tutorial 7 on your Student Disk, and then save it as New Office Memo.

2. At the beginning of the third paragraph, delete the bracketed phrase "[insert chart]" and embed the chart called Rent from the Cases folder for Tutorial 7.

3. Reduce the size of the chart to 30% of its original size, position it against the left margin, and wrap the text on the top and bottom. (*Hint:* If you have trouble placing the chart in the correct place, open the Format Object dialog box, and on the Position tab, change the Horizontal position to 0" from margin and the Vertical position to 0" from paragraph.)

4. Using Excel tools, click the vertical axis, and eliminate the two decimal places in the figures. Enlarge the axis font size to 16 points.

5. Link a copy of the Logo file (located in the Cases folder for Tutorial 7) to the top of the document.

6. Save and close the memo file, open the Paint program from the Start menu, and then open the Copy of Logo file. Change the red bar at the bottom of the logo to a light turquoise, save the file, and exit Paint.

7. Reopen the New Office Memo document, and make sure the color change was automatically made to the linked version of the logo.

8. Animate the "Interoffice Memorandum" heading with Las Vegas Lights. Format the document with a solid tan background.

9. In the second paragraph, just after the sentence that ends with "...downtown business district," insert text that reads "See Recent Downtown Developments for a listing of recent renovations in the area." Make "Recent Downtown Developments" a hyperlink, targeting the Devel file in the Cases folder for Tutorial 7 on your Student Disk.

10. Open the Devel file by clicking the hyperlink to it, insert a hyperlink at the end that takes users back to the New Office Memo, place a descriptive title in the title bar, give it a tan background, and save the file.

11. Return to the memo, save it. Print the online layout screen you see. Close the Devel and Memo files.

2. Wasatch Tours Brochure Alisha McClure is a sales representative for Wasatch Tours, a company that offers guided tours to many of the popular tourist sites in the western United States. She is preparing a flyer describing upcoming tours to selected western National Parks. She asks you to help finish the project and then convert it to HTML so she can post it on the company's home page and make it available to prospective tourists.

1. If necessary, start Word, make sure your Student Disk is in the appropriate drive. Open the file NatBroch from the Cases folder for Tutorial 7 on your Student Disk, and then save it as National Parks Tours.

2. Position the photograph of the arch against the left margin, wrap text around it, and enlarge it so that the entire second paragraph wraps to the right of the photo.

3. After the second paragraph, embed the Excel worksheet WasTours from the Cases folder for Tutorial 7. From within Word, edit the worksheet so there is a 25% gray shading in the two title rows. Change the ending date of the Shoestring Tour to August 10.

4. Create a logo of your own design at the top of the document. Open the Paint program from the Start menu, and use the text, rectangle, and fill tools to create a logo. (*Hint:* Make a small logo in the upper-left corner of the window, and use the Attributes command from the Image menu to prevent the white space around the logo from being linked to Word. Make the size about 200 dots wide by 100 dots tall.) Save the logo as a 16-color bitmap file in the Cases folder for Tutorial 7. Link a copy of the logo at the top of the National Parks Tours flyer. After saving the flyer, double-click the logo and edit it any way you want to improve its appearance.

5. Save the flyer in HTML format with the name National Parks Tours 2. Adjust the placement of text and graphics as necessary. Give it an appropriate background color or pattern, and add one or two lines. Adjust the size and color of the text headings so they go well with the background.

6. Place a hyperlink at the bottom of the document that reads "Click here to see a photo of last year's tour!", and have the hyperlink display the WasPhoto 2 HTML document in the Cases folder for Tutorial 7 on your Student Disk.
7. Format the WasPhoto 2 text and background so it's compatible with the flyer.
8. Place a hyperlink at the bottom of the WasPhotos document that takes the user back to the flyer.
9. Save both files, view them in a browser, and test the links. Print the files from your browser.

3. Zeke's Sales Organization Report Charles Turner is vice president of marketing for Zeke's Sports Equipment, a national distributor of sporting goods headquartered in Birmingham, Alabama. Because of the enormous volume of sales in California, Charles has decided to reorganize the sales regions. To lessen the load on the western region, he has decided to enlarge the southeast region to include Texas. He will explain this change in a report to all regional sales representatives. He asks you to create an integrated document that includes an Excel chart and a Paint image file of a map. He wants you to prepare the file for online viewing because he plans to post it on his company's network. Then he wants you to save and format the file for posting on the Web.

1. If necessary, start Word, and make sure your Student Disk is in the appropriate drive. Open the file ZekesRep from the Cases folder for Tutorial 7 on your Student Disk, and save it as Zeke's Sales Org.
2. After the first paragraph, embed the Excel chart Zekes97, and reduce it to 30% of its original size.
3. Center the chart between the left and right margins, with Top & bottom text wrapping.

4. Format the chart so the bars contrast more with the background. After double-clicking the chart, double-click any bar, and select the fill color of your choice. Then double-click the background and choose a contrasting color. Double-click each axis and the title and select a font size that makes the figures more readable.
5. At the end of the document, link a copy of the Paint image file ZekesReg, naming the copy Zekes Regions Map. Center the map between the left and right margins with no text wrapping.
6. Edit the linked Paint image from within Word: Fill the state of Texas with the blue color that matches the other southern states. Save the image and close Paint.
7. Save, preview, and print the document.
8. Switch to online layout view, and apply an appropriate background. Animate text with an animation of your choice. Save the Word document.
9. Save the report in HTML format. Adjust the placement of text and graphics. Change the font sizes and colors to make the on-screen document more visually appealing. Print the file from your browser.
10. Create another Word document containing additional information that readers of this report might want to see. It might contain text, a chart or graphics; avoid using Word tables. (If you are using floppy disks to save your files, be aware that graphics files can be quite large. You might want to use only text.) Save it as an HTML document, and format it so it is compatible with the report. Create hyperlinks to move the user back and forth between the two documents. Save and preview the documents in a browser and test the links. Print the file from your browser.

4. Educational Expenses Your local community education program is hosting a seminar for adults who want to return to college. The program coordinator has asked you to write a report outlining the current cost of going to college. Write a report about the average educational expenses—tuition, books, meals, etc.—for a student for a typical school year. Open a new, blank document in Word, and then do the following:

1. In several paragraphs, explain the various types of expenses that a student faces.

2. Embed a chart that categorizes these expenses by name. Use Excel if you are familiar with it; otherwise, create the chart using Microsoft Graph: Click Insert on the menu bar, point to Picture, and then click Chart. Enter expense categories and amounts for a one-year period, and then click the chart behind the grid window. Click your report document to embed the completed chart.

3. Link a picture or diagram that would enhance your report's content. For example, if you have access to a scanner, you could scan a picture of one of the buildings on campus or your own picture. You can use Paint to modify the map of the United States in the graphics file ZekesReg, showing the location of selected educational institutions.

4. Create a hyperlink at the top of the document that links to a location at the bottom of the document. Format the document with animated text and an appropriate background.

5. Create an online version of the document that you can post on a Web site. Create another file that supports your report's content, and create a link to it from your document to the supporting file. Create a link from the supporting file back to the main document.

6. If you have access to the World Wide Web, use a search engine to find relevant information about college costs, and either incorporate the information in your report, crediting the source with a footnote, or create a hyperlink to the Web address in your report.

7. Save the Word document as School Expenses, and then preview, print, and close the document.

Lab Assignments

These Lab Assignments are designed to accompany the interactive Course Lab called Internet World Wide Web. To start the Lab, click the Start button on the Windows 95 taskbar, point to Programs, point to Course Labs, point to New Perspective Applications, and click Internet World Wide Web. If you do not see Course Labs on your Windows 95 Programs menu, see your instructor or technical support person.

The Internet: World Wide Web One of the most popular services on the Internet is the World Wide Web. This Lab is a Web simulator that teaches you how to use Web browser software to find information. You can use this Lab whether or not your school provides you with Internet access.

1. Click the Steps button to learn how to use Web browser software. As you proceed through the Steps, answer all of the Quick Check questions that appear. After you complete the Steps, you'll see a Quick Check summary report. Follow the instructions on the screen to print this report.

2. Click the Explore button. Use the Web browser to locate a weather map of the Caribbean Virgin Islands. What is its URL?

3. Enter the URL **http://www.atour.com**. A SCUBA diver named Wadson Lachouffe has been searching for the fabled treasure of Greybeard the pirate. A link from the Adventure Travel Web site leads to Wadson's Web page called "Hidden Treasure." Locate the Hidden Treasure page, and answer the following questions:
   a. What was the name of Greybeard's ship?
   b. What was Greybeard's favorite food?
   c. What does Wadson think happened to Greybeard's ship?

4. In the Steps, you found a graphic of Jupiter from the photo archives of the Jet Propulsion Laboratory. In the Explore section of the Lab, you can also find a graphic of Saturn. Suppose one of your friends wants a picture of Saturn for an astronomy report. Make a list of the blue underlined links your friend must click to find the Saturn graphic. Assume that your friend begins at the Web Trainer home page.

5. Jump back to the Adventure Travel Web site. Write a one-page description of the information at the site, including the number of pages the site contains, and diagram the links it contains.

6. Chris Thomson, a student at UVI, has his own Web page. In Explore, look at the information Chris included on his page. Suppose you could create your own Web page. What would you include? Use word-processing software to design your own Web page. Make sure to indicate the graphics and links you would use.

Answers to Quick Check Questions

SESSION 5.1

1 a Word feature that contains a list of words and their synonyms and antonyms

2 arranged, organized, orderly, ordered, regulated, classified, tidied, reorganized, rearranged

3 Right-click the marked phrase to display the Grammar shortcut menu, and click Grammar.

4 A serif font is a font with a small embellishment at the tips of the lines of a character; sans serif fonts lack these embellishments. Serif examples: Century Schoolbook, Courier, Garamond, Times New Roman. Sans Serif examples: Arial, Arial Narrow, Century Gothic, Franklin Gothic Book.

5 Click Format, click Style, select the style, click Modify, make the desired modifications, click OK, click Close.

6 (1) Click Format, click Style, click New, give the style a new name, specify the style type, define the style as you would change a style definition, click Close. (2) By example: select a paragraph or characters, apply formatting, click Format, click Style, click New, specify the style type, click Close.

7 A paragraph style applies to a complete paragraph; a character style applies to a single character, a word, a phrase, or a larger set of characters.

8 Select the tab alignment style, and then click the desired location on the ruler.

SESSION 5.2

1 to change the organization of the outline, and hence the organization of the document

2 Promote: to increase the level of the heading (indent less). Demote: to decrease the level of the heading (indent more). Click the Promote or Demote button on the Outline toolbar.

3 False. You can add outline paragraphs in Outline view, and Word will automatically apply the appropriate heading style.

4 10, 25, 45, 75

5 Border: a box that frames tables or table cells. Rule: horizontal or vertical lines

6 Click Table, click Cell Height and Width, click the Row tab, click the Center option button, click OK.

7 to identify a table with a number and name so that a reader can determine the table contents

SESSION 5.3

1 Change the paragraph style of the Normal style to double spacing.

2 A blank area that runs down a page and can distract readers.

3 The amount of space at the right margin within which a word will be hyphenated. If you increase the hyphenation zone, the number of hyphenated words will decrease.

4 Word numbers the footnotes automatically; Word automatically formats the footnote text at the bottom of the pages; you can edit the footnote; Word automatically keeps the footnote reference and the footnote text on the same page.

5 True.

6 Click the Select Browse Object button, click the Browse by Heading button, click the Next Heading or Previous Heading button.

SESSION 6.1

1 a. letter containing similar content but with personal information in specific locations; b. document containing merge fields where personal information will be inserted; c. document containing individualized information; d. instructions for retrieving specific information from data source; e. all the information about one customer or individual; f. specific category of information in a record

2 b. and d.

3 record

4 True

5 Type "Gender" in the Field name text box of the Create Data Source dialog box, and then click the Add Field Name button.

6 to make it easier to enter, edit, or delete data records

7 by using the Record arrow buttons

SESSION 6.2

1 prints the current data no matter when document is printed

2 Click the Insert Merge Field button on the Mail Merge toolbar, and then click a field name.

3 by the chevrons around the merge field

4   a. a document created after merging a main document and a data source; b. rearrange order of records; c. selecting specific records from a data source; d. mathematical or logical expression used to include or exclude certain records in a query

5   Use the filtering operator Equal to, and enter the zip code desired in the Compare to field.

6   Click the View Merged Data button on the Mail Merge toolbar, or click the Print Preview button on the Standard toolbar, click the Zoom Control list arrow, and then click Page Width.

7   23

8   No

SESSION 6.3

1   b. and d.

2   True

3   Create main document of type Envelopes, specify the main document and data source, select the type of printer, create a sample envelope with merge fields in the Create Envelopes dialog box, and then create a new merge document and print.

4   False

5   a dotted line extending from text on left margin to text at tab stop

6   Click the Edit Data Source button on Mail Merge toolbar, and then click View Source.

7   Display data table, move insertion point to LastName field, and then click the Sort Descending button on the Database toolbar.

SESSION 7.1

1   a. An item in Office 97 and other Windows programs that you can modify and move from one document to another. b. The program used to create the original version of an object that is being inserted into a document created in another program. c. The program into which objects from other programs are integrated.

2   With embedding, you place an object into a document and retain the ability to use the tools of the source program. With linking, you place a representation of an object into a document. With embedding, there is no connection maintained between the source file and the destination file; with linking, there is. Choose linking when your data might change over time.

3   Object linking and embedding. An OLE-enabled program is one whose objects can be integrated into other documents using OLE technology.

4   To embed an existing worksheet, use the Insert Object command, click the Create from File tab, select the file, but don't click the Link to file check box. To link, you can also use Insert Object, but this time, you click the Link to file check box.

5   Right-click it, click Copy, then click Ctrl + V.

6   Double-click it.

7   False

SESSION 7.2

1   A hyperlink is a word, phrase, or graphic image that you click to move to another location.

2   False

3   False

4   b. Executive Summary, because it has a space

5   The hyperlink has already been used.

6   The target document is in the same folder as the current document.

7   Any three of the following: a. In normal view, words wrap to the printed page; in online layout view to the width of the screen. b. Text appears larger in online layout view. c. In online layout view, documents can be displayed with background effects. d. Page setup elements are not displayed in online layout view. e. Document Map automatically appears.

8   You jump to that heading in the document.

SESSION 7.3

1   a. A program that allows you to find, view, and interact with Web pages. b. On the Web, a computer that stores Web pages and makes them available to the Web. c. HyperText Markup Language, used to describe to format of a Web page to a Web browser. d. GIF format is a graphics format commonly used on the Web.

2   Any three of the following: a. The name in the title bar changes. b. Words wrap to the width of the screen. c. Embedded and linked objects are converted to graphics. d. Graphics are treated as text characters. e. Spacing between paragraphs increases. f. Special characters are converted when HTML doesn't support them. g. Animated text effects and other formatting are lost.

3   False

4   HTML documents have fewer available font sizes.

5   Convert target Office documents to HTML format if you want all browsers to be able to read them.